Reality, Religion, and Passion

STUDIES IN COMPARATIVE PHILOSOPHY AND RELIGION

Series Editor: Douglas Allen, University of Maine

This series is based on the view that significant and creative future studies in philosophy and religious studies will be informed by comparative research. These studies emphasize aspects of contemporary and classical Asian philosophy and religion, and their relationship to Western thought. This series features works of specialized scholarship by new and upcoming scholars in Asia and the West, as well as works by more established scholars and books with a wider readership. The editor welcomes a wide variety of manuscript submissions, especially works exhibiting highly focused research and theoretical innovation.

Varieties of Ethical Reflection: New Directions for Ethics in a Global Context, by Michael Barnhart

Gandhi's Experiments with Truth: Essential Writings by and about Mahatma Gandhi, edited by Richard L. Johnson

To Broaden the Way: A Confucian-Jewish Dialogue, by Galia Patt-Shamir

Reality, Religion, and Passion: Indian and Western Approaches in Hans-Georg Gadamer and Rūpa Gosvāmi, by Jessica Frazier

Reality, Religion, and Passion

Indian and Western Approaches in Hans-Georg Gadamer and Rūpa Gosvāmi

Jessica Frazier

LEXINGTON BOOKS
A division of
ROWMAN & LITTLEFIELD PUBLISHERS, INC.
Lanham • Boulder • New York • Toronto • Plymouth, UK

LEXINGTON BOOKS

A division of Rowman & Littlefield Publishers, Inc.
A wholly owned subsidiary of The Rowman & Littlefield Publishing Group, Inc.
4501 Forbes Boulevard, Suite 200
Lanham, MD 20706

Estover Road
Plymouth PL6 7PY
United Kingdom

British Library Cataloguing in Publication Information Available

Library of Congress Cataloging-in-Publication Data

Frazier, Jessica, 1975–
Reality, religion, and passion : Indian and Western approaches in Hans-Georg Gadamer and Rupa Gosvami / Jessica Frazier.
p. cm. — (Comparative philosophy and religion)
Includes bibliographical references and index.
ISBN-13: 978-0-7391-2439-0 (cloth : alk. paper)
ISBN-10: 0-7391-2439-0 (cloth : alk. paper)
ISBN-13: 978-0-7391-2440-6 (pbk. : alk. paper)
ISBN-10: 0-7391-2440-4 (pbk. : alk. paper)
ISBN-13: 978-0-7391-3219-7 (electronic)
ISBN-10: 0-7391-3219-9 (electronic)
1. Gadamer, Hans-Georg, 1900–2002. 2. Rupagosvami, 16th cent. I. Title.
B3248.G34F73 2009
193—dc22 2008032470

Printed in the United States of America

∞™ The paper used in this publication meets the minimum requirements of American National Standard for Information Sciences—Permanence of Paper for Printed Library Materials, ANSI/NISO Z39.48–1992.

Contents

Acknowledgments

I would like to extend my profound thanks to the following:

Professor Julius J. Lipner for his patience and generous support throughout, Professor George Pattison for his unfailing encouragement, the Oxford Centre for Hindu Studies for the sustenance of many kinds that it has provided from 2004 to the present, the Cambridge Faculties of Divinity and Anthropology for grants that facilitated my period of research in India, Chris Ryan for his unshakable philosophical generosity, Rembert Lutjeharms for his incisive reading, Zadie Smith for her oblique guidance, Robert Craven for his editorial help, and Joan Davis and Douglas J. Frazier for, in every way, making this possible.

Notes on Presentation

Non-English texts are either from published translations where specified, or from my own translations where only the original text is given in the reference.

Introduction

The word for belief, which has become so technical a word, is etymologically linked to the language of desire, love, and libido.[1] Yet we are increasingly coming to see it once again in terms not only of rational assertion, like a scientific theory waiting to be verified, but also of the life lived in the reality that the assertion describes, a rich web of relations and values woven into the fabric of truth. This book aims to contribute to the contemporary reformulation of "reality" and "belief" in ways that alter the very landscape of the lives that we lead, linking them to ontologies that acknowledge the place of the passions. The goal is to suggest ways to safeguard meaningfulness in the face of scepticism, applying a heightened self-critical awareness to the foundations of our beliefs so that we can—as Badiou puts it—discover "a figure of our destiny in relation to the destiny of being itself."[2]

In the first of the Duino Elegies, Rainer Maria Rilke poetically portrays the ideal human situation as that of the bereaved lover whose desire is most fully actualised where there is no hope of fulfilment: when the beloved has died. "[T]hose forsaken . . . ," he writes, ". . . you found/so far beyond the requited in loving. Begin/anew their never-attainable praise."[3] Here the very hope of fulfilment is denied, and Rilke advocates the perpetuated, unsatisfiable desire of which the world, after all, appears to consist.[4]

In the *Gītagovinda,* Jayadeva tells the story of how the amorous Goddess Rādhā, tormented by her fickle lover's absence, weeps deliriously for his return. However, when her anxious friends do indeed deliver him to her side, she continues to cry for him in a fever of longing even as he embraces her. She cannot be comforted by his presence. Krishna, her divine lover, is sadly led away and Rādhā is worshipped and exalted; the intensity of her love has transcended its object.[5]

Each of these stories, the first an inspirational text for Hans-Georg Gadamer, and the second a canonical text in the religious tradition to which Rūpa Gosvāmi belonged, describes a kind of "belief in" or "desire for" that does not follow the conventional economies of absence, presence, and fulfilment. In each the absence of the desired object inversely correlates with a heightened passion for it, such that the fulfilment of the original desire gradually becomes subsumed to this flourishing of passion. Desire becomes a gift, disassociated from its fulfilment, and the truest love for the object becomes allied with a philosophy of infinite deferral. Thus each also implies something about the relation of religious beliefs to the reality of their objects; these are stories with implications at every level (commonsensical, linguistic, ontological, religious) for the relation of our selves, our thoughts, and our hopes to whatever is our touchstone for "truth."

REDEFINING "REALISM"

This book argues that both of these stories point to an underlying realisation of fundamental epistemological and metaphysical principles, which in turn has had a pervasive effect on attitudes about life in general, and reality as a whole. As intuitively basic as we have sometimes thought the substantialist notion of reality to be (i.e., the idea that there are two sorts of things: *physical substances*, and *thoughts* about physical substances), on the widest geographical and historical scale thinkers have nevertheless often reasoned that all our talk of "existence" refers only to thoughts. On this alternative account, the only ontological division is *within* this sphere: an analytic division between the single ontological *fact* that the thoughts exist, and the plural ontic *forms* that they take—from sense impressions, abstract ideas, emotions, memories, and intentions to perceived "things" and, not least, our perceived "selves." The difference between the two models may seem academic, located on the level of invisible foundations, affecting few of life's exigencies. Yet how we experience the world, how we communicate with each other and seek or judge truth all depend on the distinction between these two models.

To call the first "realism," and the second "idealism" is a fundamental philosophical error to which this study is opposed. It will use two examples from diverse cultural and historical contexts to show how the latter model can also spring from what we will call a "realist" process of reasoning and epistemological rigour; a process that seeks by some epistemologically secure method to arrive at assured truths that are taken as the basis for an account of reality and a concomitant ethos of how to live. It will then show how such models are also equipped (a) to answer many of the post-Enlightenment criticisms of realist metaphysics and religious faith, and

(b) to provide the foundation for viable and powerful models of how we should live. Much of our confidence about meaningful discourse across subjective and cultural boundaries has been debilitated by the epistemological critiques that arose in the wake of the Enlightenment, and subsequently under the influence of Heideggerian philosophy. Meanwhile sincere discussion of religious ideas has widely been replaced by a psychologism that seeks to understand realist belief in terms of its moods and motivations, whilst ignoring the truth claims that are so essential to the believers. Given the wide criticism of classical models of realism in metaphysics and religion, new models of ontological and ethical realism can be discovered by exploring thinkers who stand outside of the mainstream Western metaphysical tradition. To this purpose, the goal of this book is both analytic and constructive, seeking to deconstruct traditional questions and construct newly accurate answers. Yet the method will often be exegetic, bringing to light aspects of each thinker's ideas that have hitherto been overlooked, or worse, misunderstood.

As an exploration of philosophical and religious realism, many features have had to be excluded from this investigation: in-depth historical, social, or psychological accounts of the genesis of the views recounted here about "what is the case" (truth) and "how we should live" (ethics), and comprehensive arguments for and against their philosophical validity. These are not the questions with which this study is concerned. Here the questions are about the "realist" process of reasoning by which inquiry seeks well-grounded certainties, and uses them to arrive at models of what is true, and how it therefore makes sense to live. How have these thinkers reasoned to what is most certain? By what processes of reasoning do these particular certainties generate broader accounts of reality? By what logic do those accounts show us how we should understand ourselves as part of that reality, and take decisions and actions within it? Granted the ontological starting points adopted by these two thinkers, what alternatives do they offer to the classical Western metaphysics of "onto-theological" substantialism?

As will become clear, this book also focuses on one characteristic that it sees as common to philosophical reflections on reality and ethics in the wake of radical sceptical critiques. This is the concern to rejoin a strong sense of certainty with a strong sense of engagement, vitality, or passion; some of the most debilitating effects of radical doubt can be a general confusion about what is true or good, and a consequent general apathy. We have not yet overcome this problem, but we will see that the contemporary West is not the only culture that has sought what Alain Badiou calls "the passion of the real." The interreligious dialogicians of sixteenth-century India, inhabiting a critically self-aware and multicultured society, also sought an ontological answer to the relativistic and nihilistic critiques of radical scepticism, hoping thereby to heighten their own experience of reality.[6]

The introduction will lay foundations for this inquiry by staking out a set of concerns by which to define "realism" and "realist" inquiry, and then discussing possible methods for seeking new options. The discussion is divided into two parts structured in parallel, but maintaining continuous development of increasingly sophisticated answers to the central riddle.

The first section frames the problem of realism arising in the twentieth-century Western tradition of philosophy,[7] as it is reformulated in the work of Hans-Georg Gadamer (1900–2002). Chapter 1 explores the postmodern problem of realism as an unsolved problem that persists throughout contemporary Western philosophical traditions, interrogating the basis of our religious beliefs and our everyday actions. Like Gosvāmi, Gadamer transforms his own influences and authorities, transmuting old beliefs into new and subtler insights. Chapter 2 shows how Gadamer refines past sources into a self-grounded "realist" metaphysics. Chapter 3 examines the way in which he applies this ontology to "real-life" experience, deriving an ethos of human flourishing: a "vitalistic" approach to life that encourages us to engage eagerly and urgently in each teleological movement, or "game" that characterises Being's[8] true, dialectical nature.[9] In summary, we hope to show that Gadamer's position entails a "pantheistic" ontology on which he grounds an ethos of vitalistic engagement in plural, finite, but ultimately valuable ends.

The second section looks to sixteenth-century India and the work of Rūpa Gosvāmi for fruitful reflection on the same issues. Chapter 4 looks at the paradigms according to which Indian philosophy formulates its inquiry into the nature of reality. It argues that the conditions that have weakened classical Western realism—increasing methodological rigour acknowledging that human knowledge is circumscribed by its own sphere of experience, the promotion of humanistic concerns, fear of nihilism, and resentment of the apparent retreat of the divine from scientific inquiry—that these were also present in India where they have similarly yielded sophisticated metaphysical alternatives to naive dualism. Chapter 5 outlines Rūpa Gosvāmi's synthesis of his own contemporary and canonical sources into an ontology with axiomatic similarities and telling differences from Gadamer's ontology. Chapter 6 looks at Rūpa Gosvāmi's literature and religious theory for a picture of his ideal life. This, it turns out, is devoted not to a succession of vital "plays," but rather to a radical commitment to one object that heightens experience beyond the merely passing interest of Gadamer's ethics. Through a leap of faith, the playing of "games" proposed by Gadamer is elevated into a single-minded, unquenchable passion that utterly transforms the believer.

Seen as a pleasant but sometimes complacent thinker, Gadamer is rarely recognised as encouraging us toward a greater transformation than that of increased dialogue and fused horizons. His own inspirations were revolutionary figures anticipating a change that would sweep through the modern consciousness and galvanise our thought. He speaks of how Heidegger was a keystone of philosophy's renewal in that period from when "the theological break with historical and liberal theology took place in Marburg to when the philosophical abandonment of Neo-Kantianism occurred, the Marburg School dissolved, and new stars arose in the philosophical heavens."[10]

> I find it unforgettable the way he concluded his contribution to the discussion of Thurneyson's address. After evoking the Christian scepticism of Franz Overbeck, he said it is the true task of theology, which must be discovered once again, to seek the word that is able to call one to faith and preserve one in faith. . . . In speaking these words Heidegger seemed to be posing a task for theology.[11]

Heidegger's statement was meant as a response to a period of intense critique and philosophical change, but it addresses all theologies and particularly those in which the challenge of scepticism and the impetus of increasing cultural pluralism draw forth a need for a new ethos.

We need only read the newspaper to confirm that religious realism is not suffering the same universal debilitation that philosophical realism has suffered at the hands of post-Enlightenment scepticism. Rudolf Bultmann has raised the flag for the "common-sense" rejection of religious realism by philosophically minded thinkers across the disciplines, insisting on the superiority of an existential, more human and *humane* hermeneutic of religious claims over a stubbornly literalist one. He insists that

> We cannot use electric lights and radios and in the event of illness, avail ourselves of modern medical and clinical means and at the same time believe in the spirit and wonder world of the New Testament.[12]

Yet believers of every faith make daily confessions of belief in that "spirit and wonder" world, and conduct activities that are predicated upon them. Bultmann opposes religious truth to the scientific truth paradigm of facts. But Heidegger's redefinition of "reality," which has endured through two generations of successors, means aligning that opposition in new ways. Gadamer writes that Bultmann's humanistic existential hermeneutic of religion stood in tantalising contrast with Rudolf Otto's affirmation of mystery and holiness.[13] Indeed, given that religion incorporates both metaphysical and ethical concerns, it is difficult to mark a clear line between the everyday and the sacred—a line that is itself only part of the paraphernalia of "studying religion."

In part, the problem is that the phenomenon we want to speak of when we talk about belief is subtle and can only be obliquely observed, making a very poor object of study. It is difficult to identify the vast but elusive differences between a linguist analysing the semantic content of the sentence "Christ is the immortal son of God, begotten not created," an agnostic repeating it with mystified incredulity, Don Cupitt reciting it in church as an edifying (but factually false) ethical rhetoric, Rudolf Bultmann citing it as the formula for an irreducible existential truth about the human condition, a biblical exegete mining it for symbolic meanings, a negative theologian who states it with firm faith, affirming he knows not what, and a believer for whom it is no less a historical and transhistorical truth than that London is in England, and that one plus one is two. Questions are begged about the nature of our truth assertions in different discursive contexts, about their foundations, weak or strong, and about the nature of the state of "untruth" against which they are defined. Ethics are involved here; the duality of truth and untruth, however defined, is an implicitly prescriptive one, and the characteristics of truth, on any given model, guide our ideals and actions.

If, armed with a variety of rigorous philosophical perspectives on reality, we return to the primary facts of the phenomena constituting the actuality that we encounter day to day, we should be able to reconstruct a realism that assesses our experience in ways that are newly precise and newly intuitive. Post-Heideggerian philosophy is attempting to hermeneutically translate the old marks of ultimate reality (permanence, independence, transcendence, etc.) into new metaphysical terms. Hannah Arendt once said of Heidegger's hermeneutic thought that in it

> thinking has come to life again; the cultural treasures of the past, believed to be dead, are being made to speak, in the course of which it turns out that they propose things altogether different from the familiar, worn-out trivialities they had been presumed to say.[14]

Few positions are more in need of such a resurrection than that of the realist. In many cases, questions of *value* seem to be laid aside or reduced in favour of semantic accounts of truth, leaving the problems of ethics (e.g., ideals of human flourishing) unresolved. Wilfred Cantwell Smith notes that to see religions merely as propositional belief systems is already to obscure the phenomenon of faith and the way to understand it.[15] The affectivity of faith is a major theme of anthropological study,[16] and plays a role in many prevalent modern theological views of religion as expression, figuration, and metaphor.[17] With this new hermeneutic approach comes a newly rigorous emphasis on the place of the emotions and the passions in human reasoning.[18] This relation of the propositional and the affective, or, in this study, the metaphysical and the ethical, is a persistent problem for human thought.

One of the most important ingredients of realism that has been challenged and in many cases dispensed with, is the ideal of a transcendent reality that grounds meanings, truths and the value of human actions. From the ground of the relativist insight, all conceptions of absolute transcendence appear as nothing more than elaborate acrobatics of the human imagination. Yet it is this ideal of transcendence that is widely figured as the essence, or future, or substitute for religion.[19] The problem now encountered by the West—both in philosophy and in actual religious attitudes—is how to retain the inspirational elements of the idea of a transcendental reality in what is widely supposed to be a wholly finite world of immanent values. As we will see, confronted with a critique of radical transcendence, many schools of thought have sought to replace the certainties of a God or ground, with the certainties afforded by *transcendental arguments*—necessary and eternal truths about our own, meaning-filled, finite world. Such argument needn't be attested through revelations bridging the abyss between creation and creator; they are meant to be self-evident truths inherent in the very fabric of the world that we inhabit.

Relative to the parameters of the present inquiry, basic criteria for a "realist" position have been distilled from conventional models of metaphysical and commonsense realism, and adopted for the purposes of this study. These are the following: realism is concerned with ascertaining, by whatever tools of analysis we choose to use (relative to underlying criteria), what is "real." Realism further holds that truth and ethics are dependent upon the results. From our idea of what is particularly and certainly the case, arise our general ideas of how we are and must be. Of course, "truth," "ethics," "reality"—these are vague terms indeed, and in a comparative context the use of these terms must reflect the debates and discussions that determine them in the particular cultural contexts under examination. But the kind of reasoning that looks at the world to see what is the case, and decides what to do according to what it sees, is at the heart of realism's remarkable combination of the metaphysical and the ethical. In addition to outlining an alternative realist ontology, this inquiry addresses a further unanswered question: we habitually reason from "is" to "ought" as a part of our deepest rational analyses and as an intuitive way of generating values in our everyday lives. Natural orders, social structures, psychological inclinations—all of these are states that we might take as the pattern for our lives. But when the "is" is predicated on *ontological* (i.e., necessary and universal truths), is the leap to an *ethical* "ought" justified? What can it mean to say that we should *be more* and *do better* what we always innately *are*? This "realist" pattern of reasoning involves a progression from the contextual question about reality (chapters 1 and 4) to the attempt at a definitive description (chapters 2 and 5), to the task of deriving from it a *prescriptive* model for action (chapters 3 and 6). This progression furnishes the structure of this study.[20]

Thus the aim of this book is fourfold: (a) to offer two metaphysical alternatives to the traditional notion of realism, (b) to show how these metaphysics themselves yield ethical positions that are both predicated upon and inspired in ethos by these truths, (c) to establish hitherto unexplored insights into the Western and Indian philosophical traditions, and new axes of comparison between them, and (d) to give an example of a "comparative philosophical" study in which philosophy's analytic and hermeneutical capacities can be deployed to support cross-cultural comparison, and show how cross-cultural comparison hones our insight into philosophical questions.

IDENTIFYING INDIAN "REALISM"

Chapter 4 will map out the parameters of Indian philosophical realism in order to provide a framework for exegesis of Rūpa Gosvāmi's ideas, and comparison with those of Gadamer. But in order to anticipate in the first (Western) part the direction that this intercultural comparison will take in the second (Indian) part, we must fully appreciate certain issues and aporias that underpin the tradition of realist inquiry in the Indian tradition.

Philosophically understood, "realism" goes beyond simple thought about reality; it entails self-critical reflection on the very notion of realness. The conditions for realism and a realist debate arise where a thinker or circle of thinkers begin to suspect the possibility of something that is "more" real—even "ultimately" real, above and beyond the self-evident, everyday reality that is merely "there." They may come to refute this supposition or abandon it as an unattainable subject of knowledge or misconceived goal, but the questioning of "realness" is what brings reality into being as a topic of philosophical investigation. Through this questioning reality becomes hierarchally divided into the speculatively "more" or "less" real, lending force to our fantasies of living in a more compelling and less treacherous world. This idea of a hierarchy of possible "reals" culminating in what is ultimately true is ubiquitous in attempts to discuss and determine what is truly real. It is so deeply ingrained in the fabric of language about truth and reality that it often persists as an unspoken ghostly presence in metaphysics, muddling otherwise perspicuous debates. Yet it is the essence of ontology as an enquiry into what it *really* means to "be."

In Indian culture the question of the ultimately real has enjoyed a singular prominence throughout history, the question being raised in the very earliest and most seminal texts, with various answers being championed or denied through successive generations of competing traditions, sustained through the leitmotif of what is *parama*—highest, furthest—and what is *sat*—true or existent.[21] This motivation lies behind much Indian metaphysical thought, and although the way in which it is developed in epistemology and logic varies in interesting ways from routes taken by many Western thinkers, it nevertheless manifests in many of the usual philosophical questions. What counts as good evidence? What are the rules of good reasoning, and how should we deal with the problem of perspectivalism?[22] What is the reality status of universals? What accounts for the identity of particulars given the universal changefulness of their properties? What, if anything, is universally true? In particular, as Flood notes, "apart from a concern with language and its relation to being, Hindu theologies have been interested in the relation of 'the one' to 'the many.'" He continues:

> That is, Hindu revelation and yogic experience refer to an absolute reality that is unitary and without a second, yet experience of the world tells us that existence is manifold and diverse. What is the relation to this unique one and this diversified many? . . . Hindu theologies arrive at different positions with regard to this fundamental question.[23]

The formulation of the problem in terms of "the one" and "the many" will have particular significance for comparison with Gadamer's Platonic ontology in chapters 2 and 5, and its relation to the *ontological* notion of dialectic will be explored in chapters 3 and 6.

A particularly distinctive feature of Indian inquiry into the nature of reality is that it proceeds not only by means of much-celebrated inductive tools (by means of which contemporary scholars like Bimal Matilal and Jonardon Ganeri have hoped to advance dialogue between Indian and Western philosophy), but also from the basis of an epistemological position that has only come to self-awareness and general recognition in Europe in the twentieth century. In preparing to compare Gadamer's ontology and ethics with the Indian tradition that provides a background to Rūpa Gosvāmi's work, it is essential that we observe the largely phenomenological methodology that Indian thinkers applied to problems of reality. The cosmogonic accounts found in the *Ṛg Veda* are rapidly augmented by a tradition of inquiry based on individual perceptions, the analysis of those perceptions in terms both of their form and their content, and the recognition that all questions and answers, method and content, partial and absolute truths, necessarily have their being within perceptions and are universally subject to the nature of those perceptions, whatever they are. Arindam Chakrabarti notes that the earliest extensive attempt to discover the highest truths about reality (in the *Upaniṣads*)

> shows that the enterprise was not theology but a phenomenological ontology of ubiquitous consciousness; no object "that is worshipped as a this" could be the subjective spring of action, thought, and speech, according to these Vedic proponents of transcendental subjectivity.[24]

Furthermore, in the Indian tradition as in the West, we find at least two competing methods of laying transcendental foundations (a) by postulating a mysterious "other" level of *transcendental reality* that is separate from the phenomenal world and impervious to its weaknesses, and (b) by using *transcendental arguments* to expose necessary and universal (transcendental) features of the relative and changing truths of the phenomenal world itself.[25] The resolution of this question, so important for the authority struggles that characterised Indian philosophical debate, involves resolving related aporias such as the multifaceted and changeful nature of phenomenal "things," the question of whether categories of things are themselves things, and the question of whether nonexistence is also a category (and indeed a "thing") which must be included in any comprehensive ontology. Perhaps most pertinently for the ontological issues discussed in this study, the problem of the reality status of composite wholes and of universals, has been up for debate in the Indian tradition of philosophy since the second century CE at the very latest.[26]

The movement of the current of Indian philosophy is such that, with some very notable exceptions, it has lost much of its creative impulse. Rather than asking and exploring its own questions, it contents itself largely with exegesis of the ancients, reassuring itself of its own rationalist credentials,[27] or with the application of Indian ideas to a philosophical agenda set by the luminaries of the Western tradition. And of course neither the Indian nor the Western publics are widely concerned with the realist debate, as it is coined in the philosophical language of either tradition. But the concomitant problems of relativism and its perceived debilitation of certainty, the absence of ethical direction, and concerns about the adequacy of scientific methodology as a model for all kinds of "truth," may be seen more widely. Perhaps most pernicious and widespread is their conjunction in a life that has no clear "ultimate" aims, no compelling motivation—a life that has the energy and the will to act, but lacks a foundation and a goal for action. "Reality" seems to be divested of its infrastructures of truth and ethical direction. One of the goals of this study is to explore the resources that both the Western and Indian traditions of philosophy possess for building models of reality that leave meaning, truth, and value intact, as structures that are shown to be integral at even the most "ultimate" levels of ontological analysis. Chapter 6 in particular will compare and assess the solutions proffered by our two thinkers. But throughout the first section, in which we will be focusing on Gadamer's preferred model, it is helpful to keep in mind that we are looking at writers who share an interdisciplinary interest in philosophy and the arts, are seeking to recoup and synthesise the insights of pivotal predecessors, and hope to achieve this by discovering the most basic truth and using it as the foundation for a picture of life that will revive and redirect a public demoralised by ideological pluralism, the threat of nihilism, and the inescapable ontic truths of relativism and finitude. For both men, the tension of phenomenological plurality and oneness appears to hold the key to a compelling outlook, unassailably rooted in ultimate truth.

ON COMPARATIVE PHILOSOPHICAL METHODOLOGY

On the island of Capri, at a gathering of philosophers committed to teasing out a better understanding of "postmodern" religion, Gadamer wrote:

> [W]e must learn to think on a broad scale if, under the title "Religion and the Religions," we seek to reflect on the destiny of humankind and to consider what the future may bring. We must properly ask whether other religions and cultural worlds can provide any response to the universality of the scientific enlightenment and its consequences, which is different from the "Religion" of the global economy. Will the world, perhaps, be able to discover an answer which, as yet, can only be guessed at?
>
> The participants in this discussion . . . have sought to engage with the problem of religion as it is encountered in the context of the European Enlightenment and from the perspective of our European culture. However, if the undogmatic concern with religious experience which has governed this discussion is to be thought through from a global perspective, it should be possible and indeed necessary to extend this problematic to include other world religions.[28]

The present study attempts to take up this gauntlet laid down not only by Gadamer, but also by Tracy, Derrida, Ricoeur, and Heidegger himself. Modern Western philosophy is filled with thinkers who imply that their own rebellious intuitions paralleled the radically different approaches found in other worldviews—but who possessed insufficient training to pursue the possibilities that those other traditions afforded.[29] With sufficient methodological sensitivity these possibilities can still be excavated. However, while the philosophical problem addressed here is drawn initially from characteristically Western concerns, the motivation for approaching it in this multicultured way should not solely be so. Where not long ago the judgement of Western scholars was that comparative work was fundamentally flawed in its methodology, now there can be no justification in refusing the legitimacy and need of such study. This is not because multiculturalism, the universality of human concerns and the potential dialogue in expressing those concerns, is an important fact of modern life to which we must respond. It is because these features are a fact of history, which the good scholar does not ignore, but from which they choose instead to learn. There is a crippling cultural arrogance in the view that one's own discourse is most apt for addressing philosophical meta-problems of life, and that it is also an "insider" discourse, exclusive to other views and languages.

Nevertheless, the discipline of "comparative religion" has been subject to so much criticism of both its methods and its goals that it seems necessary to turn away from its characteristic exercises in crude thematic comparison, and look for ways of doing more precise and philosophically sophisticated studies. In attempting to develop a comparative *philosophy* of religion this study places meta-questions of truth and its relation to logic and to ethics at the centre of the enterprise. The goal is no longer to point to perennial religious impulses throughout human history. It is to use historically and culturally diverse examples to illuminate and refine our understanding of the philosophical issues—in this case of truth ("is") and ethics ("ought"), which are embedded in the very structures of language, thought, and everyday action.

The main methodological criticism of comparative study is, of course, that one can never perfectly calibrate the subject of study in one tradition with an equivalent subject in another. Where there is no common historical root, it is impossible to rule out the possibility of thoroughgoing subterranean differences that undermine any equivalences made by the researcher. This spectre of semantic pluralism is omnipresent, threatening even the most provisional similarities. Yet it is ironic that a study of the aporia of reality and relativism, nominally rooted in a tradition that is at once Greek, Hebrew, and Christian, should have to defend its multicultural scope. The notion of a monolithic entity that is "Western" philosophy is more than ever being dissected into diverse and mutually illuminating strands. The singular, damning narrative of a Spenglerian twilight of the West has been challenged in the early decades of the twentieth century by the renaissance of the classical philosophers—altered, argued against, and appropriated in a humanistic spirit. Gadamer's great contribution to comparative study is widely judged to be his theory of dialogue as a fusion of horizons (*Horizontverschmelzung*). Yet when he himself brings together Plotinus, Augustine, Heidegger, and Rilke at the end of his essay "Thinking as Redemption: Plotinus between Plato and Augustine," he is not merely reviewing a series of intellectual influences. He is seeking to recoup and hermeneutically harvest culturally *distinct* insights, and to understand them in their localised context independently of their appropriation by the "Western tradition." In this way, through close attention to cultural *context* and to philosophical *content*, Gadamer sketches out in practice a method for doing comparative philosophy that is underpinned by the whole edifice of hermeneutic interpretive theory. He writes:

> Hermeneutics bridges the distance between minds and reveals the foreignness of the other mind. But revealing what is unfamiliar does not mean merely reconstructing historically the "world" in which the work had its original meaning and function. It also means apprehending what is said to us, which

> is always more than the declared and comprehended meaning. Whatever says something to us is like a person who says something. It is alien in the sense that it transcends us. To this extent there is a double foreignness in the task of understanding (*Verstehen*), which in reality is one and the same foreignness. It is this way with all speech.[30]

For Gadamer the problems of interpersonal, intracultural, and intercultural communication are fundamentally the same universal and necessary. He is himself doing comparative work within a culturally diverse tradition of mutual influences in which genuinely different worldviews competed for prominence.[31] Further exploration of "Western" philosophy in the last two hundred years shows the influence of Asian philosophies and of other disciplines in the sciences and arts. Similarly, deeper exploration of the intellectual milieu of scholastic thinkers whose proverbially Western (mis)conceptions Heidegger sought to unmask reveals Muslim, Jewish, and other influences extending beyond the bounds of "onto-theology," which have subsequently been sublimated by the writers of history.[32]

This *intracultural* pluralism can be only more apt to the lengthy and complex intellectual debates of Indian history. In general it is an insight that liquidates the rhetoric of different, distinct world-historical strands of humanity: a model that we have adhered to not least since Hegel's simplistic stab at world history. In short, it is not only the postmodern philosophers of migration and multiculturalism, but also the conscientious historians who teach us that cultural identities are more complex, and cultural boundaries more permeable than previously suspected. The interpretive sensitivity championed by Gadamer's "philosophical hermeneutics" devotes an anti-sophistic attention to both the intended meaning and its semantic complexity as complementary facets of human understanding. It is a position that affirms plurality through a constructive, Wittgensteinian approach to meaning, undaunted by the realisation that belief is capable of complex moments, manoeuvres, and positions.[33]

Reflecting the richness of this complex many-cultured intellectual landscape, the goals of comparative philosophy thus parallel the goals of phenomenological (i.e., purely descriptive) research in the social sciences: to map out more and more completely the existing and possible structures of human thought, and their application for what Aristotle famously called *phronesis*, or practical wisdom. This goal, at once modest and ambitious, has been adapted from the phenomenological project of finding "new ways of knowing and new things to know" within the limited compass of human experience. Heidegger was famously aware that such resources existed in the Buddhist traditions of Japan, Gadamer turned to the pagan religious traditions of Greece, and Levinas looked toward Judaism for an alternative to the traditional Platonic-Aristotelian "theontology" that is seen as having reached its zenith in medieval scholastic thought. In the attempt to produce a philosophy that ceases to seek an impossible foundation beyond being, framing, as it were, an Orphic comportment that should not anxiously look back for reassurance, authors like Bataille, Bourdieu, Derrida, and Zizek have looked beyond the boundaries separating the disciplines. In literature, psychology, and particularly anthropology they too have gleaned new insights from cultures that are external or marginal to the "mainstream" West.

As Jay Garfield points out in his essay on Gadamer and religious comparativism, most of the arguments against comparativism belie a sort of postcolonial xenophobia endemic to the idea of academic research as an accumulation of *knowledge* within set boundaries, like capital stored safely in a vault.[34] Certainty can stand only within cultural walls—asked to cross such boundaries, it collapses under the weight of the foregone conclusion that linguistic difference is an indicator of absolute difference, and that there are such things as "discrete" historical traditions that have always been coherent and can admit of no further cultural additions or influences. Intercultural communication between "traditions" is seen to entail problems that interpersonal and transnational do not. This assumption does not stand well against either historical or philosophical interrogation. By contrast intercultural comparison can be seen as the building of roads and bridges, producing a hard-won *understanding* that challenges those boundaries. The modern hope is that increased rigour in contextual research combined with philosophical precision (as opposed to broad thematic analogy), will assuage the methodological criticisms that threaten any nominally "comparative" enterprise, bringing them into line with the difficulties inherent in all academic work. Executed carefully, such comparative research will clarify our understanding of the concepts and cultures under examination, and enrich the dialogue that historically has served as a natural organ of philosophical and religious development—both between and within cultures.

Of course, to speak vaguely of increased comparative rigour and sensitivity is to add little that is new to the debate: Albert Reville expressed this hope in 1901 in terms that are painfully close to the working philosophy of most comparative researchers today:

> The History of Religions, like all histories, is possible only through the collective labour of all who devote their strength to it . . . what can be said is that its broad outlines have been traced, that the area of the mine has been sounded, divided, deepened, and that it is now up to each miner to excavate to the best of his ability the seam which has been allocated to him.[35]

The development of the discipline has largely consisted in honing the tools of this labour. Extending the metaphor of deep structures, one recent approach has been to apply resilient structural schemes to diverse cases, as a way of establishing a common field for valid reference and comparison. Thus we see a move from thematic studies (consider Keith Ward's comparative works on revelation (1994), creation (1996), human nature (1998) and community (2000), and the brief flurry of enthusiasm over Joseph Campbell's Jungian cross-cultural comparison), to more philosophical studies that identify contrasts, axes, relations, and conjunctions of ideas. They aim at laying the groundwork for thematic comparison by illuminating the internal logical and semantic workings of religions and philosophies. Consider the Boston Comparative Religious Ideas Project's axial dissection of religious truth into epistemology, expression, and embodiment: by establishing an analytic framework, the comparison is underpinned by a relational structure assuming not that particular themes are common, but that the process of rationally working out an idea, imaginatively expressing it, and concretely acting according to it is a universal pattern in human thought and activity. This too is controversial, but not to the same degree as, say, any purported equivalence between *duḥkha* (suffering in Buddhism and Hinduism), *pāpa* (mischief, malevolence in Hinduism), evil in Catholicism or evil in Calvinism, or other more arbitrarily related theological themes. The sophistication of the approach and our increased confidence in it depends upon how firm its *philosophical* foundations are.

Bimal Matilal has long been revered as one of the first and greatest "comparative philosophers," not least for rigorous and illuminating studies on Buddhist versions of scepticism, which clarify the basic axes according to which pan-Indian epistemology would be pursued for millennia to come. H. S. Prasad's essay "Language and Reality: A Buddhist Approach" seeks to uncover "the relationship between our language which helps us to conceptualise, and what it conceptualises"—another deep structure that underlies all intellectual endeavour and affects any results that we could hope to gain from the study of it.[36] It is essential to acknowledge the background structures, methods, and assumptions of reasoning in laying a comparative foundation while grounding his own study of Indian Semantics; E. Kahrs defends the type of research that builds on an understanding of the "deep," or "prior," structures of a system of meanings:

> My point here is simply one of logical order: the question of how something comes to mean what it means is more fundamental logically speaking [than the meaning itself], and an answer to this question may enable us to carry our investigations of Indian cultural history a step further.[37]

In analysing Western and Indian philosophical systems, Debabrata Sinha, and later Bimal Matilal and Jonardon Ganeri, has not failed to note and explore the logical processes by which each operates (according to Sinha, case-based reasoning for Indian logic, and Platonic dialectic respectively), while Arvind Sharma has more recently attempted a deep hermeneutics of Indian notions of history and of time, thereby illuminating a very wide range of disciplines (history, myth, literature, philosophy, theology, etc.) to which such assumptions are intrinsic.[38] Jonardon Ganeri notes the degree to which the Vedic faith in the philosophically foundational principle of received knowledge informs the pragmatic optimism of much Indian philosophical language use, suggesting a parallel not with formalist logic as the rigour of the Nyāya school of writers would imply, but with modern pragmatist philosophies of language.[39] His own rigorous yet expansive work on subjectivity similarly goes to an axial, philosophically succinct (if puzzle-filled) topic to stake out well-defined fields of comparative enquiry, which are to some extent shared by Flood in his comparative work on ascetic subjectivity.[40] Consider too that time and self, language and narrative have become common themes of study, revered as a hermeneutic key to other notions such as good and evil, salvation and revelation. Chandradhar Sharma's work draws on a comparative understanding of the principles of dialectic in India and the West respectively, and this comparison provides the basis for deeper insights into the importance of flux in both Indian and Western notions of identity.[41] Each of these studies, aimed at meta-themes such as processes of reasoning and enactment, of linguistic conceptualisation, of logical methodology or of identity, does the hard work of clarifying context at precisely the deeper levels of meaning that critics of comparativism have been so sceptical about. Similarly, studies on modes of perception, meaning, belief, and action all fill those elusive semantic gaps that have for so long undermined the comparative field. In many cases such studies may optionally fall within the field of anthropology, or elsewhere psychology, linguistics, even biology or aesthetics, but nonetheless we can apply to these studies the umbrella term "comparative philosophy." This, then, is what is meant by increased rigour—a contextual widening and structural deepening of our hermeneutic approach to ideas found in each culture, as if in each case we were the "outsider" mapping out the landscape.

But there are also further axes of hermeneutic sophistication with which to illuminate the cross-cultural field. Historical context is an intrinsic part of any definition, and we may reason that such references can simply be quantitatively accumulated, yielding better and better definitions. Yet this fulfils only one dimension of comparative study: it accumulates knowledge but may not yield the kind of understanding that takes into account the implicit dialogue between different positions, refracting the wider range of issues to which those positions respond, for which the information at hand has been brought to light in the first place. In this respect thematic comparison, even where it is intensified by infrastructural philosophical comparison, must be reconfigured not as an exercise in one-to-one equivalence, but as study of puzzles, issues, and aporias. In this way two things are gained.

Firstly, by exploring (for instance) the problem of epistemological authority and its application to lived conditions, we are taking a more sophisticated approach to the idea than if we had simply started by comparing two existing conceptions of truth. By focusing on an inquiry, an interrelated aporia, a problem with an inner logic as opposed to a singular theme, we have already incorporated complexity and self-interrogation into the terms of our study. By triangulating a number of related questions, we engage a space of thought rather than a single bridge, giving greater scope for contextual understanding. In addition, the study of "problems" rather than "ideas" engages not only meaning but also value—the conflicts and interests that tie together meanings and ideas and, as Heidegger might put it, bring them into the light of our discursive concern—rather than merely listing the semantic relations that constitute a definition according to the myth of neutral scientific knowledge. We are encouraged to look at the reasons why the puzzle arises, the goals of solving it, and the inner rationale that governs the way in which it unfolds as we work it out.

Secondly, this is an approach that incorporates the issues of prejudice and motivation that are at the heart of the insider-outsider critique of comparative studies. In orienting our study around the guiding concerns that attract our thought and define its contours, we acknowledge the "ethical" side of the sciences and allow the motives of the work under examination to be charted beside our own motives, whatever these may be. In this respect comparative philosophy concedes the importance of prejudice as well as complexity. In a "comparative philosophy of religion" both of these factors—far from undermining the topics under consideration—help to clarify our inquiry more effectively. Consonant with these goals, the present study approaches "realism" not as a unilateral theme to be tested against particular ideas found in given traditions, but as a bundle of related issues and aporias that are tied up with the questions of *what is,* and *what to do,* however the answers are configured.

HISTORICAL CONNECTIONS

Needless to say, these larger issues of comparison and dialogue in no way diminish the need for precision and clarity about any actual historical influences that may exist between the objects of study. In fact, while there is no evidence that Rūpa Gosvāmi came into contact with Platonic or any other brand of Western philosophy during his time of writing in sixteenth-century India, Gadamer did encounter Indian philosophy as mediated in a variety of forms by its European admirers (and indeed its European critics, such as Hegel).[42] Apart from its significant influence on Western and particularly German philosophy since Schopenhauer, Indian literature had been an important field of study in the German philosophical and philological academies. Gadamer himself pursued a brief course of study in Sanskrit at the age of eighteen before entering into the field of classical philology that came to be so formative for his own metaphysics. Scheler, whose influence on Gadamer we will see in chapter 3, writes at length on Indian philosophy (precisely in respect of the meeting between emotions, ontology, and theology that is at the heart of this investigation), and Huizinga, one of the main influences on the anthropological dimension of Gadamer's phenomenology, was *privatdozent* of Indian literature at the University of Amsterdam. Gadamer thanks Theodor Lessing's *Europa und Asien* for liberating him from the "Prussian efficiency" that surrounded him at that age, affording a partial glimpse of Asian culture. He even encountered some elements of Indian thought firsthand from Rabindranath Tagore at Stefan George's poetic gatherings in Marburg. In *Truth and Method* he credits "the study of the 'religion and wisdom of India'" (among others factors) with the rise of "historical research" which "no longer measures the past by the standards of the present, as if they were an absolute, but it ascribes to past ages a value of their own and can even acknowledge their superiority in one respect or another."[43] The passage makes it clear that he believes the same possibilities were open to intercultural research.

In the subsequent course of Gadamer's long and difficult struggle to sketch out a new metaphysics, he observed that "there are also things in the traditions of ancient India or ancient China that will rival our tradition, and discovering this will also be a good thing for the ancient Greek sources!"[44] Western philosophers had long looked to India for the clues to alternative metaphysical schemes, but for Gadamer it became clear that India was not just a sounding board providing sharp contrasts to the Western outlook; it sounded a melody that would help to identify overlooked themes within the West. The similarity of the post-Heideggerian turn of Western philosophy to the Japanese synthesis of Buddhism and Taoism is widely commented upon, and Heidegger himself was explicit about the widely acknowledged East Asian influences on his work.[45] Ray Billington's *East of Existentialism* makes such comparisons, as does George Pattison's *Agnosis: Theology in the Void*, but these works signal a more general predominance toward comparisons of Heideggerian and post-Heideggerian thought with Buddhism than with Hinduism—its ontologically more optimistic cousin.[46] There are a few counterexamples to this trend—Harold Coward provides a notable exception with his comparison of Derrida's semantics to selected Indian theories of meaning.[47] But in the main, Buddhism and Judaism have been nominated as the primary dialogue partners for postmodern metaphysics as they are often seen as anti-metaphysical religions, religions bordering on sheer "ethics," which harbour in their fundamental tenets a repudiation of ontological essentialism. Hinduism, monolithically identified with Advaita Vedānta and simplified into an essentialistic vision *par excellence,* is by contrast frequently seen as theologically dogmatic and metaphysically naive. One of the goals of this book is to contribute to the gradual overturning of those cultural and philosophical prejudices.

From the Indian side, modern Indian commentators trained in Western philosophy have often sought to compare Indian ideas with Western ones. It is highly telling that, in philosophy, these comparisons have often been oriented around features of a purported realist-idealist dichotomy. Take, for example, R. R. Dravid's attempt to give a complete history of realism throughout both traditions *vis á vis* the problem of universals.[48] That he is able to produce an even vaguely coherent study out of so large an undertaking indicates the value of philosophical problems as a comparative category. It is also a sign that—as we will see—the notion he had alighted upon was particularly appropriate to both traditions. Similarly, J. N. Mohanty has been eager to map various philosophical problems of Indian thought against the Husserlian position, inspired in part by the pairing of two perspectives that seem so far beyond the pale of Western substance ontology.[49] The comparison of Nyāya logic with modern Anglo-analytic philosophy is not uncommon,[50] and B. Matilal has also found some success in measuring Indian theories of perception against the Cartesian epistemological tradition.[51]

In choosing to explore Gadamer's philosophical hermeneutics I have not chosen the most original or provocative post-Heideggerian philosopher to represent the insights and aporias of the modern Western tradition, but rather the one who most faithfully carries on the search for ontological truth that was Heidegger's first and foremost goal. In pursuing his rigorous analysis of Being, he is inspired rather than daunted by the subversive "Nietzschean" elements present in Heidegger's thought, beguiling others into a stronger form of metaphysical scepticism.[52] In Gadamer's works a clearer picture of the modern ontological terrain comes to light than that painted by his predecessors, with more optimistic ethical conclusions than many of his contemporaries drew. This is precisely the quality that has drawn such criticism from supporters of deconstructionism, focusing on Gadamer's optimism about the foundational possibilities of the metaphysics of the finite, over and above any modest submission to the edifying rhetorics that can be attached to it.[53] His vision furnishes an important, almost unique position in the postmodern canon, shared only perhaps by a few other rigorously ontological thinkers, similarly optimistic about the philosophical potential of an approach that seeks "realist" truths.

In addition to this veridical attachment to a firm ontological grounding, Gadamer's philosophy yields further, "ethical" insights with which aspects of Caitanya Vaiṣṇavism resound. Both positions historically stand in a milieu of critical flourishing, responding to the challenges of what is seen as an outmoded transcendentalism, adopting an approach that is both "protestant" and constructively assimilative, in order to craft an ontologically grounded philosophy that affirms the conditions of necessary finitude, relationality, and immanent value that we find in all experience. Heideggerian philosophy and the Nietschean strand of critical thought in which it stands, both seek to breach the current boundaries of our thought. However, Heidegger seems to have experienced unforeseen difficulty in surmounting them—perhaps in struggling with our indoctrinated prejudices he became all the more tangled within them, caught up on this side of the wall that Nietzsche had urged him to dismantle. It may then be the task of comparative research to step briskly to the other side and beckon us through to explore and inhabit other landscapes.

Rūpa Gosvāmi is chosen, as in the case of Gadamer, because he is such an excellent representative of his tradition, because he is a philosophically responsible systematiser of his tradition, and yet because he too seeks to go beyond the tradition, saying what it is reluctant to say in order to make it genuinely coherent and accessible as a way of life for all.[54] Whilst asserting that Rūpa Gosvāmi's thought is unique and extraordinary in ways that will become clear, it is essential to this project to acknowledge that other interesting metaphysical answers to the aporia of realism could equally be gleaned from studies of many other schools of Indian philosophy that also walk the thin lines between realism and idealism, monism and pluralism, truth and ethics. The same can be said of Western thinkers such as Ricoeur, Levinas, Blanchot, Badiou, and others. The study will let the continuity of the philosophical problem of realism be its guide as it unfolds through the exposition of these two thinkers. It will seek added clarity by dealing with Gadamer and Rūpa Gosvāmi separately. Analogies will be made throughout, but generally it is not lateral comparison that is the goal of the inquiry, but the clarification and furtherance of the theme at the heart of the dialogue. Thus the logic of the problem of realism will be our guide, allowing time for proper contextualisation of the two contributors on each side. The valuable analogies between the concerns of Gadamer and Rūpa Gosvāmi will become clear in the light of the realist debate as it is transfigured through their alternative ontologies. Equally, it is their differences that will also provide a progression toward answering the problem of belief in its relation to describing objective truth, and prescribing a subjective ethos based on that truth.

NOTES

1. See in particular Donald S. Lopez Jr.'s article on "belief" in *Critical Terms for Religious Studies*, Mark C. Taylor, ed. (Chicago: University of Chicago Press, 1998).

2. See Alain Badiou, *Infinite Thought: Truth and the Return of Philosophy* (London: Continuum, 2003), 43. The *Eudaimonian Ethics* is a key Aristotelian text that introduces in a formal way the notion that ethics—the problem of what it is best to do and how we should make those decisions—should be harnessed to a model of human flourishing. Implicit in this is the idea that we have a basic nature that can flourish or wither, but in either case we are not ethically neutral agents that can be turned to any goal or ethos. We already have a nature against which our actions will always be measured, whether we like it or not. Hence the literal translation of the word indicates a coming into accordance with our "daimon"—our fateful spirit or essence. In its assumption that there is a true state and that discovering it is an intrinsic good, this "eudaimonian" position is implicitly "realist" according to the definition that we have adopted here, i.e., in the sense that it rejects ideas without basis in reality and uses whatever can be reliably ascertained as a foundational premise for (and restriction upon) other ideas.

3. Rainer Maria Rilke, *Selected Poems*, J. B. Leishman, trans. (London: Penguin, 1964), 61.

4. Maurice Blanchot tells a similar anecdote, cited by John Caputo as an exemplary postmodern approach to sustaining religious belief even after its transcendent object has been denied. The Messiah finally turns up in a modern city, but rather than welcoming him as the anticipated fulfilment of an ancient desire, the believer merely asks him with eyes full of hope: "When will the Messiah come?" This is what Derrida calls "messianicity without messianism," characteristic of a theism that has had to adapt to the philosophical problems associated with transcendence, by adopting an ontology (and soteriology) of finitude. (See John Caputo in *The Prayers and Tears of Jacques Derrida* (Bloomington: Indiana University Press, 1997), xxiv.)

5. See Barbara Stoler Miller's translation *Love Song of the Dark Lord: Jayadeva's Gītagovinda* (New York: Columbia University Press, 1977). The story is repeated in a different version in Rūpa Gosvāmi's *Ujjvala Nīlamaṇi*, chapter 15, under the heading *Prema-vaicityyam*.

6. The *Bhakti* movement of religious devotion in India that arose throughout centuries of Hindu renaissance and continues to dominate the religious experience of most Hindus today, focused on restoring fervour to religious life, and often took that engaged enthusiasm as its defining feature, seeking to meld it with the rationalism of the philosophical schools. Needless to say, others in other cultures have engaged a similar axis of passionate engagement and foundational truth, and produced different but genetically related answers that it is not within the scope of this study to explore.

7. When the term "Western" is used in this study, it refers specifically to the commonalities within the shared experiences and cultural traditions of Europe and North America. However, while this is a useful and valid designation, it will also be argued that it is not a discrete designation; this cultural historical entity includes an intrinsic identity with a range of interacting cultures that constitute and define it, within and across permeable boundaries.

8. Borrowing from Heidegger's terminology on account of its pervasive presence in post-Heideggerian thought and distinct usefulness for these purposes, this study will employ the word "being" in two ways. When capitalised as "Being" (*Sein* for

Gadamer) it refers to the whole of existence, of whatever type that existence is, in respect of its common *ontological* character. When not capitalised, it refers to individual existing beings (*Seiende*) in respect of their *ontic* character of existence, having a nature as something or other in particular.

9. The idea of "dialectic" will return as a theme of this study. It has many meanings, which of necessity will be used in this study according to context—Plato's dialectic, for instance, having a primarily methodological implication (discursive inquiry), whereas Hegel's dialectic introduces ontological connotations, claiming that dialectic is in fact ubiquitous. Where it is used in ontological discussion here, it refers primarily to any structure (of argument, object, situation, worldview, concept, Being, etc.), in which the apparent unities constituting the structure turn out to be internally complex, capable both of being divided into contradicting but interrelated entities, and of being aggregated into further and further levels of unities related to each other in similar ways. The picture produced is one of infinite division, relation, and synthesis. This conception, reflecting Gadamer's summary and development of various classical positions, is based primarily on a Hegelian model, where all apparently finite and discrete (and often contradictory) truths turn out to be complementary aspects of higher truths, which are themselves the constitutive aspects of yet higher truths, *ad infinitum*. Thus the implicit pluralism that complexifies unities, and the perspectivalism that complexifies truths are shown to be intrinsic features that are metaphysically and logically necessary. The classic ontological example of Hegelian dialectic is that of the apparent opposition of Being and Not-Being, resolved in the transcendental truths of changefulness and becoming.

10. Hans-Georg Gadamer, "Martin Heidegger and Marburg Theology," in *Philosophical Hermeneutics*, D. Linge, trans. (Cambridge, Mass.: MIT Press, 1985), 198.

11. "Martin Heidegger and Marburg Theology," in *Philosophical Hermeneutics*, 198.

12. Rudolf Bultmann, *New Testament and Mythology* (Norwich: SCM Press, 1985), 5.

13. "Martin Heidegger and Marburg Theology," in *Philosophical Hermeneutics*, 199.

14. Hannah Arendt, "Martin Heidegger at Eighty," in *The New York Review of Books*, October 21, 1971, 51.

15. Wilfred Cantwell Smith, *The Meaning and End of Religion* (San Francisco: Harper and Row, 1978), 48.

16. Anthropologists exploring this theme range from William James and Rudolf Otto to more mainstream anthropologists such as Thomas Luckmann and Peter Berger, Clifford Geertz, Roy Rappaport, and Bronislaw Malinowski.

17. Major models of this are widespread and well-illustrated by Rudolf Bultmann's notion of demythologising mythical settings for the "kerygma" of religious discourse, Paul Ricoeur's "second naivety" of religious credulousness, David Tracy's "Hidden God," Paul Tillich's and Hans Kung's insistence on the metaphorical nature of much the Bible, and Jim Robinson, Don Cupitt, Albert Schweitzer, and Thomas Altizer's arguably "non-realist" concepts of God. Other contemporary thinkers have taken this "liberal" theological theme along new interdisciplinary paths.

18. See, for instance, the work of Robert Solomon, Robert Gordon, Ronald de Sousa, Michael Stocker, Martha Nussbaum, Simon Blackburn, Jerome Neu, Richard Wollheim, and Christine Tappolet in this field.

19. See, for example, *Transcendence in Philosophy and Religion*, James Faulconer, ed. (Bloomington: Indiana University Press, 2003), *Transcendence: Philosophy, Literature and Theology Approach the Beyond*, Regina Schwarz, ed. (New York: Routledge, 2004) (with particular reference to Charles Taylor's essay "A Place for Transcendence"), and also Henk Vroom's essay "How May We Compare Ideas of Transcendence? On the Method of Comparative Theology," in *Comparative Theology: Essays for Keith Ward*, T. W. Bartel, ed. (London: SPCK, 2003).

20. The problem of reasoning from the metaphysical *is* to an ethical *ought* is an extremely common one in Indian thought, formalised in the tensions within the hierarchies of cosmological, social, and ethical order (e.g., *ṛta, dharma*). In a recent paper on the fissures within the ideologies represented in the Mahābhārata, Simon Brodbeck focused on precisely this aporia of Krishna *describing* what is the case to Arjuna, and then *prescribing* that he act in accordance with it. This tension, it is suggested, is lodged within the basic structure of the theology of *dharma* and *karma* (see Simon Brodbeck's paper "Observations on the Idea of Non-attached Action (*aśakta karman*) in the Mahābhārata" given at the 2005 session of the Spalding Symposium).

21. On the other hand, Indian thinkers have rarely equalled Western thinkers' frequent concern to bridge the gap between descriptive metaphysical foundationalism and prescriptive ethics. Nor have they expended much energy on harnessing the arguments of philosophical realism to an agenda of religious literalism; the realities of karma, reincarnation, gods, heavens and hells are considered "ontic," or "phenomenal" realities—more of the order of scientific cosmology than of ontology proper.

22. Not least of these, the problem of sophism and the annexing of correct reasoning to questionable ethical positions plagued Indian scholars as it did Greek scholars struggling to bring order to early instances of the multireligious, multiethnic, socially divided metropolis. While there is no exact equivalent concept to sophism in Sanskritic philosophy, Jonardon Ganeri succinctly cites the influential fifth-century philosopher Vātsyāyana Pakṣilasvāmin's categorisation of "bad" philosophers into those guilty of *jalpa*, using intellectual tricks to defend one's own position at all costs, and of *vitaṇḍa-*, employing reason in a purely negative and destructive way (see *Classical Philosophy in India: The Proper Work of Reason* (Oxford: Routledge, 2001), 11).

23. Gavin Flood, *An Introduction to Hinduism* (Cambridge: Cambridge University Press, 1996), 229–30.

24. Arindam Chakrabarti in "Indian Philosophy," in *The Oxford Companion to Philosophy*, Ted Honderich, ed. (Oxford: Oxford University Press, 1995), 401.

25. Again, the present study's principal focus on the second method of pursuing transcendence, is not meant to cast aspersions on the first, which also entails virtues of many kinds, philosophical and otherwise.

26. See the discussion of these questions in Gautama Akṣapada's *Nyāyasūtra*.

27. The reassertion of India thought's "rational basis" (see Ganeri's *Philosophy in Classical India: The Proper Work of Reason*) and its "argumentative" capacity (see Amartya Sen's *The Argumentative Indian: Writings on Indian History, Culture and Identity*)

is undeniably a useful project, given the history of prejudices with which it has had to contend, and which will be discussed in chapter 4.

28. "Dialogues in Capri," in *Religion*, J. Derrida and G. Vattimo, eds. (Cambridge: Polity Press, 1998), 204–5.

29. Even the turn in Levinas and in Derrida toward a Hebraic "anti-metaphysics" of the spoken word and the direct encounter, is based in part on a rejection of what is seen as a Christian "onto-theology" apotheosising substantialist Being. David Tracy once answered, in response to Scott Holland's comment "I think I once heard you say that 'Christian theology began when Greek questions were asked about a Hebrew narrative,'" saying "Yes, and now it seems to me that we theologians must be as interested in Asian thought as the early church was about Greek questions" ("This Side of God: A Conversation with David Tracy," in *Cross Currents*, Spring 2002).

30. "Aesthetics and Hermeneutics," in *Philosophical Hermeneutics*, 100–101.

31. Gadamer's extraordinary range of interests take different forms, from studies such as "Semantics and Hermeneutics" in which he draws on the early twentieth-century anthropological methodology of works by Charles Morris (1938, 1955) and Johan Huizinga (1938) taking in both Western and Asian cultural phenomena (see *Philosophical Hermeneutics*, 90), to the tradition-specific essays such as "The Nature of Things" in the same volume, in which he compares a key idea from Husserlian phenomenology with relevant ideas from other strands of the varied Western history of ideas, from Greek metaphysics to medieval scholasticism to Kantian idealism and German Romantic poetry. Six years after the publication of *Truth and Method*, Gadamer shows that his methodological prioritisation of language and its primeval sources is nothing less than an attempt to transcend cultural particularism by discovering "the prehistory of the human spirit" (see "Man and Language," also in *Philosophical Hermeneutics*, 61).

32. Increasingly, non-Western influences on the ancients, on the scholastic philosophers, and on the German and English Romantic traditions are being recognised and documented. Not least, the extent of the German tradition of Sanskritic study, and the far-reaching influence of Schopenhauer's representations of Indian thought, are becoming more widely acknowledged. Recent publications relevant to Gadamer's influences include Reinhard May's *Heidegger's Hidden Sources: East Asian Influences on his Work*, Graham Parkes, trans. (Oxford: Routledge, 1996), and *Heidegger and Asian Thought*, Graham Parkes, ed. (Honolulu: University of Hawaii Press, 1990), and *Nietzsche and Asian Thought*, Graham Parkes, ed. (Chicago: University of Chicago Press, 1996).

33. Gadamer's account of truth and language has frequently been likened to that of Wittgenstein, as by Chris Lawn in *Wittgenstein and Gadamer: Towards a Post-Analytic Philosophy of Language* (London: Continuum Press, 2005), Richard Shusterman in "The Gadamer-Derrida Encounter: A Pragmatist Perspective," in *Dialogue and Deconstruction: The Gadamer-Derrida Encounter*, Richard Michelfelder and Diane Palmer, ed. (Albany: State University of New York Press, 1989), Ulrich Arnswald in "On the Certainty of Uncertainty: Language Games and Forms of Life in Gadamer and Wittgenstein" and Jens Kertscher in "'We Understand Differently, If We Understand At All': Gadamer's Ontology of Language Reconsidered" (both in *Gadamer's*

Century: Essays in Honour of Hans Georg Gadamer, Jeff Malpas, Ulrich Arnswald, and Jens Kertscher, eds. (Cambridge, Mass.: MIT Press, 2002)), and not least by Gadamer himself in *Truth and Method* and his paper "Text and Interpretation" (in *Dialogue and Deconstruction: The Gadamer-Derrida Encounter*).

34. Jay Garfield, "Philosophy, Religion and the Hermeneutic Imperative," in *Gadamer's Century: Essays in Honour of Hans Georg Gadamer*, Jeff Malpas, Ulrich Arnswald, and Jens Kertscher, eds. (Cambridge, Mass.: MIT Press, 2002).

35. Albert Reville in *Actes du Premier Congres International d'Histoire des Religions* (1901), Eric Sharpe, trans., in *Comparative Religion* (London: Duckworth, 1975), 141.

36. H. S. Prasad, "Language and Reality: A Buddhist Approach," in *Religions and Comparative Thought: Essays in Honour of the Late Dr Ian Kesarcodi-Watson*, Purusottama Bilimoria and Peter Fenner, eds. (New Delhi: Sri Satguru Publications, 1988), 39.

37. Eivind Kahrs, *Indian Semantic Analysis: The Nirvacana Tradition* (Cambridge: Cambridge University Press, 1998), xiv.

38. See D. Sinha's *Understanding in Human Context: Themes and Variations in Indian Philosophy* (New York: Lang, 1996), any of Bimal Krishna Matilal's collections of essays, but particularly *Language, Logic and Reality: An Introduction to Indian Philosophical Studies* (New Delhi: Motilal Banarsidass, 1985), Jonardon Ganeri (2001 and 1999, as cited below), and Arvind Sharma's *Hinduism and Its Sense of History* (New Delhi: Oxford University Press, 2003).

39. See Jonardon Ganeri's *Semantic Powers: Meaning and Means of Knowing in Classical Indian Philosophy* (Oxford: Oxford University Press, 1999).

40. See Jonardon Ganeri's *The Concealed Art of the Soul: Theories of Self and Practises of Truth in Indian Ethics and Epistemology* (Oxford: Oxford University Press, 2007), and Gavin Flood's *The Ascetic Self: Subjectivity, Memory and Tradition* (Cambridge: Cambridge University Press, 2004).

41. See Chandradhar Sharma, *A Critical Survey of Indian Philosophy* (New Delhi: Motilal Banarsidass, 1987), 21–22.

42. One could argue that there is a strong potential for some indirect influence of Greek philosophy on Rūpa Gosvāmi, via the "scholastic" theology that would have prevailed in the Islamic philosophy of the court in which he and his brother were employed. This may indeed have been an influence. However, there is as yet little to mark out such influences from the wide range of other theological positions that were also present in the society of his time, of which he was such an avid connoisseur.

43. *Truth and Method* (London: Continuum, 1997), 275.

44. In conversation with Glenn Most, in *Gadamer in Conversation*, Richard Palmer, trans. and ed. (New Haven, Conn.: Yale University Press, 2001), 102.

45. See Graham Parkes, *Heidegger and Asian Thought*, and Reinhardt May, *Heidegger's Hidden Sources: East Asian Influences on His Work*.

46. For examples of comparisons between Indian philosophy and post-Enlightenment pre-Heideggerian philosophers, see Roger-Pol Droit's *The Cult of Nothingness: The Philosophers and the Buddha* (Chapel Hill: University of North Carolina Press, 2003), Gummaraju Srinivasan's *The Phenomenological Approach to Philosophy, Indian and Western* (New Delhi: Caravan Publishing Co., 1980) with regard to

Husserl, Hutchings, and Bilimoria's essay "On Not Having Regards for Fruits: Kant and the Gīta," in *Religions and Comparative Thought: Essays in Honour of the Late Dr Ian Kesarcodi-Watson*, Purusottama Bilimoria and Peter Fenner, eds. (New Delhi: Sri Satguru Publications, 1988), Robert Morrison's *Nietzsche and Buddhism: A Study in Nihilism and Ironic Affinities* (Oxford: Oxford University Press, 1999), Rāma Prasad's *Rāmānuja and Hegel: A Comparative Study* (New York: Prometheus Books, 1984), and Douglas Berger's *The Veil of Maya: Schopenhauer's System and Indian Thought* (Binghamton, N.Y.: Global Academic Publishing, 2000).

47. Harold Coward, *Derrida and Indian Philosophy* (Albany: State University of New York Press, 1990).

48. Raja Ram Dravid, *The Problem of Universals in Indian Philosophy* (Varanasi: Motilal Banarsidass, 1972).

49. J. N. Mohanty, *Essays on Indian Philosophy: Traditional and Modern* (Oxford: Oxford University Press, 2002).

50. E.g., J. L. Shaw's essay on "Singular Existential Sentences: Contemporary Philosophy and the Nyāya," in *Religions and Comparative Thought*, Purusottama Bilimoria and Peter Fenner, ed. (New Delhi: Sri Satguru Publications, 1988), John Taber's "Is Indian Logic Nonmonotonic?" in *Philosophy: East and West* 54, no. 2: (2004), Jonardon Ganeri's *Semantic Powers : Meaning and the Means of Knowing*, Frits Staals's *Universals: Studies in Indian Logic and Linguisics* (Chicago: University of Chicago Press, 1988), and other works mentioned in this book.

51. Bimal Matilal, *Perception: An Essay on Classical Indian Theories of Knowledge* (Oxford: Oxford University Press, 1986).

52. Derrida in particular accused Gadamer of wilfully disregarding the more critical, anti-metaphysical, "Nietzschean" aspects of Heidegger's works, an accusation that Gadamer succinctly undercut and assimilated with his own "philosophical" position (see the transcript of their 1981 debate in *Dialogue and Deconstruction*).

53. See Derrida, John Caputo, and others in the collected works within *Dialogue and Deconstruction.*

54. Whereas in the study of Gadamer I will draw on a wider range of his prolific writings, Rūpa's Gosvāmi's contribution to this thesis will be primarily through some of his most accessible texts: the *Bhaktirasāmṛtasindhu* and the *Ujjvala Nīlamaṇi,* his analyses of devotional theology, his two epic love poems, the *Haṃsadūta* and the *Uddhavasaṇdeśa,* and his plays, *Vidagdha Mādhava* and the *Lalita Mādhava*. Other texts such as the *Upadeṣāmṛta*, the *Padyāvali*, the *Prayuktākhyata manjari*, the *Śrīkṛṣṇa Janmatithividhi*, and the *Dāna Keli Kaumudi* expand upon the ideas found in the *Bhaktirasāmṛtasindhu,* and will be drawn upon to illuminate their author's ideas; nevertheless they are less comprehensive and significantly less available than the former works.

I

GADAMER'S REALISMS

Part I—Introduction

Gadamer's Realisms

> The nullity of what is merely there around us, of that which is said to exist in the "real" world, brings forth the higher truth of "what is the subject or the concept."[1]
>
> Hegel, determined as he was by modern circumstances, found his own philosophical endeavour confronted with a problem precisely the opposite of that which the Ancients faced. His concern was to "make fluid" the fixed suppositions of the Understanding, "to infuse them with Spirit."[2]

Alain Badiou writes that the twentieth century has been marked, in contradistinction to the scientism of the preceding century, by a search for the "passion" of the real.[3] He identifies this desire to elevate us to a more impassioned engagement with reality—above and beyond the mundane passing of the everyday world—as a goal common to many of the thinkers and events of the post-Heideggerian landscape, wherein it seems to have taken the place of the obsolete foundationalist agenda of which philosophical "realism" was a part. "Is it not," asks Badiou, "a major characteristic of all contemporary thought to challenge the theme of the ground [*fond*], of grounding, of foundation?"[4] Contemporary thought seems to agree with him, and Gadamer's attempt to alleviate "the distinctly frantic search for orientation that confronted the young people of [his own] time" is undiminished in its significance today.[5] Others go further; Lyotard insists that "[t]he project of modernity (the realisation of universality) has not been forsaken or forgotten, but destroyed, 'liquidated,'"[6] referring to the deflation of subject and object, and the dissolution of truths into Gadamer's hermeneutic "web"[7] or Badiou's mathematical infinity.[8] Badiou shows how the very framework of the foundational project is indeed not overturned but dissolved into a metaphysic that affirms both plurality and univocity as identical, making all fixed determinations "fluid." Yet contrary to Badiou, who adopts the Heideggerian narrative of philosophy's misdirection by Plato, Hegel, Descartes, and Kant, adding Heidegger himself to the list of culprits, Gadamer proposes an ontology that is similar to that of Badiou, but mines the same thinkers for an alternative understanding of Being and its "ground." Through a philosophical discourse that is both descriptive and prescriptive, direct and oblique, Gadamer supplants the analytically naive ingredients of conventional "realism"—which itself appears in the wake of Kant to be a position of faith—with a soteriological pursuit of an elusive "reality," redefined in post-Heideggerian terms. Gadamer's hermeneutics modifies Badiou's narrative of the search for the real, challenging his pessimistic prognosis that it will lead to an inevitable deflection of thought back toward mere appearance rather than unthinkable reality. He seeks a genuine passion for a genuine "real" *within* the metaphysics of European philosophy.

Yet after a career committed to transforming the extraordinary breadth of his intellectual heritage into a synthesis designed to make philosophy and its puzzles more "liveable," Gadamer was disappointed that both Heidegger and Derrida showed little sign of appreciating the importance of his project. The object of a subdued but steadily increasing acclaim, it is perhaps because his philosophical significance does not lie primarily in being *provocative* that he sometimes "flies below the radar."[9] Reappropriative rather than explicitly revolutionary, the significance of Gadamer's position is that it is already the position in which we find ourselves in modernity; more clearly described and more hopefully displayed from core to consequence than we had previously enjoyed. By the sixteenth century CE, Indian culture had enjoyed two millennia in which to accustom itself to the presence of a major strand of epistemological nihilism propounding ultimate finitude and anti-essentialism in commonsensically compelling terms. In the twentieth-century West, philosophers were still struggling to assess the validity of the transcendental ego and its inferences, and the public was still aghast at the notion that there might be no arbiter of truths and no basis for certainties. Beyond even Heidegger, Gadamer makes a major step forward in so optimistically asserting that truth can be rehabilitated as the foundation for our lives.

Thus, while Gadamer is widely hailed as a philosopher whose thought is illuminating for the various interpretative projects in which the human sciences are engaged, it is the depth of his enquiry into fundamental ontology that makes these practical applications possible. On this basis he restores an epistemological and semantic optimism that Richard Rorty's pragmatist interpretation of Gadamer's work refracts into viable philosophical applications, but of which it fails fully to reflect the moral and ontological implications.[10] Contrasting in important respects with Nietzsche, Heidegger, and Derrida, Gadamer "does not understand his position to signal the end of philosophy, but a new beginning of sorts."[11] The question for those struggling to move beyond philosophy's critical era of deconstruction and suspicion is: "What kind of 'new beginning' does Gadamer have in mind?" When William Hamilton writes of the problematic of religiosity after the "death of God," that "We move to our neighbour, to the city and to the world out of a sense of the loss of God. . . . And, for the time of our waiting we place ourselves with our neighbour and enemy in the world,"[12] must we then think of Gadamer's "urbanisation of the Heideggerian province" in this context? Or does he draw on an alternative well of resources for a "postmodern" faith that is not attendant on God in the style of a Semitic theology of the interim, but hermeneutically attentive to Him in the immanent realm of the real?

The first chapter will review Gadamer's position *vis á vis* traditional and contemporary notions of realism. The second will seek to establish the nature of the "fundamental" ontology that underlies his philosophical hermeneutic project. The third chapter explores how Gadamer developed this ontological realism into an ethical discourse in which the "passion of the real" manifests as a vitalistic approach to the finite tasks and concerns of human life. The section as a whole will not only ask what is the fundamental ontological nature of the real, but how it also entails an ethical, applied dimension that contributes to the possibility of a post-Heideggerian religious realism.

NOTES

1. Hans-Georg Gadamer, *Hegel's Dialectic: Five Hermeneutical Studies*, P. Christopher Smith, trans. (New Haven, Conn.: Yale University Press, 1976), 16.

2. *Hegel's Dialectic: Five Hermeneutical Studies*, 31.

3. See Badiou's article "One Divides into Two," Alberto Toscana, trans. (Malden, Mass.: Polity Press, 2007). Zizek had brought this term into common usage, deploying it to interpret the response to the events of September 11 in his essay "Welcome to the Desert of the Real: Reflections on WTC" (2001). *L'Etre et L'Évīnement*, published in 1988, was declared to be "the first book, since *Being and Time* that again dares to ask the question 'what of being qua being?'" (Dominique Janicaud), while tackling "the whole of philosophy from Parmenides to Heidegger" (Philippe Lacoue-Labarthe)—evidently Janicauld had not looked very closely at Gadamer's ontology. Badiou derives a great deal from the French Hegelian school with which Gadamer was in dialogue through his Hegel studies, yet himself also largely misinterprets Gadamer, identifying his goals with Heidegger's goals as an interpretative "vocation devoted to the open" (Alain Badiou, *Infinite Thought: Truth and the Return of Philosophy* (London: Continuum, 2003), 43)—the opening of

meaning folded within received reality. He neglects the ontological dimension of Gadamer, subsumes him to Heidegger's work, and claims that he is uninterested in the metaphysics of truth. The exposition in chapter 2 shows that the opposite is the case: Gadamer's ontology reaches fundamentally similar conclusions to those of Badiou's ontology, both drawing on mathematics (Pythagorean Platonism for Gadamer and set theory for Badiou), and both seeking to revive the place of truth as a centre of modern philosophy.

4. Alain Badiou, *Deleuze, The Clamor of Being*, Louise Burchill, trans. (Minneapolis: University of Minnesota Press, 2000), 42.

5. Hans-Georg Gadamer, *Philosophical Apprenticeships*, R. Sullivan, trans. (Cambridge, Mass.: MIT Press, 1985), 7.

6. Jean-Francois Lyotard, *Moralitīs Postmodernes* (Paris: Gallilee, 1993), 30.

7. See B. Wachterhauser's *Beyond Being: Gadamer's Post-Platonic Hermeneutical Ontology* (Evanston, Ill.: Northwestern University Press, 1999), 67.

8. See A. Badiou, *Être et Evènement* (Paris: Seuil, 1988) or forthcoming in translation as *Being and Event*, Oliver Feltham, trans. (London: Continuum, 2005).

9. Jean Grondin's *The Philosophy of Gadamer*, Kathryn Plant, trans. (Montreal: McGill-Queens University Press, 2003) examines the reasons why *Truth and Method* received such a restrained reception in the French philosophical sphere, suggesting that his hermeneutic topic had been largely usurped by Ricoeur, Derrida, and Foucault by the time Gadamer's unfashionably peaceable and reappropriative hermeneutics began to be widely read. The challenging text-oriented and issue-driven approaches of the younger thinkers were more in vogue than Gadamer's rather generalised and sometimes long-winded history of philosophy.

10. See Richard Rorty on Gadamer in "Being That Can Be Understood is Language," in *Gadamer's Repercussions: Reconsidering Philosophical Hermeneutics*, Bruce Krajewski, ed. (Berkeley: University of California Press, 2003), and in *Philosophy and the Mirror of Nature* (Princeton, N.J.: Princeton University Press, 1981).

11. Brice Wachterhauser, "Getting it Right: Relativism, Realism and Truth," in *The Cambridge Companion to Gadamer* (New York: Cambridge University Press, 2002), 56.

12. See W. Hamilton, "The Death of God Theologies Today," in *Radical Theology and the Death of God*, T. J. Altizer and W. Hamilton, eds. (London: Penguin Books, 1968), 59–60.

Chapter 1

Gadamer in the Realist Debate

FROM NON-REALISM TO A NEW REALISM

Gadamer, who prior to his death in 2002 was surely the most senior living member of the German phenomenological tradition, has been many things to many people. The product of his allusive style and his elusive metaphysical stance, this Protean quality is one of the features that has made him both "modern" and "classical," useful to all—exemplifying the Socratic virtue of remaining intellectually "on the move" in accordance with the exigencies of context. It also reminds us that Gadamer is a close philosophical cousin of Derrida, that his hermeneutic readings characteristically strive to question and refigure the categorising rationality by which philosophy understands itself.[1]

Within the confines of a single essay Gadamer's longstanding critic Hans Albert has charged him with "radical historism," "anti-naturalism," both "epistemological" and "analytic" relativism, and of espousing something akin to transcendental idealism (a distant cousin of Putnam's "internal realism"). Further, Albert criticises him severely for not being satisfied with the conservative task of advancing traditional "metaphysical realism as well as the notion of truth going along with it."[2] Jean Grondin controversially designates Gadamer as a "critical rationalist" of a Popperian mould, while Richard Rorty has most famously, and perhaps most misleadingly, portrayed him as a nascent pragmatist.[3] Performativity and pragmatism, not correspondence with an existing state of affairs, is how philosophers such as Christopher Norris and Richard Bernstein have characterised the modern anti-realist[4] notion of truth defined by thinkers like Rorty, and Norris is particularly quick to lump Heideggerian thinkers like Gadamer in not only with Rorty, but also with supposed continental relativists like Jean-Francois Lyotard, Gaston Bachelard, and Jacques Derrida.[5] At an opposite extreme Gadamer "has been accused of 'linguistic idealism,' of making language an autonomous creation." Here his metaphysical implications are acknowledged, but mistaken for an outmoded idealistic position that recent Gadamer scholars such as Christopher Lawn feel to be "bizarre and counter-intuitive."[6]

The range of Gadamer's metaphysical appellations extends throughout and beyond the range of positions that have been classified under the umbrella term "non-realism." Indeed, as we have seen, the post-Heideggerian tradition is increasingly understood from the perspective of a metaphysics that transcends the implicit subject-object framework onto which such designations have previously been mapped. "Non-realism" is the term that has been coined to embrace the new landscape that lies beyond the old dualistic, assertorial metaphysics.

Like Rūpa Gosvāmi, his predecessor by some five hundred years, at a distance of four and a half thousand miles, Gadamer begins by inheriting a polemical opposition to the alienating ideal of radical transcendence both in metaphysics and in religion. Through a rich dialogue with the seminal texts of their predecessors, both Gadamer and Rūpa Gosvāmi develop, refine, and eventually alter this opposition. As we will see, the range of positions on the reality of phenomenal and transcendental "things" is as wide in the Indian debate as in the modern West, although they are somewhat differently aligned in the way they figure the alternatives, and Rūpa Gosvāmi's ideas thus challenge the traditional European framework of opposed immanent and transcendent Gods, idealist and realist metaphysics, objectivist and subjectivist truths. Yet, at the risk of precluding some of those tantalising ambiguities that make his work so varied and versatile, it is important to note that Gadamer himself considered the traditional opposition of realism and idealism as "perverse," "precritical," and "pretranscendental," something already obsolete in metaphysical discourse by the time Husserl's logical investigations became influential.[7] When we understand how close Husserl comes to abolishing the reification of the contents of our experiences, it becomes clear that any "realistic elements" in subsequent phenomenology can only be understood from the perspective of an assertorial epoche.[8] For philosophers in Husserl's wake, acting as if ideas correspond to independent objects that anchor them in an objective reality, is merely a remnant of scholastic cosmology and a by-product of certain practical but imprecise functions of our language. But Gadamer goes much further than this. Biographically, Gadamer's rejection of realism came as a rejection of Hartmann in favour of Heidegger. Realism and idealism do appear as a polar pair in his commentaries on Hegel and on phenomenology, but in those rare works in which, rather than hermeneutically borrowing the tools of others, he tries to coin his own more accurate language, that traditional pair is replaced by the opposition of objectivist transcendental realism and "facticity" (*Sachlichkeit*).[9] In this opposition a more human battle is fought between varying ways of schematising our experience of phenomena. Henceforth Gadamer raised the flag of a crusade against "the prose of alienated reality against which the poetry of aesthetic reconciliation must seek its own self-consciousness."[10] The alienation of reality is a schism from which the "phenomenological criticism of the psychology and epistemology of the nineteenth century" finally liberates us by healing the divide between the speculative imagination, and the experience of the real, thus:

> [Phenomenology] has shown the error in all attempts to conceive the mode of aesthetic being in terms of the experience of reality and as a modification of it. All such ideas as imitation, appearance, irreality, illusion, magic, dream, assume a relationship to something from which the aesthetic is different. But the phenomenological return to the aesthetic experience teaches us that the latter does not think in terms of this relationship but sees, rather, actual truth in what it experiences.[11]

We will see in chapter 6 how extraordinarily close this desire to reunify us with reality through aesthetic experience is to Rūpa Gosvāmi's synthesis of the language of ontology and aesthetics.[12] For Gadamer this is in many respects a radical thesis—not because a permeable boundary between art and reality is a particularly revolutionary idea, but because, as we will see, the suggestion is underlined by a comprehensive ontology that rejects this provisional polarisation. The redirection of "truth" toward ideality was soon to be refracted by a widening of the field of candidates for the "real," restricted only by the limits of the imagination. The hermeneutics of the formulation and deconstruction of oppositions that characterises philosophical inquiry into "reality" is a leitmotif of Gadamer's covertly reconciliatory hermeneutic works.

On one level, Gadamer's quest is to eliminate our attachment to any reality from which we have the intuition that we can awaken, or any dependent paradigm of the real that can "be disappointed by a more genuine experience of reality."[13] A correct self-understanding *(sich Verstehen)* is the key to salvaton: He hopes to make us at home in the reality in which we habitually dwell, recognising it as the sole and thus ultimate reality, in which truth also has its home. This apparent "non-realism," that prefers the authority of self-presentative being (*Selbstdarstellung*) over the semiotic relation of dependence entrenched in traditional correspondence realism, fits not only with the anti-metaphysical epoché of phenomenology; it also looks forward to the growing optimism and quiet humanism represented by other hermeneutic thinkers such as Paul Ricoeur.[14] It is part of what Charles Taylor identifies as "the affirmation of ordinary life," a recovery from the Enlightenment's fragmentation of reason and its concomitant pessimistic diagnosis for psychic health.[15] The post-Heideggerian "non-realist" rejection of ontological dualism puts away the ideal of transcendence as a child puts away an inspiring but misleading fairytale. With this change goes a parallel affirmation of *phronesis*, practical wisdom rather than eternal knowledge, as a "transvaluation of values" meant to replace what was lost. *Phronesis* escapes the dialectical equivocation of "ideologies" precisely because it is not a system; it does philosophy in a different way.

Gadamer is a key figure in explicating the rationale behind this newly "realistic" and responsible adulthood, a late hero in the mythos of Heideggerian philosophy. In broad accordance with Richard Wolin's judgement that Gadamer is "Heidegger's most talented and original disciple,"[16] it is the widespread belief that Gadamer rarely really departs from the terms of Heidegger's "metaphysic," i.e., the purely descriptive analysis of what is the case.[17] Even Alain Badiou, who is perhaps the only other contemporary Western writer sharing Gadamer's metaphysical principles, places him at the same location as Heidegger on the path of Western philosophy's self-understanding.[18] Hence, while he may diverge from the Heideggerian provenance of his work in terms of the rhetorical emphasis he gives to certain ideas or aspects of life, and may vary from him in his extra-metaphysical concerns, such as the place of aesthetics or religion, his philosophical picture is consonant with that of Heidegger and draws its conclusions based on the same underlying model of being.[19] He is the Aaron to Heidegger's Moses.

The present study both supports and contends with this belief—the same ontological truths stand before both writers, but different degrees of fidelity to the implications of those truths characterise the worldviews that they derive from them. Where Gadamer has sought to clarify and resolve past puzzles, Heidegger often approached the same ambiguities with a judicious allowance of wilful mystery and mythology. It must be recognised that where Heidegger struggles with his own philosophy, Gadamer strove throughout his career to realise the full metaphysical implications of Heidegger's work by reconciling it with the history of philosophy.[20] Jean Grondin's attempt to chart their divergence is a good example of the misunderstandings that can result.[21] Differences such as "Understanding is mainly 'To know one's way around, to be up to a task' [Heidegger]/'To agree on the thing itself' [Gadamer]" are minimised when one sees that "the thing itself" in Gadamer's perspective is a thematic designation that always includes the contextual structure of understanding that incorporates the "task" in which the "thing" is involved.[22] Gunter Figal's essay in the same volume makes this very point.[23] Equally, the event *(Ereignis)* of agreement that Gadamer takes as the central research question that motivated the philosophical hermeneutic project is not a digression from the Heideggerian project; it implies all of human understanding and action, not merely interpersonal communications—although this is indeed the paradigmatic model that Gadamer uses to express this universal truth. Gadamer himself characterises their differences in terms of their media of expression, and their respective distances from Husserlian phenomenology and from Plato:

> The hermeneutics I developed was also based upon finitude and the historical character of Dasein, and it tried to carry forward Heidegger's turn away from his transcendental account of himself, albeit not in Heidegger's direction of an inspiration from the poetic mythos of Holderlin but rather in a return to the open dialectic of Plato.[24]

It is true that Heidegger orients *Dasein* toward the future and the primacy of death for self-understanding, whilst Gadamer characteristically avoids the topic of death and instead refers us to the determining and enabling prejudice of "effective history" as the seal on our finitude.[25] But again, as his response in the debate with Habermas is meant to show, his notion of "prejudice" *(vorurteile)* which is all too easily misjudged, is as much a matter of futural possibility as of past determination, and this too is a point of correspondence between them for which Gianni Vattimo argues.[26] In referring us to conversation rather than to death for an indication of our finitude, Gadamer is certainly choosing a different theme, but is not making a philosophically different claim from Heidegger.[27] Gadamer is highly familiar with the tendency in philosophy for diverse philosophers to derive their positions through different *analytic approaches to* or *thematisations of* the same logical insights. The differences that Heidegger and the whole philosophical establishment saw as paradigmatic—between Aristotle, Plato, Hegel, Kant, and Heidegger himself—are minimised from this perspective. The opposed paradigms of philosophical "schools" can then be seen as divergent, interwoven voices in a dialogue on common themes. This model is crucial for clarifying broad topics of inquiry (such as realism) in any tradition, and applies equally to the different narratives of Indian philosophical discourse (such that a narrative of philosophers deriving different views from the same reality is a commonplace fable in classical Indian thought).[28] Gadamer writes of his conversion to the Heideggerian narrative of philosophy as having been initiated through his apprenticeship in the study of Aristotle, that it

> brought a complete about-face for me. All at once I saw how misleading the whole scholastic conceptual grid was. I saw how, by means of this, people loved to represent Aristotle's philosophy as "realistic," even when they themselves were not Thomists.[29]

Dissatisfied with every trace of conventional realism, Gadamer abandoned the terminology of *Dasein* and developed his own tropes for doing phenomenological justice to the relation of individual beings to Being per se.[30] Again and again Gadamer expressed his frustration with Heidegger's "half-poetic attempts at discourse [which] are sometimes more expressive of a linguistic need than of its overcoming."[31] Thus talk about persons, things, the world, "us" and "it" is liberally scattered throughout Gadamer's major texts, implicitly drawing on the metaphysics of subject and object, and sowing the seeds of extensive misunderstanding. Yet his hermeneutical position, so insistently termed "philosophical,"[32] commits him unequivocally to the primacy of Being, swatting away the anthropocentrism of traditional epistemology through his rejection of post-Kantian subjectivism and what he calls "subjectism," our philosophically naive, commonsensical orientation toward the subject. Hence, at the threshold of the phenomenological project aimed at describing the structures of the world but not its ontological status (a project taken up with such success by Ricoeur and Merleau-Ponty, among others), Gadamer lingers in abandoned metaphysical territory in pursuit of foundations for the difficult ontology of the later Heidegger.

His most famous and successful trope of *Spiel*, or "play," is one of the main tools for reopening this territory to exploration, providing an apt interface for the phenomenological and the ontological. He writes:

> As far as language is concerned, the actual subject of play is obviously not the subjectivity of an individual who, among other activities, also plays, but is instead the play itself. But we are so accustomed to relating phenomena such as playing to the sphere of subjectivity and the ways it acts that we remain closed to these indications from the spirit of language.[33]

Play is one of the many images that Gadamer employs to transcend the objective and the subjective with a meta-entity that incorporates the two; as an ontological term it takes the place of *Dasein*, and is, as we will see, the framework for Gadamer's metaphysical realism. Gadamer's urbanisation of the inhospitable Heideggerian province is at once ontological and anthropological; "the spirit of language" is the communication from being, its "skin," so to speak, and here it communicates to us the view from within Being, as opposed to the view of it from a transcendental point outside of it. It is the difficulty of discovering, expressing, and formulating a liveable ethos based on the view from within Being that is one of Gadamer's main challenges, and the task that will distinguish a successful postmodern philosophy from a merely capricious, imaginative one. It is the striking parallel between *Spiel* and *līlā*, Gadamer and Rūpa Gosvāmi's respective metaphor models for Being as "play," that is, the axial premise for bringing both together to address the problem of a post-sceptical "realist" brand of belief.

GADAMER'S "REALISM"

Having extensively criticised the old mythos of realism imposed on past philosophers, Gadamer himself employs a language of the real that is often equally vague, but resonant with the rhetoric of liberty. His own ideals are made evident in the theme of the real:

> [W]e are moved in the space of freedom. . . . This space is not the free space of an abstract joy in construction but a space filled with reality by prior familiarity.[34]

In endowing our experience of freedom with a realistic ethos, Gadamer references the doctrine of "historically determined consciousness" to which he attributes our experiences, views, and truths—precisely the doctrine that Habermas criticises as a deterministic denial of freedom, and which others construe as a culturally constructivist account of meaning (*Vollzug*). Yet in contrast to this, Wachterhauser portrays Gadamer as combating the umbrella anti-realism of coherentism (e.g., pragmatist truth-accounts based on semantic or functional agreement of terms), with a view according to which

> "true" means something more like the way things actually are and not something merely "consistent," "warranted" or "useful in the way of belief."[35]

Gadamer writes that

> when we speak of the "nature" of things or the "language" of things, these expressions share in common a polemical rejection of violent arbitrariness in our dealing with things, especially the mere stating of opinions, the capriciousness of conjectures or assertions about things, and the arbitrariness of denials or the insistence of private opinions.[36]

Gadamer's account of language certainly does not warrant manipulation or imposition of arbitrary truth-values; language is beyond the bounds of the merely subjective powers of awareness. This autonomy of reality is further reflected in the ontological trope of the game, a metaphor (and more than metaphor) for Being according to which "even for human subjectivity the real experience of the game consists in the fact that something that obeys its own set of laws gains ascendancy in the game."[37] If realism were, practically speaking, above all an opposition to subjectivism in the question of the truth and reality of objects, Gadamer would unquestionably be a realist, although Wachterhauser is then over-quick to claim that this liberates Gadamer completely from deflationist or coherentist accounts of truth—both of which have an important place in the proper hermeneutic understanding of discourse.[38] The character of Gadamer's realism borrows much from the basic self-definition of phenomenology, as an attendance to "that which shows itself in itself" (*das Sich-an-ihm-selbst-zeigende*). Gadamer's work is laced, as is that of Heidegger, with an injunction to attend to the implicit order of Being, from within the subjective space of our "letting beings be" (*sehenlassen*). In some cases Gadamer expresses this order in the language of our everyday experience, appearing to imply a linguistic relativism and a consonant prelinguistic realism. Thus, in seeking to explain the intuitive origins of his thinking in his intellectual autobiography *Philosophical Apprenticeships*, he writes:

> All too well known are those prelinguistic and metalinguistic dawnings, dumbnesses and silences in which the immediate meeting with the world expresses itself. And who would deny that there are real conditions to human life? There are such things as hunger and love, work and domination, which themselves are not speech and language but which circumscribe the space within which speaking-with-each-other and listening-to-each-other can take place.[39]

The real conditions that reveal themselves in our "dawnings, dumbnesses and silences" can appear in Heideggerian terms as the "clearing" of our dialogue with the world, a clearing being not an absence of things, but a visibility of that which exists, including oneself. Otherwise defined, it is precisely our "immediate" encounter with the world that furnishes the contents of the speaking and listening "that we are." Although he may be, on the basis of his theoretical position and its affirmation of polyvalent texts, accused of semantic relativism, Gadamer's work is always moderated in these theoretical cases by a direct reference to "real" (in the sense of actual, "biographical") circumstances that affirm the intuitive possibility of right and wrong meaning. In his direct discussion of such conflict of meaning in the test case of modern poetry, he resolves a conflict over the interpretation of a Celan poem by reference to the response of the author, stating that by chance he "happened to be in Paris with Celan when this mistaken interpretation [was published]" and that it "made him very angry."[40] This sort of commonsense reaction should act as balm to any fears that he conceals a relativism pernicious to the activities and concerns of everyday life. But with a characteristic hermeneutic sophistication of the debate over the Celan poem, he points out that the resulting mistake does not consist in obtaining an incorrect rather than a correct meaning, but rather that it results in an inferior poem to the "right" one, just as, in theory, wrong meaning in law results in social disarray, wrong meaning in science results in failed experiments, and wrong meaning in religion results in unhappy or unethical lives. One should not confuse simple polyvalence with the radically unstable *ecriture* of Derrida's grammatology, he says.[41] Rather, the notions of right and wrong must also defer to the transcendent (in the sense of "universally necessary") notion of the Good.

Of course, these questions of semantic truth and realism ultimately defer to an idea of the Good that has an ontological pedigree but not an absolute content. Truth is a multiplicity that does indeed entail an order of relativism. However, not only because of his model of deference to an edifying order innate to the "world," but also because of its working out on an ontological scale in the dynamics of Gadamer's "play-ontology," he has been variously and justly described as a metaphysical realist of one kind or another. Wachterhauser gives an extensive exposition of Gadamer's "post-Platonic" realist ontology, and on Paul Gorner's account Gadamer's work falls under the same category of transcendental *realist* phenomenology as does that of Heidegger.[42] Despite Gadamer's ticklishness over providing explicit and complete accounts of belief and individualism, Caputo complains of him that he is a "closet essentialist" where meaning and being are concerned. He complains (in respect of Gadamer's model for interpreting modern art in *The Relevance of the Beautiful*) that Gadamer's hermeneutics is a thematising domestication of what is intended to be disruptive.[43] Karl-Otto Apel more cautiously labels him a realist who is "critical of meaning."[44] Thus what is ontology is typically misinterpreted as discourse analysis, owing to the continuance of an idealist way of thinking that makes interpretation appear as an order *imposed* on the world. The mistake is a persistent and pernicious one against which Gianni Vattimo warns, aware that it leads to a misplaced transcendentally absolute ontological realism.[45]

Gadamer writes that his turn from Nicholai Hartmann's "critical realism" to Heidegger's "facticity" was a relief, a movement from what was a purely imitative philosophical method to what fitted his deepest intuitions. He writes:

> When I found confirmation for my contrariness in Heidegger, especially in respect to the interpretive deepening of the historical uniqueness of the expressions of thought, my old schoolboy understanding with Hartmann broke down.[46]

However Gadamer, so influenced by the "realist" inclinations of phenomenological thinkers like Hartmann, Scheler, and Pfander, is quick to point out that their directive to return to the things themselves was less a securing of objectivist method, than a modest directing of attention away from the mere objects (*Gegenstand*) and toward the phenomena in all their numinous significance and imperviousness to human will.[47] Both limiting and enabling our freedom, Gadamer's "world" has an innate value, deflating the usual problems of assertion and truth. "The appeal to the nature of things refers to an order removed from human wishes," he writes, and directs us to

> remember what things really are, namely not a material that is used and consumed, not a tool that is used and set aside, but something instead that has

existence [*Existenz*] in itself and is "not forced to do anything," as Heidegger says. "[I]ts own being in itself is like a language it is vital for us to hear."[48]

The old problems of realism are increasingly subsumed to the problem of will—the phenomenological issue of what does and does not succumb to our manipulation, and how this power structure frames our worldview.[49] Gadamer assures us that his "real concern was and is philosophic; not what we do or what we ought to do, but what happens to us over and above our wanting and doing."[50] Chapter 3 will argue that the discourse of "ought" does indeed permeate his language of "is." Yet this too is a reflection of the profound realism of his philosophy.

Ironically, it is the "unifying," "regulative" function of Gadamer's realism, so conducive to pragmatic and *phronetic* applications, that often leads those interested in Gadamer's hermeneutics back to the ontological question of the regulations, the hermeneutic rules (*ḥermeneutische Regel*), the forms and determinations of the "real." In Wittgensteinian language these are the threads that tie the "bundle" of meanings into a language game, in Hegelian terms the finite spirit that leads the particular toward the absolute, or, in Platonic and subsequently Deleuzian language, the problem of the One as opposed to that of the Many. In the genesis of these questions we see that the speculative problem of foundations seems to follow hard on the heels of every successful bout of theorising. In this respect Gadamer is perhaps the most faithfully Heideggerian participant in what Derrida sees as "the long and slow trajectory" of a project to fill in the gap left by Heidegger's substitution of *Dasein* for subjectivity, such that Gadamer too seeks to strengthen the fragile "ethical, juridical and political foundations of democracy" left structurally unsound on the margins of this fundamental (Heideggerian) turn.[51] Finally foundationalism seeks to become not a tool for restricting human (or divine) freedom, but rather a precondition for the proper administration of human freedom, such that it avoids irresponsible capriciousness, while allowing the free play necessary to "authentic" decisionmaking. This realist foundationalism is a crucial part of the Gadamerian project in both its meta-physical and meta-ethical dimensions.

Gadamer characterises his own philosophical quest—half descriptive metaphysics, half reconstitution of lived reality by restoring the epiphanic, meaning-filled indeterminacies of experience—as the lived unification of Hegelian order and Kierkegaardian indeterminacy. This juxtaposition aims to maintain us as both aware of the fluidity and vitality of Being, and also refreshingly awake to it. Hegel and Kierkegaard both urge the reader to acknowledge that there are importantly paradoxical or indeterminate truths at the heart of metaphysics and human experience respectively. As we will see, this philosophical legacy lays the ground in Gadamer's work for a metaphysics acknowledging indeterminacy as well as order, plurality as well as unity. He excavates Western philosophy for ideas that name in other language the same "inconceivable identity and difference" (*acintyabhedābheda*) that is the cornerstone of Rūpa Gosvāmi's philosophical tradition. Chapters 4–6 will show that Rūpa Gosvāmi also gleans answers to the riddles of indeterminacy, paradox, and identity from the philosophical history on which he draws, and seeks to refine them into comprehensive, firmly grounded accounts of truth and human flourishing. For both thinkers, it turns out that this insight has implications on many levels. Thus Gadamer's realism is fragmented into complementary facets; an ontology that seeks to be truly fundamental, a renewed attention to the order that is "given" to us in our experience of the world, the revivification of that order through the complex energies of ambiguous interiority, seeking to milk a "higher truth" from "the nullity of what is merely there around us," and an affirmation of the brave, exploratory, vigorous, and vital lives that he had witnessed and most admired.[52] According to this worldview, there is nothing from which we need to be "saved," except the nullity and meaninglessness that can result from our ontological misconceptions. Realist reasoning based on the establishment of certain truths will show us in the next chapter that the "world" itself is not flawed, and has no "other" to which we can flee. Our goal must be to understand this world, reconcile ourselves with it in understanding and in action, and learn to appreciate it adequately. Thus Gadamer's ethics will tend not toward "soteriology," but rather toward the eudaimonian ethos of a model of human flourishing.

NOTES

1. Gadamer's philosophical proximity to Derrida is acknowledged not only by those who sought to transform his monologue *vis á vis* Derrida into a dialogue, but by more recent commentators such as Zoran Jankovic, who clarifies the way in which it is their critical response to the fundamental problems of Heideggerian philosophy that unites them (see *Au-dela du Signe: Gadamer et Derrida: Le Depassement Hermeneutique et Deconstructiviste du Dasein?* (Paris: L'Harmattan, 2003)). Despite charges of covert conservatism from thinkers such as Habermas, Gadamer's more general *critical* qualities come clearly to the fore wherever one consults his writing on any given issue or definition, contributing to the nuanced hermeneutic richness of his thought.

2. Hans Albert, "Critical Rationalism and Universal Hermeneutics," in *Gadamer's Century: Essays in Honour of Hans Georg Gadamer*, Jeff Malpas, Ulrich Arnswald, and Jens Kertscher, eds. (Cambridge, Mass.: MIT Press, 2002), 18–22.

3. Further, it is now clear that Jürgen Habermas's seminal critiques of Gadamer from the perspective of socio-political theory, reflected a fundamental failure to comprehend the profoundly ontological position from which any such application of his work must derive.

4. Anti-realism, broadly speaking, is the position that opposes itself to traditional Western realism by claiming that we cannot know about supposed thought-transcendent realities, and that our questions about them fail to recognise that none of our concerns can validly refer to or relate to such realities. Truth and meaning take on an exclusively human dimension.

5. See Christopher Norris's *Against Relativism: Philosophy of Science, Deconstruction and Critical Theory* (Oxford: Blackwell Publishers, 1997), and Richard Bernstein's *Beyond Objectivism and Relativism: Science, Hermeneutics and Praxis* (Oxford: Basil Blackwell Publishers Ltd, 1983).

6. Chris Lawn, *Gadamer: A Guide for the Perplexed* (London: Continuum, 2006), 84.

7. "The Phenomenological Movement," in *Philosophical Hermeneutics*, 165.

8. "The Phenomenological Movement," in *Philosophical Hermeneutics*, 147.

9. E.g., Hans-Georg Gadamer, *Truth and Method*, trans. G. Barden and J. Cumming (London: Sheed and Ward Ltd., 1975), 74, 104, 307.

10. *Truth and Method*, 74.

11. *Truth and Method*, 75.

12. David Haberman, in particular, shows the degree to which Rūpa Gosvāmi flew in the face of authorities such as Bhārata and even Abhinavagupta in his assertion that art was not only a means for bringing the observer to a higher appreciation of ultimate reality culminating in union with it, but also a reality in which the image and the actor themselves participate in that ultimate truth (see *Acting as a Way of Salvation: A Study of Rāgānuga Bhakti Sādhana* (New Delhi: Motilal Banarsidass, 1983)).

13. *Truth and Method*, 75.

14. Other less prominent contemporary thinkers whose works share these characteristics include Emilio Betti (1890–1968), Karl-Otto Apel (1922–present), and Gianni Vattimo (1936–present).

15. See Charles Taylor's *Sources of the Self: The Making of the Modern Identity* (New York: Cambridge University Press, 1989).

16. Richard Wolin, *Labyrinths: Explorations in the Critical History of Ideas* (Amherst: University of Massachusetts Press, 1995), 152.

17. Gadamer has on numerous occasions described his own work as a development of the "turn" toward linguisticality in Heidegger's ontology. See *Philosophical Hermeneutics*, 178.

18. See A. Badiou, *Infinite Thought: Truth and the Return of Philosophy*, trans. and ed. O. Feltham and J. Clemens (London: Continuum, 2004), 42. More recently Christopher Lawn has strongly asserted Gadamer's indebtedness to Heidegger's "crucial phenomenological and existential turn in hermeneutical thought" (Chris Lawn, *Gadamer: A Guide for the Perplexed* (London: Continuum, 2006), 12).

19. Clearly, "metaphysics" is a problematic word, in that it is taken up by Heidegger as expressive of a particular substantialist mode of ontology prevalent in Western culture, and has been used as shorthand for this perspective by many thinkers since. But insofar as both Heidegger and Gadamer do indeed make assertions about the way things are, as we shall see, *non-relativistically* (and yet without falling into the trap of dualistic substantialism), it seems to me both useful and appropri-

ate to be able to speak of "metaphysics" in the plural, in much the same way that Putnam assumes the right to speak of "realisms." This has particular application and validity when looking at the plurality of philosophical accounts of reality with which one must deal in intercultural philosophical research.

20. Here again, in his respect for his pedagogical predecessors, Gadamer shares an important methodological motivation with Rūpa Gosvāmi, but on the Indian side this instinct toward constructive reappropriation of historical sources and authorities runs throughout the tradition, as we will see in chapter 4, facilitating (often fruitful) means for "standing on the shoulders" on past thinkers and texts.

21. Jean Grondin, "Gadamer's Basic Understanding of Understanding," in *The Cambridge Companion to Gadamer* (London: Cambridge University Press, 2002), 49–50. In the same volume Robert Dostal characterises them thus: "Stylistically and substantively, the main difference between their two modes of thought is the difference between a meditative thinker (Heidegger) and a dialogical one (Gadamer)" (247).

22. In a fuller exegesis of his thought Grondin concedes that Gadamer spotted and developed aspects of Heidegger's thought that he himself had forgotten or recanted after his *Letter on Humanism* (see *The Philosophy of Gadamer*, Kathryn Plant, trans. (Guildford and King's Lynn: Acumen Publishing Limited, 2003)).

23. See 123 of "The Doing of the Thing Itself," in *The Cambridge Companion to Gadamer*.

24. Hans-Georg Gadamer, "The Heritage of Hegel," in *Reason in the Age of Science*, trans. F. Lawrence (Cambridge, Mass.: MIT Press, 1981), 56.

25. See Hans-Georg Gadamer, *Gadamer on Celan: "Who Am I and Who Are You?" and Other Essays*, ed. and trans. R. Heinemann and B. Krajewki (Albany: State University of New York, 1997), 86, for an exception.

26. See Vattimo in "Gadamer and the Problem of Ontology," in *Gadamer's Century: Essays in Honour of Hans-Georg Gadamer*.

27. This is a hermeneutical observation that, as we will see, will also illuminate certain philosophical differences between Gadamer and Rūpa Gosvāmi.

28. There is an oft-repeated Indian fable of the seven blind men who tried to discover the nature of a single reality by means of their imperfect senses, all seeking to identify the same elephant by touch alone. Each comes to a different conclusion, inferring that it is a rope from the tail, a tree from the leg, a wall from its side, etc. Just so, we are told, do those philosophers proceed who seek to concretise and formulate ultimate reality.

29. Hans-Georg Gadamer, *Gadamer in Conversation: Reflections and Commentaries*, trans. and ed. R. Palmer (New Haven, Conn.: Yale University Press, 2001), 90.

30. On this point, Gadamer questions the later Heidegger's "poeticising mode of speech," insisting: "I am opposed to creating a special language and want to make the language which we normally use say what Heidegger speaks about" (*Gadamer on Education, Poetry, History: Applied Hermeneutics*, ed. D. Misgeld and G. Nicholson, trans. L. Schmidt and M. Ruess (Albany: State University of New York Press, 1992), 128).

31. "The Heritage of Hegel," in *Reason in the Age of Science*, 57.

32. Gadamer writes of his conscious and subversive decision to call his own position *Philosophical Hermeneutics,* despite the outmoded air of his claim to be undertaking a "philosophical" inquiry (see Hans-Georg Gadamer, *Philosophical Apprenticeships,* trans. R. Sullivan (Cambridge, Mass.: MIT Press, 1985)).

33. *Truth and Method,* 93.

34. "The Heritage of Hegel," in *Reason in the Age of Science,* 51.

35. See Wachterhauser's *Beyond Being: Gadamer's Post-Platonic Hermeneutic Ontology* (Evanston, Ill.: Northwestern University Press, 1999).

36. "The Nature of Things and the Language of Things," in *Philosophical Hermeneutics,* 69 –70.

37. "On the Problem of Self-Understanding," in *Philosophical Hermeneutics,* 53.

38. It is perhaps proper to say that for Gadamer truth depends not on coherence to other meanings; this linguistically structuralist model is inappropriate and more aptly describes the mechanisms by which sophists are able to distort discourses to reflect what we would not wish to call "true." Rather, truth depends on coherence with the much wider hermeneutic circle not only of meanings, and apparent "things" but also the actions that enliven statements and circumscribe the world. Hence Gadamer's stress on the unity of *logos* and *ergon* in Greek debate. In this respect Gadamer is a coherentist, but requires coherence with what happens externally in the world, not only with the language system in which statements are made. Rorty of course reads this, controversially and I think wrongly, as pragmatism in an effort to give voice to the determining role of the "good" toward which a discourse is aimed in the truth-value of that discourse. However, he does too little to overturn the subjectivism of the pragmatist viewpoint and acknowledge the sense toward which the *ergon* helps to *constitute* the world of which discourse is a part (see Hans-Georg Gadamer, *The Beginning of Philosophy,* trans. P. Christopher Smith (New Haven, Conn.: Yale University Press, 1983), 7–8, for the harmony of *logos* and *ergon*).

39. *Philosophical Apprenticeships,* 178. We will return to the relation of such intense phenomenal concerns as hunger and desire, to the space of "speaking-with-each-other" in the final chapter of this study. However, it is a telling foretaste of the ethical decisions to come that for Gadamer the former provides the framework for the latter rather than vice versa, implying a priority of the principle of encounter over the particular concern that motivates it.

40. *Gadamer on Celan: "Who Am I and Who Are You?" and Other Essays,* 183.

41. *Gadamer on Celan: "Who Am I and Who Are You?" and Other Essays,* 181.

42. See Wachterhauser's *Beyond Being: Gadamer's Post-Platonic Hermeneutic Ontology,* and his essays "Gadamer's Realism: The Belongingness of Word and Reality," in *Hermeneutics and Truth* (Evanston, Ill.: Northwestern University Press, 1994), and "Getting It Right: Relativism, Realism and Truth," in *The Cambridge Companion to Gadamer.* See too Paul Gorner, "Heidegger's Phenomenology as Transcendental Philosophy," in the *International Journal of Philosophical Studies* 10, no. 1 (February 2002), 17.

43. See John Caputo, *More Radical Hermeneutics: On Not Knowing Who We Are* (Bloomington: Indiana University Press, 2000), 41–56.

44. See John Caputo in *Radical Hermeneutics: Repitition, Deconstruction and the Hermeneutic Project* (Bloomington: Indiana University Press, 2000) and Apel's *Transformation der Philosophie, Band I: Sprachanalytik, Semiotic, Hermeneutik* (Frankfurt am Main: Suhrkamp, 1973).

45. See Vattimo in "Gadamer and the Problem of Ontology," in *Gadamer's Century: Essays in Honour of Hans-Georg Gadamer*.

46. *Philosophical Apprenticeships*, 37.

47. "The Phenomenological Movement," in *Philosophical Hermeneutics*, 145.

48. "The Nature of Things and the Language of Things," in *Philosophical Hermeneutics*, 71–72.

49. The question of will in everyday interaction has become bound up with the instrumentalist critique that Gadamer confesses himself to have in common with his predecessors and the Frankfurt school (see *Gadamer in Conversation*, 82–83) and within which his realism which prescribes an edifying attendance to the language of "things" has a vital role.

50. *Truth and Method*, xxviii.

51. Jacques Derrida, "'Eating Well,' or the Calculation of the Subject: An Interview with Jacques Derrida," in *Who Comes After the Subject*, Eduardo Cadava, Peter Connor, and Lean-Luc Nancy, eds. (New York: Routledge, 1991), 104.

52. *Hegel's Dialectic: Five Hermeneutical Studies*, 16.

Chapter 2

Gadamer's Ontology of Telos

In the slim commentary on Celan, which Heidegger pronounced his favourite of his pupil's works, Gadamer praises Celan's poetic figuration of Being in terms of

> the "breath-crystal," which is nothing but the configuration of pure, delicate geometry that falls from the soft nothingness of breath. . . . Where one is far enough away from the trends of human activity one is close to the ultimate goal, the goal of the true word. . . . "You" are what it testifies to ("Your" witness)—the intimate, unknown You which, for the I that here is the I of the poet as well as the reader, is its You, "wholly, wholly real."[1]

Here, two contrasting images are combined in Gadamer's words: on the one hand in seeking to capture the nature of language's signifying capacity, Celan's imagery evokes the crystalline geometry of Platonic formalism. This is an analysis of the structures of experience that constitute intelligibility and thus the "mathematical order of Being, structured like the lattice of a crystal [which] is the true content of the doctrine of ideas."[2] On the other hand, for Gadamer Celan also deploys the more organic, elusive imagery of breath as an inner essence of language that brings speech into existence.[3] This complex reality of the organism that speaks is never fully exhausted in the crystalline structures of its language. The breath is a fecund nothingness, a non-substantial source of infinite (aural, linguistic, conceptual) forms, which does not *create*—but rather *becomes* the infinitely varied, tangible forms of language, the meaning of which is bestowed by the infinitely varied life of the breathing, speaking organism. And yet contrary to the actual structures of language, the interiority of the breath remains itself unspeakable and unknown.[4]

The mystery of the obscure and ambiguous interiority of meaning, language, and Being, will be explored in chapter 3. We will see that Gadamer applies the same optimistic essentialism to the problem of indeterminacy that *āstika* (orthodox) scholars like Rūpa Gosvāmi maintained in the face of *nāstika* (unorthodox) critiques, drawing on classical Indian philosophies such as Sāṃkhya and Vedānta—a further story that will be told in part II. However the "pure, delicate geometry" of Gadamer's formal ontology, so poorly or partially represented in existing scholarship, requires prior analysis with particular regard to its Platonic and Aristotelian roots. In particular, the "Platonic" feature of the ontology reveals its foundationalist essence as a description of universal truths formulating the same ontological insight that chapter 4 explains through the doctrine of *acintyabhedābheda*, "inconceivable difference and non-difference" in the work of Rūpa Gosvāmi. Meanwhile, it is Gadamer's Aristotelian affirmation of teleological identity-in-change that will be shown to share important insights with Rūpa Gosvāmi's cornerstone concept of *rasa*.

GADAMER'S "POST-PLATONIC ONTOLOGY"

Levinas provides a pithy formula for the ontology that Heidegger inherits from his Greek predecessors and passes on to his pupil.[5] He observes that

> meaning qua meaning is a manifestation of being. (But "a manifestation of being" is a tautology for the Greeks! . . . and Heidegger preserves this position.)[6]

Or, as Gadamer even more succinctly puts it, "being is a verb, an insight Heidegger had arrived at only very slowly."[7] Throughout the modern period the increasing reductions of an epistemology driven by the desire for certainty, resulted (via Descartes, Kant, Hegel, Husserl, Heidegger, and their peers) in an ontology of experience alone, shorn of subject and object.[8] Like Heidegger, Gadamer sees Greek philosophy as the point at which the possibility of a subject-object dualism was realised from within the deep analysis of the metaphysics of unity and plurality in which Parmenides, Pythagoras, Plato, and Aristotle were engaged.[9] But this does not mean that he, like Heidegger, lays the blame at their feet. Rather he views it as a time in which the complicity of Being and discourse was realised within the ordering and dividing framework of an increasingly systematic philosophical method. Where Plato and Aristotle tempered their theories of truth with "soft" notions of knowledge (*aletheia* and *phronesis*, respectively) that emphasised the contextual value and edifying application of "true" meanings as well as their potential for stability and certitude, subsequent social conditions developed these human-centred, practical wisdoms in ways that facilitated the pragmatic, technological control demanded by the *polis*. Throughout the development of Western thought in its many neo-classical varieties, this scientific "method" of thought, *techne*, flourished in affinity with what Gadamer calls the "Pythagorising aesthetic"[10] and the "Pythagorising, mathematical mind"[11] of absolutism.

He is passionate about his reappropriation of Plato from the grip of both the absolute realists and the constructivist idealists, claiming with pride that toward the end of Heidegger's life the pupil finally managed to convince the teacher that he had underestimated the radicality of Plato's metaphysics. Gadamer's intellectual biography is a truly fascinating one, into which we will look deeper in chapter 3, but the elements which relate strictly to the discipline of metaphysics themselves present a narrative of the twentieth-century struggle between the desire for revolutionary steps forward and the desire for secure roots; the Odyssean urge to reclaim one's identity and the Promethean urge to change it. Originally trained as a classicist, with a great love for his material, Gadamer was always an open-minded, interdisciplinary thinker who was taught by contemporary approaches to classical texts (inspired not least by Lutheran hermeneutics) to pay attention to issues of authorial intention, historical context, and the negotiation of multiple meanings. His interests and his sheer location at that place and time in the German academic system brought him into contact with Heidegger, who had also been a Plato scholar, but had propelled himself forward through two millennia of Western thought (and some Eastern) to a post-Nietzschean, post-Husserlian philosophical position. Heidegger was already an academic star, and always inclined toward respect for his luminary predecessors in philosophy, Gadamer developed a pedagogical relationship with him that meant immersing himself in his worldview as well as his philosophical conclusions. It was a somewhat uneasy relationship, marred by Gadamer's discomfiture at seeing a host of thinkers to whom he retained a great hermeneutic sensitivity being repudiated and possibly misunderstood by his teacher. From Heidegger's side, it seemed that his polite pupil would never overcome the limitations of his reappropriative instinct and reach any new and groundbreaking conclusions. As we will see, there were a range of other contemporary influences on Gadamer's thought, and an even wider range of post-Platonic influences. But he never yielded his first sympathy with Plato's thought to the fashion for Nietzschean critique, while on the other hand as a rather secular-minded Protestant, he felt no compunction about eliding the notion of a transcendent God and contenting himself with more "pagan" modes of thinking. *Truth and Method* was, in its way, a complete rebuttal of Heidegger's rejection of the post-Platonic tradition of metaphysics and Heidegger's attempt to strike out with a new philosophical language, preferring instead a meticulously historical and exegetic approach in which helpful metaphors play an important part, and past perspectives are sympathetically reassessed.

This approach has sometimes had the deleterious effect of obscuring Gadamer's true aspirations. Famously and controversially, Gadamer's philosophical hermeneutics makes a "universal claim"—a claim that has not ceased to inspire attempts at clarification. Metaphysicians and Gadamer scholars remain ambivalent about the precise status of these insights. Grondin assures us that there is no "phantom of an absolute foundation—that child of positivism and ultimately of metaphysics" in the framework that Heidegger passes down to Gadamer, exceeding the strictures and transcendental goals of Husserl's phenomenology.[12] Thus, despite his meticulous explication of the Platonic framework of Gadamer's ontology, Brice Wachterhauser remains cautious in attributing to Gadamer the "metaphysical views about the inherent intelligibility of word and language that I ascribe to him," namely, that he can be "legitimately called an idealist in a certain realist (and, we might add, Hegelian sense)."[13] He assuages his own confusion with a suggestion that Gadamer himself is confused, and his reasoning correspondingly slapdash:

> Gadamer's metaphysical picture is, like all metaphysical pictures, a kind of inference to the best explanation. It is a sober account of what we must assume is the case given our experience as knowers.[14]

Yet we can compare this with what Gadamer writes when confronted by his own Husserlian and Heideggerian roots. He is attempting the "programme of a new science of consciousness" that is made possible by the realisation that "the unilluminable obscurity of our facticity . . . sustains and does not merely set limits to the project character of human Dasein." Contemporary metaphysics needed "to bestow a new weight on the historicity of human Dasein."[15] He was irrepressibly optimistic about the possibility of doing positive philosophy. Gadamer felt it essential that we should not be, as Hegel says (paraphrased by Gadamer), "a people without a metaphysics . . . like a temple without a sanctuary, an empty temple, a temple in which nothing dwells any longer and hence is itself nothing any more."[16] Gadamer himself abjured the scholastic idea of a source of absolute being, as something that "we cannot go along with," but he nevertheless also confesses a fascination with the idea of "the power of the concept of maximal reality that carries its existence with it."[17] In this respect the philosophies of Dilthey, Yorck, and Husserl all seek ontological foundations by going "back beyond the abstraction of neo-Kantianism."[18] Yorck "achieves even more" because he "maintains the metaphysical connection between life and self-consciousness worked out by Hegel," and Dilthey and Husserl gestured toward a self-grounding of ontology by "going back beyond the objectivity of science to the life-world . . . based methodically on the self-givenness of experience."[19] This attempt at furnishing a foothold in reality for philosophical thinking is not destroyed by the Heideggerian turn in phenomenology, but altered:

> [I]t soon emerged that what constituted the significance of Heidegger's "fundamental ontology" was not that it was the solution to the problem of historicism, and certainly not a more original grounding of science, nor even, as with Husserl, philosophy's ultimate grounding of itself; rather the whole idea of grounding itself underwent a total reversal.[20]

In order to understand the nature and function of grounding here we must negotiate between different conceptions of philosophical certainties and goals. In this vein, Georgia Warnke, prefiguring Jean Grondin, argues that Gadamer is indeed "closer to a foundationalist enterprise than any of them [i.e., Habermas, Apel, and Rorty] admit."[21] J. M. Baker argues for "the positive ontological stake" in Gadamer's work, which mimics "Mallarmé [and] Hegel's most radical intentions in the field of logic: both push predication to its limits, but both intend something that will not be falsified, something indeed that both called the idea."[22] Elsewhere, Wachterhauser too argues after his many caveats that "[w]hile Gadamer acknowledges that the later Heidegger can still offer us brilliant insights, it is simply a mistake to think that he occupies ground that is really beyond metaphysics."[23] Rather, for Gadamer, Heidegger's whole project is to provide foundations. His "paradoxical demand" was that "phenomenology should be ontologically based on the facticity of Dasein, existence, which cannot be based on or derived from anything else, and not on the pure cogito."[24] Here Gadamer is rejecting the remains of Cartesianism, but reassuring us that Heidegger's reversal of the project of grounding does not mean its repudiation. Rather it effects a radical deflation of foundation into what it purports to ground—of life into foundation, of word into meaning, and, as we will see, of meaning into meaning*fulness*.

In all of this, Gadamer's restoration of Platonic metaphysics was the keystone for his project of rediscovering transcendental truths throughout the tradition. He writes unequivocally that "[t]he vulgar concept of Platonism . . . holds without qualification to be a transformation of Plato's intentions."[25] He puts the case against Platonic dualism even more strongly:

> With a persistence bordering on the absurd, the prevailing form of interpretation in which Plato's philosophy has been passed onto us has advocated the two-worlds theory, that is, the complete separation of the paradigmatic world of ideas from the ebb and flow of change in our experience of the sense perceived world. Idea and reality are made to look like two worlds separated by a chasm, and the interrelationship of the two remains obscure.[26]

Instead of the apparent dualism to which the allegories of the *Republic* lend credence, Gadamer holds to a more Parmenidean Platonist ontology in which the forms must be understood not as entities in another realm *imitated* by our mundane reality, but rather as the various forms and patterns that reality *instantiates*. This more complex intermingling of idea and reality is, according to Gadamer, citing the Plato scholars of the Tubingen school, what is really implied in the difficult ambiguities of the doctrine of ideal numbers with which Plato struggles from the earliest dialogues.[27] This model of reality is far from the ontological criteria of "realness" in what Heidegger famously terms the "onto-theological" sense of *existentio*. Rather, as we will see, it is the reappropriated ontology of form as repetition in diversity, of "harmonic intervals" and patterns. It describes the constitutive *qualities* of which Being consists, as opposed to the mistakenly reified "things" of which, when misunderstood, those qualities appear to be only a predicate.[28]

It is remarkable how often this version of Plato's ontology, of which Gadamer charts the long history and pervasive presence in Western philosophical thought, both ancient and modern, analytic and continental, is misunderstood and criticised by the most laborious of misdirected arguments. Gadamer's infamous exchange with Habermas was based on a failure to comprehend the ontological depth of Gadamer's position.[29] This was merely sustained and repeated during Gadamer's encounters with Derridean deconstruction during the 1980s, throughout which Gadamer's Platonism was frequently taken as evidence that he had abandoned Heidegger's Nietzschean critique of Plato, and betrayed his own tradition.[30] In his "Three Questions to Hans-Georg Gadamer," Derrida complains that Gadamer's position remains subject to the dictates of tradition and the Kantian "will," while Derrida's subsequent defenders accused Gadamer of a Hellenistic, Hegelian absolutism revering Plato as the "aboriginal essentialist."[31] In the same volume Joseph Margolis, Fred Dallmayr, and Josef Simon similarly see in Gadamer's work an affirmation of conservative values, rather than an attempt to frame a metaphysical *truth*. G. B. Madison, David Farrell Krell (in the same volume), Carsten Dutt (in *Gadamer in Conversation*), and Jean Grondin in his recent excellent biography of Gadamer all indicate more clearly Gadamer's true position, but never to the extent of setting out a clear statement of that position in terms of its ontological foundations, and why it thus is impervious to such criticism. Like so many philosophers in both India and the West, including Rūpa Gosvāmi, his realist ontological underpinnings are all too often undervalued, ignored, or unsuspected.

It is Wachterhauser who offers perhaps the most exhaustive explanation of Gadamer's "Post-Platonic" ontology, although in explaining it through the lens of Platonic philosophy he has to combat the widespread prejudices and ontological misunderstandings from which Plato's works also suffer.[32]

Gadamer was one of the earliest scholars to try to archaeologically uncover the often-subversive literary and philosophical techniques that complicate the simple mythologies found in the *Republic* and elsewhere.[33] A significant degree of Gadamer's importance for contemporary philosophy lies in clarifying, with the help of these overlooked subtleties, the continuity that lies between many of the pre-Socratic thinkers, Plato, Aristotle, Hegel, Husserl, Heidegger, and others. In Gadamer's works, as in those of Gosvāmi, what appears to be regard for the authority of tradition is also a great regard for his predecessors' insights into a central metaphysical truth on which he believed them all to converge.

Nevertheless, the persistence of the dualistic picture of Plato is still in evidence in secondary literature on Gadamer. Wachterhauser, one of the most vigorous champions of his ontology, himself has some difficulty in countering the predominance of the idealist interpretation of Platonism that is so hard to avoid thanks to the subject-object structure of the language that he must use to explicate his philosophy.[34] Heidegger's later philosophy, in which Gadamer sees many similarities with Plato, suffers from the same difficulty of expression. Thus in the *Seventh Letter*, one of the texts in which Plato pursues his philosophy to what, as we will see, is (nearly) its most fundamental level in the analysis of the One and the Two, Gadamer writes of the objectifying influence of his discourse that "this appearance of rigidity may be the reason that Plato thought it ill advised to put this doctrine down in writing."[35] Certainly Gadamer's hermeneutic predisposition to proceed by example and commentary, rather than by direct explication, should not be dismissed as a merely stylistic device. It is one of the ways in which he attempts to improve upon the Heideggerian heritage and its awkward use of language—finding ways to express those "facts" of being which slip through the net of language's predicative abilities. At the same time he is able in this way to maintain an insistent realism *vis á vis* the forms, which corrects the traditional idealist (mis)reading of Platonic philosophy without falling foul of the misleadingly dualistic "objectivism" that Husserl risked when coining the motto "to the things themselves," and that ultimately prompted Heidegger to turn away from *Being and Time* toward a more ambitious ontology. It is this realism of analytic truths to which Gadamer sought to give a voice, and which we will clarify as the position for which he does indeed make claims of universality and necessity.

THE FORMS

In his wide range of philosophical commentaries and original insights, Gadamer offers various ways in which to understand this difficult "turn" (*Kehre*) of perspective to which Heidegger strove to remain true in his later works. The model that Gadamer most favours as a clear and original framework for explanation, that of "play" (*Spiel*) understood in the widest sense as a structural analogy both for cultural game-playing (including language games), and for the "play" of phenomenal forms of all kinds, also helps to illuminate the "Platonic" core of his metaphysics. He refers us to the natural world and the forms that light or water take on—e.g., ripples that have their own individual structural identities, but not a substantial identity *independent* of the water that provides a medium for them. He cites the patterns of light and shade that have no substantial existence; their identity lies in sheer form, defined in relation to each other. The playing of a piece of music appears to present another challenge to a dualistic substantialist ontology, for music is an excellent example of an entity that is defined not by its substance or medium (sound, marks on a page, perceptions, or memories), but by the transiently instantiated arrangement of form in which it consists.[36] It is the "shape" of the vibrations in the air, cast into a particular pattern of notes that we see symbolically represented in the score, never the same from one performance to the next, but always going by the same title. Gadamer seeks to show how universal and varied such entities are, citing

> [t]he play of light, the play of the waves, the play of gears or parts of machinery, the interplay of limbs, the play of forces, the play of gnats, even a play on words.[37]

But, as he points out,

> it is by no means merely a metaphor when we speak of the "play of the waves," or "the playing flies" or of the "free play of the parts."[38]

It is precisely the iteration of the structural pattern through diverse moments and contexts that describes a determinate form in the midst of radical flux. Repetition of analogous forms across a wider context of diversity is the true nature of identity—an insight that, as we will see, is itself repeated in different dimensions.

Gadamer avidly deploys such philosophical metaphors throughout *Truth and Method*, but the metaphor is never merely an analogical digression from the issue: it is a concrete instance of the philosophical principle at hand. The metaphors of play, music, waves, and light are not only analogies by which to clarify the nature of ideas, forms, things, beings, and Being. They are also exemplary, lucid specimens of that very universal principle. Grondin complains about the polysemic use of the notion of "universality" in *Truth and Method*, yet this pervasive polysemy is an accurate reflection of the pervasiveness of the truths that Gadamer is uncovering. It is important to clarify what Grondin is getting at when he says (rather vaguely) that hermeneutics possesses the universality of a *dimension*, not of a particular philosophical position.[39]

The universality of the hermeneutic perspective of which Gadamer boasts is such that it not only applies to every discrete application of the hermeneutic method, but to all phenomena at every (microcosmic and macrocosmic) level. This is true of his discussions of play, of language, of revelation, of art.[40] At times it can make his metaphysical tenets appear difficult to pin down, as each example is open to the different interpretations that one finds on either side of what Wachterhauser calls "the hermeneutic fork"—between Rortyan relativism and a genuinely Heideggerian ontology.[41] The proliferation of metaphor examples also reflects the pains that Gadamer takes to avoid an overemphasis on form and unity rather than instantiation and plurality. That—in the mind of certain contemporaries—would have cast him as a neo-Hegelian enemy of individualism, and leave him open to the sort of criticisms that Kojeve makes of Hegel's bias toward absolute rather than finite spirit.[42] In commentary on the later Heideggerian philosophy, Gadamer makes it clear that Heidegger's interpretation of the work of art as the unique manifestation of the concept in an *event* of truth, succeeded in checking any lingering tendency toward overly abstract, concretising philosophical conceptualisation.[43] Thus, long before Caputo had accused him of pursuing "the aigle of savoir absolue" through "an essentialistic, Hellenistic sky," Gadamer already had a cautious eye out for any suspiciously abstracted, absolutising discourse.[44] For Gadamer, as for the later Heidegger, both the unifying common form and the multiplying particular instance are real. In short, Gadamer's formal realism, like that of Rūpa Gosvāmi, includes a healthy affirmation of the reality of the particulars of our commonsense phenomenal world, while bringing their structural patterns or forms into focus.

THE ONE AND THE MANY

Gadamer's deployment of "play" as a model (and an actual example) of the nature of "form" (*Idee*), has its correlates elsewhere. It could be likened to a Derridean exposition on difference by semantic pessimists, or to a Wittgensteinian bundle theory by semantic optimists. But in reality what it demonstrates has an ontological dimension that goes beyond both of those theories of meaning; indeed, his use of *Spiel* is much closer in meaning to the Sanskrit word *līlā* than the English word "play," as which both are rather inadequately translated. The proliferation and complexity of "plays" makes concrete the Platonic problem of the One and the Many. Gadamer is quite explicit again and again that this is the problem to which all reason turns:[45]

> In any order in which a many becomes a unity, in the state and in the soul, in knowledge and in the structure of the world, it sees the law of the One and the Many, of number and Being.[46]

Precisely this doctrine of the One and the Many has often been ill served by neo-Platonism with its two-worlds interpretation of the doctrine of the forms, and by the perception that Plato was further from Aristotle than in fact he was. Gadamer categorically repudiates this position: "It is, as we know, precisely this doctrine which Aristotle above all represents and criticises as Plato's actual philosophy" for it is "not a step beyond the doctrine of ideas which would negate the latter but a step behind it which expresses its actual basis."[47] Whereas Rūpa Gosvāmi's philosophical language for addressing the problems raised by the self-evident plurality of phenomena (both among objects, and between the properties and moments of their individual existence) was provided by ongoing debates in Advaita and Sāṃkhya philosophy, Gadamer foreshadowed Alain Badiou's use of set theory as an ontological model, by unambiguously asserting the importance of Plato's Pythagorean ontology.[48] This is not to deny that the Pythagorean interpretation of the doctrine of the forms can seem to lend itself to the classical Platonist model of realism that has dominated the philosophies of mathematics, language, and Being. As Gadamer concedes, the mathematical entities in which Pythagorean philosophy trades are a powerful idea throughout the history of Western philosophy (and theology) "because here something permanently fixed and stable 'beyond' the flood of appearances comes into plain view . . . the pure genus, the pure meaning, or however one might choose to explain the 'universal' in modern concepts."[49] Badiou accounts for this cast in Plato's thinking by reference to the fact that, historically, the Sophists were his main interlocutors, practising a problematically deconstructive rhetoric that he took it upon himself to combat in his own philosophy with a model of a stable and determinate truth.[50] Yet the Socrates of the *Parmenides, Theaetetus, Sophist, Philebus, Timaeus,* and the *Seventh Letter* leads us toward a less mythological, more complex notion of the One—not as an uncontestable unity, but as the principle of structural similarity to which we have referred, the relative stability of form that in every identity marks a particular nexus in the infinite "web of ideas."[51] The foundation, fabric, and terrain of this web reveal the true nature of Being. Gadamer picks up on Plato's Parmenidean portrayal of all things, identities, or unities as being ambiguously one and many, existing and not existing as such simultaneously, pointing to the same ambivalence championed as a solution to the problem of the One and the Many by those Hindu philosophers who "maintain that both identity and difference are true of the relation between the one and the many."[52]

On this Platonic reading, reality is infinitely plural: the progress of time divides every being at each moment from its previous and future selves—an insight Heidegger applauded in Bergson's 1928 "The Metaphysical Foundations of Logic" in his notion of qualitative plurality. In addition, the many-propertied constitution of each object is a plurality that has puzzled innumerable philosophers, and with which Plato was much concerned. Finally, there is a sense in which each identity can be dissolved into an external plurality with an infinite horizon, for as Plato laboriously shows, each identity or essence (*Wesen* in German) is implicitly defined in reference to the pool of all other identities, similar and different in their various degrees. This is an insight now familiar to us through the semantic theories of the structuralist movement, but Plato refers us to this insight every time he has a character pose riddles about relative qualities, such as how geometrical values are determined, or how the tallest and the shortest man in a group are to be defined and what happens when a yet taller or shorter man arrives on the scene. This relativity of all properties to other properties and multiple instances points us toward the unending hermeneutic circle of reference that complicates any given unity. Hence the "universality" of the forms, their exact repeatability across diverse contexts, is revealed as a myth.[53]

Gadamer does indeed accept the Platonic account of the forms as repeated structures, but given this thoroughgoing plurality to which they are subject, he indicates that we should look at their relative similarity of structure through the course of change as a developing *theme* in which true identity lies, in order better to understand the indwelling of the *eidos* in plurality. He gives an Aristotelian example according to which:

> The living thing which emerges from the seed does not simply assume another eidetic determination, and it is not simply something "different," something defined by essentially different determinations, though if viewed mathematically it would be.[54]

The "living thing" here is an entity in the same way as the piece of music described earlier. And the instability of the organism's identity throughout its development, and of the artwork's identity throughout its history of performances is only the tip of the iceberg. The plurality of identity that we see in the changing essence of the thing reflects the plurality of the whole "world." Indeed, although we look toward the similarities between different phenomenal instances of what we identify as the object in question to provide an account of its essential structure, in fact the whole situation in which it is located is implied in this structural similarity (e.g., its accidental properties relative to other things, spaces, situations, times). On Gadamer's reading of Aristotle's metaphysics (understood as a refinement of Plato's doctrine of the forms, developed to better accommodate identity in change), the transformation of the living being synthesises one set of changing forms (seed, sapling, tree, mulch) with another (a similarity of situation in relation to place, time, things, persons, and ideas) to yield an apparent "identity." To identify an object or identity is to detect a thematic similarity or continuity that runs throughout the ongoing structures of the whole world.

This Aristotelian picture, which refigures the stable "thing" as a thematically linked phenomenon of change, is more dynamic than its Platonic precedent: a dynamic that highlights the importance of Gadamer's Hegelian paradigm for thinking the nature of the "thing"—a concept rendered more richly as the *Sache* in German. *Sache* expresses an idea not only of the physical object, but more generally and insightfully it also designates the "topic," the "subject matter" of discussion, the topos or concern that draws consciousness to it in the first place. When we pass the *Sache* from context to context, whether in conversation or in physical motion, it is at every moment transformed by that varying contextuality, and yet unified by its "theme," which has the structure of an analogy. Thus Ricoeur speaks of metaphor and Derrida of thematisation as endemic to Being. By way of providing an example for this Platonic, Hegelian, and also Heideggerian metaphysic, Derrida draws on Ricoeur's law of intentional analogy to trace a thematic path,

> [m]oving from the azure to the windowpane, to the blank paper, to the glacier, to the snowy peak, to the swan, to the wing, to the ceiling.[55]

Whereas the commonality that links the transformations in Aristotle's organism seems to be located in time and space, and the commonality threading through Derrida's conceptual transformations seems to be located in the imagination, from an ontological perspective, the two have the same reality status as themes in the flow of phenomena. Derrida's example poetically illustrates both the fragmentation and the thematic continuity that are the nature of Being. He calls this the problem of rebinding "the question of *life death* to the question of the position."

Hence to understand the reality of things we must understand the thread of analogy that connects the infinite instantiations into a broad *theme*, a structural continuity relative to what surrounds it—which from this perspective is what all "real objects" really are. When, to borrow Heidegger's terminology, we see items as "present to hand" (*vorhanden*) we focus on their singleness and particularity. It is when we see them as "ready to hand" (*zuhanden*) that we understand their true complicity in the context, their "enrootedness" in the situation. The same insight is true of people and our-"selves." In Gadamer's world picture the One and Many and the *Sache* reveal Being as a structure in which every identity is dialectical, a triangulation of multiple relations that furnishes the profound "realness" of any "self."

> Only now can the great dialectical puzzle of the one and the many which fascinated Plato as the negation of the logos and which received a mysterious affirmation in medieval speculation on the trinity, be given its true and fundamental ground. When Plato realised that the word of language is both one

> and many, he took only the first step. . . . But there is another dialectic of the word, which accords to every word an inner dimension of multiplication: every word breaks forth as if from a center and is related to a whole, through which it alone is a word. Every word causes the whole of the language to which it belongs to resonate and the whole worldview that underlies it to appear. Thus every word, as the event of a moment, carries with it the unsaid, to which it is related by responding and summoning.[56]

The "word" here is ontologically equivalent to the *Sache*, both possessing a flexible and nebulous structure that reminds us of the ubiquitous plurality and indeterminacy of the universe, but also has positive implications for understanding. It affirms analogy and imaginative construction while also policing the boundaries of possible inaccuracy and misuse. Thus it is in the prospective rightness and wrongness of the analogy defining a particular *Sache* that one also observes the regulative function of the form as a directionality that can either be followed in pursuit of truth, or abandoned in digression and falsehood. Thus the theme with its simultaneously limiting and enabling importance for humanity is not just the idea, the number, the form, the subject matter—it is also the objects we encounter empirically making up the "real world"; those objects which we use, listen to, and which, though they are intrinsically related to us also have an unmanipulable essence; they offer resistance to our will and desires.[57]

FORMAL ONTOLOGY AS FUNDAMENTAL ONTOLOGY

Thus the doctrines of the One and the Many and the *Sache* provide a way of characterising individuals, such that the idea, at once ancient and postmodern, of the simultaneous unity-and-multiplicity of all things is accommodated without sacrificing our sense of being located in a world of truths that are beyond the subjective whims of our will. Thus Grondin observes that "[w]hen all is said and done, it is finitude which is the new 'transcendence.'"[58] While Gadamer felt he could not look beyond the boundaries of Being as Levinas seems to do, nor wait expectantly by them as Derrida recommends, he remained attached to the "transcendental" truths that he explicitly equates with the "formal concepts of logic."[59] But the question remained of whether transcendental analysis could delve behind these truths to yet more basic analytic features of Being. The One and the Many furnished an important realisation about Being, but did not seem to strike the deepest level of things; some more foundational truth seemed to be implied. He writes: "With the thematisation of language as it belongs indissolubly to the human life world, a new basis for the old metaphysical question about the whole seems to be available."[60] Gadamer asserts that what qualifies Heidegger's philosophy as "fundamental ontology" (*Existenzial-ontologie* or *Fundamental-ontologie*) is its "ontological priority" (*ontologische Priorität*).[61] But what is meant by "priority"? The phenomenological tradition sought to determine what is *necessarily* presupposed by the one and only starting point is the one that is self-evident: the plural, changing, meaningful presence of phenomena as the content of our perception.[62] But Heidegger left his students the riddle of where, and whether, a totally foundational level might be found.

In effect, this Heideggerian notion of "priority" really means "necessary ontological precondition." From within the framework of a substantialist ontology, Jonathan Schaffer has tried to offer a notion of "fundamental levels" that illuminates how we think of fundamentalness and ontological foundation in general. Quoting Jaegwon Kim's schema, he defines that which is "fundamental" as lying on a level in a mereological (part-whole) structure that does not "have an exhaustive decomposition, without remainder" into lower levels.[63] One analyses each "unit" of Being into its composite parts until one discovers a level that is omnipresent and necessary to the existence of the higher levels but cannot be further divided or reduced into any more simple feature. By this reasoning one discovers what is fundamental in the sense of being "basic," irreducible, necessary, a universal precondition of all things. Thus as one deconstructs, one rises to increasing levels of universality and also of non-composite simpleness and purity—qualities traditionally considered (in both India and the West) to be the mark of an ontologically sovereign, primordial level.

Wachterhauser brings to light an apt example of this mereological analysis in Plato's reasoning to the "transcendentals"—universal, necessary, and ontological rather than ontic qualities, called "transcendental" because they belong to all existing things by the sheer fact of their existing at all, and thus "transcend" any other particular property that the individual existent might have. The beautiful, the good and the true, motion, rest, unity (or the One) and plurality (or the Many), likeness (or participation) and unlikeness (or separation), and Being itself—all of these are the fruit of a mereological analysis of intelligibility itself, marking a fundamental level beyond which thought itself cannot go, although they are universally present in thought.[64] The transcendentals "are always already there whenever we become aware of our own thinking. . . . Such a grasp is 'primitive' in that we must always presuppose them and can never break such intuitions down into more basic units of meaning."[65] In his works on the Platonic dialogues, Gadamer strives to clarify the ways in which Plato sought deeper and deeper mechanisms of analysis in his dialogues, arriving at an initial level of universality in the transcendentals, which "function across all distinctions of genera and species, universal and particular."[66] Indeed, he writes that "[t]ranscendental means that [the greatest classes] may not be thought according to the order of genera and species"[67] The transcendentals are not themselves categories or regulative principles of things; rather, each describes a necessary principle of what it is to be a principle, each is a principle of universality itself. What comes into relief here is the attempt to identify "syncategorematic" qualities—universals of a yet more universal kind.

Gadamer is keen to pursue Plato's insights to their most fundamental level, sifting through the many more and less obscure doctrines that fill his texts.[68] His exegesis of Plato's fragmentary ideas on the One and the Many lead him to the elusive doctrine of the indeterminate two (*hê aoristos duas*, as paraphrased by Simplicius) ascribed to Plato by his successors.[69] Gadamer writes:

> If we are indeed forbidden to seek a fixed system of deduction in Plato's doctrines and if, on the contrary, Plato's doctrine of the indeterminate Two establishes precisely the impossibility of completing such a system, then Plato's doctrine of ideas turns out to be a general theory of relationship from which it can be convincingly deduced that dialectic is unending and infinite.[70]

This doctrine reduces the previous duality of unity and multiplicity to the underlying, preconditional principle of relationality that, paradoxically, enables any single thing to be itself. The indeterminate two encapsulates the mystery that any identity of any kind (name, object, idea, property) is intrinsically and essentially constituted by relationality. Here "it is this question of the meaning of being which leads [Plato] to the One and the Two, an entirety of the logoi in which reality, according to its ordering principle, both unifies and unfolds itself."[71] Indeed, in Aristotle's account of Plato's doctrine, the Two plays almost exactly the same role as that played by the ontological concept of *prakṛti* (the primordial level of proliferation of forms, in the Sāṃkhya school) in Rūpa Gosvāmi's metaphysical source texts. Plato's primordial One combines with the prolific relational principle of the Two to produce the range of transcendentals, which combine in the same way to produce universals, and in due course the multiplicity of particulars. Difference within a context of reciprocally determining relations is the essence of identity. On this model, everything that is, both *is* and *is not* the same as itself, is and is not the same as others, consisting of a relationality which dialectically subsumes and transcends those very concepts.

Characteristically, Gadamer paraphrases this whole account as if it were a hypothetical speculation—nevertheless, he leaves little room for doubt about his own philosophical convictions. He attributes foundational qualities to this dyad of the One and the Two:

> The principles of the One and the Two are able to generate the series of all numbers—just as they make all discourse possible. The entire series of numbers, the even as well as the odd, can be explicated according to these principles. . . . This special status of the One and the Two could be what is indicated by the "outside of the First" in that famous Aristotelian text.[72]

The One and the Two are preconditions facilitating the possibility of any form, structure, or pattern at all; they are relationality itself, and the very material of Being.[73]

But Gadamer shows that the One and the Many, the indeterminate dyad of the One and the Two, and the *Sache*, still do not yet represent the deepest level of analysis—perhaps because it is not clear that these are truths which can play a constructively foundational role for our understanding of meaning, truth, identity, and action. Drawing on a different set of thinkers, Gadamer shifts his approach from the synchronic analysis of form according to its mereological levels to the diachronic analysis of form in terms of temporality. For this approach, proceeding from the facts of time and change, Gadamer looks to other sources.

The diachronic analysis of Being is less prominent in Gadamer's works, but one of the thinkers through whose work this question arises is Husserl. Gadamer does not feel that Being as a whole begs the question of an efficient cause, for causation is something observed *within* the world and not something that we can speak of as external to it. In this he is again in line with the Vedāntic sources of Rūpa Gosvāmi's thought—there is a continuous thread in the Vedic tradition of portraying the cause of the world as a continual arising without temporal beginning. Speaking in terms of the Husserlian paradigm of Being as consciousness, Gadamer too feels that we cannot delve before or beneath the sheer, upwelling present in all its "immediate" "primal source":

> The core of the problem lies exclusively in the self-constitution of temporality in its primal source of the present. Hence it lies in that deepest level of the problematic of constitution for which even the transcendental ego and the stream of consciousness (the ultimate source of all accomplishments of constitution) is transcended in the sense that the immediate flow of the living present, as the real primal phenomenon, lies at the basis even of the stream of consciousness.[74]

Gadamer's account of reality as an actuality that is immediately encountered complements the Husserlian model of the primal present with Dilthey's notion of experience as *erlebnis*, which "suggests the immediacy with which something real is grasped."[75]

The primal constitution of cognition lies in immediacy (*Unmittelbarkeit*), and this is meant to illuminate an alternative notion of creation, never past, always part of the "immediate flow of the living present."[76] As in the Caitanya Vaiṣṇava assertion that the relation of God and world is *acintya*, literally "unthinkable," so Gadamer uses the notion of "immediacy" for the opaque, basic level of things in Husserl's thought.[77] Gunter Figal paints a convincing picture of the "turn" in Gadamer's later work away from the evasions of a historical approach, toward an explicit acknowledgement of the elusive nature of Being as that which "withdraws" from understanding, and "cannot be gotten behind" (*unhintergebare*).[78] Once again, in phenomenological terms, this points us toward the "unilluminable obscurity of our facticity."[79] Yet elsewhere he challenges the awed retreat before this apparent primordiality. This immediacy is not itself a static foundation of Being but its dynamic presence (*Anwesenheit*). For Gadamer, genesis is "revealed perhaps in every reduction properly understood."[80]

In order to undercut Husserl's "false hyposticising of inner processes" he returns to an ancient thinker with a strong intuition of the dynamic for a genetic account of Being—not to Plato, but to Aristotle. The constant primal upwelling of Being is widely associated with Aristotle's concept of *physis*, or "nature." But Gadamer also focuses on Aristotle's work regarding the *epagoge*, the genesis of the form. As we have seen, Gadamer acknowledges that Heidegger's philosophy proceeds by the "consistent carrying out of the transcendental thought in Husserl's phenomenology." Yet he identifies the crux of the divergence between the two thinkers in "the completely different dimension of origin [*Ursprung*] of the process of Being's manifestation that proceeds and lies at the basis even of metaphysics."[81]

> In his first apperception, a sensuously equipped being finds himself in a surging sea of stimuli, and finally one day he begins, as we say, to know something. Clearly we do not mean that he was previously blind. Rather when we say to know [*erkennen*] we mean to "recognise" [*wiedererkennen*], that is, to pick something out [*herauserkennen*] of the stream of images flowing past as being identical.[82]

Sensitive to the continuing, fruitful, perennial problems of history, like Aristotle Gadamer asks:

> How does one arrive at a universal? [which is the same, he says, as arriving at a general concept or indeed a word]. . . . Can we really say that there is a single event in which a first knowing extricates the child from the darkness of not knowing?[83]

In the text in which he raises the question, Gadamer immediately answers himself with a terse gesture of philosophical surrender: "It seems obvious to me that we cannot." But as usual, other answers are scattered within the fabric of his diverse hermeneutic studies. While Aristotle is most famous for those accounts of change and development that focus on natural forms, Gadamer focuses on an Aristotelian analogy in which the development of the unified concept is likened to the movement of an army:

> He says it is the same as when an army is in flight, driven by panic, until at last someone stops and looks around to see whether the foe is still danger-

> ously close behind. We cannot say that the army stops when one soldier has stopped. But then another stops. But then another stops. The army does not stop by virtue of the fact that two soldiers stop. When does it actually stop, then? Suddenly it stands its ground again. Suddenly it obeys its command once again.[84]

It changes its position as a whole dependent on the multiplicity that constitutes it, and because of the multiplicity the whole is never univocal. Thus it is impossible for the aggregate concept "army" to identify the moment at which "it" came to a stand. This reflects the view that there is no "first moment" of knowing, prior to conceptualisation. Yet the army does indeed stop, move, and stop again with an innate complexity that defies categorisation and partakes rather of the logic of the Wittgensteinian language game. Gadamer speaks of Being's coming to a stand in a particular form as an *Einfall*, a sudden idea that drops lightly into any given moment. The metaphor of the army is popular with Gadamer, turning up when the problem of the source arises again in an essay of the same year, "Man and Language."

The changeful energy that Gadamer via Aristotle is attempting to describe can be equated with what Plato calls "motion" (*Bewegtheit* for Gadamer): the flux that, as we have seen, weaves plurality through even the most stable identities. Wachterhauser judges the realist features of Gadamer's metaphysics to be compromised by the inclusion of motion in the list of transcendentals, enabling Gadamer "to see in Plato a tacit acknowledgement that some aspects of the 'real' world do change."[85] But this reflects an old "two-worlds" notion of Platonic realism that assumes that motion and change are necessarily deconstructive and destabilising forces, excluded from a "real" world. This is not Gadamer's position at all. By contrast, one of his most distinctive features is that he draws on the notion of flux as the positive *energeia* by which Being is, and is *such as it is* in the forms. He says that Aristotle's "highest speculative concept" of *energeia,* influenced by Plato's laws and influential on Hegel's dialectic, is "that which properly speaking *is* in the highest sense."[86] Indeed, Gadamer writes that "the petrified tranquility of a cosmos of ideas cannot be the ultimate truth for Plato. For the soul, which he co-ordinates with these ideas, is motion."[87] The soul is yet another microcosm/metaphor of Being, in which an underlying *dynamis* is invested.[88] Gadamer argues that the soul, as envisioned by the ancients and contrary to our individualistic notion of the *psyche,* is all things,[89] and particularly is *motion* in all things. Understood as a universal principle of identity, it is each entity as an action, as event, "The Doing of the Thing-Itself," as Gunter Figal puts it.[90] Thus *energeia* is also a fundamental level that itself assumes the status for Gadamer of *anwesenheit,* "pure presence."

This new perspective implies an ontology not merely of entities founded in substance, or structures founded in difference, nor merely of sheer synchronic, structural relationality, but of relational, mutually constitutive *dynamics*. Yet *energeia* as ever-present first cause does not serve alone as the foundation stone of ontology. What is the cause of the army's coming to a stand and the shift into movement again? In connection with this metaphor, Gadamer notes that it is appropriate that in Aristotle's Greek description of the process of the coming to a stand (*Anstoss*) the "'command' means *arche*, that is, *principium*. When is the principle present as a principle? Through what capacity? This question is in fact the question of the universal."[91] Here, the army does not merely stand and move on again in blind flux from form to form. It pivots on the "command," requiring that the mystery of teleology be installed firmly at the heart of being. *Phronesis* can be interpreted as not a practical but an ontological category, insofar as it assimilates the teleology of question (past) and answer (potentiality) to the present moment of decision, which microcosmically is the formation of the universal: a coming to stand of Being. In Platonic terms, this teleology is called the "Good," but in order to clarify this (so unclear) notion it is important to recognise that the Good for us must have the shape of human life, just as "Plato's Pythagoreanism is a Pythagoreanism not of the world but of human beings"—which is not opposed to, but *inclusive of* that same world.[92] This is a truth of Being as a whole (and what kind of Being is there other than human Being?), and paints a picture in which the turn of events, the choice of actions and the taking of any stand is also the coming to be of reality. There is a tacit admission of the dynamic and elusive changefulness of this central teleology in Gadamer's explanation that *tou agathon* in Plato means not an objectified idea of the Good, but a *looking to* the regulative principle of Goodness,[93] just as the whole project of our self-understanding must be called not *sophia* (wisdom) but *philosophia* (the love of wisdom).[94]

Correcting and completing thought's attempt at self-analysis in these ways, allows us to take more seriously Gadamer's assertion that *wirkungsgeschichtliches Bewusstsein*, the "consciousness in which history is ever at work" that consists of the fabric of inherited "prejudices" or "anterior influences" (*Voreingenommenheiten*) defining any present determination, really is the answer to the question of origins.[95] What was seen negatively as prejudice can be seen positively as the teleological dynamic that is our ontological essence. In this light the Platonic idea, mediated through the individual "thing," takes on the character of a question, or, as Gadamer characterises it, an invasion by reality which is more like a passion than an action (*mehr ein Erleiden als ein Tun*).[96] We do not merely have the option of applying a spirit of passion to Being, nor is passion merely interwoven into the Being's phenomenal fabric; our passions, understood as teleologies, correspond to the teleological essence of all forms and things.[97] This is true for Gadamer much in the way that the world for Rūpa Gosvāmi is explained as form (*rūpa* and *prakṛti*) proliferating through the "dialectical dynamic of love."[98]

For the latter thinker, the idea that reality is inherently (and necessarily) dynamic and imbued with value is no great stretch of the imagination, but Gadamer's contemporaries still had the unchallenged authority of the fact-value divide to contend with. Seen from the perspective of Gadamer's emerging post-Heideggerian realism, the apparently passive, autonomous, unmanipulable objects that we perceive are endowed with an implicit dynamism, which is itself governed in the themed continuity of its manifestations by their teleological directionality. In chapter 3 we will see how this inspires an ethos of movement, development, growth, and vitality in Gadamer's own philosophy. Here, we will explore the cosmological and soteriological world-picture that Gadamer develops from his realisation of the true nature of the One and the Many and the *Sache*, and the fundamental status of the Indeterminate Two, of motion and teleology.

GADAMER'S APOTHEOSIS OF FINITE BEING

Gadamer's altered view of "things" corresponds with a changed view of the whole of Being—no longer as a set of objects that are ontologically independent of each other and ourselves, but rather as aspects of a larger, multifaceted single set of existence. It is important here, not least for comparative reasons, to note not only how Gadamer arrives at this notion, but also how he characterises it and the values that he attributes to it. Through the language that Gadamer employs, and through its "fundamental" and "transcendental" character, this model of Being as the flux of unified and divided forms is subtly but surely apotheosised in Gadamer's philosophy. Here, as in the case of various post-Vedāntic schools that arose in India, a holistic, fundamental analysis of existence based on the evidence of sheer phenomena, yields a view of reality that must eschew radical dualism, and locate *foundational* and *divine* value in the finite, immanent world.

The fundamental structure of Being as "[ontologically] One and [ontically] Many" is what Gadamer discovers in Leibniz in the idea that the monad is itself a universe, reflecting the world within itself. For Hegel who figures it as "Spirit" (*Geist*) and as the dialectic of history and of reality in his *Logic*, it can also be thought more qualitatively in terms of beauty.[99] In Gadamer's discussions of Kantian aesthetics, he notes that Kant's conception of "genius" is not unlike the successful play of the player, and relates these conceptions of art and play.[100] In Heidegger the "formal" worldview appears first in terms of *Dasein* and later as language (here, *Sprache*) and also as the *Kunstwerkes*, the work of art. As we see in *Truth and Method*, Gadamer also privileges language and particularly the work of art as a paradigmatic metaphor instance of the nature of Being. The relation of the viewer to the work of art had already raised issues of submission and submergence, union, and sacrifice of self to higher truths in the thought of writers like Schiller. In his treatment of each of these examples, Gadamer has identified an idea—*Dasein*, dialectic, language, beauty, play, genius—through which a philosopher struggles with the intellectual materials available at a given point in history, to articulate a medial paradigm that incorporates subject and object into a single reality. Each is the vehicle for a new, more accurate metaphysics marked by a decentring shift in perspective toward a concept into which both subject and object are subsumed.

Grondin writes that students of Gadamer were resigned to a semantic and systematic haziness, illustrated in Walter Schutz's observation that

> [h]istory, language, dialogue and game—all of these, and this is the decisive thing, are interchangeable quantities.[101]

But, on the contrary, Schultz's statement recognises that this is not a vague but a decisive equivalence, essential for getting to the bottom of things. Thus reason, for Gadamer as for Hegel, is not a power held by subjects over/against their environment; it is rather the "unity of thought and reality"—a unity that must be asserted over every inner limit of the real:

> The dichotomisation of reality into universal and particular, idea and appearance, the law and its instances, needs just as much to be eliminated as does the division of consciousness into consciousness on the one side and its object on the other.[102]

Gadamer stresses both the unity and the "inner infinity" applicable to each of the medial concepts such as truth, beauty, art, language, mathematics, and play,[103] in respect of which, "insofar as that which differentiates itself from within itself is not limited from the outside by the boundary of something else from which it differentiates itself, it is infinite in itself."[104] Gadamer does not claim that Being is absolute in the Hegelian sense of closure as a completed picture or quantity. But he does assert its absoluteness as both universal and necessary, and he does assert its infinity, both in the sense of infinite possibility and of infinite inner division into unities and relations. Again we are reminded of Badiou's paradigm of number, progressing forever, and infinitely divisible.[105] Thus whatever model we favour, the picture we have is of an infinite whole, single in type, infinitely plural in different dimensions (synchronically, semantically, diachronically), encompassing all things and ourselves in reciprocally defined relational quiddity.

In relatively early texts Gadamer uses suggestively religious terms for this universal inner unity, although for precisely the opposite reasons to those for which the Pythagoreans, aspiring to the purity and immutability of number, also thought of the reality of the logos in religious terms. Gadamer by contrast is interested in the close connection between the dynamic, pluralistic truth of reality and ourselves, speaking of the relation of self and object in terms of the correspondence, or "pre-established harmony" of "world and soul." He approvingly observes that

> Hegel sees the unity of the speculative and reasonable in everything, and, as is well known, he said of Heraclitus's cryptic utterances, which are manifold variations on this principle of speculative unity, that there was not a single one which he had failed to incorporate in his Logic.[106]

Here he seems sympathetic to ancient worldviews in their emphasis on holistic unity and harmony of the self with its cosmic context, and some of Gadamer's Christian theological imagery also seems by implication to theophanise this more accurate, medial version of Being. In his comments on Christian scripture his preferred trope for discussion of reality is the divine "Word."[107] His relation via the romanticism of Schleiermacher and Dilthey, among others, to Reformation hermeneutics is well established, and his philosophy of language led him by Lutheran, Romantic, and Heideggerian routes toward a sense that language possessed more than *merely* historical or human significance.[108] Again and again language brought him to profound correspondences and unities that were prefigured by thinkers with clear, if sometimes unorthodox, religious interest.

Understood in terms of the divine word, reality assumes the eminent status of a divine counsel, addressed to each of us in the infinite particularity of our own situation, and drawing on the horizon of its infinite possibility. The theological Word becomes, for Gadamer, not only a piece of practical wisdom, but a meditation on Being's context-specificity and at the same time a reminder of its eminence, foundation-fulness, importance, and soteriological efficacy. While Heidegger "waits" for a god, Gadamer's worldview weaves divine communication into the finite plane of everyday phenomena, just as Rilke advises him to do in the caption that Gadamer chose for the beginning of *Truth and Method*:

> Catch only what you've thrown yourself, all is
> mere skill and little gain;
> but when you're suddenly the catcher of a ball
> thrown by an eternal partner
> with accurate and measured swing
> towards you, to your center, in an arch
> from the great bridge-building of God:
> why catching then becomes a power
> —not yours, a world's.[109]

Almost nowhere in his broad body of work is Gadamer so explicitly theological about his philosophy as in this short verse, and nowhere could he hope to make a more telling and pervasive statement than in the caption of his magnum opus. It is a curious quote, presenting a single vision in which the isolated individual is assimilated into the divine play, exchanges his passive position (as catcher) for the position of power, and finally discovers that the power assumed belongs to the world as a whole.[110]

This points to the ambiguity of Gadamer's appropriation of theistic ideas and images. Like Kant's noumenal "object," any idea of purely transcendent, wholly independent divinity, whether Christian scholastic or postmodern Judaic (e.g., Levinas, Derrida), would seem to fall outside the remit of Gadamer's cautiously delimited ontology.[111] Thus his position opposes that taken by Levinas in preserving space for the unknowable beyond of Being, and also Derrida's flirtation with concepts of radical transcendence. Indeed he even implicitly eschews the rhetoric of Heidegger's final, most famous wish in his posthumously published *Der Spiegel* interview of 1966, for the intervention of a/the saving god/God. For Gadamer, the soteriological efficacy of the "god" is always immanent and accessible to us when we successfully "catch" the ball, or embrace the telos, of the divine play of Being.

To some extent, Gadamer's resistance to the idea of a wholly transcendent, and thus absent God as divine Giver of Being reflects his commitment to the "given-ness" of Being. He holds out for an ontology that is not created or founded, but merely and magically "gifted." It demands an Orphic comportment—we must learn not to feel that nagging need to look back for reassurance. Arguing that the "given" nature of Being is such that we must abjure the search for origins, Gadamer likens this cherished ideal to the madness of a Kaspar Hauser–like tale, or to the folly of a tower of Babel. "What is mad about such ideas," he says, "is that they want to suspend in some artificial way our very enclosedness in the linguistic world in which we live."[112] Rather, "we are always already encompassed by the language that is our own."[113] To some extent the Lutheran paradigm for thinking the "sacred" place of language in relation to human subjects was juxtaposed with a slightly divergent Romantic model that led him to the controversial figures of a more nature-oriented German perspective. On such models the world took the place of the divine partner, not throwing messages to the finite human realm *through* words, but *itself* creating and delighting those within it with the self-sufficiency of a playful work of art:

> [I]t becomes finally meaningless to distinguish between literal and metaphorical usage. . . . Thus Friedrich Schlegel writes, "All the sacred games of art are only remote imitations of the infinite play of the world, the eternally self-creating work of art"[114]

He contrasts the unhealthy and misguided search for origins with the sense of vigour and independence that we find under the conditions of the self-forgetfulness of Being (*Seinsvergessenheit*) or language. This is an experience that is "alive": "The more language is a living operation, the less we are aware of it."[115] This vigour replaces spirituality with a "spiritedness" in which the self-consciousness of spirituality dissolves as we are absorbed into the energy and teleology of the play of the world. This revivification of "spirit" recalls the Hegelian language of spirit as much as the theological imagery of the soul. This is our reward for giving up absolute transcendence: a pantheistic vitalism that aims to legitimise and commend the finite realm with which rigorous truthfulness leaves us. Gadamer could not help but have a sympathy with Heraclitus for whom the soul—which to Plato is the motion of being, and for the Milesians is mere breath—is rather an integral part of "the great mystery of the unfathomable limitlessness within which the thinking soul moves."[116] For Heraclitus, he argues, cosmology is really "the whole of human/political life," which, given "the unity in that which changes itself . . . turns all of the Heraclitean propositions into one truth of unfathomable depth."[117] In Heraclitus universal flux is acknowledged as both motion and rest, and epitomised in the powers of fire.[118] What falls to humanity is "the total animation and free interplay of all our spiritual powers."[119]

By recognising both indeterminacy and flux we are led to "the intensification of the *Lebensgefuhl* (life-feeling)"[120] In theology this intensification is seen in[121]

> the word that is a *singulare tantum*. That means the word that strikes one, the word one allows to be said to oneself, the word that enters into a determinate and unique life-situation; and it is good to be reminded that behind this *singulare tantum* stands ultimately the linguistic usage of the New Testament.[122]

The gospel, "far from being evidence documenting something bygone that we may not care to interpret and make our own, is already speaking to us and every other person in history in a way that is uniquely appropriate to that particular place and time."[123] This mediatory theology is intended to walk a thin line between theological positions that seemed inadequate in the thought of many of his peers. Heidegger's "turn" stripped theology of its theological justification in hoping to refer to an external authority, and left Heidegger facing either a pagan attention to the daemon of everyday existence or, as seems to have been Heidegger's final preference, a more "Abrahamic" decision to await the intervention of a "God," in the face of encroaching nihilism.[124] But Gadamer's Christian paradigms are always used in ways that universalise the Christian message, often quite explicitly. He writes:

> Does not the intended meaning of the New Testament authors—even what they may concretely have in mind—move in the direction of the meaning of

> salvation for which one reads the Bible? . . . Their honour should lie precisely in the fact that they proclaim something that surpasses their own horizon of understanding—even if they are named John or Paul.[125]

The transcendence of self to a wider horizon in the immediate situation, the world, and Being as a whole, is a soteriological tenet of Gadamer's philosophy. In these examples ontology performs a foundational function not only by providing a point of reference for meaning, truth, and action, but also by taking on the characteristics of lost divinity. Whatever is foundational so often takes on a divine status—this is borne out in the Indian context and has provided some philosophical fuel for the Buddhist critique of Hindu philosophy. It is interesting to note that Gadamer's metaphor of play as a tacitly *religious* image reoccurs in reference to Rilke, Schlegel (who incidentally had published a book on Indian thought), and Heidegger, favouring forms that are self-fulfilling—like the play of light or the Rilkean play with a ball or toy. Derrida provides the analogy of a constellation for the post-Heideggerian ontological framework that he shares with Gadamer:

> This absence of any border or closure of propriety gives to this textual music what I will call . . . its galaxic or galactic structure. By galaxy here one must understand, at least, a multiplicity in a space of perpetually deployment, which has no external limit, no outside, no end, a constellated autonomy referring to nothing but itself, nurturing itself, inseminating or nurturing itself from its own milk.[126]

This image is meant to counter the foundationalist hunger for an external point of reference with images of self-sufficiency, and indeed a nurturing fecundity. Gadamer's ontology reflects this "galactic" structure of Being while maintaining the rhetoric of foundationalism. Grondin is one of those commentators who has been sensitive enough to perceive this:

> We certainly cannot say that Gadamer is hostile to foundations. Rather, he is opposed to an easy fundamentalist solution, to foundations that are too convenient, that can be tamed or explained, because to explain foundations is to cut them off from their essential dimension, or the basis from which everything else flows.[127]

Mark Taylor cites the trope of play as a "solution" to the problem of a philosophy and theology that do not take refuge in the philosophically dubious ideal of radically transcendent foundations:

> Instead of a conclusion, we are left with an Interlude, which, it appears, is always already playing. Inscribed between an Origin that never was and an End that never is, the Interlude is the Inter Ludus of scripture itself.[128]

We are to understand ourselves as themes contributing to the harmony and counterpoint of Being, players devoting ourselves to the goals of the game, and teleological trajectories that dialectically shift and advance at every moment. Yet Gadamer's interludic position leaves us with the unanswered question of whether action can successfully be restricted to finite goals, like Gerald Bruns's *phronesis* of concrete situations, satisfied by an ethos of inherent fulfilment reminiscent of aesthetic enjoyment.[129] This is an issue that Rūpa Gosvāmi also addresses, borrowing the model of aesthetic teleology and fulfilment, as we will see. What appears problematic in Gadamer's philosophy is any radical ethical question of a Camusian sort, which asks "what is it all for?" unless the answer is to be fundamentally an aesthetic one—beauty inspiring in us spiritual powers to instantiate and appreciate further beauty. Note that "beauty" here becomes a term that designates the value that it itself predicates and thus bestows—without any external parameters of "taste," it becomes almost a theophanising term.

Taking into account certain key features such as the implicit but radical rejection of independent absolute transcendence, Being's single ontological kind and its self-grounding, the deflation of fact and meaning, and of substance and idea, and the inadequacy of all such attempts at typology, it is tempting to align Gadamer's position more closely with pantheism than with theism. The attraction of a pantheistic position has a long precedent in Western thinkers for whom Gadamer professes great appreciation, such as Heraclitus, Spinoza, Leibniz, Hegel, Goethe, and Dilthey, whose complex world-pictures pictured from outside of the traditional substantialist camp have challenged any simplistic univocal definitions of this fraught word. Gadamer draws on many of the thinkers implicated in the *Pantheismusstreit*, or pantheism controversy that rocked eighteenth-century Germany, and must have been aware of this debate over the Spinozistic pantheist position that Toland, Lessing, and Mendelsohn had implied was a superior perspective to dualistic Christian theism on primarily *rational* grounds. Gadamer himself declines to use the term and certainly did not see himself as a Spinozist *tout court*, or a pantheist in quite the mould of these thinkers. Instead he charts his own path, drawing selectively on thinkers with positions that are often far from the mainstream of Christian theism, such as Schleiermacher, Goethe, and Oetinger, in whom he applauds the idea that

> the presence of God consists precisely in life itself, in this "communal sense" that distinguishes all living things from dead—it is no accident that he mentions the polyp and the starfish which, though cut into small pieces, regenerate themselves and form new individuals. In man the same divine power operates.[130]

He himself was wont to discuss explicitly theological ideas (except insofar as they concerned Lutheran hermeneutics) as little as possible. One could not have failed to learn from Heidegger the lesson that to "onto-theologise" is to amass power, and to claim it over and against other positions, particularly given Heidegger's fall, which Gadamer had witnessed, and the consequent damage to Heidegger's own complex faith commitments. But while Gadamer declines to make a religious stand, signalling perhaps that such stands are unnecessary for the pursuit of truth and the practice of philosophy, the implications and applications of his position are hinted at and they remain to be fully explored.

In the ever-cautious tone of his assessment of the many thinkers with whom he felt an evident sympathy of outlook, one can guess that no philosopher had quite expressed his own worldview in terms that he could fully approve, for his own delicate ontological balance between what he called "subjectism" and dualistic realism had not yet been clearly formulated by another thinker. Gadamer affirms that "Hegel defines reason as the unity of thought and reality," and without a dualistic conception of transcendence, all that *is*, is indeed only thought and reality.[131] Assimilating and surpassing elements of the systems of Hegel and Schelling and other thinkers (Feuerbach, Fichte, Schleiermacher) Gadamer's ontology implies a pantheism of the structures of Being—of essences not substances. Here we think not of the crude pantheism conceived as an identity of God and Nature, or an omnipresent pervasive substance, which many dictionaries give as its definition. Rather, this is the philosopher's pantheism, seen as a recurring answer to so many metaphysical problems, and described as the idea that everything that exists constitutes an all-inclusive unity that is in some way "divine,"[132] such that "all other forms of realities are either modes (or appearances) of it or identical with it."[133] Gadamer's paragons for this model are the pre-Socratics and Hegel, but it is intended to assimilate aspects of Christianity with which Gadamer seems most concerned. Rather, he sees Hegel's formulation as uniting ancient religious forms with the essence of Christianity in a way that judiciously redressed the imbalances in contemporary philosophy and solved its key dilemmas:

> [T]he concept of spirit, which Hegel appropriated from the Christian spiritualistic tradition and raised to new life, is still the basis of every critique of subjective spirit, as this critique is posed for us as our own task by the experience of the post-Hegelian epoch. This concept of spirit that transcends the subjectivity of the ego has its true counterpart in the phenomenon of language, which is coming increasingly to the center of contemporary philosophy.[134]

Hegel's mistake is to be mystified and seduced by the less philosophical tenets of Christianity:

> The reason is that in contrast to the concept of spirit that Hegel drew from the Christian tradition, the phenomenon of language has the merit of being

appropriate to our finitude. It is infinite as is spirit, and yet finite, as is every event.[135]

Gadamer makes an important implicit distinction here between what is finitely infinite (language) and what is transcendently infinite (Christian conceptions of spirit), which we will encounter again in the Indian Advaitic debates between those pitting dualism against monism, immanence against transcendence. It is a philosophical distinction that informs Rūpa Gosvāmi's Caitanya Vaiṣṇava formulation of the relationship between the divine as the ground of Being, and the world as its manifestation. In Gadamer's case, the implication is that non-finite absolute transcendence is a powerful religious ideal, but a false one, whereas Being as ubiquitous form, energy, telos, indeterminacy, meaning, beauty, and spirit—these are ideals into which we should be happy to assimilate our own identities. It has been written of Rūpa Gosvāmi's conception of the divine that it is really a "concentrated form of Being"—on a sufficiently attentive hermeneutic reading, the same might be said with regard to Gadamer.[136]

GADAMER'S POSTMODERN PANTHEISM

To interpret this ontology according to a pantheistic rather than a theistic framework is also to alter its religious and ethical implications for the individual. As we have seen, Gadamer parallels the mystery, indeterminacy, and telos of being with the mystery, indeterminacy, and telos of the soul. The key to understanding the relation of this new realism to that which we experience day to day, and to improving our lives through its understanding, is to see how the medial whole appears to individual subjectivity. We can schematise the whole as Gadamer has done with notions such as "play," but it is essential to connect this with our actual experiences and actual beliefs about reality by giving account of the individual's view from within Being. Importantly—and intriguingly, given Gadamer's apparently descriptive goals—this yields both a notion of the kind of experience from which subjectivity hopes to be liberated, and that ideal experience toward which it should strive; Gadamer's fundamental ontology gives rise to a soteriology of absorption and assimilation.

In the old type of realist attitude the subject and the object enter into an economy of power relations that governs the dynamics of subjectivity. With particular reference to the determination of self-consciousness through the dialectic of the "master" and the "slave" in Hegel's work, Gadamer shows how the slave experiences its own radical freedom in relation to the resistance and challenge of the master's command or task.[137] The slave willingly "disappears," in Foucault's sense, into the medial reality of dialectic. Here again we observe the glimmer of a Gadamerian soteriology:

> The history of freedom has by no means come to an end here, but in the history of the consciousness of freedom the decisive step has been taken. That is demonstrated by what follows: as the "total dissolution" of self-consciousness, this being-for-self has become "a new form of self-consciousness, a consciousness which thinks, i.e., a consciousness which is free self-consciousness." What we have here is something truly universal in which you and I are the same.[138]

From what we have called the "pantheistic" perspective of the last line, subjectivity itself is just a theme within the matrices of being, a theme that Gadamer says is "only a flickering in the closed circuits of historical life."[139] Gadamer wants to assimilate individual subjectivity into the "genuine universality of spirit" such that "[i]t finds itself there and to its satisfaction, it knows its singleness was wrong."[140] Far from the "ubiquitous coercion of things" in traditional realism, "the experience consciousness has is that all handiwork is a matter of the spirit."[141] Explaining himself with recourse to the usual model, Gadamer elaborates on the subject's experience of the other thus:

> Whatever is brought into play or comes into play depends on itself but is dominated by the relation that we call the game. For the individual who, as playing subjectivity, engages in the game, this fact may seem at first to be an accommodation. He conforms to the game or subjects himself to it, that is, he relinquishes the autonomy of his own will. For example, two men who use a saw together allow the free play of the saw to take place.[142]

Will, in Gadamer's way of thinking, is contrary to freedom as it too concretely fixes to a particular prejudice or structural context within being, and does not allow the "free play" of the theme to maintain its priority. The exaggerated authority of the will is a perversion of the activity of "listening" to the things themselves, and the equivalent of sophism rather than Platonic dialogue. In this telling passage, Gadamer continues:

> [M]ovement to-and-fro obviously belongs so essentially to the game that there is an ultimate sense in which you cannot have a game by yourself. In order for there to be a game, there always has to be, not necessarily literally another player, but something else with which the player plays and which automatically responds to his move with a countermove. Thus the cat at play chooses the ball of wool because it responds to play, and ball games will be with us forever because the ball is freely mobile in every direction, appearing to do surprising things of its own accord.[143]

The ball of wool might as well be another person, a road, a movie, an idea, or God. Gadamer seeks to replace the language of resistance with that of "response" and "surprise," indicating the dialogical challenge of the world around us (i.e., the "game," the "goal," the "theme," the "question"), through which the identity and aim of the subject are defined in a forward-moving and fruitful dialectic. Gadamer's remembrance of Being is more dialogical than that of Heidegger or Levinas, or even Martin Buber, whose meditative "I"-oriented attitude to the other he also criticises, and his ideal of the good life is immanent in all actions and interactions.[144] Each play-like, art-like, task-like interaction, according to the Gadamerian ideal entails, at the level of subjective experience, a *realist* attitude, reflecting the nature of the "thing" not as a dominated or dominating "object" but as a *Sache* in which the "will" is engaged, unified with everything and transformed. Thus *techne*, "technology," the craft of human action, is famously for Gadamer, as for Heidegger, the "constellation of truth," which is the "truth of the saving power."[145] It is in learning to submit to the theme, the task or game, the free-play of the real "object" that we are ourselves constituted, which is also to say transformed and "saved." The eudaimonian destiny of humanity is for our particular subjectivity to understand and embrace its part in the medial unity of Being. Thus, as we will see, we must be passive and passionate at once, in order to play our proper part and "be played" (*Gespieltwerden*) by Being.

In this chapter we have seen that Gadamer continues the classic metaphysical project of establishing certainties, and deriving from it an ontology of what is universally, necessarily true. It turns out that this ontology has curious and extraordinary characteristics; it is monistic in its ontological kind and plural in its phenomenal manifestations, it is its own immanent foundation. In the sphere of ethics it has the capacity to furnish us with new identities, and to validate the ultimacy of our values. But Gadamerian realism does not end here. Just as Rūpa Gosvāmi is the sort of thinker who must provide a practical as well as a theoretical philosophy, so Gadamer awards himself an applied as well as a theoretical responsibility. An important facet of the realist debate to which he is responding is the critique of traditional realist theory's objectivising effects, so he must make account of how these truths can take up a place in our actual lived realities, not merely in our "metaphysical" schematisation of them. In the next chapter we will see how he seeks to incorporate his ontological realism into the pressing everyday reality of our lives.

NOTES

1. *Gadamer on Celan: "Who Am I and Who Are You?" and Other Essays*, 125–26.

2. Hans-Georg Gadamer, "Amicus Plato Magis Amica Veritas," in *Dialogue and Dialectic*, trans. P. Christopher Smith (New Haven, Conn.: Yale University Press, 1980), 208.

3. We will see in a later chapter how it is that the Sanskrit word for "spirit" or "soul" also can mean breath.

4. From a more comparative perspective, part II will show us how this inner spirit of language, so Hegelian in its influence, philosophically parallels the Hindu cosmogony of multiplicity from a primeval unity (chapter 4), and more specifically the dialectic of Krishna's manifestation in phenomenal reality in Rūpa Gosvāmi's Caitanya Vaiṣṇava ontology (chapter 5).

5. Wachterhauser's fullest statement of what he considers to be Gadamer's ontological position is to be found in *Beyond Being: Gadamer's Post-Platonic Hermeneutical Ontology* (Evanston, Ill.: Northwestern University Press, 1999), 58. More general accounts are given in Weinsheimer's commentary *Gadamer's Hermeneutics: A Reading of Truth and Method* (New Haven, Conn.: Yale University Press, 1985), James Risser's *Hermeneutics and the Voice of the Other: Re-reading Gadamer's Philosophical Hermeneutics* (Albany: State University of New York Press, 1997), Lawrence Schmidt's *The Epistemology of Hans-Georg Gadamer: An Analysis of the Legitimization of Vorurteile* (Frankfurt am Main: P. Lang, 1987), and Georgia Warnke's *Gadamer: Hermeneutics, Tradition and Reason* (Cambridge: Polity Press, 1987), and other studies relating to specific non-ontological themes.

6. Emmanuel Levinas in "Being and Meaning: Friday, November 14 1975," in *God, Death and Time*, 126.

7. See the text of Gadamer's 1992 conversation with Alfons Grieder, in *Gadamer in Conversation*, 111. The verb in question is the verb "to be," or, in Levinas's words, "to manifest."

8. The word "experience," like almost all of the terms that can be used to describe the post-Heideggerian ontology, is suspect in that it implies a subject to whom the experiences belong. This, however, is not intended in the Heideggerian context where it encompasses everything that we are or could be aware of (granted that we cannot know of anything other than through some kind of experience), including the experience of an apparent subject's self-awareness. Thus used, it does not necessarily imply an actual subject and object, although the experience itself may have the structure of a subject-object relationality, such as is variously formulated in theories of the "intentional structure" of experience.

9. In *The Beginning of Philosophy* Gadamer makes it clear that he believes Plato and Aristotle to be "the sole philosophical access to an interpretation of the Presocratics" (10). This continuity is further elaborated in Gadamer's essays on the Good in Plato and Aristotle and he is further at pains to show the connection between the pre-Socratics and the burgeoning ontological revolution in Hegel (for whom the pre-Socratics provided the architectural support, see 11 of *The Beginning of Philosophy*), in Schleiermacher and later in Heidegger.

10. "Heidegger and Marburg Theology," in *Philosophical Hermeneutics*, 209.

11. "Aesthetics and Hermeneutics," in *Philosophical Hermeneutics*, 98.

12. Jean Grondin, *Introduction to Philosophical Hermeneutics*, trans. Joel Weinsheimer (New Haven, Conn.: Yale University Press, 1994), 107. Robert Dostal writes of how Gadamer's philosophy is indeed a transcendental phenomenology on the model of Heidegger's *Being and Time*, while avoiding the key characteristics of the Husserlian transcendental project. This is correct, and when I speak of Gadamer following through the spirit of Husserlian phenomenology I refer rather to Husserl's

transcendental rigour such that it gave rise to Heidegger's refinement of the reduction or epoche of reference to an experience-independent reality. See "Gadamer's Relation to Heidegger and Phenomenology," in *The Cambridge Companion to Gadamer* (New York: Cambridge University Press, 2002), 252, for Dostal's account.

13. Brice Wachterhauser, "Getting It Right: Relativism, Realism and Truth," in *The Cambridge Companion to Gadamer*, Robert Dostal, ed. (New York: Cambridge University Press, 2002), 75–76.

14. Wachterhauser, "Getting It Right: Relativism, Realism and Truth," in *The Cambridge Companion to Gadamer*, 76.

15. "The Heritage of Hegel," in *Reason in the Age of Science*, 41.

16. "On the Philosophical Element in the Sciences and the Scientific Character of Philosophy," in *Reason in the Age of Science*, 3.

17. Hans-Georg Gadamer, "Kant and the Doctrine of God," in *Hermeneutics, Religion, and Ethics*, trans. Joel Weinsheimer (New Haven, Conn.: Yale University Press, 1999), 14–15.

18. *Truth and Method*, 244.

19. *Truth and Method*, 245.

20. *Truth and Method*, 256–57.

21. Georgia Warnke, *Gadamer: Hermeneutics, Tradition and Reason*, 141.

22. J. M. Baker Jr., "Lyric as Paradigm: Hegel and the Speculative Instance of Poetry in Gadamer's Hermeneutics," in *The Cambridge Companion to Gadamer*, Robert Dostal, ed. (New York: Cambridge University Press, 2002), 147.

23. Wachterhauser, *Beyond Being: Gadamer's Post-Platonic Hermeneutic Ontology*, 170.

24. *Truth and Method*, 245.

25. Hans-Georg Gadamer, "Between Phenomenology and Dialectic," *Gesammelte Werke* (Tübingen: J. C. B. Mohr, 1991), 13–14. Gadamer has frequently restated his belief in the importance of Greek thought for the modern mind, in careful studies such as *The Beginning of Philosophy* (and *Dialogue and Dialectic: Eight Hermeneutical Studies on Plato*) and his comments in interview with Glenn Most (see *Gadamer in Conversation: Reflections and Commentary*).

26. "Idea and Reality in Plato's *Timaeus*," in *Dialogue and Dialectic: Eight Hermeneutical Studies on Plato*.

27. "Idea and Reality in Plato's *Timaeus*," in *Dialogue and Dialectic: Eight Hermeneutical Studies on Plato*, 157.

28. Of course, the notion that substances do not exist, but only properties, is not unfamiliar in analytic philosophy. We will also find that Rūpa Gosvāmi's synthesis of Sāṃkhya and Vedānta philosophies yields a metaphysics in which apparent substances such as physical matter are themselves only forms of the one true ultimate substance that is the divine (*brahman* or Krishna). In chapter 5 we will see how some of the source texts of Rūpa Gosvāmi's tradition, such as the *Brahmavaivarta Purāṇa*, play with the possibility that the proliferation of forms have a more foundational existence than the apparent ubiqity of substance.

29. See Habermas and Gadamer's critique, defence, and countercritique in *Hermeneutics and Modern Philosophy*, Brice Wachterhauser, ed. (Albany: State Uni-

versity of New York Press, 1986).

30. Gadamer and Derrida had their first real academic encounter in 1989 at the Goethe Institute in Paris, but this encounter was generally seen (certainly by Gadamer) to be a failure—an encounter but not an exchange, largely as a result of Derrida's apparent feeling that his own position could not enter into dialogue with Gadamer's own. The encounter furnished the inspiration for a number of later exchanges between the adherents of hermeneutics and deconstruction however, most notably the volume *Dialogue and Deconstruction: The Gadamer-Derrida Encounter*, Richard Michelfelder and Diane Palmer, eds. (Albany: State University of New York Press, 1989).

31. John Caputo in "Gadamer's Closet Essentialism: A Derridean Critique," in *Dialogue and Deconstruction: The Gadamer-Derrida Encounter*, 259.

32. See the comments in the last chapter of the present text, and Wachterhauser's *Beyond Being: Gadamer's Post-Platonic Hermeneutic Ontology*.

33. The literary and Parmenidean Plato has since received attention from a range of scholars seeking to balance the scales. These include Derrida's analyses of Plato, and those of Catherine Pickstock, Robert Wood, and Kenneth Dorter. As Wood observes, "Platonic philosophy is not concerned with some 'heaven of forms' separated from human experience—though there does indeed remain the problem of the relation between *eidos* and instance debated intensely throughout the history of philosophy." "Self-Reflexivity in Plato´s *Theaetetus*: Toward a Phenomenology of the Life-World," in *The Review of Metaphysics* 52 (1998), 832.

34. These are still in evidence in Joel Weinsheimer's *Gadamer's Hermeneutics*, where he writes that from Plato to Hegel truth consists in the complete revelation of the thing, its full presence to an infinite mind. It is no wonder then that for Weinsheimer "the differences [between them] quickly become clear" (250). This is one of the axes of cultural and philosophical difference that so forcefully differentiates Gadamer's concept of the One and the Two from Rūpa Gosvāmi's formulation of universal (i.e., encompassing and individually characterising all things) unity. Rūpa Gosvāmi never had to defend the idea that consciousness is universally and necessarily present, as it is a tenet discussed and recommended by some of India's earliest and most authoritative philosophical texts.

35. See "Dialectic and Sophism in Plato's *Seventh Letter*," in *Dialectic and Dialectic: Eight Hermeneutical Studies on Plato*.

36. I.e., Mozart's *The Magic Flute* exists in no person's imagination, in no performance, nor on any piece of paper or tape eternally—unless it does indeed exist either in a realm of eternal and unchanging Platonic forms, or in the mind of God, which some have hoped to be the case. Yet *what* it is, its defining essence, seems to transcend its temporary and divergent instances of existence.

37. *Truth and Method*, 103.

38. "Man and Language," in *Philosophical Hermeneutics*, 66.

39. See Jean Grondin in *Introduction to Philosophical Hermeneutics*, 120–21.

40. Gadamer's universality of play is universal at all loci in Being and across all micro- and macro-cosmic levels in precisely the same way that the Platonic One and the Many, Hegelian dialectic, and the Caitanya Vaiṣṇava doctrine of "inconceivable

difference and non-difference" are universal—since as we will see, they are features of the same logical-phenomenological insight.

41. Furthermore, as Wachterhauser points out, by attempting to proceed within the confines of everyday language, Gadamer's statements are at all times subject to two different interpretations; it is this which has made it so easy to ignore the degree to which his position is not a dualistic one (see Wachterhauser's "Getting It Right: Relativism, Realism and Truth," in *The Cambridge Companion to Gadamer*.

42. Gadamer's hermeneutic dialogue is meant to correct the "passive, contemplative and descriptive character of the 'scientific' method," but clearly it retains these characteristics in admixture with a respect for the transitive and finite—that which Hegel seems to lack in Kojeve's *Introduction to the Reading of Hegel: Lectures on the Phenomenology of Spirit*, James Nichols, trans. (Ithaca, N.Y.: Cornell University Press, 1980).

43. See "Heidegger's Later Philosophy," in *Philosophical Hermeneutics*, 224. Wachterhauser argues that Gadamer's work grows from the earlier Heideggerian thought of works such as *Being and Time* when Heidegger appeared comparatively optimistic about the phenomenological methods, and language that he attempted to use before giving them after his *kehre* or "turn." Yet Gadamer makes it clear that while he shares an enthusiasm for the possibilities afforded by normative language and philosophy with the earlier Heidegger, it is the ideas of the later Heidegger that are more sophisticated and come closer to his own conclusions.

44. John Caputo, *The Prayers and Tears of Jacques Derrida* (Bloomington: Indiana University Press, 1997), xxx.

45. The binary concepts of the One and the Many, and the One and the Two should not be confused; they are two different ideas, the former representing what Gadamer (and Plato) see as a universal truth, the latter being a more basic, fundamental level of analysis to which that truth can be reduced.

46. *Dialogue and Dialectic*, 92. In "Plato's Unwritten Dialectic" in the same volume he further expounds the centrality of number to Plato's philosophy, as he does in other works in his *Gessamelte Werke* cited below.

47. "Dialectic and Sophism in Plato's *Seventh Letter*," in *Dialogue and Dialectic*, 118–19.

48. Gadamer writes: "What *is* revealed [by Plato] is that the number of the unity of many is the ontological paradigm. These dihairetical classifications point to a whole of explications, as it were, a whole which is incapable of ever being completed" ("Amicus Plato Magis Amica Veritas," in *Dialogue and Dialectic: Eight Hermeneutical Studies on Plato*, 203).

49. "Amicus Plato Magis Amica Veritas," in *Dialogue and Dialectic*, 207.

50. See Badiou's arguments in his essay "Platonic Gesture," in *Manifesto for Philosophy*, N. Madarasz, trans. and ed. (Albany: State University of New York Press, 1989).

51. B. Wachterhauser's *Beyond Being: Gadamer's Post-Platonic Hermeneutical Ontology*, 67.

52. Gavin Flood, *An Introduction to Hinduism* (New York: Routledge, 1996). For comparison with Plato's formulations of the same *philosophical* problem, see the

final line of the Parmenides: "[W]hether one is or is not, one and the others in relation to themselves and one another, all of them, in every way, are and are not, and appear to be and appear not to be."

53. As the Buddhists observe, reality can be characterised as an infinitely variable succession of unique instants that have no duration and no substantial essence, in respect of which common notions of identity have no purchase.

54. "Amicus Plato Magis Amica Veritas," in *Dialogue and Dialectic*, 210.

55. Jacques Derrida, *Dissemination*, B. Johnson, trans. (London: Athlone Press, 1981), 249.

56. *Truth and Method*, 454.

57. We will see in chapters 5 and 6 how Rūpa Gosvāmi expresses this "thematic" essence of "things" from a different perspective, by ontologising the Sanskritic notion of *rasa*.

58. Jean Grondin, *The Philosophy of Gadamer*, Kathryn Plant, trans. (Guildford and King's Lynn: Acumen Publishing Limited, 2003), 77.

59. "Plato's Unwritten Dialectic," in *Dialogue and Dialectic*, 133.

60. "On the Philosophical Element in the Sciences and the Scientific Character of Philosophy," in *Reason in the Age of Science*, 4.

61. "Heidgger's Later Philosophy," in *Philosophical Hermeneutics*, 215.

62. A fascinating aspect of Gadamer's method of ontological analysis is that in proceeding by way of metaphors and historical example and commentary, he saw these illustrations as tools for revealing the inner structures of meaning *and Being*. By forcing us to realise the common thread between two disparate examples, each metaphor performs its own analysis. Speaking of his main metaphor, play, he writes: "Here as always the metaphorical usage [of the word 'play'] has methodological priority. If a word is applied to a sphere to which it did not originally belong, the actual 'original' meaning emerges quite clearly. Language has performed in advance the abstraction that is, as such, the task of conceptual analysis" ("Man and Language," in *Philosophical Hermeneutics*, 66). Language then is not a veil over truth at all, nor merely the fabric; it is a tool of hermeneutic analysis, and poetry is not the other of philosophy, but rather a sieve in which elusive meanings and values are caught. In holding language up to itself as in a mirror, its inner "dialectical" constitution is brought into relief (we will see that Rūpa Gosvāmi also uses poetry as a dialectical tool for engaging with *metaphysical* truths). Thus the difficulties of expressing this form of ontology through language do not frustrate Gadamer as they did Heidegger, since he sees language itself as the slide on which the contents of Being are to be dissected.

63. Jonathan Schaffer in "Is There a Fundamental Level," *Nous* 37 (September 2003), 500.

64. See Plato's statement of his doctrine of the transcendentals in the *Republic*, developed further through Plato's own countercritique in the *Parmenides*.

65. Wachterhauser, *Beyond Being: Gadamer's Post-Platonic Hermeneutical Ontology*, 86.

66. Wachterhauser, *Beyond Being: Gadamer's Post-Platonic Hermeneutical Ontology*, 85.

67. Gadamer, "Dialektik ist nicht Sophistik: Theatet lernt das im Sophistes," in *Gessamelte Werke*, 363.

68. Gadamer's commitment to showing the full ontological implications of Plato's analysis, and its special transcendental mode of truth, is a fine example for any attempt to make sense of a thinker whose ideas may not immediately appear to have rigorously reasoned ontological implications, or whose ideas may not fit with our normal ideas of a metaphysical scheme. Certainly, it is a lesson for understanding Rūpa Gosvāmi's ontological insights that similarly seek to discover basic (foundational) and universal (transcendental) features of Being, and develop them into rich themes with aesthetic and ethical connotations.

69. Aristotle (in his *Metaphysics*) and other subsequent philosophers, referring to Plato's "unwritten doctrines," characterise Plato's thought in terms of the two fundamental principles the one and the indeterminate two. Hints toward this doctrine may be seen in chain of reasoning that fills the later sections of the *Parmenides*, culminating in the final assertion of the dialogue: "Let thus much be said; and further let us affirm what seems to be the truth, that, whether one is or is not, one and the others in relation to themselves and one another, all of them, in every way, are and are not, and appear to be and appear not to be." It is important to note that the "two" in question here is not just shorthand for the notion of plurality; it signifies the principle of differentiation, of relative difference within a bond of relationality (for which "great" and "small" are the paradigmatic example), which underlies any plurality.

70. "Plato's Unwritten Dialectic," in *Dialogue and Dialectic: Eight Hermeneutical Studies on Plato*, 152.

71. "Dialectic and Sophism in Plato's *Seventh Letter*," in *Dialogue and Dialectic*, 120. The "One and the Many" and the "One and the Two" are broadly interchangeable phrase both used by both Gadamer and Plato.

72. "Plato's Unwritten Dialectic," in *Dialogue and Dialectic: Eight Hermeneutical Studies on Plato*, 152.

73. They are foundational not in the sense of providing a first, for creation can no longer be understood as the act of a transcendent creator, but in terms of a material cause, in which we simply find the materials for Being. This is the kind of "giving account" of creation that is given in chapter 4 of the Sāṃkhya concept of the *guṇas*.

74. "The Phenomenological Movement," in *Philosophical Hermeneutics*, 166.

75. *Truth and Method*, 61.

76. "The Phenomenological Movement," in *Philosophical Hermeneutics*, 167.

77. In answer to the very pointed question which Hyppolite posed in Royaumont as to whether in Husserl there is a basic level that is egoless, van Breda correctly answered "for Husserl this solution is unthinkable." "The Phenomenological Movement," in *Philosophical Hermeneutics*, 168.

78. Gunter Figal, "The Doing of the Thing Itself," in *The Cambridge Companion to Gadamer*, 122.

79. "The Heritage of Hegel," in *Reason in the Age of Science*, 41. Heavily influenced by Husserl, Derrida too supports the notion of a transcendental genesis that

is "resistant in principle to every reduction." Indeed, Bernasconi elsewhere observes that Derrida can envision genesis only on the extra-historical model of the "gift" understood in Levinasian terms as an interruption from outside of Being. See Jacques Derrida, *The Problem of Genesis in Husserl's Philosophy*, Marion Hobson, trans. (Chicago: University of Chicago, 1990), xix, and Robert Bernasconi, "What Goes Around Comes Around: Derrida and Levinas on the Economy of the Gift and the Gift of Geneaology," in *The Logic of the Gift: Toward an Ethic of Generosity*, Alan Schrift, ed. (New York: Routledge, 1997).

80. Jacques Derrida, *The Problem of Genesis in Husserl's Philosophy*, 176.

81. *Truth and Method*, 148–49.

82. "The Universality of the Hermeneutical Problem," in *Philosophical Hermeneutics*, 14.

83. "The Universality of the Hermeneutical Problem," in *Philosophical Hermeneutics*, 14.

84. "The Universality of the Hermeneutical Problem," in *Philosophical Hermeneutics*, 14.

85. *Beyond Being: Gadamer's Post-Platonic Hermeneutical Ontology*, 131.

86. *Hegel's Dialectic: Five Hermeneutical Studies*, 14.

87. *Hegel's Dialectic: Five Hermeneutical Studies*, 14.

88. Wachterhauser, *Beyond Being: Gadamer's Post-Platonic Hermeneutical Ontology*, 135.

89. See *Truth and Method*, 455.

90. See Gunter Figal's essay, "The Doing of the Thing Itself," in *The Cambridge Companion to Gadamer*.

91. "The Universality of the Hermeneutical Problem," in *Philosophical Hermeneutics*, 14.

92. "Dialectic and Sophism in Plato's *Seventh Letter*," in *Dialogue and Dialectic: Eight Hermeneutical Studies on Plato*, 121.

93. Hans-Georg Gadamer, *The Idea of the Good in Platonic-Aristotelian Philosophy*, trans. P. Christopher Smith (New Haven, Conn.: Yale University Press, 1988), 28.

94. "Plato's Unwritten Dialectic," in *Dialogue and Dialectic: Eight Hermeneutical Studies on Plato*, 155.

95. "The Scope and Function of Hermeneutical Reflection," in *Philosophical Hermeneutics*, 19–21.

96. *Truth and Method*, 366.

97. To this point the word "passion" has been used primarily in its everyday sense, but this will be increasingly stretched to designate a whole attitude, present in Gadamer's thought, and prevalent in Rūpa Gosvāmi's. This meaning will be defined by the uses, ethical and metaphysical, to which these two thinkers put it. However, the word "passion" is employed here because, better than any other available word in English, it draws together relevant associations: a strong but potentially ambivalent emotion that can equally be desire, pleasure, and passion; etymologically, the "passivity" of being mentally and physically altered by their forceful desires; sometimes violent suffering undergone for one's faith, often entailing staking one's whole life on it (this will be particularly apt in Rūpa Gosvāmi's depictions of

passion); and intensity of attachment to a specified external object that is like an external agency; barely within the subject's own control.

98. See D. Haberman in *Bhaktirasāmṛtasindhu of Rūpa Gosvāmi*, D. Haberman, trans. and ed. (New Delhi: Motilal Banarsidass, 2003), lvi.

99. "To be sure the Hegelian definition of beauty shares with Heidegger's own effort the fundamental transcendence of the antithesis between subject and object, I and object, and does not describe the being of the work of art in terms of the subjectivity of the subject" (see "Heidegger's Later Philosophy," in *Philosophical Hermeneutics*, 223).

100. "For Kant himself, to be sure, the determining factor was still the mysterious ambiguity that obtained between the beauty of nature and the subjectivity of the subject. In the same way, he understood the creative genius who transcends all rules in creating the miracle of the work of art to be a favourite of nature." "Heidegger's Later Philosophy," in *Philosophical Hermeneutics*, 219.

101. Grondin cites Schultz in *Introduction to Philosophical Hermeneutics*, 118.

102. "Hegel's Dialectic of Self-Consciousness," in *Hegel's Dialectic: Five Hermeneutical Studies*, 56–57.

103. "The Universality of the Hermeneutical Problem," in *Philosophical Hermeneutics*, 17.

104. "Hegel's Dialectic of Self Consciousness," in *Hegel's Dialectic: Five Hermeneutical Studies*, 57.

105. It is *precisely* in order to express this mirroring of inner and outer infinity that Badiou employs mathematical set theory as a system that allows for "infinite, infinitely divided infinities."

106. "Hegel and Heidegger," in *Hegel's Dialectic: Five Hermeneutical Studies*, 111.

107. Gadamer most famously and most fully expounds the ontological universality of language in part III of *Truth and Method*, and considers the special authoritative test case of theology in his sections on Schleiermacher repeating his interpretation of the divine "Word" more succinctly in the 1962 essay "On the Problem of Self-Understanding" (see *Philosophical Hermeneutics*, 57–58).

108. For further details on the philosophical hermeneutic parallels with early Lutheran tenets, see "Hermeneutics as a Theoretical and Practical Task," in *Reason in the Age of Science*.

109. From Joel Weinsheimer's translation in *Truth and Method*.

110. Again, commonalities with the ambivalent dualism and non-dualism of Rūpa Gosvāmi's tradition are striking and will be followed up in chapters 4 and 5.

111. Gadamer's main discussions of theology, excluding his purely historical studies on theological hermeneutics, concern either the nature of the divine message in scripture and preaching (see many works, including *Truth and Method* and "On the Problem of Self-Understanding" in *Philosophical Hermeneutics* for seminal discussions of this), or the relation of the parts of the Trinity in comparison to pre-Socratic influences on Christianity (see *The Beginnings of Knowledge*).

112. "Man and Language," in *Philosophical Hermeneutics*, 63.

113. "Man and Language," in *Philosophical Hermeneutics*, 62.

114. *Truth and Method*, 104–5.

115. "Man and Language," in *Philosophical Hermeneutics*, 65.

116. *The Beginning of Knowledge*, 17. Indeed, while it is not the topic of the present study, there is much to consider in the possible philosophical commonalities between the *acintyabhedābheda* concept that is the foundation of Rūpa Gosvāmi's assertion that individuals both are and are not God and the World, and the Heraclitean maxim that "[t]he wise, being one thing only, would and would not take the name of Zeus [or 'Life']" (see Heraclitean fragment DK22B32, Diels, Hermann and Walther Kranz, *Die Fragmente der Vorsokratiker* (Zurich: Weidmann, 1985)).

117. Hans-Georg Gadamer, *The Beginning of Knowledge*, trans. R. Coltman (New York: Continuum, 2002), 19.

118. See Gadamer's interpretation of Heraclitus in *The Beginning of Knowledge*, 31–32. Interestingly, Richard Gombrich notes the Indian use of "fire" as a metaphor for consciousness as an insatiably intentional force, both in the early Vedas, and in the earliest Buddhist writings (see R. Gombrich, paper given to the Oxford Centre for Hindu Studies "Consciousness" seminars, March 1, 2005). Regardless of Heraclitus's original intentions, there are clear parallels with Gadamer's reference to this trope.

119. "Heidegger's Later Philosophy," in *Philosophical Hermeneutics*, 219.

120. "Heidegger's Later Philosophy," in *Philosophical Hermeneutics*, 219.

121. By and large, Gadamer's assumption is that his reader is Christian and takes the New Testament and the Lutheran paradigm of preaching as paradigmatic. As he himself confesses, his observations pertain in some measure to all scriptural or "eminent" texts, but his theological hermeneutic heritage maintains a strong influence on his hermeneutic approach.

122. *Gesammeltes Werkes* 2, 192.

123. *Truth and Method* (1989), 289.

124. Heidegger's position in its turn was also an explicit movement away from Bultmann's theology of salvation as a power of transcendental self-analysis toward authenticity—this too was a merciful escape for Gadamer. This, says Gadamer, is why Bultmann remained married to the Heideggerian philosophy of *Being and Time*, which still appears as an empowering analytic of human nature. See "Heidegger and Marburg Theology," in *Philosophical Hermeneutics*, 206–7.

125. "Heidegger and Marburg Theology," in *Philosophical Hermeneutics*, 210.

126. Jacques Derrida, *Psychī* (Paris: Editions Gallilee, 1972), 99.

127. Jean Grondin, *The Philosophy of Gadamer*, 18–19.

128. Mark C. Taylor, *Erring: A Postmodern A/theology* (Chicago: University of Chicago Press, 1987), 16.

129. See Gerald Bruns, "The Hermeneutical Anarchist: *Phronesis*, Rhetoric and the Experience of Art," in *Gadamer's Century: Essays in Honour of Hans-Georg Gadamer*, Jeff Malpas, Ulrich Arnswald, and Jens Kertscher, eds. (Cambridge, Mass.: MIT Press, 2002).

130. *Truth and Method* (London: Continuum, 2006), 25.

131. "Hegel's Dialectic of Self-Consciousness," in *Hegel's Dialectic: Five Hermeneutical Studies*, 55–56.

132. See Alastair Macintyre's definition under "pantheism," in *Encyclopedia of Philosophy*, Paul Edwards, ed. (New York: Macmillan, 1967), Vol. 6, 31–35.

133. See H. P. Owen, *Concepts of Deity* (London: Macmillan, 1971), 65.

134. "The Philosophical Foundations of the Twentieth Century," in *Philosophical Hermeneutics*, 128.

135. "The Philosophical Foundations of the Twentieth Century," in *Philosophical Hermeneutics*, 128.

136. David Haberman, *Bhaktirasamṛtasindu of Rūpa Gosvāmi*, lvi.

137. See "Hegel's Dialectic of Self-consciousness," in *Hegel's Dialectic: Five Hermeneutical Studies*, 70–74.

138. "Hegel's Dialectic of Self-Consciousness," in *Hegel's Dialectic: Five Hermeneutical Studies*, 72. This is a strong optimism regarding the ability of the individual to rise above the will, not rejecting it, but channeling it into a level that transcends subjectivity. This is precisely what Habermas, Gadamer's longstanding critic, is sceptical of, claiming that "Surrender and Letting be remained as chained to the desire for control as the rebellion of counterpower does to the oppression of power. Those who would like to leave all paradigms behind along with the paradigm of the philosophy of consciousness, and go forth into the clearing of postmodernity, will just not be able to free themselves from the concepts of subject-centred reason and its impressively illustrated topography" (Jurgen Habermas, "An Alternative Way Out of the Philosophy of the Subject: Communicative versus Subject-Centred Reason," in *The Philosophical Discourse of Modernity*, Frederick Lawrence, trans. (London: MIT Press, 1980), 309). Habermas's pessimism brings Gadamer's optimism into relief.

139. *Truth and Method*, 245. Gadamer's own account of the subject will come under examination in chapter 3.

140. "Hegel's Dialectic of Self-Consciousness," in *Hegel's Dialectic: Five Hermeneutical Studies*, 72.

141. "Hegel's Dialectic of Self-Consciousness," in *Hegel's Dialectic: Five Hermeneutical Studies*, 73–74.

142. "On the Problem of Self-Understanding," in *Philosophical Hermeneutics*, 53–54.

143. *Truth and Method*, 106.

144. See Gadamer's comments on Buber in his 1961 letter to Leo Strauss published in *The Independent Journal of Philosophy* 2 (1978), 8.

145. Martin Heidegger, "The Question Concerning Technology," in *Basic Writings* (Oxford: Routledge, 1978), 338.

Chapter 3

Gadamer's Ethics of Play

If philosophical hermeneutics tells us anything about discourse, it is that every statement or position has a teleological structure, illuminated by the light of a particular question and a particular ethics of human flourishing. It sets the paradigms for the answer, even as it asks the question. In this chapter we will explore Gadamer's much neglected discourses on reality, such as it is understood not as the topic of ontological inquiry, but as the actuality in which we dwell and in the context of which ontological truths must be translated into ethical ones. For a thinker much affected by Kierkegaard, Nietzsche, Dilthey, Scheler, Heidegger, and others who had struggled to revivify our engagement with the world, it is essential to complement the systematising discourse of metaphysics with an exploration of the "reality" of our experiences in all their elusiveness to discourse, and in the omnipresent ethical urgency of everyday actions. By exploring other dimensions of Gadamer's "realism," we can more fully reconstruct the "ethics" that accompanies his post-sceptical "metaphysics." The resulting picture of human flourishing both complements and contrasts with the ethical ideal that Rūpa Gosvāmi derives from a similar ontological outlook.

INDETERMINACY AND VITALITY IN THE PRACTICE OF PHILOSOPHY

Commensurate with the "realism" of philosophical hermeneutics as an approach that always looks to the "actual" or "real" concerns of the author and audience, Gadamer's ethical position also informs the way in which he elaborates his "realist" philosophy in terms of the actuality of the thinking, writing philosopher. The Platonic studies with which he began his career were not only a philological exercise, but also a biographical project. Plato's works offer the doubly fascinating insight of a portrait of one life (the reported life of Socrates as canvas for the search for *arete*) refracted through the dialogically rich works of another (Plato). In the drama of the dialogues, which form an episodic biography, we see the interweaving of system with the more complex dynamics of a portrait of real life.[1] In this "actuality," which the dialogues seek to portray, philosophy is pursued through reflection and conversation, while the whole is subjected to the pervasive debate over the ultimate good. In his discussion of Plato's *Lysis* it is to the deed, the *ergon*—the work or act of experience—that the concept—*Idee* or *logos*—must have reference if it is to have meaning. It is only in relation to this actuality that our metaphysical "realist" discourse can be complete and accurate. Thus, as in Rūpa Gosvāmi's integral interweaving of poetry, narrative, and philosophy, Gadamer's talk *about* actuality is not a complementary consideration of an additional theme. It is an integral modification of Gadamer's whole project of talking about the real, necessary to bring the discourse in line with its object and make it more able to render both the hard structures of system and the soft structures of indeterminacy. Thus in his own "autobiography," he writes that hermeneutics is meant to be deployed "not in the sense of a methodology, but as a theory of the real experience that thinking is."[2]

In Gadamer's attentions to the priority of biography and lived life for any project of philosophising, he tries to come closer to what is "truly real, *to ontos on*."[3] He also emphasises this implicit reference to reality throughout Plato's dialogues—from the arguments of the *Meno* to his scene-setting evocations of the pedagogical forum. By way of example, Gadamer writes with reference to Plato's discussion of the concept of friendship:

> One must know what friendship is if one is to grasp once and for all that in it sameness and difference, longing and fulfilment, growing intimacy with others and with oneself, are all one and the same thing. And this the boys [i.e., Socrates' pupils] do not yet know.[4]

Gadamer is trying to indicate the omnipresence of lived truths in Plato—both as a limitation on knowledge and discourse, and also as an infinitely open and vitalising extension of both. On one hand this reminder has a bearing on the practice of interpreting a body of thought, such that we must keep the realities from which it is written and into which it is read in mind when interpreting that corpus. What Gadamer intends, however, is to offer historical demonstrations of dialectic as the continually transforming momentum of reality, both individual and social. He elaborates this content through the hermeneutic interpretation of intellectual history.

Contrary to the character of the systems to which logics of different kinds and cultural origins lead us, reality is difficult to bring into discourse without its being limited by the conclusiveness of our ideas and the closure of our practical, habitual means of expression. It is partly for this reason that both Gadamer and Heidegger hold poetic discourse in such high regard. We have seen that Gadamer is wary of any "Hegelian" overemphasis on the *Logischreelles* (the logical concept as preeminent reality).[5] It is partly in pursuit of balance, and as a counteradvocate of Hegel's "bad infinite," that he turns to the hermeneutics of Dilthey's notion of the *Lebenswelt* (life-world) and its organic structures in *Truth and Method*.[6] For similar reasons, Gadamer writes that "[i]n contrast to Hegel, Schleiermacher had a particular feeling for the individuality of phenomena," which he considers, in line with the Romantics, to be *ineffabile*.[7] On Gadamer's reading the two approaches coalesce in the Hegel who prefigures Gadamer's own concerns in observing that "[i]n the modern period . . . [man] directly forces the inner essence into the open without the mediatory experience of the natural consciousness. Thus the generation of the universal here is cut off from the manifold of existence."[8] The Hegel who makes this complaint is Gadamer's Kierkegaardian Hegel, a conciliatory figure who played a formative role in the intellectual development of the young Gadamer. Hence Gadamer's autobiographical reminiscence that

> [a]lready, however, one of my earliest experiences in thought—by way of a detour through Kierkegaard, together with a paradoxical enthusiasm for the assessor, William in Either/Or—had led me to Hegel, without my completely having realised it.[9]

Here a somewhat different axis of philosophical influence leads him to unexpected insights that stand—if not in opposition, then in counterpoint to the search for structure and certainty that we observe in his ontology.

Jean Grondin recounts how a particular aporia that had been puzzling him was finally resolved in the course of a conversation with Gadamer in a Heidelberg pub. In requesting clarification about the precise nature of the universality of the hermeneutic insight, he might have expected the sort of answer that we have anticipated in chapter 2, and that Gadamer gives in the foreword to the very book that the conversation is cited in: Gadamer writes that hermeneutics draws its universality from "the universality of logic, the logos, and language."[10] By contrast, the answer Grondin actually received from Gadamer pointed to what is ineffable, elusive, and "inner," and drew on a (Augustinian) theological precedent. The universality of hermeneutics, he contends, lies

> [i]n the verbum interius. . . . This universality consists in inner speech, in that one cannot say everything. One cannot express everything that one has in

> mind, the *logos endiathetos*. That is something I learned from Augustine's *De Trinitate*. This experience is universal: the *actus signatus* is never fully covered by the *actus exercitus*.[11]

The inner word suggests precisely those aspects of experience that cannot be said, ambivalent, unformulated feelings, thoughts, and impressions that resist the crude warp and weft of conceptual analysis.

Grondin, like Wachterhauser, gives an exegesis of Gadamer that seeks to fill in the gaps that are left by the common, crude stereotype of hermeneutics as a sort of hopeful relativism, useful for the applied sciences of interpretations and translation. Where Wachterhauser attempts to show the extent to which determinate truths feature as a positive value in Gadamer's thought, Grondin seeks further to fill out our understanding of the Gadamerian metaphysic by restoring its positive affirmation of indeterminacy in everyday life. From this basis we can see how Gadamer's philosophy is meant to restore not only confidence in our access to truth, but also aims to restore "the passion of the real."

A study of Gadamer's ontology shows how it is possible within the system of "a personalised, dialogical Hegel" to maintain "the daily, thoughtful intercourse with the Platonic dialogues,"[12] and also make space for Kierkegaard's concept of existence, characterised by Gadamer as "the emergence of what is really up to us . . . not a fuzzy, emotional event, but an illumination."[13] The connection between Kierkegaard's ideas and the importance of *phronesis* as an ethical decisionmaking process was brought to Gadamer's attention by Heidegger. Both indicated other rationalities through which to think out the problems of philosophy. Along with Freud's "unconscious," Marx's analysis of production, and Dilthey's historicism, Gadamer recognised Kierkegaard's notion of existence as one of the "interpretive standpoints that our century has developed as ways of going behind what is meant in subjective consciousness."[14] Kierkegaard himself writes that "[e]xistence is the spacing that holds apart; the systematic is the conclusiveness that combines."[15] In the analysis of the One and the Many Gadamer shows the sense in which this definition of existence fits the terms of his *ontological* realism. But it is also crucial at the phenomenological level of what we experience—the reality that we all first and foremost have and in which realist truths manifest as ethical decisions. The microcosmic structure of the One and Many sketches out the indeterminate momentum of immediate everyday experience: just as Parmenides reveals to Socrates that the One is in fact a Many, so "the words we find capture our intending, as it were, and dovetail into relations that point out beyond the momentariness of our act of intending."[16] In his Platonic exegeses Gadamer sought "the inner tension and energy of Plato's philosophising," that part of lived reality that *cannot* enter into the concept.[17]

This affirmation of indeterminacy at the phenomenal, personal level is complemented by Gadamer's celebration of those who celebrate the motion, energy, and telos of life—all kinds of life. According to Gadamer, life philosophy—which encompassed the legacy of Nietzsche, Bergson, and Marcuse, as well as Schleiermacher and Dilthey's historicism—derived its view of reality from a Schellingian vision of life "as the potency of the organism."[18] From diverse vantage points these writers saw that the life of the individual, its very persistence through time, is its power of change. For Gadamer, this Schellingian potency also manifests in Celan's image of the organism as an indistinct but vivifying interiority (of breath), which we can only observe in the forms of its manifestation (i.e., crystallised in form and language).[19]

Again and again, we encounter thinkers, images, and ideas associated with aspects of "vitalist" philosophy. Vitalism is generally seen to originate in Aristotle's account of the growing, transforming self, for which he was perhaps the first thinker to appropriate the paradigm of biology. He introduced key ideas that have continued to resonate in the systems of various thinkers throughout the long history of the Western tradition, including philosophers such as Bergson, who was a direct influence on Gadamer. These tenets include the idea that beings are truly to be identified with vital forces or energy that account for their activity, rather than the static forms and mechanisms into and out of which they change; that the immanent teleology of beings lies in their fulfilment of natural processes; the striving of the "forms" of the world to actualise themselves; humanity's contextualisation in terms of the world at large; an optimism about transformation and development; a preservation of a sense of mystery about the "interior" force from which life, in all its change and diversity, springs. Gadamer seems to recommend such an ethos when he approvingly cites Bergson's

> passionate appeal to the "inner energy of an intelligence which at each moment wins itself back to itself, eliminating ideas already formed to give place to those in the process of being formed" . . . the constant task of "renewed adaptation to new situations."[20]

In short, this vitalist ethos, which came to a practical, ethical expression in Bergson's philosophy of *le bon sens*, imagines and advocates life as a constant "fusion of horizons." Elsewhere, Gadamer shows how such "vitalist" ideas took on a historical and political dimension in the anti-technological movement of his time:

> Schleiermacher's appeal to living feeling against the cold rationalism of the Enlightenment, Schiller's call for aesthetic freedom against mechanistic society, Hegel's contrast between life (later, spirit) and "positivity," were the forerun-

> ners of the protest against modern industrial society, which at the beginning of our century caused the words Erlebnis and Erleben to become almost sacred clarion calls . . . the influence of Friedrich Nietzsche and Henri Bergson played its part, but also a spiritual movement like that around Stefan George. . . . The life philosophy of our own day follows on its own romantic predecessors.[21]

He goes on to stress features of Bergson's philosophy that fit with "pantheistic" elements of his own thought. Here, he writes, the concept of "life" comes to express the "undivided concretion" and "absolute continuity of the psychic" as the mode of being of living things in which "every element is representative of the whole." Gadamer notes approvingly that Bergson "compares the inner interpenetration of all elements in consciousness to the way all the notes intermingle when we listen to a melody . . . then, defends the anti-Cartesian element of the concept of life against objectivising science." All this he characterises by an "'organic' relationship of part and whole."[22] The fascination with Bergson's, as with Aristotle's, vitalism is clear, and is emphasised repeatedly throughout his writings by the linking of these ideas to themes of nature, health, life, thriving, change, and the organic world in the work of other writers.

Yet, while this is a motif that merges well with Gadamer's concerns to stress the metaphysics of movement, the ethics of self-transforming encounter, and the anti-systematising struggles of modern thought, the further "vitalistic" theme of fruitful interior energy is less pronounced, buried in more marginal works such as the monograph on Celan, and newly excavated by Gadamer's biographer Jean Grondin. Grondin's presentation of Gadamer puts the "*verbum interius* . . . the conversation with oneself that every person is . . . an inner deliberation" at the heart of the hermeneutic insight in all its universality.[23] Thus he thematises the "interiority" of the changeful self as an inner word, or borrowing Celan's organic image, that "pausing for breath" that Benjamin designates "the mode most proper to the process of contemplation."[24]

The self that we cannot capture in determinate discourse, system, and theory—the self that should be treated as "alive" and in transformation rather than transfixed under sedation and under the lens—is not meant to be merely a topic for discussion. The portrait of "life" that Gadamer painted in the exegetical practice of philosophical hermeneutics is intended to go beyond the late Heidegger's "almost tragic grappling with the language of metaphysics."[25] The hermeneutic method is intended to be ontology at work—the reality of which our discourse speaks is never as real as the reality which our discourse instantiates. Our powers of analysis could only catch up with this present, which always outstrips the contents of our thought, by including the fact of our thinking, and its reference to the infinite and ever-unfolding world.[26] Thus, as Plato already recognised, in trying to do justice to reality, the philosopher is himself the field of demonstration.

But Gadamer provides the insight that we can speak *as* the real, pro-actively instantiating it at the raw forefront of its coming-to-be. In this way he replaces self-reflexivity, which he characterises as "subjectism" (objectivised subjectivity), with engaged activity. His hermeneutic exercises show the "thought-forming labor of life" as Plato's "universal-forming motion of soul."[27] Gadamer thus seeks to maintain avenues for speaking of soul without capitulating to what Ricoeur warily calls the "philosophies of the cogito." This effort is also the effort to do justice to reality.[28]

Gadamer's early academic training came at a time and place in which the nature and goals of philosophy were being actively questioned by the proliferation of new approaches. The wide purview of *Truth and Method* is a testament not only to Gadamer's thoroughness, but also to the richness of the culture that he assimilated, and its readiness to engage with questions that unify the different disciplines. While the growing hegemony of science advanced a model of truth whose manifest efficacy would win the minds of the masses, other disciplines also developed important models of truth whose tenacious influence would shape the hopes of those for whom scientific methodology left much to be desired. The poetic and mythological sensibility of Gadamer's generation widened the ambit of philosophical reflection. He notes how, in the rise of anthropology, as of classical philology, the influence of writers such as Vico, Herder, Goethe, Novalis, Holderlin, and Dante promoted "myth's reawakening claim to religious validity" in contrast to the truth-claims of scripture.[29] Gadamer's autobiographical comments later in his career reflect the sense of a "new" way of doing philosophy that he harvested from this fertile modern fracturing of the tradition. For Gadamer, as in the Kantian notion of genius, the practice of philosophising was not meant to be an imposition on nature, but an outgrowth of it.[30] By engaging in philosophical reflection one is first and foremost instantiating the dialectical reality under examination (just as Rūpa Gosvāmi's ideal devotee, in worshipping Krishna, better instantiates the relational reality that Krishna is), and in this respect all such description itself was to be newly understood not as mimesis but as *physis*. Toward the end of his life Gadamer advised that

> one ought to work descriptively, creatively—intuitively and in a concretising manner. Instead of simply applying concepts to all sorts of things, concepts ought to come forward in movements of thought springing from the spirit of language and the power of intuition.[31]

Note that this account of descriptive work is itself prescriptive. Gadamer's portrait of the philosopher is not a mere description—it describes the ideal philosopher and the ideal work of the philosopher as one that best reflects the structures of reality that he has already discovered.

This combination of description and prescription is a reminder of what it is to talk of a realist ethics, and a reminder that Gadamer's realism, while it is a search for universal truths, never claims to be a neutral, purely descriptive enquiry. Gadamer cites one of the lights of German philosophy:

> Difficult though it might be to detect it, a certain polemical thread runs through any philosophical writing. He who philosophises is not at one with the previous and contemporary world's ways of thinking of things. Thus Plato's discussions are often not only directed to something but also directed against it.[32]

Goethe's comments on Plato, here quoted in a paper that Gadamer presented to the Humanistic Gymnasium at Marburg, apply equally to the speaker himself. Zizek complains of Heidegger that his ontological solution to the ontic problems of contemporary thought failed to escape the pull of the discourse of objective theorising that it sought to transcend. The mode of his rebellion suffered what Zizek calls "in Hegelese: [a] 'speculative identity'" with its dialectical opposite (which in Zizek's opinion accounts for Heidegger's misplaced faith in a particular finite perspective: National Socialist ideology).[33] The hermeneutic concern is that the particular content of the prescription will maintain a dialectical identity with its preconditioning polemic, regardless of the attempt to provide an ethics that is as universal as the fundamental ontology. Gadamer learned a great deal from the mistake of Heidegger's particularism, and the gist of his ethics is thus to show us not what to choose, but rather how to choose.[34] In retrospective essays Gadamer claims that his own moral-political quest was to prevent an *over-hasty* democracy, derived from an over-hasty interpretation of the Greeks, from disastrously holding sway and undermining its own goals by pretending to an impossible objectivism. He sought to return to democracy a "concretely real content" and a "new solidarity within our society."[35] His concerns relate as well to questions of religious choice as to questions of political choice; it is not an objective weighing of neutral facts or factors that determines our orientations and acts; religious choice is, as we have observed and as most theologians of the Indian devotional traditions would agree—by definition—as much a passion as an action. His portrayal of democracy as a passion of choice reflects the awkward combination of finitude and innate teleological energy that we are. In this he affirms our plural, finite passions.

GADAMER'S HUMANISM

The portrait of choice as nothing but a polemic-induced passion limited to the parameters of the immediate situation, is not denigrated but affirmed in Gadamer's way of thinking.[36] The peregrinary motif in Derrida's writings depicts a fear that admitting this necessary combination of prejudiced passion and its finite object will leave us confused and indifferent, nostalgic for the touchstone of independent absolutes—that it will in fact nullify "the passion of the real":

> Wandering texts, errant signifiers, signs gone astray, uncertain points of departure, indifference towards destinations . . . sometimes we wander amidst the uncertain play of the world, sometimes an uncertain future wanders toward us.[37]

But this fear is itself confused about the relation of universal truths to ethical prescriptions, with Ian Almond noting that "some passages depict 'wandering' as the ineluctable fate of all communication, others extol it not just as a consequence of the instability of the sign but as the only way of confronting positively the unpredictable 'play' of the world."[38] Similar issues are raised if one approaches Gadamer's notion of "play" as an ethical model: If each round of the game is finite, and each game just one of many, why do we play at all? Why do we uselessly expend passion and energy in such arbitrary choices?[39] One answer is that the playing of the game is the way in which, through such "dialogue" we constitute ourselves. But of course this is not merely a prescription but a description of the present state—such playing is already what we are. "Playing better" will merely constitute "better" selves. We become not wanderers, but explorers by embracing the relativistic aspects of our passion for truth.

Thus Gadamer observes that "[t]he language of philosophising was not made for philosophising," but operates rather as a richly multifaceted tool for shaking up, and throwing light on the horizon of communication. His ethos of growth through healthy exploration and discovery sees inquiry in the human sciences as the "weak afterglow of the rhetorical tradition," where rhetoric is a positive term, and sophism is its self-serving, errant negative other.[40] As rhetoric, the human sciences are the ways in which we negotiate our choices. They instantiate truth as *aletheia*, the opening up of compelling insights relative to certain issues and situations, rather than truth as *techne*, rigid models intended to achieve particular goals. Gadamer tantalisingly recalls Vico's own determination to reveal "God's providence under humankind's most characteristic property, which is its essentially social nature."[41] On the model of Vico's *New Science* Gadamer affirmed the "other" logics of thought reflected in the wide range of disciplines, which included "the authority of religion and the wisdom of the poets."[42] These other discourses, affirmed in their exemplary *relativity* and concomitant *relevance*, are at the heart of Gadamer's humanism as an ideology that explores and champions what is uniquely *human* about the universe.

Of course, Gadamer's own training was deeply "humanistic," both in the sense of combining a healthy range of the human sciences, and in that it encompassed the lessons of classical and Renaissance humanism. This wider context of debate and religious concern was taken as an essential key to the understanding of the Socratic dialogues, and with the assimilation of this contextual worldview, a model for the modern academy was born.[43] This yielded not only canonical texts for philosophy, but also models for the life and methods of the philosopher, meanwhile elevating hermeneutical concerns to a more pervasive presence within the discipline. As with the (differently motivated and aligned) flourishing of philosophical positions in Rūpa's time, the result was an enhanced self-awareness, diversity, and subtlety in the philosophical outlooks that filled Gadamer's intellectual milieu. Gadamer identifies this "rise of the new humanism" as one of the driving forces in the growth of hermeneutical concerns in the German academy of the early twentieth century, putting the lessons learned from Lutheran theological hermeneutics to new "humanist" uses:

> the famous *querelle des anciens et modernes* belongs to the prehistory of hermeneutics insofar as it awakened a hermeneutical reflection upon the ideals of humanism.[44]

Thus the reawakening of the classical tradition provoked interpretive questions that honed current thinking on historicity, while demanding an engagement with humanistic ideals. Bultmann's influence on Gadamer, as on Heidegger, dealt a powerful blow to the philosophical desirability of a traditional realist interpretation of theological matters, and contributed to the sense that a new thinking was needed in respect of the spiritual—a thinking that appreciated the parameters of human life and concern. Gadamer did not hesitate to characterise Bultmann himself as a "truly convinced humanist," and much of Gadamer's own distinctiveness as a philosopher lies in his "striking vindication of humanistic tradition."[45] It is with a reviving interest in the *pre-Enlightenment* philosophical foundations of modernity that Richard J. Bernstein says of Gadamer that he:

> fits directly into the tradition of humanistic thought that traces its origins back to Greek philosophy. . . . His entire philosophical project can be characterised as an apologia for humanistic learning.[46]

Of course this "humanist" orientation was much in keeping with certain threads of contemporary concern, while being famously problematic for the philosophical self-definition of Heidegger (as, of course, of previous existentialists). It can easily appear that humanism involves subjugation of the "world" with man at its centre—Heidegger expresses such concerns in his famous *Letter on Humanism* of 1947. And yet the thinker who first published this letter, Ernesto Grassi, has himself felt compelled to make a defence of humanism as containing a "specifically philosophical essence" holding much in common with Heidegger's existentialism.[47] In Gadamer's retrospective view, the Renaissance humanist inquiry after truth incorporated both Vico's path toward poetic truths and Descartes' path toward certainty; Gadamer's hermeneutics assimilates aspects of both.[48] This affirmation of the concerns and character of human experience is shared by Rūpa Gosvāmi, and is crucial to what he sees as a fulfilment of our (human-shaped) reality. Yet, while Gadamer and Gosvāmi affirm engagement with actuality, rather than some negation of finite reality, nevertheless, both construe the essence of the "play" of actuality in subtly different ways.

Here Gadamer is polemically if not materially in conflict with Heidegger who gives the impression of having never fully reconciled himself to the sovereignty of the finite realm. His emphasis on death is not echoed in Gadamer,[49] and his waiting for a saving god, as attested in his final interview with *Der Speigel*, was also not shared with Gadamer. Heidegger's stronger affinity with Nietzsche was further a major difference between them. In a 1993 conversation with Carsten Dutt, Gadamer insisted that he was "sceptical of every kind of pessimism. . . . Because no one can live without hope."[50] Thus Gadamer, who is named by Hermann Heidegger as his father's oldest and truest student, himself confessed that during the writing of *Truth and Method* he sensed Heidegger looking over his shoulder all the time, and—referring to his *magnum opus* many years later as an introduction to the later Heidegger—also confessed that, in contrast to his teacher, he never felt any personal interest in the pessimistic philosophy of Nietzsche. He writes:

> Don't we all run the risk of a terrible intellectual hubris if we equate Nietzsche's anticipations and the ideological confusion of the present with life as it is actually lived with its own forms of solidarity? Here, in fact, my divergence from Heidegger is fundamental.[51]

As Rūpa Gosvāmi's "humanism" is tempered by the prior, more reactionary "humanism" of Indian Buddhism, so in Gadamer's work we see that his hermeneutic humanism necessarily assumed a new postclassical incarnation after the Second World War; as Gianni Vattimo says, forced to choose between transcendence and charity, hermeneutics chose charity. But it does so not merely as an attempt to choose a more morally edifying position. It does so because what is the case (conversations embedded in finitude and human concern) is what ought to be the case, but more vigorously instantiated, without dissent, unifying action with intention. For Gadamer then, it would seem that salvation is merely ceasing to feel alienated from our own indeterminate human natures.

FUNDAMENTAL ONTOLOGY AS FUNDAMENTAL MORALITY: *IS* AS *OUGHT*

But if all of this is founded on a merely descriptive analysis of what Being consists of, then on what basis can we speak of what is better and what is worse for humankind in general? What can ontology tell us about human flourishing?

In essays published after *Truth and Method*, Gadamer takes a rhetorical position on a range of specific concerns about how we do and should live. But how does this rhetoric sit with his ontological, value-neutral exposition of transcendent truths? How is it, for instance, that Gadamer can justify calling us to recognise the "true nature" of Being rather than to misconstrue it, when in both cases we are equally well instantiating Being itself? From a "transcendental" perspective all of our actions are forward movements of dialectic. Thus all positions should be equal, and Gadamer's could only be justified in making such prescriptions relative to specific personally and historically prejudiced concerns.

One could try to argue that more thematised Being is better than the "bad infinity" of disintegrated, fragmentarily structural relations in which there is little "Oneness" and little subjective meaningfulness to be found. Engaging with a theme, as we have argued, can be seen as a robustly "realist" enterprise. Of course, one (a Marxist theorist, for instance) might argue that actually the disruption of themes and discourses has a beneficial (e.g., liberating) effect. This would not challenge that position—one could counter that the criticism of the content of a certain theme, or even of its fundamental principles, is not a breaking of the theme at the higher level of the *Sache*, but a continuation of it in new ways. Indeed, a conservative adherence to the theme's content might involve abandoning the inner concerns that it addresses—the *real* theme. Thus, for instance, dogmatic adherence to particular doctrine might be a tangent that actually betrays the inner themes of the New Testament.[52] Even on the most basic and minimal assessment, the pluralistic, chaotic actuality of real life is always at least unified by the structure and teleology of the "self." This "self" is the shape that the themed immediacy of Being takes. Gadamer must advise that we use our self-awareness to contribute to whatever theme is most compelling in our particular self and situation. And when that theme changes, or to put it another way, a different theme rises and predominates, there should be no compunction about switching our energies to this new work (of art), life project, or "game" that has come "into play." We will be playing such a game anyway, but from our subjective perspective on things from *within* Being, we will be happier because our self-reflexive consciousness will be better assimilated to Being's essence. The point is to embrace each theme with the proper qualities of absorption, passion, attentiveness, and vitality.

This would suggest that the "good life" is merely a matter of making subjective experience more satisfying according to subjectivity's own particular yardstick. Making the right choice makes us more subject to an "ecstatic self-forgetting"[53] through a monistic structural identity with the whole, relieving "the abysmal ignorance about ourselves in which we live," and reducing the likelihood of being disappointed by an ethos based on an inaccurate theory of Being.[54] But all this would make Gadamer something of a pragmatist, like Rorty, content for people to follow a particular good of their own "choosing" according to their own hedonistic needs. By grounding this ethics in Being as a whole, we seem to lose any foundation for the particularity of its content. Here, for instance, moral actions would be advisable based only on their propensity to gratify the individual who acts (albeit at a deep level, oriented to the truths of Being *per se*). One might, however, choose ignorance and its benefits and by way of the status of his ethical position, Gadamer would have no ontologically grounded answer as to why this ought not to be the case. Ignorance and blind, wilful fantasy are yet further themes for Being to instantiate.[55]

In order to defend the priority of his insights Gadamer would have to argue that accuracy (with regard to the reality of things) was an innate good, and it is not clear on what basis he might do this. By this argument, his version of the Good, which tries to avoid being caught up in the particular dialectical contents of Being, would mereologically subsume other theories of the Good. But unless accurateness can be lauded as anything more than a favourite prejudice of his, Gadamer could have no leverage against other positions.

Can one understand the priority of Gadamer's advice to pursue the theme not from the perspective of subjectivity as discussed, but from that of Being, of the *game* itself? Generally, and this is where he begins to diverge most significantly from the ideas that we will see Rūpa Gosvāmi developing, Gadamer takes the position that medial awareness is always superior to subjective awareness. Much of his language suggests this. Subjective self-understanding is subsumed to the "unconscious teleology" of the game, through which "the unified form of movement as a whole" takes up the individual self "into a higher determination that is really the decisive factor" and is analogous to faith as "a gracious act of God that happens *to* the one who has faith."[56] It is in this connection that Gadamer speaks of "ecstasy" and "free buoyancy," and of the theological event in which "a new man is established."[57] Grondin characterises the subsuming of the subjective in the medial as a participation "composed of activity, passivity and wonder. We are there but without ever seizing everything."[58] This characterisation sums up many key aspects of Gadamer's ethics, including their applicability to religious belief-choice, and their divergence from Rūpa Gosvāmi's vision of flourishing.

Yet while lauding this happy state, Grondin cannot help but ask: "What exactly is transfigured: reality, or us?"[59] Is this tantamount to a soteriological transformation at the level of "the whole of our being, the totality of our being-in-the-world"?[60] In Gadamer's depiction of game, the "back and forth movement of the game has a peculiar freedom and buoyancy" as "something that obeys its own set of laws [and] gains ascendancy in the game." It is "a condition of weightless balance" that merits Rilke's laudatory lines.[61] At this level human individuals are subsumed to the "life of language," almost as if language were an organism to be protected and encouraged to flourish.[62] The individual profits by a feeling of "enrichment" and "elevation," in an event that for him or her appears as "accident, favor and surprise."[63]

Once again we are thrown back on the idea that a special attitude of participation will not only make us happier, but also make us better "players," thus improving the game itself, and the state of Being in general relative to the theme of human flourishing. Is it right to say that a game full of good players is better than a game full of bad players precisely because the nature of the game is a gathering and teleological movement of players, rather than an event of fragmentation and strife? Is there some "objective" sense in which a good game is good *per se*, or is it that, only insofar as it is understood as a game, its success at being a game is a good thing? Are Being's themes intrinsic such that their successful development is an intrinsic good, or is meaning "only" human, and not in any way rooted in Being itself, which is neutral? From Gadamer's perspective, this latter position remains a false dichotomy based on the old, mistaken idea of a basic, primal level—it imagines a level of Being that is not veined through with the forces of human concern. As the investigation of motion and teleology in chapter 2 argued, Gadamerian meaning and meaningfulness are "human-shaped," and intrinsic in the very fabric of things.

On this picture of Being, value finally sits not lightly among other objects, but sinks in and assumes a transcendental significance. In his oblique way, Gadamer is attempting to point out that our very existence is proof that vitality *is*, not sheer fragmentation, which itself is an impossibility for Being in any case. Derrida's philosophy is most insightful, fruitful and effective when he is most ably doing precisely that which Gadamer prescribes, following the "theme" of deconstruction (although he might disagree), interpreting "theme" in a more limited way. Gadamer's position thus is truly ontological, while Derrida's, when all is said and done, is merely a critical method for elucidating aspects of the unity and vitality that Gadamer advocates. Plurality, complexity, fragmentation, and space are, as the Kierkegaardian side of Hegel reveals, key factors in the existence of the dynamic, practical, teleological, Aristotelian Oneness of reality.[64]

Thus Gadamer affirms the whole in its transcendental constitution and its essential nature, which is to grow in constant becoming—which, however, is not mere proliferation of an identical meaningless substance, but rather a growth of forms, themes, and essences according to their unforeclosed rubric. This links with a number of rhetorics that Gadamer deploys; firstly, of an innate "order" of things, and its intrinsic value. In this way of thinking, echoing Heidegger and, indeed, Rilke and Holderlin, humanity participates in a larger *order* of being, according to which it has an *essence*, and thus a destiny that it is its duty to fulfil. For Heidegger this means that instead of merely existing in isolation, we must "ek-sist," the "fundamental character of ek-sistence [being] ecstatic inherence in the truth of Being."[65] But whereas Heidegger prefers a somewhat mystical language for this implicit order, Gadamer's conception recalls the teleology of the organism according to Aristotle.

This affirmation recalls Heidegger's notion that technological thought (*techne*) is not just a short-sighted distortion of Heidegger's model of truth as *aletheia*—insight, but also part of the essence of man—an essence that both *is*, and can *save*. While on the one hand Gadamer wants to affirm the medial perspective, he finds he must simultaneously affirm immersion in finite ends. Thus he writes:

> Illusion, forgetfulness of death, is essential to life and creativity . . . life is unliveable without its being partly illusion. . . . We can appeal to the Spanish term illusion which could intend to say that we have a goal, a hope, a joy, an ideal, something that makes us live (a use which perhaps explains the joie de vivre of the Spanish) . . . Jean-Paul Sartre came close to this phenomenon when he spoke of the mauvaise foi inherent in all language.[66]

This reveals one of the paradoxes of life: in order to be true to the nature of Being as not null matter but motivated teleological movement, we must adopt the "illusion" entailed in living. If life is the playing of (serious) games, we must adopt the rules of a particular game as a fulfilment of the "essence" of Being, which entails submission to orders. This is crucial—we will see that when Rūpa Gosvāmi thinks through the problem of how we are best to enact Being's finite dynamic trajectories, he too must affirm finite focuses (facets, ornamentations, details, episodes, and digressions of his characters and stories) in order to properly address our attention to Being.

Here too, we develop through smaller themes while contributing to a larger one, as in a symphony, or the Popperian notion of scientific progress through trial and error, an example that Gadamer raises. Yet according to Grondin "Gadamer acknowledges this [latter] conception of experience, but thinks that it perhaps stresses too much the voluntarist aspect of experimentation, ignoring the passive and passionate (*leidenschaftlich*) character of the whole experience of life."[67] This *leidenshaftlich* character of individual experience is perhaps where Gadamer's ethics comes closest to that of Rūpa Gosvāmi, for whom the act of engaging with something, our being assimilated to a theme becomes more than mere vitality. It becomes a focused and intensifying passion when we see the dialectic not only as broadening but also deepening the scope of our play. For Gadamer we are an organism that grows—not by choice, but as a natural flourishing. We too are a product of our environment, of wind, rain, and sun, as it were. Rūpa Gosvāmi champions the same passivity—in being saved we become the vehicles of an over-riding passion that is knit into the fabric of reality. We merely "incarnate" the passions of which reality consists. Already we see that there are a number of different ways of talking about this innate teleological dynamism that constitutes Being. It can be an order in response to which we, the army, take our stand in one or another formation. It can be an inner "essence" that we are forever moving toward, like the growing plant. It can be a game that we must become increasingly immersed in and enthused by. It can be a passionate force that overwhelms us, transforming the individual into a passive part of a larger play of Being.

FROM OBJECTIVITY TO VITALITY

Ever sensitive to the human and historical moods behind philosophy, Gadamer writes:

> [O]ne should not fail to note that the motives that compelled Heidegger to his so-called Kehre ("turnabout") harmonised with a new sensibility or style of the epoch, which, exhausted from the subtle sensuality of impressionistic enchantment, called out for a new, constructive objectivity.[68]

"Constructive" is the key word in this new objectivity. Kierkegaard had passed through the grain of German thought and left no movement untouched. The solipsistic introspection of much Romanticist thought had provoked a counterinstinct toward making decisive steps forward on firm ground—in philosophy, much as science and technology had begun to do. In this respect the phenomenological clarion call to return *Zu den Sachen selbst* was a summons to business, to the real issues or "matters" (*Sachen*) at hand.[69] It sought to declare both an epistemological strategy for defying the Kantian riddle of the "thing-itself," and a philosophical agenda according to which thinkers would not pursue such purely academic concerns in isolation. In this sense Heidegger and his followers saw themselves as following quite the opposite of what we now think of as an anti-realist agenda; they were seeking to reground us in certainties, and to assure us that our philosophical inquiry has a powerfully "meaningful" dimension. Philosophy was to be concerned not merely with marginal, purely technical tasks of clarification, but always with vital considerations of what we should do in immediate everyday situations. *Zu den Sachen selbst* said, "let us get back to the real issue, that which is truly there, and upon which the quality of our own lives depends." It was for this philosophical clarity and commitment that Gadamer held up Socrates as his hero, an exemplarily serious philosopher "player," in respect of whom he observes that "Plato's magnificent writings are dedicated in their entirety to showing that the Socrates who had to drink the cup of poison was no sophist."[70]

It is interesting to note how the language of objectivity and that of subjectivity were combined and alternated by twentieth-century thinkers influenced by phenomenology, as if, cast somewhere between the two, many were not sure which title promised greater philosophical leverage. In many respects, Heidegger was eager to reclaim the virtues of objectivity in the wake of romanticism. By contrast, foreshadowing Levinas's portrayal of what is subjective as precisely that which has relevance and meaningfulness for us, Gadamer writes censoriously of objectivity. In so doing he wishes to contrast objectivity's neutral information and its capacity of freedom with that which gives our freedom its content: motive and care. Contrary to the null freedom of choice, which is mere "method," he sketches out an ethical arena in which free choice goes hand in hand with the passions that determine us, and over which we have little or no control.

> Is it at all true that we follow our own free decision whenever we try to investigate or interpret certain things? Free decision? A neutral, completely objective concern? At least the theologian would surely have objections here and say, "Oh no! Our understanding of the Holy Scripture does not come from our own free choice. It takes an act of grace. And the Bible is not a totality of sentences offered willy-nilly as a sacrifice to human analysis. No, the gospel is directed at me in a personal way. It claims to contain neither an objective statement nor a totality of objective statements but a special address to me."[71]

The phrase "sacrifice to human analysis" reminds us that emphasis on the human will and its powers was vehemently resisted. The defence of a vitalising objectivity merged with the defence of a vitalising subjectivity in the intention to carve out a new discourse that was at once personal and answerable to the real. For Gadamer this concern had a personal as well as an academic dimension, rooted in his father's criticism of the "prattling classes" of the bourgeoisie. Thus even in what counts as his academic autobiography, Gadamer complains that the

> calm distance from which a middle-class educational consciousness takes satisfaction in its educational achievements, misunderstands how much we ourselves are immersed in the game and are the stake in this game.[72]

For Gadamer the middle classes were like Nietzsche's philosophers of whom the latter wrote:

> They think that they [the philosophers] show their *respect* for a subject when they de-historicise it, *sub specie aeterni*—when they turn it into a mummy. All that philosophers have handled for thousands of years have been concept-mummies; nothing real escaped their grasp alive.[73]

Gadamer writes of how the *critical* Nietzsche, for whom he had no special sympathy, nevertheless became a collaborator in the postwar quest for "new grounds and new standards" of value, rather than a destroyer of them.[74] Nietzsche's words resonate throughout the work of subsequent thinkers in the experience of a fear of "nullity" or "something bygone" (Gadamer), of "worn-out trivialities" (Arendt), "concept mummies" (Nietzsche), "distanciated knowledge" (Kierkegaard), and "mere knowing" (Levinas), as opposed to what is *einleuchtend*, "illuminated/ing" (Gadamer), or what "has weight" (Levinas). Indeed, according to Gadamer, the whole of nineteenth-century Germany was led through the works of Goethe to feel that "All theory, O noble friend, is grey."[75]

Gadamer never abandons the importance of conversation as a guarantee that personal ideologies and the passion with which we pursue them will not compromise our moral conduct toward others. Nevertheless, it is important to note that on Gadamer's wider ethical model, the criteria for "judging" other viewpoints is primarily according to their vitality. In terms of the "game" or "technology" of ensuring benevolent relations and social order, we can judge each attitude and activity accordingly. But in terms of their own innate value, we assess them in terms of the passion with which they are pursued, and their affective power in the life of those who hold them. Indeed, it is this affectivity that provides a framework for understanding the truth-content of those perspectives, and indeed, for understanding religious truth-discourse. It invests truth into the affectivity and intensity of the belief, without (by its own lights) falling into anti-realist reductionism. In understanding truth discourse we must balance out the understanding of "theoretical knowledge" with a sensitivity to "the brightness, sharpness and pressure of conscience."[76]

GADAMER'S ETHICAL EXEMPLARS: PHILOSOPHERS AND POETS

Gadamer writes:

> Life experience and the study of Plato had led me quite early to the insight that the truth of a single proposition . . . depends upon the genuineness of

its enrootedness and bond with the person of the speaker in whom it wins its truth potential.[77]

Many of the philosophers whom Gadamer saw around him provided concrete examples of this ethos, which he recorded in his biographical (and semi-autobiographical) writings—largely compiled in *Philosophical Apprenticeships* and scattered throughout his work in the form of observations on his contemporaries. These are distinctive in their (often unphilosophical) detail and attention to the mood in which the thinker in question pursues his or her work. They are philosophically telling enough to have merited exclusive compilation but are generally seen as little more than a footnote to his interpretative theory, yet it is in these portraits that Gadamer best displays his ethical ideals. The volume forms a unique autobiography in that it remains silent about himself, yet throughout its richly described memories, Gadamer's own experience emerges.

The academy of which Gadamer was such a keen observer acts as yet another microcosm of Being, in which concepts are passed down dialectically—whether through synchronically stable "systems" of philosophy, or through the already complex, dialogical or parataxic logic of aphorism, literature, and life. Gadamer writes of his development during this period that

> I sought to overcome the historical self-estrangement with which historical positivism deflated ideas into opinions and philosophy into doxography. I was helped by the theory of contemporaneity that Kierkegaard, for religious and critical theological reasons, had set up against "understanding at a distance" and that attained in 1924 a persuasive effectiveness.[78]

Gadamer's doctoral research into the intellectual culture of ancient Athens held up a mirror to the intersection of moral and metaphysical philosophy in his own academic milieu. Like the intellectual arena of Athens with its Platonic propositions, metaphors, and myths, its Aristotelian morals, metaphysics, aesthetics, and natural sciences, and its Heraclitean fragments, Marburg saw a number of different modes of reasoning at work.[79] As genuine as Gadamer's search for a fundamental ontology was, it was by his own admission not "the sincere concern for transcendental self-grounding that Edmund Husserl viewed as his life's work" that inspired him, but "to be sure, the sweeping insatiability and demonic possession with which Max Scheler followed out his brilliant intuitions."[80] Scheler's alternation between philosophical ecstasy and "a sinking back into the dull stress of life" was a microcosm for all human experience.[81] In 1920s Marburg, Scheler's charismatic, personalist phenomenology was in fierce competition with Husserl's revolution in metaphysical thought, and, according to Gadamer, the former was an equally powerful influence on students. Phenomenology, which now is most characteristically understood as the philosophy of

Edmund Husserl and his successors, then included Scheler's phenomenology of the emotions, the "existence philosophies" of Bergson, Jaspers, and Marcel, and the "life philosophies" of Dilthey, Scheler, and Simmel. In the thought of thinkers like Scheler, such concerns even took on an explicitly spiritual dimension, and there was a clear indication that the pursuit of philosophy was not a neutral choice, but an overwhelming destiny. At Gadamer's first meeting with Scheler, he was asked: "Don't you think philosophy is something like pulling puppets on a string?" Gadamer writes:

> I understood suddenly what he had meant. Pulling strings, pulling on puppets—no, it was more like being drawn along, a nearly satanic sense of being possessed that led the speaker on to a true furioso of thought.[82]

Scheler's phenomenology, expounded in works such as *On the Eternal in Man,* and *Man's Place in Nature,* was a far cry from that of Husserl and Brentano. Scheler's schema of value-types and their operations (inhering in things and ideas just as colours inhere in objects) explicitly examines the way in which *value* is mapped onto the apparently neutral *contents* of thought which were Husserl's primary interest. He too offered up a realism in which values were inherent. He explored the realms of the personal and the ethical in a way that for Gadamer was reminiscent of the scarlet-bound editions of Dostoevsky's works that he recalls as sitting like the flags of a new ethos on so many desks in Marburg at that time. Gadamer implies that Scheler's philosophy naturally brought to bear new hopes and ideals on the phenomenological tradition that Husserl's post-Cartesian concern for certainty had rendered so dry: "His brilliance was overwhelming." Gadamer writes: "What was to become of philosophy as a rigorous science within the fired-up essence of this man?"[83] The "*elan vital* that drove him on so powerfully was not a muddying of his high intellectuality but the supporting stream from which he nourished himself."[84] Gadamer's language makes it seem almost as if Scheler himself were one of the metaphysical metaphor/examples that Gadamer employs.

Goethe is another important exemplary figure for Gadamer, described as having "concentrated in the unity of his own person that substance of spiritual and intellectual life which constituted the unity of the Western world, and which precisely at this time was on the point of disappearing."[85] Gadamer observes that "[i]n his encounter with things philosophical [Goethe] is basically looking for the same thing he is seeking in all his experiences of the world: an expansion of his activity, a vital increase in the unfolding of his own creative and formative powers," which in turn he calls an "augmentation of being."[86]

Gadamer's philosopher-heroes—Scheler, Goethe, and others—are "fired-up" "furiosos" seeking a vital increase of their activity through unfolding powers. They are passionate in the sense that they pose a clear counterpoint to the "dull" realism of everyday life and the passive realism of Husserl's phenomenological epoche. But their passion is not directed at a particular object—rather the goal is precisely to bring about their own increase, albeit within the framework of the wider world's natural growth and development.

Yet Scheler argued in early works against the self-transparent transcendental ego as the core of the individual, in favour of the human heart, distinguished above all by its capacity for love. He opposed an ecstatic, almost kenotic "I" (which seems so religious and, as we will see, very Hindu) to the self-consideration of Husserl's transcendental ego. Thus beside the model of *homo poeticus* advanced by Vico, and that of *homo ludens* evoked by Huizinga, Gadamer thus encountered the idea of humanity as the *ens amans*, the loving being. Scheler also offered in his later work *Man's Place in Nature*, a modern vision of world, man and God as a monistic whole, constantly emergent in the "becoming" of the present.[87]

The son of a natural scientist, sharing the "common opposition among young people to throne and altar," Gadamer seems to have entertained little religious inspiration in his philosophical thought. But he is by no means untouched by "the spirit of Luther, German Mysticism, and the Pietist heritage of his homeland" that had also left its mark on Hegel, and the religious consciences of his contemporaries made a powerful impression on him.[88] Of course, his immediate German religious context was itself a pluralistic one, and beyond both Heidegger and Scheler's troubled relations with Lutheranism and Catholicism, many more unorthodox forms of religion were popular in the "Athens" of Marburg. These included the "corporate consciousness at a high spiritual level" of Stefan George's circle, which became "an increasingly powerful presence" in Gadamer's life.[89] To this was added the "deep mystical sense" that he discerned in Rabindranath Tagore, with whom he attended drama readings in Marburg. Heidegger meanwhile was exploring the spiritual potential of neo-classical sources (and was beginning to give them darker applications that Levinas would later associate with all "pagan" religious impulses in the West). Religious brands of monism, pantheistic, panentheistic, or otherwise were an omnipresent influence in Gadamer's formative years. The notion of a personal God barely features in his thought, but the "gods" of Holderlin's poetry, and the "angels" of Rilke's elegies express an ideal of eudaimonia that sheds light on the ethos of causing the self to realise and accord with its true essence. As we saw briefly in chapter 2, Gadamer saw poetry as the discourse that, in his opinion, best reflects the true nature of Being as *aletheia*, unifying form and indeterminacy. But poetry is not merely a descriptive "realist" discourse—Gadamer, like Heidegger, values poetry for its capacity to *inspire* the vitality with which we are to participate in Being. Just as both men draw on exemplary role models to demonstrate the ideals of human flourishing which they advocate, so both Gadamer and Rūpa Gosvāmi, who riddles his treatises with verse quotations, draw on poetic examples—to draw us into the proper attitude of engagement, vitality, and listening to everyday life, and to enthuse us into an aesthetic state of immersion and self-forgetting.

Where Heidegger felt the need to attempt a poetic style in his later works, Gadamer seems pleased to find that many poets had already done much of the talking for him. Unlike philosophy, poetry did not close itself within the limitations of conceptuality—rather it had long explored resources for disrupting and expanding the apparent Pythagorean rigidity of language. It seemed more able to resolve the aporia wherein

> the part of lived reality [*Erleben*] that can enter into the concept is always a flattened version—like every projection of a living bodily existence onto a surface.[90]

Indeed, in his study of Rilke's fourth Duino Elegy, Gadamer shows how Rilke uses "mytho-poetic inversion" not to press the expansive "inner word" into too-small concepts, but to open it out into the rich and unravelling semantic language of imagery and myth. It is the more difficult work of writers like Celan, Mallarmé, and Rilke that suit Gadamer's hermeneutic concerns better than that of Holderlin, precisely because the metaphors and images they use are open, uncertain, and resonant without requiring the closure of an easy sentimentality or a simple interpretive "key." The engagement that these writers demand is a microcosm of the yielding attention with which Gadamer advises us to approach the world in general. In many respects the language of Rilke and Mallarmé's poetry would seem to destabilise notions of order with the ambiguity and parataxic dialogicism that characterises their style. Yet, analogous to Rūpa Gosvāmi's perpetual deferral of closure in the poetic narratives about Rādhā's passion, and in the riddle-like stanzas of his verse, "the negativity of modern poetry" that is cherished by Gadamer is meant to be "not a wholesale denigration of the world but, much rather, a rethinking and rearticulation of worldliness."[91] Even the narrative structure of the Platonic dialogues could be interpreted as replacing the wisdom of doctrine with the wisdom of poetry. Stanley Rosen writes with regard to Gadamer's analysis of the Platonic Dialogues on the nature of the soul:

> If there is an answer in the Platonic dialogues to the question "what is the soul?" that answer is not a rational account of determinate structure but rather the dialogues themselves, as we come to understand them through the exercise of recreating them in our discursive imagination.[92]

It is at this point, as Rosen points out, that the failure of mathematics gives way to poetry which traffics in the "tension and release that structure all understanding and understandability."[93] Poetry presents (and instantiates) a "gnomic present," occurring "again and again," characterised by "pure expectation."[94]

Gadamer also writes that

> [t]he poet must dismantle the scaffold of everyday words syllable by syllable. He must fight against the ordinary, customary, obscuring and levelling function of language in order to lay open a view of the glimmer above.[95]

Again we see that this discourse, which is "language in a preeminent sense," struggles against the apparent valuelessness of everyday realism.[96] Thus Gadamer follows the view, along with Mallarmé, Valery, and Holderlin, among others, that poetry is a discourse that is self-validating, a deflated truth-discourse in which meaning and reference are unified. Of course, poetry does not refer to "the world nor this or that thing in the world."[97] He is quick to criticise "correspondence" and "verification" as mechanisms that are ill at ease in the province of the poem.[98] He says of the poetically transfigured word that

> it would be misleading to think that this represents an enfeebled consciousness of reality or a weakening of the positing power of consciousness. The reverse is true. The realisation that occurs by means of the word eliminates any comparison with whatever else might be present and raises what might be said above the particularity of what is usually called "reality."[99]

In such poetry we discover direct "indications from the spirit of language."[100] This emotive listening diminishes "the utilitarian scepticism of a massive realism which despises the luxury of the emotions."[101] Paul Celan's image, already cited in chapter 2, of "the 'breath-crystal,' which is nothing but the configuration of pure, delicate geometry that falls from the soft nothingness of breath"[102] denotes that which is "wholly, wholly real."

Valery speaks of the poetic discourse as like the old gold coin—not merely referential like its paper note heir, but rather innately possessing the value (twenty dollars) that it signifies ("twenty dollars"). Thus the poetic word does not refer outward, but rather, as Gadamer says in relation again to Celan's poetry:

> Here there are no allegories. Everything is itself.
>
> The poetic word is "itself" in the sense that nothing other, nothing prior, exists against which it can be measured. . . . But this means that it is an answer. Answers comprise questions as well as answer them. Thus the utterance [*Gesagte*] is not made up only of itself, even when nothing else beyond its realisation in language is otherwise apparent.[103]

Again the self-grounding character of Being (here as "language") comes to light. For Mallarmé this indicates a lamentable "*theological* powerlessness," but for Gadamer, who devoted much of his work to justifying the passion of being taken up into a theme, however finite, it becomes at once a fact of life, a source of salvation, and a cause for celebration.[104] The "glimmer above" that Gadamer posits behind the language of the poem echoes Celan's repeated use of the word "glimmer" with images of nature and body, and of inanimate objects (the mulberry leaves, the flowers), emphasised and often anthropomorphised to suggest the goal of something higher to which we aspire in our finite environment. The ethos of this poetic realism is the feeling that, as Rilke puts it,

> Now it is time that gods emerge
> From things by which we dwell.[105]

But the paradigm for these "gods" are the daimon of which Heidegger writes, the *ethos* of humanity itself. In realising our identity with them and our manifestation of the divine we achieve *eudaimonia*.

Thus Gadamer gives the cheerful advice that

> one ought to work descriptively, creatively—intuitively and in a concretising manner. Instead of simply applying concepts to all sorts of things, concepts ought to come forward in movements of thought springing from the spirit of language and the power of intuition.[106]

Such an ethos can only succeed on the prior ground of a complete faith in the value of a reality that is "not the world of the first day but one that is always already handed over to us."[107] Gadamer's position in sum is a sort of "pantheist" soteriology that advocates a universal monism in which we realise our fundamental identity with the whole, learning to see ultimate value in our self and situation. Human flourishing is seen in terms of an Aristotelian vitalism, realising and embracing our true nature. Again it is essential to keep in mind that the Western history in which Gadamer's thought is rooted is *not* a monolithic tradition of theistic dualism. It is a tradition in which his first academic experience was of a pre-Socratic universe in which Heraclitus considered the truth underlying all phenomena to be single and unified; in which Pythagoras taught that the rationality of the cosmos was a subject for religious concern, and that the world, which was considered to be both living (i.e., possessed of a moving, developing vitality) and divine, was in fact akin to the human soul.

Gadamer's soteriology is a eudaimonian one because he is an ontological and ethical realist: the realisation of ultimate truths shows us who we are and how to live in accordance with that identity—as ultimate reality. It is interesting to note that his eudaimonian monism yields vitalistic engagement, movement, and change, rather than the quietism that we might have expected. Already we begin to see the kinds of differences that can characterise an ethics based on an epistemology that has survived scepticism, as opposed to a "naive" ethics that maintains an ideal of values rooted in a world-transcending ontological "other."

None of the views mentioned in this chapter are identical to any particular Indian philosophical position, just as they are not identical to each other. But in them there is a family resemblance based on the results of reasoning from questions about the necessary conditions of phenomena and the underlying unity of the *fact* that phenomena exist. It is historically clear that not only were Gadamer and his contemporaries profoundly familiar with and evidently compelled by a range of ontological models and their ethoses, they were also familiar with a range of Indian worldviews from firsthand study. The next section will argue that Rūpa Gosvāmi's worldview, which is widely claimed to constitute a dualistic theism, in fact also formulates truths about the fundamental constitution of reality as form, motion, and teleology, and takes it as the ground of a *eudaimonian* ethics not merely of self-augmenting vitality, but of focused and intensifying passions.

In the *Duino Elegies* Rilke's ethical exemplar is the lover who has lost the object of his love forever—a Dante desiring the dead Beatrice without hope of satisfaction. Only in this love is the desire "purified" of its finite object and elevated into a saving engagement with reality. This is a teleology divorced from its telos, which must of necessity find its painful satisfaction in its own intensity. Gadamer too gives voice to this ideal of desire:

> Is all longing really of such a nature that it depends upon a deficiency, upon what I lack? . . . is all longing a need which has passed when it is satisfied in the way that thirst is quenched when one has drunk something? . . . Or is there a mode of attraction which is not governed by the law of self-termination but which of itself nourishes and augments itself, as it were?[108]

Paralleling the image of a galactic ontology, here we find the metaphor of a self-nourishing desire, that does not invest itself wholly in particular goals, but rather avoids the closure of satisfaction, instead maintaining the bittersweet intensity of longing. This latter model challenges the vitalist ideal of engagement with an ethos that sacrifices the health of the individual for a more full absorption in the telos of which Being consists. We have seen that a "eudaimonian" self-flexive sensitivity to the place of the individual being in Being as a whole, can transform the acknowledgement of indeterminacy, changefulness, and non-fulfilment into a positive philosophy of pantheistic immersion and vitality. Now we see that the soteriology of speculative recognition that is adopted here, leads us to a second strand of "realist" reasoning that shows us what can happen if we think through a monist pluralist realism and its consonant ethics from an altered starting point. This will be discussed further in the next part of the book.

NOTES

1. We will return to Gadamer's depictions of the life of the philosopher as ethical role model later in this chapter.

2. *Philosophical Apprenticeships*, 178.

3. See "Logos and Ergon in Plato's *Lysis*," in *Dialogue and Dialectic*, 17, for discussion of the "different mode of reality or Being" indicated.

4. "Logos and Ergon in Plato's *Lysis*," in *Dialogue and Dialectic*, 20.

5. In this regard, Gadamer praises Spinoza's hermeneutics as a pre-Hegelian insight into the importance of dialectical detours through the particulars of history, for illuminating the essence of an idea: "The operation of the understanding requires that the unconscious elements involved in the original act of knowledge be brought to consciousness . . . Spinoza's work makes it quite evident that the way of historical understanding is a kind of unavoidable detour that the person who understands must take when immediate insight into what is said in the tradition is no longer possible for him" ("On the Problem of Self-Understanding," in *Philosophical Hermeneutics*, 45–46). For Gadamer, Spinoza more obviously (if more crudely) avoids the naïve universalism that Kojève criticises in Hegel, thanks to the hermeneutical influence of his biblical criticism in the *Tractatus-Theologico-Politicus*.

6. See "The Heritage of Hegel," in *Reason in the Age of Science*, 40.

7. *The Beginning of Philosophy*, 12. In a later epoch of response to Hegel, Deleuze seeks to resolve this perceived danger in Hegel's thoughts by recourse to a similar attention to particularity.

8. From Hegel's *Phenomenology of the Spirit*, quoted by Gadamer in "Hegel and the Dialectic of the Ancient Philosophers," in *Hegel's Dialectic: Five Hermeneutical Studies*, 8.

9. "The Heritage of Hegel," in *Reason in the Age of Science*, 44.

10. *Introduction to Philosophical Hermeneutics*, Joel Weinsheimer, trans. (New Haven, Conn.: Yale University Press, 1994), ix.

11. *Introduction to Philosophical Hermeneutics*, xiv.

12. "The Heritage of Hegel," in *Reason in the Age of Science*, 44.

13. "The Philosophical Foundations of the Twentieth Century," in *Philosophical Hermeneutics*, 124. Gadamer briefly comments on the difficulty experienced by classicists, including himself, in balancing these two perspectives in the interpretation of Plato.

14. "The Philosophical Foundations of the Twentieth Century," in *Philosophical Hermeneutics*, 117.

15. *Concluding Unscientific Postscript* (Princeton, N.J.: Princeton University Press, 1992), 33.

16. "The Scope of Hermeneutical Reflection," in *Philosophical Hermeneutics*, 56.

17. *Plato's Dialectical Ethics: Phenomenological Interpretations Relating to the Philebus*, R. M. Wallace, ed. and trans. (New Haven, Conn.: Yale University Press, 1991), 7.

18. "The Heritage of Hegel," in *Reason in the Age of Science*, 55.

19. Here too, we will see an analogy in chapters 6 and 7 with the dialectic of Rūpa Gosvāmi's interpretation of *śakti* as unfolding not only in the plurality of created forms, but in the dialectic of relation between them.

20. *Truth and Method* (London: Continuum, 2004), 26.

21. *Truth and Method* (London: Continuum, 2004), 63.

22. *Truth and Method* (London: Continuum, 2004), 69.

23. Jean Grondin, *Introduction to Philosophical Hermeneutics*, Joel Weinsheimer, trans. (New Haven, Conn.: Yale University Press, 1994), 143.

24. Walter Benjamin, quoted by Gerald Bruns in "The Remembrance of Language: An Introduction to Gadamer's Poetics," in *Gadamer on Celan: "Who Am I and Who Are You?" and Other Essays*, 1.

25. "The Heritage of Hegel," in *Reason in the Age of Science*, 56.

26. This was a criticism that Yorck made of Dilthey's distanciated, almost transcendental historicism, and which was influential upon both Heidegger and Gadamer.

27. Gadamer quotes Dilthey in summing up his philosophy in *Reason in the Age of Science*, 160.

28. See Paul Ricoeur, *Oneself as Another*, 4. Zizek writes that "the point, of course, is not to return to the cogito in the guise in which this notion has dominated modern thought (the self-transparent thinking subject), but to bring to light its forgotten obverse, the excessive, unacknowledged kernel of the cogito" (Slavoj Zizek, *The Ticklish Subject: The Absent Centre of Political Ontology* (Guildford and King's Lynn: Verso, 1999)).

29. "Myth in the Age of Science," in *Hermeneutics, Religion, and Ethics*, 91.

30. This notion of the role of humanity harmonises with Heidegger's sometimes self-contradictory affirmations of the spirit of technology as an innate and positive part of the being of humanity (see "The Question Concerning Technology," in *Basic Writings* (Oxford: Routledge, 1978), 338).

31. In conversation with Alfons Grieder in *Gadamer in Conversation*, 113.

32. Goethe, quoted by Gadamer in "Plato and the Poets," in *Dialogue and Dialectic: Eight Hermeneutical Studies on Plato*, 39.

33. Zizek, *The Ticklish Subject: The Absent Centre of Political Ontology*, 14.

34. We will see how this degree of moral relativism is reflected in Rūpa Gosvāmi's emphasis on the intensity of the relation with Krishna rather than on the moral character of the relation.

35. *Gadamer in Conversation*, 94.

36. Gerald Bruns applauds this situational, applied character of Gadamer's implicit ethical position in "The Hermeneutical Anarchist," in *Gadamer's Century: Essays in Honour of Hans-Georg Gadamer*, Jeff Malpas, Ulrich Arnswald, and Jens Kertscher, eds. (Cambridge, Mass.: MIT Press, 2002).

37. Ian Almond, "Religious Echoes of the Errant Text: Darker Shades of Derrida's Pathless Way," in *The Heythrop Journal* 44 (2003), 294.

38. Ian Almond, "Religious Echoes of the Errant Text: Darker Shades of Derrida's Pathless Way," in *The Heythrop Journal* 44 (2003), 294.

39. The same question can be asked of God's "divine play" in manifesting the world.

40. *The Idea of the Good in Platonic-Aristotelian Philosophy*, 169.

41. Giambattista Vico, *New Science*, David Marsh, trans. (London: Penguin, 1999), 2.

42. See Vico's Prolegomena to Book Two of the *New Science*.

43. See *Dialogue and Dialectic*, and Catherine Zuckert's essay " Hermeneutics in Practice: Gadamer on Ancient Philosophy," in *The Cambridge Companion to Gadamer*, Robert Dostal, ed. (New York: Cambridge University Press, 2002).

44. "The Heritage of Hegel," in *Reason in the Age of Science*, 96–97.

45. Jean Grondin, *Hans-Georg Gadamer: Eine Biographie* (Tubingen: J.C.B. Mohr, 1999), 327.

46. Robert Bernstein, *Beyond Objectivism and Relativism: Science, Hermeneutics and Praxis* (Oxford: Basil Blackwell Publishers Limited, 1983), 180.

47. Ernesto Grassi, *Heidegger and the Question of Humanism: Four Studies* (Albany: State University of New York Press, 1983), 50.

48. Jean Grondin, in his exposition of Gadamer's philosophy makes a case for the similarities between Gadamer and Descartes (see *The Philosophy of Gadamer*, Kathryn Plant, trans. (Guildford and King's Lynn: Acumen, 2003)). Gadamer himself cites Vico as one of the few early modern systematic thinkers to maintain the Aristotelian insight into that distinction between practical and theoretical thinking, which Gadamer in turn takes up as his theme in *Truth and Method* (see *The Idea of the Good in Platonic-Aristotelian Philosophy*, 169).

49. The theme of death arises in his discussions of Heidegger, but outside of this exegetical context he takes a primarily anthropological approach to death, focusing on its paraphernalia, consonant with a view of it as no more than a particular theme of a particular discourse. Such *rituals* of death (rather than psychological attitudes such as anxiety toward it) are interpreted as reflecting on the contents of life—the idea of death itself receives short shrift. See *Reason in the Age of Science*, 75, where Gadamer portrays death rituals on the one hand as "a way of cherishing human existence," and on the other as a turning of humanity "against the natural vital instincts of survival."

50. *Gadamer in Conversation*, 83

51. "A Letter by Professor Hans-Georg Gadamer," in *Beyond Objectivism and Relativism: Science, Hermeneutics and Praxis* (Oxford: Basil Blackwell Publishers Limited, 1983), 264.

52. This principle is what Habermas fails to recognise in his allegations of a covert conservatism in Gadamer's idea of a present that is "determined" by the past.

53. "On the Problem of Self-Understanding," in *Philosophical Hermeneutics*, 55.

54. "On the Problem of Self-Understanding," in *Philosophical Hermeneutics*, 55.

55. My aim is not to criticise what might be seen as "blind, wilful fantasy" in religion—not all positions are "realist" in the way that I have outlined, and surely such flights of imagination and leaps of faith are often at the heart of religious faith.

56. "On the Problem of Self-Understanding," in *Philosophical Hermeneutics*, 54.

57. "On the Problem of Self-Understanding," in *Philosophical Hermeneutics*, 55.

58. Jean Grondin, *The Philosophy of Gadamer*, Kathryn Plant, trans. (Guildford and King's Lynn: Acumen Publishing Limited, 2003), 43. Here we see the exploratory ethos of philosophical hermeneutics once again at work, ably expounded by one of the most sensitive of Gadamer's expositors.

59. Grondin, *The Philosophy of Gadamer*, 43.

60. Grondin, *The Philosophy of Gadamer*, 43.

61. See "On the Problem of Self-Understanding," in *Philosophical Hermeneutics*, 54.

62. See "On the Problem of Self-Understanding," in *Philosophical Hermeneutics*, 56.

63. See "On the Problem of Self-Understanding," in *Philosophical Hermeneutics*, 57.

64. I will argue that the same insight is formulated in Caitanya Vaiṣṇava theology through the synthesis of Advaita Vedāntic unity, the Sāṃkhya notion of *śaktis* and the identification of this dynamic, creative unity with the value-filled concept of *rasa*, the "relishing" of things.

65. Martin Heidegger, "Letter on Humanism," in *Basic Writings* (Oxford: Routledge, 1978), 229.

66. Grondin, *The Philosophy of Gadamer*, 117.

67. Cited in Grondin, *The Philosophy of Gadamer*, 117.

68. "The Heritage of Hegel," in *Reason in the Age of Science*, 42–43.

69. See Husserl's motto to *Philosophical Investigations*.

70. *The Beginning of Philosophy*, 5.

71. "Hermeneutics as Practical Philosophy," in *Reason in the Age of Science*, 106.

72. *Philosophical Apprenticeships*, 178.

73. Friedrich Nietzsche, *The Twilight of the Idols* in *The Portable Nietzsche*, 479. The surrounding text prefigures much of Heidegger and Gadamer's ontology and the value-judgements on different ways of thinking about reality that is attendent upon it. He writes:

You ask me which of the philosophers' traits are really idiosyncrasies? For example, their lack of historical sense, their hatred of the very idea of becoming, their Egypticism. They think that they show their *respect* for a subject when they de-historicize it, *sub specie aeterni*—when they turn it into a mummy. All that philosophers have handled for thousands of years have been concept-mummies; nothing real escaped their grasp alive. When these honorable idolators of concepts worship something, they kill it and stuff it; they threaten the life of everything they worship. Death, change, old age, as well as procreation and growth, are to their minds objections—even refutations. Whatever has being does not become; whatever becomes does not have being. Now they all believe, desperately even, in what has being. But since they never grasp it, they seek for reasons why it is kept from them. "There must be mere appearance, there must be some deception which prevents us from perceiving that which has being: where is the deceiver?"

"We have found him," they cry ecstatically; "it is the senses! These senses, which are so immoral in other ways too, deceive us concerning the true world. Moral: let us free ourselves from the deception of the senses, from becoming, from history, from lies; history is nothing but faith in the senses, faith in lies. Moral: let us say No to all who have faith in the senses, to all the rest of mankind; they are all 'mob.' Let us be philosophers! Let us be mummies." Let us represent monotono-theism by adopting the expression of a gravedigger! And above all, away with the body, this wretched *idée fixe* of the senses, disfigured by all the fallacies of logic, refuted, even impossible, although it is impudent enough to behave as if it were real! With the highest respect, I except the name of Heraclitus. When the rest of the philosophic folk rejected the testimony of the senses because they showed multiplicity and change, he rejected their testimony because they showed things as if they had permanence and unity.

74. See "The Ethics of Value and Practical Philosophy," in *Hermeneutics, Religion, and Ethics*.

75. See "Goethe and Philosophy," in *Literature and Philosophy in Dialogue: Essays in German Literary Theory*, Robert Paslick, trans. (Albany: State University of New York Press, 1994), 3.

76. "On the Possibility of a Philosophical Ethics," in *Hermeneutics, Religion, and Ethics*, 20–21.

77. "The Heritage of Hegel," in *Reason in the Age of Science*, 44. Here we see again how reality and truth are not just about correctly reflecting a certain extraneous ontology, or about fitting into context. Rather, it shows that the very essence of truth involves relatedness to that to which the truth relates. There is no objective truth "in itself." Note that Gadamer does not omit to show that his theoretical knowledge of Plato is also transfigured into a practical understanding through his own "life experience."

78. "The Heritage of Hegel," in *Reason in the Age of Science*, 44.

79. The richness and simultaneous confusion yielded by the diversity of types of discourse in Platonic and Aristotelian philosophy is one of the underlying hermeneutical themes of Gadamer's *The Idea of the Good in Platonic-Aristotelian Philosophy*.

80. See "The Ethics and Value of Practical Philosophy," in *Hermeneutics, Religion, and Ethics*.

81. *Philosophical Apprenticeships*, 31.

82. *Philosophical Apprenticeships*, 28–29.

83. *Philosophical Apprenticeships*, 27–28.

84. *Philosophical Apprenticeships*, 31.

85. "Goethe and Philosophy," in *Literature and Philosophy in Dialogue: Essays on German Literary Theory*, 3.

86. "Goethe and Philosophy," in *Literature and Philosophy in Dialogue: Essays on German Literary Theory*, 7.

87. Interestingly, Scheler makes reference to Buddhism around this period, to be found in his collected works on this subject.

88. *Hegel's Dialectic: Five Hermeneutical Studies*, 33.

89. *Philosophical Apprenticeships*, 9–10.

90. "Who Am I and Who Are You?" in *Gadamer on Celan: "Who Am I and Who Are You" and Other Essays*, 82.

91. J. M. Baker Jr., "Lyric as Paradigm: Hegel and the Speculative Instance of Poetry in Gadamer's Hermeneutics," in *The Cambridge Companion to Gadamer* (New York: Cambridge University Press, 2002), 149.

92. Stanley Rosen, "Are we such stuff as dreams are made on? On Reductionism," in *Gadamer's Century: Essays in Honour of Hans-Georg Gadamer*, 263.

93. "On the Scope and Function of Hermeneutical Reflection," in *Philosophical Hermeneutics*, 19.

94. See *Gadamer on Celan: "Who Am I and Who Are You?" and Other Essays*, 83.

95. *Gadamer on Celan: "Who Am I and Who Are You?" and Other Essays*, 82.

96. Hans-Georg Gadamer, *The Relevance of the Beautiful and Other Essays*, trans. N. Walker, ed. R. Bernasconi (Cambridge: Cambridge University Press, 1986), 106.

97. *The Relevance of the Beautiful*, 115.

98. *The Relevance of the Beautiful*, 112.

99. *The Relevance of the Beautiful*, 112.

100. *Truth and Method*, 104.

101. Hans-Georg Gadamer, "Mythopoetic Inversion in Rilke's *Duino Elegies*," in *Hermeneutics Versus Science*, ed. Gadamer, Stegmuller, and Specht (Notre Dame, Ind.: University of Notre Dame Press, 1988), 83–84.

102. *Gadamer on Celan: "Who Am I and Who Are You?" and Other Essays*, 125–26.

103. *Gadamer on Celan: "Who Am I and Who Are You?" and Other Essays*, 130.

104. *Gadamer on Celan: "Who Am I and Who Are You?" and Other Essays*, 8.

105. *Jetzt war es Zeit, das Gotter traten/aus bewohnten Dingen*, Rilke (*Insel* ed. II, 185).

106. In conversation with Alfons Grieder in *Gadamer in Conversation*, 113.

107. *Philosophical Hermeneutics*, 181.

108. See "Logos and Ergon in Plato's *Lysis*," in *Dialogue and Dialectic: Eight Hermeneutical Studies on Plato*, 18.

II

RŪPA GOSVĀMI'S REALISMS

Part II—Introduction

Rūpa Gosvāmi's Realisms

Bhaktānāṃ hṛdi rājantī saṃskārayugalojjvalā
ratirānandarūpaiva nīyamānā tu rasyatām[1]
Passion, which governs in the heart of devotees as paired sacraments joining [us] to the luminous [Krishna], has bliss as its true form, leading us to dwell in rasa.
or:
Passion, shining in the mind of devotees, manifested as past and present sense-impressions, has bliss itself as its true form, defining religious feeling/defining enjoyment/leading to a state of aesthetic pleasure/leading to a gratifying state of fluidity.[2]

Rādhā: Enough with these jokes! You are all very lucky because you can, without pausing, drink the wonderful nectar of Krishna with your eyes again and again. Because I have not performed even the slightest pious action, it is very difficult for me to even hear about Krishna.

Kuṇḍalāta: Rādhā, your words are like the thirst of someone who is drowning in an ocean of nectar.[3]

Part II explores a sixteenth-century North Indian Hindu devotional alternative to Gadamer's "formal" ontology and his eudaimonian "vitalist" ethics. It will seek to put Rūpa Gosvāmi's views into their historical and intellectual context, and show the vital relevance of his ideas to underlying questions about reality and ethics. The sixteenth century was a time of great dialogue and cultural growth in India. It was a period that inherited the sophisticated philosophical treatises of great Vedantic thinkers such as Śaṃkara,[4] Rāmānuja,[5] and Madhva,[6] as well as polymaths such as Abhinavagupta, and saw the issues that they addressed brought into vibrant new arenas of debate by new thinkers such as Vallabha[7] and the Gosvāmis, who reworked them under the vibrant influence of a culture that was growing ever more religiously diverse and syncretic. Many contemporary sects and theologies, blending art and aesthetics, religious practice, and ecstatic possession with philosophy, were aimed at restoring popular engagement to Indian religiosity. It is almost impossible to determine the precise beginnings of the popular devotional form of predominantly Hindu religion known as *bhakti,* but the title is used now as then for a constellation of approaches which tended to prioritise the particularism of the divine in its form as "God" (Īśvara), which in the self-designated "Vedantic" forms channelled this personalism into a practice of complete absorption in the divine identity, and in the "emotional bhakti" forms sought to inspire a strong emotional feeling in the devotee. In some schools this involved eliding the distinction between the human and divine identity in some way, whether through philosophical realisation, metaphysical union, role-play, possession, or other nuanced senses of participation in the divine—the word *bhakti* deriving from the Sankrit root *bhaj*, meaning "to share in" or "be part of." Bhakti is often characterised by a focus on the arts as media for worship, and certainly in the powerful poetry that was produced one finds a literature that frames strong emotions in intensely evocative ways, often, as we will see, commenting with great self-awareness on their own emotive aims.

The notion of bhakti as an affective devotional movement that stands in contrast with the renunciatory asceticism, pragmatic ritual, and dry philosophy of an earlier period has been fruitfully problematised as a sample of Western wishful thinking and modern Hindu revisionist propaganda, by scholars from Biardeau[8] to Prentiss[9] and more recently Jack Hawley, a scholar who had brought some of its most florid and distinctive literary products to a wide audience.[10] The result is that, as when the myth of an Aryan "invasion" was downsized into the more modest proposal of a possible long-term Aryan immigration, so we must see the "bhakti movement" as the gradual, dispersed development of a family of characteristics that did indeed gather pace at certain periods of heightened activity, but were as much marked by fluidity, syncretism, and creative variation as by the traits of a unified identity. Yet that very creative diversity was part of what continued to be seen as a fresh and vibrant religious alternative that broke social barriers (in theory at least) and demanded ecstatic enthusiasm.

Thus Rūpa Gosvāmi himself writes in his treatise on the theory and practice of cultivating religious emotions, that "those who are burned out by worthless asceticism, those who possess dry knowledge, the logicians and especially the Mīmāṃsākas [broadly pragmatist philosophers of language concerned with the correct actions proceeding from injunctive discourse] are all incapable of experiencing devotion."[11] His heroes and heroines, like those of most North Indian poets, were all distinguished by their soft hearts and emotional sensitivity, often eliciting jealous looks from the yogis and ascetics who strove with such self-denying difficulty to achieve the kind of mental focus that these passionate devotees achieved at the mere reminder of their god. Asked about the flourishing of bhakti in India (by an interlocutor who stood within a Hindu movement that sought to use Rūpa Gosvāmi's conception of bhakti to reinvigorate Western religiosity), Shrivatsa Gosvāmi cites the account that Bhakti, personified as a young woman, gave of herself in the *Devī Mahātmya*. Bhakti says:

> I was born in the Draviḍa land and grew up to maturity in Karṇāṭaka. At some places in Māhārṣṭra I was respected, but after coming to Gujarat I became old and decrepit. . . . I was subject to live in that stage for a long time and I became weak and sluggish. . . . But after reaching Vṛndāvana I became rejuvenated, and endowed with enviable beauty.[12]

Here we find the emergent voice of a self-designating "bhakti" religiosity that, in both its ancient and modern, Indian and Western forms, has seen itself as an organ of regeneration.

But what is often missing from this picture, prevalent both then and now, of bhakti as a burst of religious enthusiasm is the degree to which it was also a rationally synthesising influence and a tool of reflection. In his introduction to the topic of "Hindu theology and philosophy," Gavin Flood writes that "[w]hile there are undoubted similarities between traditional Hindu thinking and modern Western philosophy, what traditional Hindu thinkers do would only be partially recognised in contemporary departments of philosophy in western universities."[13] Of course the same is true of the philosophy done in many periods of "Western" philosophy, and indeed of the different brands of philosophies currently done on neighbouring continents. What is rarely affirmed is that unexpected discourses and techniques are used to engage with philosophical questions in a wide range of texts—furthering the debate. Thus the development of bhakti was not only a religious renewal aimed at what Heidegger called "the true task of theology, which must be discovered once again, to seek the word that is able to call one to faith," but also a philosophical project that sought to "preserve one in faith."[14] By these lights Rūpa was part of a very well established tradition of what Lipner succinctly calls "philosophical theologians."[15] But it is important to keep in mind that while the prevailing view is that "[i]t was no virtue to be seen 'doing theology in an original way,'" it was also true that thinkers who could provide new answers to ongoing debates, or make new appeals to aspects of experience, religious and otherwise, naturally attracted support and favour—this is a basic principle of intracultural historical competition that is not to be controverted by any degree of reverence for the tradition.[16] Indeed, Gadamer's summary of Hegel also throws light on this geographically distant case, reminding us that for Rūpa Gosvāmi as for Hegel, "determined as he was by [contemporary] circumstances, found his own philosophical endeavour confronted with a problem precisely the opposite of that which the Ancients faced. His concern was to 'make fluid' the fixed suppositions of the Understanding, 'to infuse them with Spirit.'"[17] While Rūpa Gosvāmi, like Gadamer, has received little hermeneutic attention to his more metaphysical concerns, he too was an optimist who sought to bring practical and theoretical clarity to the work of a charismatic teacher, using the resources of past authorities. He too is a thinker who synthesises and redefines our disciplinary, metaphysical, and religious categories.

Chapter 4 will give an introductory review of the "realist debate" in the Indian philosophical context. Chapter 5 will explore the implicitly "realist" dimensions of Rūpa Gosvāmi's Caitanya Vaiṣṇava, neo-Sāṃkhya, neo-Vedāntic and neo-purāṇic metaphysics. Finally, chapter 6 will explore his eudaimonian ethos, replacing Gadamer's vital engagement with an uncompromising passion that seeks to bring the individual into accordance with the infinitely dialectical nature of Being.

NOTES

1. *Bhaktirasāmṛtasindhu*, Southern Section, 1.9.

2. The meanings for the sentence are hugely enriched by the possible translations of *rasa*, based here both on Caitanya Vaiṣṇava theological interpretations and on the range of commonplace connotations of the word.

3. *Lalita Mādhava*, 2.2.

4. Śaṃkara's traditional dates are 788–820 CE.

5. Rāmānuja's traditional dates are 1017–1157 CE.

6. Madhva's exact dates are not known but are believed to be circa thirteenth century CE.

7. Vallabha's dates are usually cited as being 1479–1531, making him a direct contemporary of Rūpa Gosvāmi.

8. Madeleine Biardeau, *Hinduism: The Anthropology of a Civilisation*, Richard Nice, trans. (New Delhi: Oxford University Press, 1989).

9. Karen Pechilis Prentiss, *The Embodiment of Bhakti* (New York: Oxford University Press, 1999).

10. John Stratton Hawley is currently working on a project to explore the ways in which a conception of a "bhakti" movement was constructed and why—the implication being that a degree of anti-colonial (whether Muslim or Hindu) sentiment was involved. Yet he himself has repeatedly illuminated the ways in which key religious and philosophical figures have framed their own identities and ideas within an explicit understanding of bhakti as a traditional as well as a mode of religion (see his discussions of saints such as Ravidas in his *Songs of the Saints of India* (New York: Oxford University Press, 1988)).

11. Rūpa Gosvāmi, *Bhaktirasamrtasindhu* v. 129–30, translated by David Haberman in "A Selection from the Bhaktirasamrtasindhu of Rupa Gosvamin: The Foundational Emotions (Sthayibhavas)," in *Krishna: A Sourcebook* (New York: Oxford University Press, 2007), 431–32.

12. Shrivatsa Gosvāmi in *Hare Krishna, Hare Krishna: Five Distinguished Scholars on the Krishna Movement in the West*, Steven J. Gelberg, ed. (New York: Grove Press Inc., 1983), 211.

13. Gavin Flood, *An Introduction to Hinduism* (Cambridge: Cambridge University Press, 1996), 224.

14. "Martin Heidegger and Marburg Theology," in *Philosophical Hermeneutics*, 198.

15. Julius Lipner, *The Face of Truth: A Study of Meaning and Metaphysics in the Vedāntic Theology of Rāmānuja* (Hong Kong: State University of New York Press, 1986), 1.

16. Lipner, *The Face of Truth: A Study of Meaning and Metaphysics in the Vedāntic Theology of Rāmānuja*, 3.

17. *Hegel's Dialectic: Five Hermeneutical Studies*, 31.

Chapter 4

The Realist Debate in Indian Philosophy

While it is true that "the realistic systems of Indian Philosophy have generally received less attention than they deserve," it remains helpful to explore what is meant by such "realistic systems" in the Indian context.[1] The epithet "realist" has been diversely defined and variously applied to many doctrines within the major schools of Indian philosophical thought and to those that lie between and across their boundaries.[2] In mapping out the terrain of Indian classical debates about what is ultimately real and what soteriological significance it has, this introductory chapter will attempt to bring to light the issues that underpin and define Indian realism from within, rather than attempting a simplistic translation of the term from its Western particularities into the Indian idiom. By triangulating the defining issues of inquiry into the nature of reality in each tradition, it is possible to build a bridge between Indian and Western metaphysical "realisms"—not through strict categorisation, but through an understanding of the conceptual tensions and aporias that create the different realist debates. Such issues include the practical problem of falsity, our ideals of ontological ultimacy and ontological foundation, the possibility (or impossibility) of radical scepticism, and philosophy's faculty for self-interrogation of its methods, assumptions, and goals.

Naturally, these questions take on a very particular hue in the light that illuminates the Indian arena of debate. It is an arena in which, arguably, dualistic substantialist models, such as that so roundly criticised by the Heideggerian tradition, found little foothold because monistic cosmogonies predominated in early Indian mythology; *creation ex nihilo* is almost nowhere to be seen. The rigorous application of logical processes of reasoning from the earliest periods of Indian philosophising helped to realise the implications of that primeval picture. We will see that *ex nihilo* dualism was not the main "world picture" presiding throughout the complex defence and denial of Indian metaphysical debate. These other views paved the way for Rūpa Gosvāmi's extraordinary synthesis of metaphysics with aesthetics, poetry, practical theology, and his own portrayal of what he saw to be the heart of religious belief. Thus the chapter will conclude by following the threads of this debate through the interweaving of religious ideas in the purāṇic literature and into the texts of Rūpa Gosvāmi, a young emigrant scholar of South Indian origin, preparing to take leave of the sophisticated Muslim courts of sixteenth-century Bengal for the fresh territory of Uttar Pradesh in Northern India.

THE CRITICAL DIMENSION OF INDIAN PHILOSOPHY

Hindu philosophy has too often been portrayed as the paradigmatic opposite of Western secular reason: a tradition with a tendency to submit to the dictates of orthodox religion, free of the self-critical, radical questioning of foundations that punctuates the movement of Western philosophical thought. In his introduction to Guha's exposition of the Navya-Nyāya school, Ingalls tells an anecdote in which a Western philosopher pronounces that Indian philosophy "always leads to a religious or mystical goal, which is all very fine, I daresay, but it is not what I call philosophy."[3] In a 1997 volume dedicated to Bimal Matilal, J. N. Mohanty traces the same extraordinary attitude back to Hegel: "[A]s Hegel bluntly put it, the Indians did not *think*, they did not raise their intuitions to concepts, so how could they have philosophy?"[4] These tales illustrate the common misconception about Indian philosophy that contemporary scholars have so often felt a need to refute. In addition the conscientious scholar of Indian thought must struggle with the debilitating simplifications made by the "present-day critic who is fond of applying to it sweeping epithets."[5] Such critics are often influenced by what Ingalls calls the "cultural 'tourist trade'" of which Indian studies consisted at an early stage, in which translations of Indian *religious* texts predominated, rather than those following a more explicitly rigorous method of *philosophical* inquiry. The popular notion of Indian philosophy often retains this bias, influencing its perception within Western academic disciplines. In support of the "dogmatic" image of Indian philosophy, one may point to various factors that set authoritative controls on the development of ideas over time: the *gurūparamparā*—the lineages of teachers that oversaw the transmission of doctrine—the presumed "complete indifference of the ancient Indians towards personal histories" (another conclusion based on the corporate and oral authorship of many *religious* texts), and the hermeneutic continuity supposedly entailed by the commentarial method of writing.[6] An uncritical coherence can appear in this way to be preserved and fossilised, far from the Copernican revolutions that are thought to characterise modern Western thought. These crude cultural stereotypes of "Asian" thought introduced by thinkers such as Vico and Hegel remain influential, and one observes many patterns of Orientalist prejudice (academic and social) vested in the proverbial continuity and uncritical religious optimism of Indian thought.

In this light, it is *complexity* that scholarly rhetoric has combined with prejudice to obscure in the Indian philosophical context, although that same complexity is so widely recognised among the Indian languages and histories, sects and arts. It is only more recently that sensitive scholars have come to recognise the "richness and variety" of Indian thought, of which, conversely, it is said, "[T]here is practically no shade of speculation that it does not include."[7] It is illuminating to realise that where the Western tradition opposed a strongly predominant theistic tradition with a marginalized classical "pagan" or Spinozistic "pantheist" unorthodoxy, and another demonised non-Christian unorthodoxy of (philosophically very similar) Semitic theisms, India effortlessly balanced at least six different traditions (the *ṣaḍ darśanas*) in its formative "classical" stage that we would now call broadly "Hindu" (Vedānta, Sāṃkhya, Yoga, Nyāya, Vaiśeṣika, Mīmāṃsā,), with at least four different thriving unorthodox schools (Cārvāka materialism, Buddhism, Jainism, and the sceptics). Many more schools within each of these traditions would follow in the millennia to come.[8] The dissenting tones of the schools who departed from the orthodox sphere of social brahmanism around the time of the Buddha, explored a wide range of views in a way that is intensely reminiscent of the early Greeks.[9] The unorthodox schools in particular—the Buddhists, the Jains, the materialists and the sceptics (who refused even to refute other views, so wary were they of the claims made through philosophical reasoning)—yielded enormous fruits for the intellectual clarity and richness of the others. Noting in reference to Advaita what has been observed about almost every Indian school in relation to Buddhism's "liberal and catholic" character,[10] King writes that "no system of thought can be completely autonomous and it is important to recognise that in India, as much as anywhere else, the dynamic interplay between differing religious and philosophical traditions is a major factor in the development of any system of thought."[11] By contrast with the monolithic cultural caricatures of Western thought sketched by so many historians of religion from Vico down to the present day, the Indian contemporary philosopher may justifiably complain to his colleagues "we have completely forgotten that we are Aryans and Dasas mixed, and we have only 'Prasthanas' or 'Panthas' but no religion."[12]

Of course, any writer faces a difficult task in "introducing" a tradition to a reader who has few prior points of orientation for understanding it, and with so many traditions running parallel the problem is amplified. M. Hiriyanna laments of Indian philosophical views that "the history of so unique a development, if it could be written in full, would be of immense value; but our knowledge at present of early India . . . is too meagre and imperfect for it. Not only can we not trace the growth of single philosophic ideas step by step; we are sometimes unable to determine the relation even between one system and another."[13] Prejudicial views are often instinctive to the academic who is ill equipped to respond to this "looseness of perspective."[14] Every scholar in the field knows only too well that Indian studies is an exercise in shepherding richly complex information. The challenge to the modern scholar is to find ways of making sense of this complexity by staking out flags for revealing deep structures of deeper meaning. A conscientious and minute comparative philosophical method has great potential for achieving precisely this task of navigation.

Far from the staid transmission of ideas from guru to pupil, text to ur-text, the tradition can be seen as a hugely vigorous forum of "systems in endless dialogue amongst themselves."[15] Matilal describes Indian philosophy as "the result of an intellectual climate pervaded by public discussions, debates, arguments and counter arguments."[16] Here, as in Athens, scholars sat before both their teachers and their opponents, benefiting from a warm climate in which to circulate freely and debate fervently in an arena of formalised competition on matters touching both truth and ethics. Here too, to speak was both to refute one perspective and to assimilate another—and sometimes to do both in respect of one and the same position. Here too, thinkers vied for the sympathies of the audience and had to counter consequent threats of sophism. Here too, ideas could be adopted, elaborated upon, and overturned within a single exposition. The dialectical path from the ideas of the imaginary opponent (the *pūrva-pakṣin*, reminiscent of Plato's convenient interlocutor) to the newly established truth or conclusory *Siddhānta* involved critical organs of thought that were no less sophisticated in India than in the West.[17]

A seemingly self-evident point, this is rarely fully recognised by either Indian or Western academic sources. Often too, it is a historical truth that gets muddled within the defences or denials of academic apologetics. Thus J. N. Mohanty writes:

> Philosophising in the Indian tradition was fundamentally hermeneutical when you consider each system of philosophy separately. Each such system thought and questioned from within a conceptually defined tradition, and not in an open logical space.

This is a valid observation, yet it does not single Indian philosophy out as itself any more tradition-bound than its Western equivalent; it is a valid criticism of philosophy in general. Realising this, Mohanty adds with belated caution:

> (How open this space can be, and whether Greek questioning took place within an open space, not delimited by any conceptual framework, are questions I will not ask for my present purpose.)[18]

The misconception is that a tradition proceeding by exegetic commentary must be innately, methodologically orthodox in a manner that outweighs the intra- and intertradition context of dialogue that shaped that very hermeneutical method of reasoning. The idea of philosophers affirming, exploring, and refining their authorities is common to both traditions, and an implicit feature of the ceaseless revisionism attributed to Western thought. Thus, the deference that is evident in Heidegger and Derrida's writings on Husserl, and in Gadamer's writings on Heidegger. Gadamer's integration and philosophical sifting of his predecessors and contemporaries into his own system of thought is happily explicit—as we have noted, the hermeneutic history of philosophy is his chosen *modus operandi*. As this chapter and the brief biography beginning the next chapter will show, Rūpa Gosvāmi not only incorporated the work of his predecessors within the philosophical and Vaiṣṇava devotional traditions, as shown by the textual references woven throughout his major works, he also explicitly courted dialogue and friendly debate, harvesting the best insights of contemporary debate on reality and its translation into ethical terms. As we will see, the contemporary debates, resulting largely from the juxtaposition of resurgences in Advaita Vedāntic ideas, the re-presentation of Sāṃkhya in seminal purāṇic texts, and Nyāya logic, combined within the process of devotional apologetic, resulted in deft treatment of some of the extreme subtleties of the question of Being.

SPIRITUALITY VERSUS RATIONALITY

One of the most persistent forms that academic prejudice toward Indian philosophy has taken is as a frequent and longstanding overcharacterisation of all Indian thought as a "unique spiritualistic cultural pattern."[19] Again, we can observe twentieth-century Indian philosophers combating this idea by way of apology, defence, or lampoon in innumerable introductions:

> [T]he very name of Indian Philosophy has sometimes been denied to Indian speculation on the ground, apparently established historically, that the Oriental intellect is not sufficiently dry and has not masculine virility enough to rise to anything higher than grotesque imaginative cosmogonies.[20]

In 1922, while staking out his own meticulous and carefully considered markers for an understanding of Indian philosophy, S. Dasgupta complained that "there are some people who think that the Indians never rose beyond the stage of simple faith," quoting Cornell Professor Frank Thilly's judgement that "the theories of Oriental peoples, the Hindus . . . are not thoroughgoing systems of thought: they are shot through with poetry and faith."[21] Caitanya himself (1486–1533), the founder of the Caitanya Vaiṣṇava movement of which Rūpa Gosvāmi was a leading member, was a figure noted for an ecstatic emotionalism that won popular converts, as well as for extensive theological debates that won scholarly converts. Caitanya attracted the following criticism by M. T. Kennedy:

> Not only did his absorption in bhakti leave no time or energy for the life of scholarship, but—what is far more to the point—the increasing strain of an impossible emotionalism upon a highly-wrought nervous system, made serious intellectual effort quite out of the question as the years went on. His whole mode of life was against his being a thinker.[22]

Modern views have moved on considerably from such prejudices, yet the task of redressing them remains. While part I of the present inquiry has sought to show how the West can yield a metaphysics "shot through with poetry and faith," one task of this introduction is to show the degree to which Indian philosophy need not be.

While few have commented extensively on the self-perceived goals of the philosophical tradition itself, the reality is that many Indian thinkers quite explicitly recognised that rational methodologies (including Nyāya logic and the practical sciences of the *śāstras*) had not only spiritual goals (*mokṣa*), but also ethical (*dharma*), material (*artha*) and hedonistic (*kāma*) ones.[23] This notion of philosophy corresponded to *anvīkṣā*, reason as a critical sharpening of those sciences intended to provide a foundation for right action. In this sense the *darśanas* (the major schools of philosophical thought) did indeed function as pragmatic tools belying a *phronetic* notion of reason, not itself to be engaged in determining the foregoing ethical questions of virtue and purpose. Ravi Gupta makes the same observation in respect of Rūpa Gosvāmi's teacher Caitanya, in the way that he opposed the emotional goals of bhakti to the dry intellectualism of his Advaita opponents.[24] Indeed, in Caitanya's case, he argues that it was less by philosophical argument that he won them over to his view, and more through the compelling force of his devotional priorities. Reason was forced to review its goals. On this model of philosophy, advocated in mainstream texts such as the *Mahābharata*, the *artha*—here used in its meaning as "purpose, goal, aim," or even more widely as "topic, subject matter, teleology"—could be many things for many thinkers.[25] Hence, just as we are so often blind to our own foundations but will easily spot where others' presuppositions lie, Indian philosophy is seen to be practical in its processes, and dogmatic at its core—as if Western philosophy were not. Chandradhar Sharma, combining both philosophical and comparative goals, characterises Western philosophy as a search for truth, while describing Indian philosophy as, by contrast, "intensely spiritual" and "practical." It is not that he is wrong, but rather that we are conflating an extreme level of methodological commitment to the formal processes of conceptual analysis (Western "reason"), with the search for "truth" that a degree of hermeneutic sensitivity shows to be innately bound up with practical methods and "spiritual" concerns.[26] From this perspective no philosophical realism could hope to be "neutral"—it would be expected to incorporate underlying decisions about worldviews, values, and ethics.

The Advaitins, as so often happens, are held up as a paradigmatic model for Indian philosophy, in exemplifying the supposed subordination of reason to religion. Yet neither Nyāya, nor Vaiśeṣika, nor Sāṃkhya philosophy appears to have been explicitly religious in their earliest stages, during which they explored logic, physics, and metaphysics and primarily left explicitly *religious* metaphysical postulates to the Mīmāṃsā and Advaitins alone. The eventual mixture of these many positions into diverse combinations shows how the wide forum of different views emerging in direct conversation and competition with each other acted as a natural organ of ideological self-reflection. As Gadamer is famous for having shown, dialogue automatically helps us to interrogate and develop our foundational views, bringing the notion of foundation itself into question. Indeed, the method of exegetical reasoning adopted by many philosophers, like Plato's dialogues, incorporated the critique of the *pūrva-pakṣin*—the opposing view—into its own perspicuous processes of self-definition. This has become the main source for much of our knowledge of unorthodox schools such as that of the materialists, which posed a radical challenge to the metaphysical and ethical assumptions of orthodox Hinduism.[27] Buddhism in particular acted as a dialogue partner for most of the classical Hindu schools at some point in the course of their development, its ideological challenges continuing into the second millennium through the assimilation of Buddhist-Hindu debates to Advaitic thought, and metaphysical speculation in general.[28] Buddhist philosophers seemed to demonstrate the application of certain "control," or "foundational" questions with such a degree of rigour that it led to what some saw as a nihilistic extreme in which all certainties and essences are undermined by universal groundlessness. Yet for those engaged in the explication or systematisation of any tradition it retained a problematic, compelling rational consistency. As a response to this methodological rigour, other schools often considered the Buddhist and atheistic thinkers to be excessively rationalistic—a trait that was clearly judged by many orthodox texts, such as the *Laws of Manu*, to be unhealthy.[29] Ganeri cites

Rāma's own warning to his brother to steer clear of rationalist Brahmins who are "lokayata"—a term that literally means worldly but also may have been used at that time, as later, to refer to the materialist school, otherwise known as the Cārvākas.

Contrary to the image of Indian reasoning as a purely applied, practical science that is uncontroversially harnessed to dogma, this warning indicates that the Indian field of philosophical debate also featured a dichotomy between emotional and unemotional religion. Reason was contrasted with devotional charisma. The opposition of the *sahṛdaya*—the one with the sympathetic heart/imagination—with the reasoner—the *haituka*—would later be shifted to a polar contrast between the *sahṛdaya* and the one who seeks *mokṣa*, detachment and liberation from such sympathies. In either case the passions were seen as controversial, needing to be defended both from the apparent authority of systematic reason, and from the religious trend toward detachment that was advocated, not least, in the *Bhāgavad Gīta* itself. Rūpa Gosvāmi himself can be cited, alongside Caitanya, as a proponent of this divide and the caution that it necessitates: he lauds the highest goal of *uttama bhakti* as "empty of all other desires and unobscured by jñāna (rationality) and karma (self-interested actions)."[30] He is very sensitive to the potential power struggle between the logic of rational assessment, and the logic of desires and prejudicial concerns. Nevertheless, as Ganeri assures us, many schools sought to synthesise aspects of both poles; the division between sentiment and reason is not abyssal, but rather acts as a rhetorical reminder to keep the right goals in mind behind all one's actions. While Gadamer is one of the thinkers in the contemporary West who has pressed this point again and again to an audience that tends to resist the influence of the passions, Rūpa Gosvāmi was one of those many philosophically sensitive thinkers of his generation who was led to combine religious and philosophical modes of reasoning in sophisticated ways.

The great danger to be avoided was that reason should be "goalless, capricious, ungrounded," "an end in itself," rather than, as Kauṭilya suggests, a lamp for the other sciences.[31] Thus the fears for the unrestricted application of reason, are moderated by reason's eventual entry into each tradition mediated by the "theologians," whether to the centre of the tradition's self-understanding, or to its margins. In the Gauḍīya Vaiṣṇava tradition, as we will see, the synthesis of passion and reason was a central dynamic in the self-determination of the movement as a philosophically refined branch of bhakti. Reason was generally considered to be a great tool, championed by the Naiyāyikas and honed by the Buddhists, adopted by the theologians, but one about which we fool ourselves if we believe that it can indicate either the origins or the goals of life.

Thus, while there is a crude equivalence between Aristotle's concept of *phronesis* and the notion of philosophy as a tool harnessed to a certain *artha* in Indian thought, the question of emotional and objective, "hot" and "cool" uses of reason is another axis of debate, dissecting the first. It includes a reflection on the place of careful thought in the project of our lives, and the question of when we should let it give way to the passions. Here, we will see that Rūpa Gosvāmi addresses issues in the hermeneutics of rational and realist reasoning that Gadamer is circumspect about—the degree to which our critical faculty is bounded by the emotional depth of the "prejudices" that lead us to choose certain games and goals. To some extent, the main way in which Rūpa Gosvāmi surpasses Gadamer in his philosophical sophistication and his usefulness for understanding stronger forms of realist religious belief is in his willingness to admit the foundationally thoroughgoing character of the prejudicial passions that constitute our ontological reality and shape our phenomenological realities. Gadamer shows that life involves a necessary and desirable shift from goal to goal. Rūpa Gosvāmi asks what this says about the depth of the passions that dictate our starting point. In chapters 5 and 6 we will see that Rūpa Gosvāmi touches on issues that are well formulated in Hegel's language of dialectic. If the being of the individual is itself a dialectical route through diversity, to what extent can our defining passions-prejudices represent a consistent trajectory or repeated commitment running through that route, and to what extent should they do so? Gadamer gives little attention to consistency and long-term, pervasive prejudices. He is not interested in the psychology through which we are bound by passions and engage in a complex interplay of choices based on them. He does not follow through the tenuous importance that prejudices have in defining us and is perhaps too ready to portray us as Odyssean wanderers from island to island, never really seeking to stay on new territory but only to return home to our own confirmed identities. This part seeks to locate discussion of reality within a cultural context in which passion, motivation, and the goals of selfhood have a wider scope of interpretation and importance.

Yet it is important to note that, just as we must read the "philosophical" works of Plato in the right tone (political, anti-sophistical, dialogical, sometimes historical and sometimes literary), or must read Aristotle with a sensitivity to the context of his writing (natural sciences, public morals), so too we must read Indian philosophy in the right way without imposing onto it the Enlightenment's notion of an isolated, objective, self-reflective apotheosis of knowledge for knowledge's sake. Indian rationality has also had its own crisis of identity, and reached its own (multiple) conclusions about the proper place of reason, and the passions and authorities that guide it.

ANALYSING REALITY IN INDIA

This prior understanding of the identities and tasks that Indian philosophy has set itself is important for a redefinition of realism in ways that will accommodate not only the range of Western but also of Indian metaphysics. This need is reinforced by the disparate and provisional treatments that have necessarily resulted from attempts to fit a Western dualist model of realism into the Indian arena of debate. One always finds that the categories of analysis do not quite fit the Indian field, and even a cursory glance into any of the major *darśanas* reveals the degree to which they ask the question of Being in a way that is quite distinct from their mainstream Western cousins.

Arvind Sharma begins his introduction to "Classical Hindu Thought" with an approach by which he hopes to bypass these problems. He presents a single concept as the key to understanding the notions of what is ultimately real in the many-stranded system of Indian thought:

> Just as Yahweh is the one ultimate reality in Judaism, God in Christianity, Allah in Islam, Nirvāṇa in Theravada Buddhism, the Buddha in Mahāyana Buddhism, heaven in Confucianism and Tao in Taoism, Brahman is the one ultimate reality in Hinduism.[32]

Immediately this strikes one as the kind of crude analogy that has given comparative study of religion a bad name. It raises innumerable questions about the parity of these ideas, and Sharma commits the common mistake of reducing the many Hindu traditions to Vedānta, which is but one of the major orthodox schools, and to Advaita Vedānta at that.[33] Yet any intuitive validity that the analogy possesses is based on the two qualifiers: "ultimate" and "real." In each of the examples given, the sense in which it is ultimately real is distinctly different from the others, or questionably imposed from an ontological perspective onto theologies that are otherwise primarily narrative or ethical. The God of the Hebrew Bible is not God because he is more "real" than the world, but because he is God, the Creator and maker of the covenant. Heaven may be better and longer lasting, but not necessarily more real. Sharma imports the philosophical self-understanding of Advaita Vedānta in its search for the most highly unified and most absolute reality into unphilosophical territory. In each of the examples this yields a different way of calculating what is "most real" relative to a particular set of governing values: ideas of illusion for instance, or notions of ontological emanation, of final human ends, or of degree of ethical importance. But with a practical eye for the phenomenological facts of how we do the philosophy of religion, Sharma gives a working definition for his approach, anecdotally sketching out the basic principle of reasoning that yields this "ultimacy" in each case. He writes:

> Just as one might first see the grass and the flowers in a garden, and then, raising one's vision, see the trees and then, moving further, see the clouds and the sky and the space that seems to extend far beyond it and then conclude, as a result, that there is nothing beyond space; similarly, with regard to the ultimate reality one may go on ascending to higher and higher orders of reality till one comes to a stop.[34]

This is not a mereological "part-whole" process of reasoning but a related method of reasoning toward the "highest" that proceeds by applying a given mechanism of analysis—determined by the underlying value system (most real, most powerful, causally first, most soteriologically important)—again and again until the innate limitations of the analytic procedure itself brings that process to an end. There it finds what is "ultimate," although the curious transparency of the reasoning process may cause the thinker to forget that this ultimacy is merely a function of the framework of truth and value applied by the reasoner.

What is revealed here is a self-governing internal structural principle, like those of mathematics and logic, which describes the process of rule-defined reiterative reasoning that governs "ultimacy" in any context. It is not about any particular content, but about the meta-structures that are necessary to content itself. At the recent end of the Western tradition, we have seen how Gadamer affirms finitude as a limiting, defining, constitutive, and enabling condition of the "real" world itself, and he arrives at this conclusion through just such a process of progressive analysis as Sharma implies. But Gadamer seeks a transcendental analysis (what is intrinsically necessary), whereas the reasoning here is toward universality. Even the famously anti-essentialist conclusions of Buddhist thinkers through the centuries, various in kind, have also proceeded by this same reasoning ("what is universal and certain?": "changefulness and uncertainty")—or have struggled to understand how to escape it. To this extent, every metaphysics is a realist enterprise in the sense that I have outlined in the introduction: it chooses the criteria of a *truest* truth, formulates a reiterative, reductive method of testing for these criteria, and applies this process to determine what is "most real." Then it explains its position and advocates its prescription according to a global rationale founded in those prior choices about what is most "true." As the result of a comparative exercise in distinguishing "idealism" from "realism," P. T. Raju quotes J. S. Haldane in noting precisely this point:

> "Since philosophy is our ultimate interpretation of reality, every philosophy must claim to be realistic." Every philosophy . . . is a search for reality, and is therefore realism.[35]

One of Sharma's oversights is that, just as the concept of "God" defined as ultimate reality, has itself varied through Western history, so the intermarried Indian systems of thought present a wide range of ultimate reals. These many "most true" realities in the Indian schools of thought reflect various logics and criteria, and scholars have seemed to see a dizzying range of metaphysical models among them. Dasgupta devotes a whole book to Indian "idealism," as Sinha does to the elements of "realism" that he discerns amongst the *darśanas*.[36] The philosopher Madhva, with whom the Caitanya Vaiṣṇavas professed a certain sympathy, and who was himself engaged in vigorous refutation of radical non-dualism, has been called a "die-hard realist" in Vedāntic debates over this issue.[37] Throwing the usual categories into disarray, Hiriyanna decides that it is the earliest Theravada Buddhists who were "dualistic and realistic."[38] For Dravid it is the problem of the reality status of universals that best sheds light onto the questions of the most real, the true, the absolute, and he categorises the six major schools according to this seminal, transcultural, and transhistorical aporia of metaphysics.[39] Focusing instead on the problem of ontological foundations, Chandradhar Sharma classifies the schools quite succinctly (despite internal variation and dissent), into those which prioritise consciousness (Vedānta and Mahāyāna), and those which prioritise atomistic matter (Cārvāka, Nyāya, Vaiśeṣika, Mīmāṃsā, Jain, and Hīnayāna), and that school for which the motion and imbalance of forms (of *prakṛti*) is the first cause (Sāṃkhya).[40] This last school he classifies as "a spiritualistic pluralism and atheistic realism"; a designation to which we will return in looking at the substrate of Rūpa Gosvāmi's thought.[41]

Yet such distinctions are significantly elided by precisely the problem that we noted in chapter 1, of trying to apply categories derived from a dualistic substance ontology (e.g., realism, materialism, idealism, subjectivism, objectivism) to cultural systems that are not governed by that orientation, a process at which we will look more closely in the next chapters. All attempts to do justice to the mysterious relation of unity and plurality in structural descriptions of phenomenology, or accounts of identity in an ontology of radical flux, require translation as much as do the basic premises of metaphysics in the wake of Heidegger. This chapter seeks to outline some of the philosophical issues that form axes around which the long and rich dialectic of Indian realist debate turns, particularly as Rūpa Gosvāmi and his contemporaries engaged it. These are the paradigms for asking the question of Being that Rūpa Gosvāmi inherited in thinking about the ontological *value* and soteriological implications of those realities. At the end we must ask what is the nature of Hinduism's fundamental ontological optimism: How does it incorporate the epistemological scepticism of Buddhism—with its necessary recognition of finitude and flux—yet finally integrate these insights into a philosophy that affirms essence and the possibility of thinking about and deriving a prescriptive ethics from Being *as a whole*?

RŪPA GOSVĀMI'S REALIST HERITAGE

A glance at a Sanskrit dictionary, or into a dictionary of Indian philosophy, will reveal that even speaking of the real, or what "is," is a complex project of translation. There are the terms *bhava* and *bhāva*, both from the verbal root *bhū*, both implying the activity of being, becoming, and abiding. There is also the word *sattā*, connected with the notion of *sat*, existence as reality, and connected with *satya*, truth in the emphatic sense (polarised with falsehood) of "what *is* the case," having an ontological and veridical tone. To this affirmative character is added the implication of what is good and noble; one thinks of the conceptual synthesis found in Plato's *agathon*, the "Good."[42] There is also the concept of *astitā*, a particularly interesting term from the verbal root *as*, from which the common verb *asti*, "it is," is derived. For this, Apte gives the meanings: "To be, live, exist (showing mere existence) . . . used as a copula or verb of incomplete predication" and also "To arise, spring out, occur."[43] This sense includes not only the idea of living but also the features of happening and becoming.[44] In this flexible definition there is a sense of that Being that is in flux, while it also plays the transparent linguistic role of referring unreflectively to anything that occurs, that we think of, discuss, etc.[45] Hence the son of a barren woman, or a unicorn, has no *sattā*, but we might refer to it as something that exists in the sense of *astitā*, for *astitā* "belongs to all entities, positive and negative, particular and universal, permanent and changing."[46] *Sattā* and *bhāva*, by contrast, could not possibly belong to something as abstract as universal categories, by virtue of their purely analytical character and their non-particularity respectively.

One might say that *astitā* has a hermeneutic character (affirming all levels and kinds of being, making no ontological distinction between the internal and external referents of thought, its structures or its contents), while *sattā*, which unlike *astitā* admits of falsehood, tends to be used in objective philosophical discussion of what exists and whether it exists. Of these terms, *sattā* most reminds us of the objectified "Being" concept associated with scholastic substantialism. Yet it is also pertinent that *sattā*, in its relation to the concept *satya*—truth—also possesses an essentialist implication: *satya* can denote that which defines a thing, furnishing its identity relative to all other beings. Mohanty imaginatively connects this concept to Heidegger's ontological notion of truth as *aletheia*—the unconcealment and coming to being/light of things.[47] In *sattā*, then, we try to speak of that special defining character that each being has in the course of its *astitā*—*sattā* seeks definitions. Meanwhile, *bhāva* in turn refers us to the entities and beings of the phenomenological world of our actual experiences, bearing a stronger relation to the notion of a soul. As a topic or theme of philosophy, designated in doctrines and titles of treatises, one sees the term *tātparya* being used to designate reality, meaning that which *is*—inquiry into "what is so." From these categories alone, one sees that there are subtle sensitivities to the different definitions of Being facilitated within the very language; one thinks with sympathy of Heidegger's attempts to milk new ontological terminologies from his own native German. Already the Indian terminology admits of different levels of being, of its implied connection with truth and falsehood, of the fact that we may want to speak differently of what *is* in the largest sense, what is specifically true, and of the particular essence according to which each thing is. We see that any thinker working with this vocabulary will already in some sense have transcended a strictly dualistic ontology of thought and thing, for it is clear that thoughts and things both exist according to a still larger meaning of that word in which the hierarchies of types of being are subsumed. These distinctions are worked out in greater detail and implication through the philosophical problems to which these concepts have been applied over the millennia.

IDEALS OF ULTIMACY IN INDIAN PHILOSOPHICAL TRADITIONS

Much like that of the West, Indian philosophical thinking about reality is focused around axial aporias such as ontological foundationalism (i.e., questions of efficient causal origins or causal sovereignty), epistemological foundationalism (arguments toward various ideals of certainty), and the question of the relationship between forms of things and the fact and kind of Being's instantiation in a particular existent. Ultimacy is in one sense merely one of these themes, indicating the intuitive idea that reality has hierarchically layered multiple levels that the philosophical imagination can, as it were, ascend in order to discover that which is highest. This idea is innate in the everyday notions of truth and falsehood—a distinction indicating that something can exist as an idea without existing "in truth" as a circumstance that we encounter. Even here, fantasy and falsehood are the symptoms of a principle of hierarchical ontology that elsewhere can attain to a far more elaborate ontological architecture. In another sense, however, ultimacy is also a meta-theme of Indian philosophy. Throughout the different *darśanas* there runs a concern with what is *para*—that which goes furthest relative to any given insight or system. *Para* is a phrase linguistically associated with ideals of metaphysical ultimacy—*paramārthika*,[48] *paramānu*,[49] and often religious ultimacy—*paramavidya*,[50] *paramita*,[51] and *paramātman*.[52] It is often translated as "highest." Yet etymologically it means furthest, implying not a value judgement but the furthest extent of a continuum, whether spatial or conceptual, and in many cases it is still a phrase that merely denotes what is beyond something in particular, further than a given boundary.[53]

Insofar as we have defined realism as a search for the furthest truth in any given system, many descriptions of the ultimately real are to be found among the Indian *darśanas*, including notions of pure consciousness (*cit*), pure (potential or actuated) form (*prakṛti*), universal categories (*sāmānya* or *jāti*), irreducible atoms (*anu*), irreducible phenomenal "moments" (*dharmas*) or pure changefulness and impermanence. If the West struggles to voice and nurture three different metaphysics (of substance, mind, and form), then India has been explicit in its metaphysical pluralism of what the contemporary philosopher Bhattācārya calls "alternative absolutes."[54] Always painfully aware of this latent plurality of interpretation, the schools showed a concurrent concern with epistemological foundations. The notion of a *pramāṇa*, a valid authority for knowledge, and of the proper processes of reasoning were almost universally adopted from resurgent Nyāya methods of logic, to the extent that for certain thinkers scriptural revelation (*śruti*, referring to what is heard) was itself categorised as testimony (*śabda*, referring to what is said) and classed as standing, theoretically at least, on an even playing field with inference (*anumāna*) and perception (*pratyakṣa*). Such foundations laid the groundwork for each tradition's reiterative processes of "far, further, and furthest" truths. Buddhism and, in a more mitigated fashion, Sāṃkhya both focus on flux rather than stability in "things." Vedāntins, by contrast, whether more or less dualistic relative to each other, tend to prioritise the unity of Brahman, and its sovereign and simple *true* reality, as prized metaphysical qualities—ultimately resistant to fragmentation and change through metaphysical or cosmological processes. Nyāya sits close to Advaita in affirming the reality and value of universals, but uses analytical rigour to delve deeper into the ambiguous nature of unity *in the finite world* of particulars, forcing a recognition of the limitations to which unity is ultimately subject.[55]

One could arrange the notions of the ultimately real according to various hierarchies of ideals: in terms of universals for instance, from the radical flux of Buddhist *dharmas*, according to which universals are considered to be purely nominal, to the notion in Nyāya that existence itself is the highest universal, subsuming both universals and particulars in the same single reality, to the Vedāntin, who judges universals to be more real than particulars because more unified, finally to the Advaitin, who looks at this highest universal of "Being" and seeks to nudge it a step further into the transcendent ideal of Brahman. Just as it is possible to look at Sāṃkhya philosophy as an analysis of what it means for there to be a consciousness or substrate of what exists (*puruṣa*) and for it to be constituted by phenomenal forms (*prakṛti*), so one can interpret Brahman as an idea containing an implicit analysis of how we can talk about existence as a whole. Here we see that Sharma's basic model of reasoning about ultimate reality shows us how analogous notions of truth in diverse systems are generated. And here, as it does in the West, it raises the questions of *whether* we can speak of Being qua Being, either in microcosm in terms of essential constitution and universal properties, or in terms of its macrocosmic character.

THE "HERMENEUTIC FORK" IN INDIAN THOUGHT

It is precisely the instinctive Hindu concern with degrees and classifications of ultimacy that nascent Theravada Buddhism both exemplified in its rigorous analysis of causality, and simultaneously lampooned by branding the results of their inquiry with the names of corresponding Hindu concepts—*dharma, nirvāṇa, nāma-rūpa,* etc. Whereas the results of Buddhist philosophical enquiry purported to yield purely analytical transcendental truths about phenomenal reality, coupled with a profound denial of ontological essentialism, the terms that they appropriated had previously designated actual existences and essences, the positive fruits produced by similar processes of reasoning by thinkers with different underlying ideals. The given, largely unquestioned criterion for the most real throughout the tradition was that which is most permanent—and the general realisation of phenomenal impermanence (formulated in Platonic terms as plurality and motion), came early in the tradition and was never forgotten, remaining a fundamental axiom of the Hindu worldview today. In the sixteenth-century Bengal of Rūpa Gosvāmi's experience, renascent Buddhism reminded contemporary thinkers of the rigours and religious "dangers" of scepticism. Hiriyanna sees Buddhism as taking to their logical conclusions certain tendencies that define the outlook of the more monistic Upaniṣads (rather in the way that scepticism, nihilism, and deconstruction generally saw themselves as bringing the logic followed by tradition to its hitherto unacknowledged correct conclusion). The true reality of self (*ātman*) and of the whole of Being (*brahman*) is devoid of attributes and lies beyond change and particularity.[56] As in all "realist" soteriologies of the kind we are examining, including those of Gadamer and Rūpa Gosvāmi, the ultimate human aim is to realise both in thought and action, our true natures as part of Being as a whole.

Yet it is remarkable that in acknowledging these factors—the radical flux and finitude of the phenomenal world—Buddhism came to the conclusion that identity as previously defined in terms of permanent essence was an impossible and misleading fantasy. By contrast, the writers of the Upaniṣads and their later Vedāntic followers never lost their faith in a transcendent principle of self-identity at the heart of flux, and thus also pertaining to Being as a whole. The Buddhists and early Vedāntins took radically different directions from a very similar starting point. What is the nature of this divide, branded by Coward as "two distinct and exclusive patterns,"[57] so like

Wachterhauser's "hermeneutic fork" in Western philosophy, between their ontological pessimism and ontological optimism? We come again to the perennial difference between the Derridas and the Gadamers of history.

In the vast majority of Indian accounts, whether philosophical or mythological, creation arises as the division or outpouring of the First. Even for Rāmānuja and Madhva, some of the most stridently dualistic of Hindu theists, God is the *material* before he is the *efficient* cause of the universe. This premise is expressed through different images: God is not the potter of Semitic theism, but rather the clay. Rāmānuja uses the God-world analogy of a body and the one who dwells in it, while the Upaniṣads describe a spider spinning a web out of itself. At some point this has acquired a phenomenological interpretation. The idea that plurality (rope, snake) results from a mistaken perception of a single object (the elephant's trunk) is a commonplace notion in Indian religious and philosophical thought. Much Indian philosophy seems to have taken the ultimate unity of ontological ground as a basic truth from its earliest times.[58] Coward points to the first manifestations of the "fundamental thought" in Ṛg Veda I.164.46: *ekam sad*, the one being (being here used in the ontological sense of "sad," not *jīva*, *puruṣa*, etc). It is this "being" that preexists plurality and the cosmological "creation" of the universe by the Gods, and thus asks the perennial religio-philosophical question of the unified understanding of the whole. Bilimoria concedes the likelihood of a shared basis of belief in Buddhism and post-Buddhist Brahminical philosophy in a single non-substantial substrate to all existence:

> The concept of ātman, as the pervasive, infinite principle of existence, without admitting to the substantive categories implicated in, say, the concept of matter on the one hand and the idea of "soul" or spirit self (jīva, dehātman, ksetrajñā, bhūtaprāṇa) on the other hand, was perhaps the brahmanical answer to the critique of the very notion of the substantial self, which had been around in India (with the Saṃnyāsins, Jains, Ajīvakās, Cārvākas and Lokāyatas or materialists) long before the Buddha and his followers came upon the scene.[59]

Hiriyanna classifies pre-Upanisadic thought as the product of a "longing for unity," culminating in the "higher conception of unity, viz. Monism."[60] On this basis, the dualities of God and world, mind and matter, substance and property, unity of existence and plurality of forms are always mitigated by a shared ontological basis.[61] This leads the Indian thinker to think the whole more effectively—not standing humbly back before the craftsman's secrets of a creator God—but attempting to think creation and Being as a unity divided by internal relation rather than an abyss spanned only by exceptional powers of sovereignty and will. To some extent this shared cosmological heritage can also be taken to explain their divergence. Indic conceptions of reality were not an archive of past evidence, but rather the tip of an iceberg in the present religious life—they were "a stage in an open-ended process of revelation."[62] And indeed, the Vedas themselves were sometimes seen to be the primordial reality itself, the "protosemantic" progenitor of linguistic creation—a heavy ontological burden was laid upon them in order to answer the philosophical questions of the whole culture.[63] Buddhism came out of a Vedic milieu that left an inevitable mark on its assumptions, despite explicitly rejecting the Vedic judgement on the value of the "first one," the precondition of a "universal witness" which is really Being as the substrate of consciousness, i.e., the *a priori* necessary precondition of all phenomena. Halbfass writes: "Followers of all religions and philosophical schools in India recognise certain Vedic premises. Even the Buddhists fall within the range of that totality of systems (*sarvadarśana*) which is ultimately dependent on the Veda: the Veda is valid insofar as it is the origin and framework of the entire Indian tradition, the condition of its possibility."[64] The Vedas established a dominant primordial monism throughout the culture as firmly as the ideologies behind the Hebrew Bible established dualism for the three Semitic cultures, even where religious cosmology had shaded into science.

Wherever these philosophical issues of foundation, essence, and the whole arose as a subject for philosophical investigation, thinkers took their cue from the methodological flexibility, pragmatism, and universalism of Nyāya logic. The fashions in thought operate in such a way that once a school or sect entered into the rhetorical and competitive arena of contemporary discourse, the organs of formalised reasoning largely set by the Nyāya school became the *lingua franca* of debate. Nyāya was the *pradīpah sarvaśāstrānam,* the "light of all the branches of learning," considered perfect for "unambiguous expression of subtle ideas."[65] Not all schools and sects reached the same conclusion, but thanks to the spread of Nyāya, each started with similar questions and asked them with similar ideals of rigour and similar organs for inference. As we will see, Rūpa Gosvāmi himself almost certainly studied Navya-Nyāya logic in the erudite environment of Mughal Bengal, inheriting a richly complex tapestry of ideas. To understand how Rūpa Gosvāmi would come to negotiate the false dichotomy of the "hermeneutic fork" in Indian ontology, one must uncover the many resources that were available to him. The combination of a monist framework with any method advocating logical rigour leads smoothly toward basic characteristics in formal ontology when addressing the existence of phenomenal plurality.[66] Traces of this framework are observed wherever we see phenomenological plurality marshalled into provisional unities of a higher ontological kind—in the categorical thinking of Nyāya, the atoms and aggregates of Vaiśeṣika, the aggregation of *dharmas* in Buddhism, the infinite forms of *prakṛti* in Sāṃkhya, and the *māyic* manifestations of Brahman in Advaita Vedānta. Many widely used concepts of Indian philosophy reveal their consonance with these principles in the process of translation: the Western concept of essence is often identified with the Sanskrit term *svarūpa*—meaning "own-form," an idea of essence that carries more formal structural implications rather than the suggestion of malleable Newtonian substances. As we will see, it is precisely the aspect of Indian thought that hasty philosophers have so often delivered into the hands of a supposed "idealism," which must be reevaluated without imposing an assumed duality of real and ideal. The debate over the ontological status of universals, which spanned the above schools, is itself a widespread recognition that a mind-matter dualism cannot do justice to the range of entities and the modes of their existence.[67]

Most of the orthodox schools can be described in a dualistic way, and have been: Sāṃkhya as a duality of spirit (*puruṣa*) and form (*prakṛti*), Nyāya of language and referent, Advaita as a duality of real and illusory levels of being, and Vaiśeṣika as an incorrigible thought-matter materialism. In Sāṃkhya, Advaita, and Vaiśeṣika, however, both physical objects and ideas or sense impressions are put together into the same category, and in the case of Sāṃkhya and Advaita are opposed to a quite different ontological dimension (*puruṣa* or *brahman*, respectively), which contains no such ideas or contents.[68] Both the Sāṃkhya ontology of qualities (*guṇa*) and the Nyāya-Vaiśeṣika ontology of atoms (*anu*—which is itself not merely physical, but also constitutes and consists of formal properties, as C. Sharma asserts in pointing out that Vaiśeṣika atomism is not materialism[69]), also seek to explain particulars in terms of aggregates of qualities. But the ontological conception is heightened precisely when an aggregation of property and *existence* is proposed. Here the controversy over universals is invoked: What is the ontological difference between generalities and the particulars that instantiate them? Is "exists" really just the largest of the universals, ontologically equivalent to Plato's Good in the hierarchy described in the *Republic*? In its atomistic worldview, Vaiśeṣika, the very name of which emphasises its focus on the enumeration and differential analysis of "qualities" admits that "the heart of reality consists in difference."[70]

In Sāṃkhya in particular we have an example of how the mapping of Western metaphysical typologies onto Indian philosophical systems can lead to substantial and enduring misunderstandings. Sāṃkhya is often spoken of as a mind-matter dualism consonant with Western Cartesian dualism, as by Richard King, Arthur Macdonell, John Davies, Arthur Keith, and others. However, this analogy is clearly misplaced because those qualities that are normally attributed to the "mind" side of the divide in the West—the ideas, sensations, and emotions that constitute the contents of consciousness—are explicitly placed within the realm of *prakṛti* by the *Sāṃkhya Kārikā*, that is, on the side allied with "matter" by those scholars. *Buddhi*, discriminating consciousness, and *ahamkāra*, the self-reflexive "I" are both part of what careless scholars have sometimes called the "material" dimension of this Sāṃkhya metaphysics which has been so influential on almost every major orthodox sect or philosophical school, and many onorthodox ones. Thus Gerald Larson described Sāṃkhya as "an eccentric form of dualism" and likened its conception of matter to a straightforward reductive materialism, adding that "[t]he term eccentric is meant to indicate simply that the Sāṃkhya dualism does not fit the usual or conventional notions of dualism," and that in comparison both to Descartes and to the more recent dualist position of Kai Nielson, "one realises immediately that Sāṃkhya somehow misses the mark."[71] In his excellent book relating Sāṃkhya to phenomenology's attempt at a metaphysics of experience divided between the contentual or intentional analysis of Husserlian phenomenology, and the transcendental analysis of Heideggerian phenomenology, Burley devotes a whole chapter to critiquing the philosophically uncritical use of terms like substance, matter, and realism in reference to this and other schools of Indian philosophy.[72]

Burley comes to the conclusion that Sāṃkhya's taxonomy of form (*prakṛti*), consciousness (*puruṣa*), and qualities (the three *guṇas* or cosmological qualities *sattva, rajas,* and tamas) "is the result of something approximating transcendental reflection upon experience."[73] Thus what is purported to be a spirit-matter dualism of *puruṣa* and *prakṛti* can be otherwise read as a sophisticated analysis of Being with regard to the kinds of its formal qualities. Here the idea of *puruṣa* represents the ubiquity of consciousness, upheld by the argument that "the physical universe, being insentient, requires a sentient principle to experience it." Hiriyanna rightly points out "such an argument by recognising a necessary relation between the two militates against the fundamental dualism of the system."[74] A similar observation arises for much Vedāntic thought on the relation of consciousness to the phenomenal world.

Vedānta encompasses innumerable positions that include many models found within the range of Western metaphysics.[75] Yet even "Advaita" (meaning "non-dual") Vedānta has been characterised as a radical dualism where all phenomenality, in its phenomenal character, is illusory, indicating a dependent yet different *type* of existence. And what do we say of Being itself when considered at its furthest, most unified, and irreducible level, the level at which Heidegger is trying originally to ask the question, of something rather than nothing? This is the level at which it comes remarkably close to the *śūnya-vāda* theory of emptiness in Buddhism but veers away at the last moment to offer a bare, blunt opposition to nihilism. Here, laced with analogy, apophasis, and negative theology, Vedāntic thought is ready to give Being a name: Brahman. Vedānta, dualistic and monistic, is then an attempt to understand how particular, formal modification of that one medial substrate of Being relates to the whole.

Vedānta has never ceased to be hugely influential on Hindu devotional thought, mixed almost from its inception with other schools through a vigorous culture of philosophical debate, dialogue, and appropriation. Like Sāṃkhya, it was not only a popular contemporary school during Rūpa Gosvāmi's lifetime, but also a major philosophical strand in the *Bhāgavata Purāṇa,* the seminal text of the Vaiṣṇava sect to which he converted. Indeed, such philosophical concerns were part of a culture of reflection that is found in poetry, practice, theology, and philosophy across the regions of India and through the wide range of vibrant contemporary religious forms, such as tantra, brahminical Śaivism, Jainism, and perhaps also interacting productively with the more syncretic forms of Islam present at the time. Many other philosophies in the Indian tradition pursued the same or similar subtle ontology questions with equal vigour, although few gave the same ontological and religious application to aesthetic thought as Rūpa.

Study of other such thinkers would furnish equally (if differently) illuminating material, and contemporary sects in contrast to which Rūpa would have defined his position, such as his brahminical precursors and the non-Vedic, so-called "unorthodox," but extremely well-articulated positions of the materialists, Buddhists, and Jains, almost certainly provided a springboard for his own ideas.

By way of an example, certain Jain metaphysicians produced a particularly precise expression of the metaphysical features that are also at the heart of Gadamer's ontology.[76] Summarised as a whole, Jain philosophy has exemplified the ambiguity, dialogism, and crossing of categories that characterises so many schools. Like Gadamer's supposed non-realism, it has posed a serious challenge to scholars trying to get a philosophical handle on its worldview, relative to that which classically sets the paradigms of realist debate. Its notorious doctrine of *anekāntavada* (literally "non-one-endedness" or "not-one-conclusion," translated elsewhere as "non-absolutism," "many-pointedness," and "pluralism") has been seen both as a philosophical shrugging of the shoulders by hasty scholars, and as a brave philosophical insight by more sympathetic ones. It has been called a "realistic and [a] relativistic pluralism,"[77] and elsewhere it has been characterised as a "relative pluralism,"[78] and a "monistic idealism."[79] But even more than the acceptance of a pluralistic monist ontology, it is the recognition of the fundamental centrality of ambiguity and motion that recalls the post-Platonic features of Gadamer's ontology. Thinkers such as Samantabhadra have confused commentators by seeming to take no definite position on important issues such as the relative reality of the universal and particular, the priority of unity or plurality.[80] But it is precisely the resistance of the Jain point of view to these poles that alerts us to the subtlety of its insight. What initially appears as a stubborn ambiguity in the Jain view eventually is revealed as a faithful attempt to highlight difficult borderline truths about the constitution of reality.

Classical Jain philosophers sought to preserve that internal limit between the particularity of a thing's identity and its relativity to other identities, which Plato referred to as the "indeterminate Two," through the view that objects are both universal and particular (*sāmānyaviśeṣātma*) indivisibly and equally.[81] As Dravid puts it, "[T]he one without the other is an abstraction having no basis in experience."[82] Samantabhadra in particular stressed the unity of all existence, necessarily lacking in difference or hierarchy in type, only in division of phenomenal content, such that "things might differ as substances, qualities, and so on, but they are all identical so far as their existence is concerned."[83] The Jain position lies directly between the unity and absolutism of the Advaitin and the plurality and nihilism of the Buddhist, establishing a "theological mean between Brahminism and early Buddhism."[84] Epistemologically, this perception of the ambiguity and indeterminacy of Being yielded the doctrine of *syādvāda*, which argues for the optative status of Being—holding many points in common with "the theory of the relativity of knowledge" that has subsequently overwhelmed the West.[85] It is interesting to note that this relativism inspired as great an outcry in contemporary India as post-Enlightenment relativism has done in the West. Yet while Jainism was seen as a heterodox philosophy, at a deep metaphysical level it sought to avoid the hermeneutical fork of ontological optimism and ontological pessimism about essences by upholding the innate ambiguity of Being and refusing to make a judgement about essence one way or the other. It was a way of responding to the debate on the true nature of reality that other later philosophies echoed in their own solutions. The *acintyabhedābheda* position of Rūpa Gosvāmi's school would be one of these.

Hence, "the universal is the stable element persisting through the changing modes which are particulars. . . . Change and stability are so intimately related that one does not exist without the other."[86] Thus, for instance, in the allegory of the six blind men and the elephant, the Jain must hold that there is no objective elephant trunk giving rise to the illusion of the rope, the snake, etc. Rather there is only the similarity observed in the long, slender, and curving structure that is common to the rope perceived by one man, the snake perceived by another, and the trunk that is perceived by the teller of the tale. From the phenomenological perspective, the Buddhist and Nyāya thinkers offered a particularly incisive analysis of the structural constitution of hermeneutic reality. The Nyāya thinkers understood what it is to define things in terms of finding an entity's identifying "mark" or *lakṣaṇa*, its analytical "essence." This is a structural or relational concept of definition, which defines a definition as the category that excludes and includes just the correct sets of things for the designated object. The Indian trope that most eloquently expresses this idea of essence, that is such a keystone of the hermeneutic metaphysic, is the anecdote of the stargazer who points out a dim star in the star-full sky by reference to its context in relation to other brighter ones. It is in this way that Nyāya, through practical linguistic concerns, expressed the mutual interdefinition of all essences toward which Plato was led by the mathematical insights of the Pythagoreans. Stars and numbers here are, structurally, the same entities, and both act as microcosmic models for the nature of Being in general. A similar insight is expressed in the Buddhist idea that identity, self, and universal are all actually constituted not by positive essences, but by *apoha*: negation of the other. The Jains add to this by noting that the self-identity that accrues to universals as general concepts (termed the *tiryak sāmānya*, the "horizontal universal"), and to particulars as entities persisting through time (the *ūrdhvata sāmānya*, or "vertical universal"), is of the same "universal" nature in both cases: similarity of development (*sadṛṣaparināma*).

In the above doctrines we can identify aspects of a formal ontology that appeared in modified forms throughout the Indian schools as they revised, rediscovered, and synthesised themselves throughout the centuries. These many attempts to formulate the deep ambiguity of essence bridged almost two millennia of Indian history to recur in the doctrine of *acintyabhedābheda*, "inconceivable difference-and-non-difference" that was brought to fruition from Vedāntic and Sāṃkhya-influenced purāṇic sources by Rūpa Gosvāmi's nephew, Jīva Gosvāmi.[87] It was in the generation after Rūpa himself (most notably in the work of Jīva) that his tradition brought these insights explicitly into line with the neo-Vedāntic debates.

The next chapter will give a short account of his own immediate historical context, but it is important to note that Rūpa inherited a complex web of metaphysical insights, synthesised in his tradition's most authoritative text, the *Bhāgavata Purāṇa* (exact date unknown, but broadly thought to date in its approximate present form from the ninth century CE), and multiplied through the rich threads of philosophy and religious practice with which he came face to face in his society. In the Bengal of Rūpa Gosvāmi's youth, his teacher Caitanya had lent an increasingly theological cast to the local tradition of devotion to the god Krishna.[88] Already, the theology of the incarnate Vishnu had encountered the theology of the Goddess that dominated in Bengal. The pluralistic theism of the Hindu cults had encountered the monotheistic ideology of Islam through the influence of the Muslim rulers (and sometime Hindu converts) of contemporary Bengal.[89] In the courts of these rulers, the renewed vigour of Navya-Nyāya (neo-Nyāya) logic was paralleled by a flourishing of the devotional arts, perhaps evidenced in audible form beneath Rūpa Gosvāmi's very window through the ecstatic singing of the devotees.[90] These were the intellectual and social channels through which the different systems met and interacted around Rūpa, further enriched by his private interest in classical Sanskrit literature, trends in vernacular literature, and the aesthetic theory of Bharata (which the Śaiva polymath Abhinavagupta (tenth through eleventh century CE) and others had already woven into bhakti's self-understanding as a charismatic religion). Far from inhabiting a monolithic and dogmatic culture, Rūpa lived in a multicultural, multireligious, geographically and socially mobile society in which his own experience had proved scholarship to be a valuable economic, social, and spiritual currency.[91] He was an Indian "Renaissance man," and in his hands the philosophy of religion was judiciously tempered both by the rigorous demands of contemporary logic on the one hand, and by a devotional readership on the other.

As we will see, Rūpa's case demonstrates the concrete reality of realist reasoning in India. Many theories were entertained, and the issues that divided and linked them were debated by those who sought new answers over the course of more than a millennium. These answers were synthetic and also novel, but all inherited basic patterns for thinking about reality on the basis of early textual paradigms. These patterns are different from the Western models, but instructively illuminate them. Realism in the Indian framework, as in the Western postmodern tradition, is not based on the ontological dualism with which we are so familiar. In the wider sense of "realism," many schools hold the "realist" belief that there are discoverable truths about Being in general and that these can illuminate the nature of our selves and lives, furnishing an ideal of human flourishing. In the same way in which Gadamer is a eudaimonian realist and optimist about ontology and ethics, so too is Rūpa Gosvāmi.[92] If the Buddhists were ontological pessimists, and the Jains were cheerful realists of a later Platonic-Parmenidean sort, then Rūpa Gosvāmi's Hindu optimism stakes out a further postmodern possibility for realist belief, not as a Derridean *waiting*, nor an uncommitted Gadamerian *vitality*, but as a transformative, all-consuming *passion*.

NOTES

1. K. Narain, *An Outline of Madhva Philosophy* (Allahabad, India: Udayana Publishers, 1962), vii.

2. There are discussions of Indian "realist" ideas to be found in many works on Indian philosophy, often tackling an unspoken assumption that Indian philosophy is predominantly idealist. See D. N. Shastri's *Critique of Indian Realism* (1964), G. N. Shastri's *Philosophy of Word and Meaning*, Dasgupta's *Indian Realism*, Stephen Phillips's *Classical Indian Metaphysics: Refutations of Realism and the Emergence of "New Logic"* (1995), Raja Ram Dravid's *The Problem of Universals in Indian Philosophy* (1972), J. Sinha's *Indian Realism* (1938), P. K. Mukhopadhyay's *Indian Realism: A Rigorous Descriptive Metaphysics* (1984), applied to the Nyāya and Vaiśeṣika by P.

T. Raju (in *Idealistic Thought of India* (Cambridge, Mass.: Harvard University Press, 1953), 20), and K. Narain (1962) in respect of Madhva's philosophy as cited above, etc. But even in 1953 as a reflection on applying the realism-idealism axis to Indian thought, Raju had cause to cite J. H. Muirhead: "The distinction between idealism and realism 'has been wearing thin of late and perhaps had better be dropped now that it has served its purpose'" (*Idealistic Thought of India*, 39).

3. See Daniel Ingalls in his introductory note to D.C. Guha's *Navya-Nyāya System of Logic* (New Delhi: Motilal Banarsidass, 1979), ix.

4. J. N. Mohanty, "Introduction: Bimal Matilal, the Man, and the Philosopher," in *Relativism, Suffering and Beyond*, P. Bilimoria and J. N. Mohanty, eds. (New Delhi: Oxford University Press, 1997), 4–5.

5. M. Hiriyanna, *Outlines of Indian Philosophy* (New Delhi: Motilal Banarsidass, 1993), 16.

6. Chandradhar Sharma, *A Critical Survey of Indian Philosophy* (New Delhi: Motilal Banarsidass, 1987), 13.

7. Hiriyanna, *Outlines of Indian Philosophy*, 16.

8. As a corrective to the common oversimplification of the Indian philosophical tradition, Julius Lipner makes a point of noting "talk of only six orthodox systems is misconceived. There are many more *darśanas* or religious perspectives on life even within high Hinduism, i.e., the traditions which formally acknowledged the religious authority of the Vedas. And 'orthodox' in this context is a highly debatable word" (*Hindus: Their Religious Beliefs and Practices* (Oxford: Routledge, 1994), 159). Gavin Flood notes that Madhva refers not to six but to sixteen schools, and points to the *sad darśana* idea's rhetorical purpose of imbuing the complex "orthodox" traditions with apparent coherence and codification in the face of "unorthodox" attack (*An Introduction to Hinduism* (Cambridge: Cambridge University Press, 1996), 231).

9. Peter Harvey makes the comparison in his *An Introduction to Buddhism: Teachings, Histories and Practices* (Cambridge: Cambridge University Press, 1996), 11. It is not only the range and critical depth of the views that suggests this, but also the evidence that it was a flourishing of urban culture that prompted these developments.

10. Ascribed to Caitanya Vaiṣṇavism by Cchanda Chatterjee.

11. R. King, *Early Advaita Vedānta and Buddhism: The Mahāyana Context of the Gaudapadiyakarika* (Albany: State University of New York Press, 1995), 2.

12. Chhanda Chatterjee, *The Philosophy of Caitanya and His School* (New Delhi: Associated Publishing Co., 1993), vii.

13. Hiriyanna, *Outlines of Indian Philosophy*, 13. Generally speaking, Hiriyanna is laudably cautious and context-sensitive in making statements about the habits of different branches of Indian thought.

14. Hiriyanna, *Outlines of Indian Philosophy*, 13.

15. J. N. Mohanty, *Reason and Tradition in Indian Thought: An Essay on the Nature of Indian Philosophical Thinking* (New Delhi: Oxford University Press, 1992), 151.

16. Bimal Matilal, *Perception: An Essay on Classical Indian Theories of Knowledge* (Oxford: Oxford University Press, 1986), 70.

17. Richard King fortifies this point, *Early Advaita Vedānta and Buddhism: The Mahāyana Context of the Gauḍapadīyakārikā*, 2.

18. Mohanty, *Reason and Tradition in Indian Thought: An Essay on the Nature of Indian Philosophical Thinking*, 151.

19. See S. N. Gupta, *The Indian Concept of Values* (New Delhi: Manohar Book Service, 1978), vii.

20. Krishnadasa Bhattacaryya, *Studies in Indian Philosophy* (New Delhi: Motilal Banarsidass, 1958), 2.

21. S. Dasgupta, *A History of Indian Philosophy, Vol. 1* (New Delhi: Motilal Banarsidass, 1922), 3–4.

22. M. T. Melville, *The Chaitanya Movement: A Study of Vaiṣṇavism in Bengal* (New Delhi: Munshiram Manoharlal Publishers, 1925), 88.

23. This fourfold division of *artha* as purpose in the *Arthaśāstra* of Kauṭilya (of which *artha* as wealth is but one of the four parts) is noted by J. Ganeri in *The Blackwell Introduction to Hinduism* as an integral part of the notion of reason as a practical tool, adaptable to all human goals.

24. See Ravi Gupta's 2004 Oxford University thesis *Caitanya Vaiṣṇava Vedānta: Acintyabhedābheda in Jīva Gosvāmi's Catuḥsutri Tika*.

25. Jonardon Ganeri notes the dual meaning of *artha* and, rather than excluding one meaning in each exegetic context for purposes of clarity, rightly seeks to retain the word's ambivalence which is itself so illuminating to the discussion (see *Philosophy in Classical India: The Proper Work of Reason* (Oxford: Routledge, 2001), 12).

26. Chandradhar Sharma, *A Critical Survey of Indian Philosophy* (New Delhi: Motilal Banarsidass, 1987), 13. Sharma's characterisation of Indian philosophy actually goes deeper, arguing that the foundation of truth in India is arrived at not as an idea but a perception; through a "direct, immediate and intuitive vision of Reality, the actual perception of Truth."

27. The Cārvākas or materialists, for instance, are best known through the descriptions made of them in the writings left by other schools (e.g., the Advaitic *Sarvasiddhanta Saṃgraha* attributed to Śaṃkara, the *Bṛhaspati sūtras*, or Jayantabhatta's Nyāya text the *Nyāyamanjari*). There, they feature along with Buddhist and other *nāstika*, or unorthodox views, as a foundational critique that many thinkers feel it necessary to overcome before proceeding with their own exposition.

28. K. Narain paints a historical picture of Vedānta's internal debate (in his view, between monism (Śaṃkara), dualism (Rāmānuja), and pluralism (Madhva)) as the natural successor to Buddhism in providing a provocation and a conceptual space for the perennial problems of Indian philosophy (*An Outline of Madhva Philosophy*).

29. See Jonardon Ganeri's concise introduction summarising Indian attitudes to rationalistic thought in "Hinduism and the Proper Work of Reason," in *The Blackwell Companion to Hinduism* (Oxford: Blackwell Publishers, 2003), 411–12.

30. *Bhaktirasāmṛtasindhu* 1.1.11.

31. Ganeri, "Hinduism and the Proper Work of Reason," in *The Blackwell Companion to Hinduism*, 412.

32. Arvind Sharma, *Classical Hindu Thought* (New Delhi: Oxford University Press, 2000), 1.

33. Nyāya, Vaiśeṣika, Purva Mīmāṃsā, Uttara Mīmāṃsā, Sāṃkhya, and Vedānta. The unorthodox schools being Buddhism, Jainism, and the Cārvākas (materialists).

34. Sharma, *Classical Hindu Thought*, 1.

35. Raju, *Idealistic Thought of India*, 38.

36. See Surendranath Dasgupta's *Indian Idealism* (Cambridge: Cambridge University Press, 1962), and Jadunath Sinha's *Indian Realism* (New Delhi: Motilal Banarsidass, 1972).

37. See Narain, *An Outline of Madhva Philosophy*.

38. Hiriyanna, *Outlines of Indian Philosophy*, 138. This statement is made as a complement to Stcherbatsky's pronouncement that the Buddhists were "pluralists." As we will see and as in the case of Badiou's mathematical model of Being, the combination of realism and pluralism is a leitmotif of formal ontology wherever it arises.

39. Raja Ram Dravid, *The Problem of Universals in Indian Philosophy* (New Delhi: Motilal Banarsidass, 1972).

40. Sharma, *A Critical Survey of Indian Philosophy*, 153.

41. Sharma, *A Critical Survey of Indian Philosophy*, 149.

42. For confirmations of this, see the definitions of *sattā* and *sattva* in John Grimes's *A Concise Dictionary of English Philosophy* (Albany: State University of New York, 1989), 326.

43. V. S. Apte, *The Practical Sanskrit-English Dictionary* (New Delhi: Motilal Banarsidass, 1965), 138.

44. There are other terms similarly used in this general way: *vṛt* for what is happening, or literally, "turning," and *sthā* denoting to "be" something, literally, "to stand" or "remain."

45. Accordingly, *astitā* is denied the status of a real universal by the Nyāya-Vaiśeṣ ika thinkers precisely because it is a synthetic concept used in the course of our thinking about the world, and not something that we think of as being observed accruing to things in the world (see Mohanty, *Reason and Tradition in Indian Thought*, 154.)

46. Mohanty, *Reason and Tradition in Indian Thought*, 154.

47. Mohanty, *Reason and Tradition in Indian Thought*, 150.

48. The highest of the three levels of reality in Advaita.

49. The most basic type of atom in Vaiśeṣika, of the nature of one of the five elements.

50. The supreme knowledge of the self as the ultimate reality in the Upaniṣads.

51. Ideals of spiritual perfection in Buddhism.

52. A phrase used both to denote the *ātman* in Advaita, and the *puruṣa* in Sāṃkhya.

53. Interestingly, such queries in translation can be the site of key theological dispute, as when Victor DiCara, a contemporary devotee, translates *uttama*, which has a similar meaning, as highest. But he filters this meaning through the assumption that what is highest is diametrically opposed (rather than at the other end of a scale from) what is low—thus taking *uttama* to mean morally and metaphysically "pure" (see Victor DiCara's translation of the Eastern Quadrant of the *Bhaktirasāmṛtasindhu*, online at www.victordicara.com). This is the sort of overtly dualistic interpretation that can lead to a misinterpretation of Rūpa's metaphysics.

54. K. C. Bhattacharya, *Studies in Indian Philosophy, Vol.1*, Gopīnath Bhattacharya, ed. (New Delhi: Motilal Banarsidass, 1983).

55. In Nyāya as for Plato, one cannot affirm the universality itself as a universal, as this leads to infinite regress. This is one of those aporias that point inward toward the constitutive features of analysing phenomena in terms of unity and plurality.

56. Hiriyanna, *Outlines of Indian Philosophy*, 135.

57. H. Coward, *Derrida and Indian Philosophy* (Albany: State University of New York Press, 1990), 7.

58. Coward states this view, citing the *Ṛg Veda*, in *Early Advaita Vedānta and Buddhism: The Mahāyāna Context of the Gauḍapadīyakārikā*, 5.

59. Purushottama Bilimoria, "On Ñaṃkara's Attempted Reconciliation of 'You' and 'I': *Yusmadasmatsamanvaya*" in *Relativism, Suffering and Beyond: Essays in Memory of Bimal Matilal*, 252.

60. Hiriyanna, *Outlines of Indian Philosophy*, 41. Hiriyanna also points toward the *tad ekam* of early Vedic texts, but reminds us that this is not pantheism in the strict sense of identifying world with God, but is panentheism: World is one with God, but God transcends and exceeds it.

61. The same could be argued of the Abrahamic scholastic God, insofar as the different categories all share an ontological dependence on the essence and existence of God, which are themselves mysteriously unified in His "simple" sovereign Being.

62. W. Halbfass, *Tradition and Reflection: Explorations in Indian Thought* (Albany: State University of New York Press, 1991), 4.

63. Halbfass, *Tradition and Reflection: Explorations in Indian Thought*, 5–6.

64. Halbfass, *Tradition and Reflection: Explorations in Indian Thought*, 25.

65. D. C. Guha, *Navya Nyāya System of Logic* (New Delhi: Motilal Banarsidass, 1979), 1.

66. It is significant that many of the philosophers with whom Indian philosophy has been most compared—Hegel, Leibniz, Spinoza—are those who themselves are seen to stand on the boundary between idealism and pantheism, possessing a strong "logical" method.

67. Raja Ram Dravid's *The Problem of Universals in Indian Philosophy* comprehensively describes this Pan-Indian debate.

68. See Hiriyanna, *Outlines of Indian Philosophy*, 270, on the mind-object duality of Sāṃkhya epistemology—although it is significant here that one speaks of mind and object, and not mind and *matter*. This is a phenomenological, not an ontological division.

69. Sharma, *A Critical Survey of Indian Philosophy*, 184.

70. Sharma, *A Critical Survey of Indian Philosophy*, 176.

71. Gerald Larson in *Encyclopedia of Indian Philosophies Vol. IV: Sāṃkhya* (New Delhi: Motilal Banarsidass, 1987), 75–77.

72. Mikel Burley, *Classical Samkhya and Yoga: An Indian Metaphysics of Experience* (Oxford: RoutledgeCurzon, 2007), 102.

73. Burley, *Classical Samkhya and Yoga: An Indian Metaphysics of Experience*, 102.

74. Hiriyanna, *Outlines of Indian Philosophy*, 279.

75. Śaṃkara's Advaita Vedānta (Non-dualism, eighth century CE) was subsequently countered and complemented by Rāmānuja's Viśiṣṭādvaita Vedānta (qualified non-dualism, twelfth century CE), Nimbārka's Dvaita Advaita (dualistic non-dualism), Madhva's Dvaita (dualism) and Vallabha's Śuddhādvaita. The philosophers of the different bhakti schools subsequently made use of a range of these positions, drawing explicitly on the Vedāntins who had expounded them.

76. Coward notes the potential fruitfulness of Jainism and its doctrines of ambiguity for comparison with the post-Heideggerian tradition in the work of Derrida. See Coward, *Derrida and Indian Philososphy*, 18.

77. Sharma, *A Critical Survey of Indian Philosophy*, 50–51.

78. Dasgupta, *A History of Indian Philosophy, Vol. 1*, 175.

79. Rādhākrishnan, *Indian Philosophy* (New Delhi: Oxford University Press, 1996), 305.

80. In his assessment of the Jain *Syādvāda* doctrine and its ambiguities, Chandradhar Sharma cites numerous complaints from scholars such as Dharmakīrti, Śaṃkara, and Rāmānuja (see *A Critical Survey of Indian Philosophy*, 54–62).

81. See the *Parīkṣamukha Sūtra, Mānikyanandī* of Samantabhadra, IV, 1.

82. Dravid, *The Problem of Universals in Indian Philosophy*, 132.

83. Dravid, *The Problem of Universals in Indian Philosophy*, 132.

84. Sharma, *A Critical Survey of Indian Philosophy*, 51.

85. Sharma, *A Critical Survey of Indian Philosophy*, 52.

86. Dravid, *The Problem of Universals in Indian Philosophy*, 132.

87. Of course, *acintyabhedā bheda* was not the only doctrine to take up this pervasive issue. It is tackled in many doctrines belonging to many schools throughout the years between Prabhacandra and Jīva Gosvāmi—not least in that of the Kashmiri Śaivas. It was, of course, often at the heart of the struggle between appropriators of Vedāntic thought seeking to defend Advaita, Viśiṣṭādvaita, or Dvaita.

88. Caitanya's traditional dates are 1486–1533 CE. There is still debate over what Caitanya added to the already rich bhakti philosophy of the South Indians as it travelled north and merged with the Vaiṣṇava philosophy of the Alvars, Ācāryas, and poets (Jayadeva, Vidyāpati, and Caṇḍidās). Chatterjee's *The Philosophy of Caitanya and His School* deals with this question in depth, observing the centralising and systematising influence he had.

89. For details of the Muslim-Hindu synthesis of sixteenth-century Bengal in its effect on the Vaiṣṇava tradition, see Richard Eaton's essay "The Bengal of Sri Caitanya Mahāprabhu," in Steven Rosen's *Vaiṣṇavism: Contemporary Scholars Discuss the Gauḍīya Tradition* (New York: FOLK Books, 1992).

90. An episode (see Richard Eaton's account in Steven Rosen's *Vaiṣṇavism: Contemporary Scholars Discuss the Gauḍīya Tradition*) recounts how even the Hindu residents of Bengal used to complain to the authorities about the loud noise made by the kīrtana-singing of Caitanya's followers.

91. Biographies tell that Caitanya had noted Rūpa and his brother Sanātana in part for their learning, and that this was to contribute to their quest to take the Gauḍīya Vaiṣṇava school west in a new, revitalised, and highly *theologised* form.

92. Even the materialists had to state their chosen pramāṇas, authorities (which

happened to be empirical evidence and the intuitive character of our practical assumptions), before proceeding to expound their scepticism about religious realities.

Chapter 5

Rūpa Gosvāmi's Ontology of *Rasa*

This chapter will give an exposition of the specific ontological synthesis that Rūpa Gosvāmi inherited, and his complex formulation of this ontology as *rasa*—a theory with which he seeks to establish the philosophical ultimacy of his position. In this apologetic subtext of his devotional works, he incorporates Advaitic monism, theistic dualism, and Vedānta and Sāṃkhya metaphysics, filters them through the logic of Nyāya, and tests them against the psychological insights of Sanskrit aesthetic theory. While this will require an exposition and reassessment of Rūpa Gosvāmi's reasoning, the goal is mainly to shed light on the philosophical problem itself by looking at the methods and results of ontological analysis in Rūpa Gosvāmi's framework, drawing out the implications for a deepening of Gadamer's formal ontological model. As a response to the interrogation of metaphysics by finitude, relativity, indeterminacy, and the infinite relationality at the heart of identity, Rūpa Gosvāmi's position complements Blanchot's "messianism" and Gadamer's "vitalism" with another option for postmodern religious realist belief: unwavering and focused passion.[1] Rather than a naive dogmatism or uncritical spirituality, Rūpa Gosvāmi's bhakti philosophy incorporates the fruits of India's own "Enlightenment scepticism" into a realistic worldview that draws added strength from the very factors that have had a demoralising influence on religious belief and realism in the West.

THE INTELLECTUAL CONTEXT OF RŪPA GOSWAMI'S WORK

Born in approximately 1489 CE, and dying seventy-five years later in his adoptive home of Vṛndāvana, Rūpa Gosvāmi is the author of devotional plays and poetry, an influential aesthetics, a renowned system of practical theology, and a less well-known metaphysics, all of which celebrate the ontology of phenomenal forms. He synthesises influences from a wide range of Indian textual sources, schools, disciplines, and religious orientations, while modifying and honing this mixture through extensive discursive engagement with other thinkers of his time. He distilled contemporary theological sources into a newly systematic, consistent, and comprehensive position by means of his own unique analysis of the nature of the divine, and of the ultimate goals of human life. The analogies with Gadamer's ontology are not unique to Rūpa Gosvāmi's work; while Rūpa Gosvāmi's career includes authorship of texts that are "canonical" for his tradition, in many respects his metaphysics refracts insights that pervade much of the Vaiṣṇava tradition, and of the contemporary intellectual and religious milieu.[2] His texts are philosophically important firstly because they reflect the contemporary environment in rich and richly critical ways; as we will see, the Vraja region in his time was a particularly vibrant and fruitful environment for philosophical and theological reflection. But they are also significant because they distil these sources, as Gadamer distils his sources, into a more precise metaphysical insight, in certain respects advancing that insight through a further stage of synthesis and analysis.

Most studies of the philosophy of the Caitanya Vaiṣṇava tradition are enormously influenced by the works of Jīva Gosvāmi (c. 1517–1608), Rūpa's nephew, who formalised the tradition's ideas and concretised certain positions with regard to common philosophical controversies in the generation *after* Rūpa Gosvāmi.[3] Yet Rūpa was at the forefront of the movement in its earliest phases of expansion and self-awareness, and was perhaps the first to bring it to written expression.[4] Yet despite this there is relatively little work on him and his complex, expansive synthesis. In many cases, it seems that precisely the interdisciplinary richness of his influences and writings, which makes him a fascinating object of research, is the feature that discourages scholars from focusing on him. Yet it is essential that writers who interweave different discourses should be studied, and one often feels that the wealth of scholarship on Jīva Gosvāmi reflects a tendency to engage with thinkers who speak a language of "philosophical" style that puts Western philosophers at ease. It is precisely the "difference" of Rūpa's approach that should call him most urgently to our interest, furnishing new insights into the other methods that were used to explore the depths of philosophical questions.[5] While there is little reliable biographical material on him, many accounts make it appear that his life and intellectual significance have their roots in the fateful meeting with Caitanya, and trail off into a list of writings that more or less merge with those of the other Gosvāmins and the later generations of Caitanya Vaiṣṇava writers.[6] Yet later concerns within the tradition he established about Rūpa's pronounced emphasis on the suffering that Krishna causes, and on the higher "esoteric" states of *rasa*—refined aesthetic or religious emotion, to which it gives access—reflect the liberties permitted by the open and unconcretised nature of the early tradition.

There was clearly a firsthand dimension to his religious education—he is said by traditional biographies to have gained his philosophical outlook in part from direct discussion with Caitanya in Allahabad, and cites his elder brother Sanātana as his personal guru. Sanātana had also gained many of his ideas directly from Caitanya in early meetings with him while Rūpa Gosvāmi still lived in the Bengali cultural centre of Navadvīpa in service to the Nawab Hussein Shah. In the Bengal of Rūpa Gosvāmi's youth, Caitanya had already lent an increasingly systematic and theological cast to the local tradition of devotion to the god Krishna. But contrary to popular perception, Caitanya was not his only direct influence. It is likely that the eventual founder of Caitanya Vaiṣṇavism was only one of many theologians, holy men, and philosophers whom Rūpa and Sanātana, renowned for their love of learning, invited to Navadvīpa. His own personal dialogues must have been diverse, as was his extensive experience of pan-Indian cultural life. Rūpa Gosvāmi's earlier writings show that the prolific religious movement that had grown around Krishna already preoccupied his thoughts, and many of the ingredients of his later theological and philosophical thought predate the meeting with Caitanya.

His own family, having travelled from Karṇāṭaka to Bengal, spanned the southern and northern traditions of bhakti and the flourishing Vaiṣṇava movement of the time, as did Caitanya's own travels. Eventually, the fellowship of thinkers whom he and Sanātana gathered in the pilgrimage centre of Vraja would come to represent influences spanning almost the whole subcontinent, from Bengal and the holy city of Varanasi to the spiritual centres of Madurai and Śrīrangam in the South. Bengal Vaiṣṇavism has a long, literarily and theologically rich history, and the tradition was flourishing with new practical and theological impetus, not least from its southern,[7] Neo-Classical, heterodox,[8] Śaiva and Śākta, Buddhist,[9] and even Muslim influences.[10] In the courts of Bengal, the renewed vigour of Navya-Nyāya logic was paralleled by a flourishing of the devotional arts, perhaps evidenced in audible form beneath Rūpa Gosvāmi's very window through the ecstatic singing of the devotees.[11] Working in an office of the Islamic government, Rūpa was a near-contemporary of Kabir (between 1398–1518), the syncretist Indian Muslim thinker, and of Guru Nanak (1469–1539), the originator of Sikhism, as well as numerous theologians, such as Vallabha (1479–1531), who stood very close to his own tradition. He was probably also familiar with the Sufi piety of the Chishti order that was popular among the Bengal Muslim elite and served as a powerful example of a charismatic religious movement that had been enthusiastically taken up by a wide popular public.[12] Demonstrating an impressive command of classical Sanskrit language and literature in his works, and an equal enthusiasm for the style and motifs of purāṇic narratives and devotional poetry, Rūpa Gosvāmi was ideally placed to synthesise the widest cross-section of Indian intellectual life. While his prescribed devotional path toward the highest human experience might have involved an "insider epistemology" of the exclusive, protected type described by Deepak Sarma, Rūpa Gosvāmi's presentation of it involved a strong and pervasive superstructure of open, dialogical reasoning.[13]

Contemporary bhakti theologies devoted to Krishna were largely mediated through the syncretic ideology of the sixth- through ninth-century CE text, the *Bhāgavata Purāṇa*. Arguably, the conscientious "realist" theologising that we can observe implicitly in Rūpa Gosvāmi's works and explicitly in those of Jīva Gosvāmi, begins in the *Bhāgavata Purāṇa*, with its authoritative reinterpretative character, seeking to philosophically sublimate and express the "essence" of the Vedas, as the *Upaniṣads* claim to do.[14] The result was a complex and sometimes contradictory, but mostly coherent theology figuring classical philosophical discourses within the framework of intensely theistic and personalistic, mythic narratives. There is a subtle humanism in these narratives, not uncommon in bhakti texts, characterised by an emphasis on the experience of the devotee, and particularly of devotees of low status. In this case, "two varieties of devotion are contained in the *Bhāgavata*: one reinforces the transcendence and exclusivity of Bhagavan, the other strengthens the reality of the devotee as an immanent form of the transcendent Deity." In order to formulate the relation of these two views both a "variegated Vedāntic vocabulary" and "a Sāṃkhya terminology" are used.[15] Rūpa also draws on other *purāṇas* (such as the *Brahmavaivarta Purāṇ a*) that also combine a mildly Vedāntic theology of Krishna as highest divinity (replacing parama Brahman) with an extended theology of *prakṛti*, the manifest reality, as *śakti*, the energy of Krishna. We will see how the worldview that Rūpa inherits combines this emphasis on embodiment, and its implicit humanist affirmation of the conditions of embodied personhood that define human life in the world (often explicitly contrasted with the ascetic practices of renouncers), with its philosophical resources.

The *Bhāgavata Purāṇa* itself, true to the purāṇic genre, is a complex composite text drawing on prior foundations in the second-century *Harivaṃśa Purāṇa* and the third- through sixth-century *Viṣṇu Purāṇa*, going on to inspire the twelfth-century *Devī Bhāgavata*.[16] Rūpa cites this as a central text, but his reference to wide-ranging sources including tantric texts (such as the *Vaiṣṇava Tantra* at *Bhaktirasāmṛtasindhu* (abbreviated as *BRS*) 2.1.6 and *Nārada Pañcarātra* at *BRS* 1.4.18, and predominantly Śaiva texts such as the *Skanda Purāṇa* at *BRS* 1.3.23) that together show how rich and diverse was the contemporary cache of purāṇic thought for thinkers in this period, who appear to have read widely across them regardless of sectarian focus, and to have felt it legitimate to draw on them at will.

These texts also provided the impetus and raw material for extraordinarily powerful poetry in both the north and south of India by writers such as Jayadeva (c. twelfth century CE), Vidyāpati (c. 1352–1448 CE), Caṇḍidās (c. fourteenth through fifteenth century CE), and others. This literary tradition was complemented in the south by the theology of the Alvars, and in the north by the practices of Bengali Vaiṣṇavism, toward which Rūpa is said to have been inclined from an early stage. Kept alive through commentary and devotional practice, all of these sources were to provide the life-blood of the movement of which Rūpa Gosvāmi became one founding member. Rupa's purāṇic reading is equalled by his literary knowledge, which he uses to illustrate his technical points in manuals such as the *Bhaktirasāmṛtasindhu*. This background encompasses epic texts such as the *Mahābhārata* (*BRS* 2.5.92), Alvar literature such as the *Mukundamālā* (*BRS* 2.5.29), and the (primarily ascetic rather than devotional) poetry of Bhartṛhari, as well as repeated reference throughout to his own literary works and his collection of Krishna-related verses in the *Padyāvalī*. In addition he also drew repeatedly on the tradition of systematic aesthetic theory, particularly the writings of Bharata (variously dated from 400 BCE–500 CE). He may possibly even have had inclinations toward the aesthetics of Persian poetry common in the Mughal court of which he was initially a member.

There are innumerable studies of the intellectual constitution of Caitanya Vaiṣṇavism, its sources, and the particular process of synthesis, sifting, and concretisation that these textual and personal sources underwent in the life of Caitanya.[17] But there is a wider pool of influence on the six Gosvāmi founders of the school than is commonly acknowledged, and this influence does not end with the pilgrimage to Vṛndāvana. That period and locale became a major milieu for debate over the interface between Vedānta and Krishna theology, and while there is little explicit engagement in Rūpa's texts with the work of thinkers such as Vallabha and Nimbārka (c. b. 1162 CE), Madhsūdana Sarasvatī (c. sixteenth through seventeenth century CE), and other Vedāntic thinkers, it is important to recognise that they were important signposts on the intellectual landscape in which he moved. It is widely noted that his interest in aesthetic theory remains particularly striking, far outweighing the quantity of theological material explicitly devoted to metaphysical concerns. It is this aesthetic interest that furnishes the keystone concept of *bhakti-rasa* as a unique class of aesthetic-religious emotion culminating in *śṛṅgāra rasa*—passion; it is through this lens that his most unique contributions both to metaphysics and to ethics are figured.[18]

Rūpa has been seen as a devotee whose works are applied manuals rather that theoretical treatises treating practice, literary inspiration, psychology, and even theology, but not philosophy proper. Contrary to the unambiguously philosophical works of Jīva Gosvāmi, it can appear that in Rūpa's works he "categorises and illustrates" rather than analyses and expounds.[19] Much that is perhaps more explicit and more systematic could be said about Jīva Gosvāmi's position on these questions, and we will draw on his thought in due course.[20] There is a school of modern scholarly thinking that seeks to remind us that these thinkers were driven by the embodied, socially located, immediate agenda of guiding a religious community and inheriting or creating a tradition of ritual. Surely there is some illuminating value in the idea that "developed metaphysical interpretations of a metaphysical nature about the unity of consciousness are a later, secondary overlay on to the basic ritual and cosmogological structure . . . metaphysical speculation sits on top, as it were, of a ritual substrate."[21] Reminding scholars of necessary caution toward colonial and modern mediations of the Hindu tradition, Vertovec notes that modern trends in seeking to understand Hinduism have tended toward the "rationalisation of belief and practice" with particular reference to Vedāntic models.[22]

Yet this touches on a puzzle that is hotly debated in the study of Hinduism—is it belief that underpins practice, or practice that underpins belief? Bourdieu has brought powerful insights to bear on the centrality of the enacted structure of human life. Yet this assumes a life without questions, without deep reflection, without the scope for interrogating one's own reasons. Such questioning is seen as all too modern, and the contemporary abandonment of practice for reasons of the "untenability" of belief in the process of secularisation is contrasted with a notion of pre-critical religiosity.

Yet Srilata Raman notes that the "search for identity and meaning in modernity, often goes hand-in-hand with an impatience towards theological doctrine . . . it is crucial that the interaction and interpenetration of theology and socio-religious practice in the creation of the religious ideology of a community be grasped."[23] The Indian religious philosophy under examination in this book is deeply entrenched in a highly questioning milieu of debate and critical reflection in which thinkers often vindicated or ceded their views in a formal arena of logically moderated disputation—in short, a very "modern" context. There is a (hagiographic) story of how Caitanya tried to peddle his religious praxis and attitude in Varanasi, and found no audience until he was able to convince his detractors and the audience of its value in reasoned formal debate. Thus one can temper Flood and Sanderson's model with the image of a "devotional edifice" that must be "constructed upon a solid foundation of philosophical argument and understanding. Once a building's architecture is visible, the foundation is sometimes forgotten or ignored, but in reality the completed edifice is only as good as its supports."[24] This may be particularly true for those positions that drew on heavily theologised narratives such as (but not exclusive to) the *Bhagavad Gītā* and the *Bhāgavata Purāṇa*.

While Rūpa and his sources were indeed practitioners in the process of (re)creating traditions, they were also syncretic, systematic, and philosophically discerning about their range of influences, and distinctively individualistic in the cast of their theologising. In the natural course of synthesis, debate, and apologetics at a time of renaissance, it is not surprising that "the Chaitanya school unconsciously picked up the liberal and catholic traits of the above [heterodox] creeds."[25] Echoing a theme in the *Bhāgavata Purāṇa* itself, Rūpa uses his portrayals of Rādhā as an apt occasion both to lampoon the other positions (e.g., Buddhism in verse 136 of the Haṃsadūta) and to assimilate their religious modes into evocative, multivalent texts—and, of course, ultimately to transcend them. In short, while Rūpa Gosvāmi does not show the explicit marks of philosophical discourse in the manner that we observe in his nephew, we can expect the same depth of critical thinking from him as from the "philosopher" Jīva Gosvāmi, or from his classical forebearers. Even the language of his poetry belies his metaphysical reasons and reasoning, although as Lipner says of the philosophical study of Rāmānuja, for the scholar "the aim is to make explicit what is only implicit in [his] way of theologising."[26]

The main difficulty that the scholar will have in treating him in this way is a hermeneutical one. As Ganeri notes, some texts need more "set-up" for intercultural philosophical discussion than others.[27] As with Gadamer's works, the metaphysical structure underlying Rūpa's literary and aesthetic modes of discourse must be triangulated and teased out of his more dialectical, imaginative means of expression. Yet the philosophical integrity of his works are widely recognised, reflecting a distinctive incorporation of theory and practice that also marked the work of his contemporaries, but is seen with particular emphasis in the Caitanya Vaiṣṇavas. In contrast to M. T. Melville Kennedy's insistence that for the bhakta "serious intellectual effort [was] quite out of the question,"[28] Friedhelm Hardy notes of Rūpa and his contemporaries that "we may sense behind the history of these philosophical schools a progressive harmony and interaction between religious thought and practice. . . . Rūpa and Jīva Gosvāmi's theology was in fact the conceptual interpretation of their bhakti."[29] We differ here only in asserting that the theology and the practice go hand in hand, just as every action goes in hand in hand with the reason for performing it, even if those reasons are not the ones that immediately present themselves on the surface.

It will be Rūpa Gosvāmi's unique formulation and development of sophisticated contemporary ontological insights that is the primary interest of this chapter, but like Gadamer, his own philosophy is a deeply hermeneutical system that assumes a history of inquiry, and uses the building blocks of existing, heavily loaded terminologies from within the tradition that he is transforming. His texts are laced through with a particularly high proportion of quotes from the *purāṇas* and texts preceding him within his own Vaiṣṇava Bhakti tradition. Thus it is helpful to sketch out the cultural cache of ideas and debates on which he drew in forming his own ontological language.

RŪPA GOSVĀMI'S POST-PURĀṆIC ONTOLOGY

Previous chapters have sought to show how rigorous ontological inquiry that is tempered by sceptical and nihilist critiques, and takes phenomena rather than assumed substances as its epistemological starting point, tends by virtue of its own inner logic to define existence in terms of phenomenological content. Thus all beings, understood in terms of the nature of their Being, exist in terms of the nature of phenomena. There is and can be no *philosophically* warranted talk of any other reality. This train of reasoning results in the basic characteristics of an ontology of "ubiquitous consciousness" (Chakrabarti), of experience, of form, qualities, patterns, of "harmonic intervals" and radical flux.[30] This model is characterised by a family of defining features, including (a) the commonality of all existence in terms of the nature of its Being, an equivalence and unity of ontological *kinds* (i.e., there is no other reality); (b) the self-grounded sovereignty of all existence (reality can have no prior foundation and requires none); (c) the infinite plurality of the forms of existence such that they are infinite in number, and each individual form is infinitely divisible into internal constitutive facets; (d) the mutually constitutive character of all individual identities, all essences being structurally determined by their relations to all other essences (as illustrated by the example of language or mathematics); and (e) the admission that there is a fundamental ambiguity in all identities, individuals, or entities (consisting of a plurality bound by an analogical theme), which can be seen in terms of the dyads of universality and particularity, similarity and difference, determinacy and indeterminacy, and from which admission follows the diachronic (i.e., "similarity not sameness") character of all identity.

The above features can be posited as symptoms of a "monist-pluralist" ontology of phenomenal forms—a worldview that sees reality as an infinitely divided unity, ontically plural, and ontologically one. But they map out a "realism" that is not itself inferior to, or—relative to cultural context—less *intuitive* than the substantialist realism that the West has inherited from certain of its Abrahamic and Hellenistic roots.[31] By contrast, in keeping with the patterns of ontological debate outlined in chapter 4, Rūpa Gosvāmi's philosophical position grew from Nyāya logical methods, and an engagement with the formal realist paradigms of Vedānta and Sāṃkhya ideas that were prevalent in the *Bhāgavata Purāṇa* and a natural part of current philosophical-theological debate.

THE ONE AND THE MANY IN VEDĀNTA

Foremost among the philosophical discourses with which the Caitanya school engaged, enjoying flourishing activity and controversy at that time, was the Vedāntic debate. The contest between ontological views was no longer limited to the schools of Vedānta itself (insofar as it ever was bounded by such an ideological identity, which is questionable). By the sixteenth century, pundits possessed of diverse sectarian affiliations throughout the subcontinent, were defending or attacking the positions of key Vedāntins. This produced a range of nuanced later Vedāntic positions (such as those of Madhva, Nimbārka, Vallabha, and Caitanya and Jīva Gosvāmi), that are evidenced in the Vedāntic debates reported as crucial turning points in the life of Caitanya and in the popularity of the movement. Sophisticated positions on the question of whether reality is dual or non-dual proliferated in contemporary intellectual life. The theological problems of theism and pantheism were cross-referenced with philosophical attempts to redefine crude dualism in terms of a reality subtly divided into various modes of ontological intrarelation. Vedāntins contemporary with Rūpa Goswami handled problems of participation, internal relation, and identity that are similar in philosophical content to many questions with which Christian philosophers of the Trinity struggle today.

The Caitanya philosophy elaborated by Rūpa Gosvāmi assumes an ambiguous place in this debate, largely inherited from the "Advaitic theism," as Daniel Sheridan calls it, of the *Bhāgavata Purāṇa*. Even in this text, so full of mythological narrative, the ultimate focus of the enquiry at which these terminological tools are directed is an ontological one: the *āśraya*,[32] that on which things are dependent or in which they are inherent, and from which creation and destruction emerge.[33] And while the ultimate human goal for the devotee in the *Bhāgavata Purāṇa* will be devotion to Krishna, defended over and above the religiosity of the ascetic, nevertheless the philosophical substructure of the text advocates that the *jīvasya . . . artha*, the goal or purpose of the living person, is *tattvajijñāsa*, the knowledge of reality.[34] In fact, the tradition based upon this text typically employs a double strategy of simultaneously rejecting and appropriating the ideas of other groups; thus the literature that develops from the *Bhāgavata Purāṇa* employs tantric, ascetic, Sāṃkhya, and other imagery, while asserting its own superiority over such forms. Caitanya, who has so often been portrayed as a purely charismatic and unphilosophical thinker, evidently took to heart the aim of doing justice to this philosophical synthesis, imbuing his immediate circle of followers with the same goal.

The lynchpin of Caitanya Vaiṣṇava thought about reality is the pivotal doctrine that, in its median position between Advaitic ultimacy and Dvaitic devotion, is so reminiscent of Jainism's refusal to choose between unity and difference. This doctrine is *acintyabhedābheda*, a doctrine that asserts that the true nature of reality is "inconceivable difference and non-difference."[35] This doctrine encapsulates the way in which the school straddles the Vedāntic divide. The origin of this doctrine is not clear; the term first appears in the work of Jīva Gosvāmi, but notions of unthinkability and simultaneous difference and non-difference as applied to Krishna's ultimate divine nature are already juxtaposed in the work of Rūpa Gosvāmi (including the *Bhaktirasāmṛtasindhu*, which Jīva Gosvāmi helped to edit), and indeed other predecessors. It has been traced back to the doctrine of *bhedābhedavāda* in the Vedānta-Sūtras, in which shared identity is described in terms of the possessed quality and the possessing entity (e.g., *śakti* and the *śaktimat*), or the identity of cause and effect (*satkāryavāda*) through their reliance on the same potency. As Shrivatsa Gosvāmi argues, contradicting Steve Rosen's interpretation, *acintybhedābheda* is not merely a "supra-rational" concept, but in fact has a firm rational basis in the sophisticated ontological analysis that runs throughout the tradition.[36] The Caitanya school seeks to maintain a paradigmatically dualist self-definition appropriate to the personalism of the *Bhāgavata Purāṇa*'s Krishna narratives that are so important for Rūpa's discussion of the role-playing divine-human relationality of the characters in them. Thus, some have portrayed Caitanya himself as affiliated with the *sampradāya* or following of the radical dualist theologian Madhva.[37]

Yet others have sparked philosophical debate by linking him more firmly with less dualistic Vedāntins such as Rāmānuja, Vallabha, and Nimbārka.[38] Certainly, Caitanya's devotional biography is sprinkled with symbolic anecdotes as well as verifiable facts, and tells of pivotal occasions on which he vanquished the Advaitins in debate and converted them to his position. During his travels in Orissa he refutes the Bengali Advaitin founder of the Navya-Nyāya school Vasudeva Sarvabhauma,[39] and later in Varanasi he similarly defeats the Advaitin scholar Prakaśānanda Sarasvatī.[40] The first encounter is said to have given rise to the doctrinal Sāṃkhya-Vedānta underpinnings of his Bhakti dualism—the highest divinity's essence as Krishna, and Krishna's essence as the self-proliferating, self-dividing *svarūpa-śakti*—which were further elaborated in later discussion with another contemporary Vaiṣṇava dualist, Ramānanda Ray. We will come back to the Sāṃkhya framework for dvaitic apologetics shortly. For believers, the encounter with Ramānanda Ray only served to confirm the definitive superiority of the path of Bhakti to the Vedāntin's path of *jñāna*, or knowledge. Rūpa himself confirms this perspective in terms of the superiority of *bhakti* over *jñāna* and *mokṣa* in the *Bhaktirasāmṛtasindhu*.[41] Jīva would later come to give his explicit approval to elements both of Rāmānuja's "qualified non-dual" philosophy and Madhva's dualism. Yet the more dualistic position elaborated in the *Brahma Sūtra* alongside *bhedābhedavada* is not taken up by the Caitanya Vaiṣṇavas: the notion that souls are currently different from God but may become one with him as the pinnacle of a soteriological process did not hold great appeal for the school that sought an eternal, intrinsic truth that is firmly rooted in metaphysics rather than in a narrative soteriological framework.

While Jīva and Rūpa clearly had much in common with the modified monisms of Rāmānuja, Vallabha, and Nimbārka, it often seems that it was in regard to Advaita Vedānta that early Caitanya philosophy was most compelled to give a philosophical account of itself—not only because of its huge appeal and consequent threat, but also because by its very nature it challenged all philosophies of manifestation, multiplicity, limitation, and finitude with the ultimate absolutist formula. Yet the manner of defending against this threat was as much through assimilation as defence. Thus in the *Tattvasaṇdarbha* Jīva Gosvāmi sets himself the task of teasing out stubbornly Advaitic statements found in the *Bhāgavata Purāṇa*, and incorporates Advaitic features in his conclusions. The *Bhāgavata Purāṇa* includes the fairly Advaitic statement that the successively more personal appellations of divinity—"Brahman," "Paramātman" (the highest self), and "Bhāgavan" (the Lord)—are all known by the "knowers of reality" to be *jñānam advayam*—"undivided knowledge." Such a statement needed to be explained in a way that corresponds with bhakti ideology and practice.[42] Interestingly, Jīva denies that this is a statement of unity, but nevertheless interprets it as an assertion of the more desirable *features* of unity. *Advaya* is said to mean not that it is "non-dual," but rather that it is *svayam-siddha* ("self-establishing"—"sovereign" in Western scholastic terms), *cidekarūpam* ("pure-consciousness in form"—wholly ideal), and *antar-abhāvat* ("ontologically non-dependent").[43] Thus, while the school went on to give consummate theological defences of incarnational dualism, there was still a great drive to discuss, assert, and defend the ultimacy of the Caitanya conception of the divine on an Advaitic model.[44] Where Sāṃkhya would provide key building blocks of a philosophical framework for cosmic plurality, Advaita was the ideology on which theologians drew for a model of divine absoluteness, sovereignty, simplicity, impassibility—in short, that which qualified the divine as not only most *lovable*, the priority of the bhakti theologian, but also most *high*, the priority of the bhakti philosopher. Clearly the school sought to harvest the benefits of Advaitic ultimacy for the bhakti movement.

Seen in the light of India's classical axes of philosophical debate, the doctrine of *acintyabhedābheda*, "inconceivable difference and non-difference," arose from the same soil as the Jain doctrine of *sāmānyaviśeṣātma*, the unity of universal and particular. Its immediate subject in the Caitanya Vaiṣṇava context is the relation of Brahman and Ātman, but this is also an ontological formulation applying to all entities in the same micro-macro cosmic manner as Gadamer's ontological insights about structures of form and play.[45] It is what Gadamer recognises:

> In any order in which a many becomes a unity, in the state and in the soul, in knowledge and in the structure of the world, it sees the law of the One and the Many, of number and Being.[46]

Indeed, the language of the One and the Many has been widely applied to Indian Vedāntic thought, beyond its similarities to the strict *acintyabhedābheda* doctrine.[47] Implicit in the very terminology is not that reality is unknowable ("knowledge" in terms of the verbal root *jñā*), as we might say of Kant's thing-in-itself, but rather that is it beyond consciousness, unreflectable-upon (from the verbal root *cint*). Like Plato's "Indeterminate Two," it is, as it were, the very building block of thought, the necessary condition for it, which thought itself cannot therefore think. Both David Haberman and O. B. L. Kapoor explain it in ways that fit wholly with the formal ontological model. Kapoor writes:

> Even the concepts of identity and difference are transcended and reconciled in the higher synthesis. Transcendence and immanence are made the associated aspects of an abiding unity in God, or, in other words, in the doctrine of acintyabhedābheda.[48]

And Haberman elaborates:

> Any tradition that calls itself by the philosophical name acintyabhedābheda is really setting one up to think about ambiguities in a particular way. It is not that they are ultimately opposing notions, but rather that they are opposites that define one another and in some inconceivable way are non-different from one another.[49]

These accounts fit well with the mutual constitution of unity and difference and universal and particular in the formal ontological model, and it is interesting to note that one could quite validly make exactly the same observation about the doctrine of the "indeterminate two." Further, the universal applicability of the doctrine, drawing all possible beings under its umbrella, indicates a monist ontology, i.e., an commonality of all beings as one ontological *kind* and thus also of ontological non-dependent sovereignty. The universality of difference in the doctrine and the pervasive character of Krishna as envisioned by the school would also imply the infinite and equal plurality of all existence. Jīva also interprets the Vedāntic statement that reality is *advaya jñāna*, "undivided consciousness," as indicating that it is also *sva-prakāśa-rūpam*, "self-luminosity in character"—indicating again that reality also enjoys the feature of self-existence that accrues to Being according to a monistic ontology.[50]

Although it seeks a different paradigm, at a higher level *acintyabhedābheda* recalls the attempts of Vedāntic scholars like Rāmānuja to find ways of expressing the subtle ontological relation of part to whole—as body to person, as limb to body, as potency to agent. Sanātana Gosvāmi, during Rūpa's own generation, explains *acintyabhedābheda* in terms of the relative being of the wave to the sea that constitutes it, precisely echoing the natural images that Gadamer deploys to describe formal Being, exemplified in the play of light, the forms of the waves, the interplay of forces or of words.[51] Ontologically speaking, Rāmānuja's *viśiṣṭa*—"qualification"—and Caitanya's *bheda*—"difference"—can refer to the ontological distinction between the subject and its attribute, which is also included in the wide remit of Plato's accounts of *chorismos*. But Jīva Gosvāmi's version of the *acintyabhedābheda* doctrine focuses on the relation of ontological difference between a subject (with the divine subject as his preeminent paradigm) and its potencies (including the *jīvas*, or individual souls which we are)—following the lead of the *Bhāgavata Purāṇa*, he calls this the relation of the *śaktimat* and *śakti*. It is on this basis that S. C. Chakravarti places him in closest proximity to Nimbārka of all the Vedāntins,[52] yet here again there are unrecognised ontological subtleties in the doctrine in question. When Jīva says that there is an inseparable and unthinkable relation between the *śakti* and the *śaktimat*, this does not only refer to the incidental relation between a subject and the potency that it may (as an active mind) or may not (as a passive and unconscious entity) possess. Rather, it also takes in the necessary and constitutive relation between any subject and the potency for Being (remembering that "Being" is not a noun but a verb) that is its very essence. In this sense the two are a profound identity within which the only difference is an analytical one.[53] The *bheda* of Caitanya Vaiṣṇavism goes deeper than is widely acknowledged, incorporating aspects both of Plato's *chorismos*—"*ontological* difference"—of his *dihairesis*—"*analytic* division." It reflects analytic divisions that can be made within unities on many different axes and micro- or macroscopic levels. Logically, it refers to the kind of mutually constitutive difference that Plato saw in the eternally paired principles of same and other, motion and rest, becoming and destruction, greater and less, limit and unlimited, and is precisely the same kind of ontologically essential, foundational, and mysterious dyad.[54]

In many respects, the differences between the Vedāntic schools reflect the range of impulses about which aspects of unity and distinction should be highlighted. It is often a question of the way in which the cake is cut, intellectually speaking; the Buddhists tended toward anti-essentialism, the Upaniṣadic Hindus toward essentialism. Heraclitus emphasised the changefulness of "motion" while the earlier Plato emphasised the stability of "rest." Aristotle emphasised the teleological unity of motion that defines beings, whereas the Buddhists emphasised the synchronic plurality to which those so-called "beings" are subject. Śaṃkara emphasised the unity of the fact of Being in all particular beings. Rāmānuja emphasised the *distinctions* between a being and its constitutive parts, and between the fact of

Being and its manifestations, while Samantabhadra, like Vallabha, emphasised the *identity* of the whole of Being with its constitutive manifestations. The list of views with similar structures but different emphases could go on and on. In this sense, different "metaphysics" may come out of the same fundamental ontology.

It would seem that the core of the metaphysical disagreement between the Advaitic and the Caitanya Vaiṣṇava point of view was that the latter prioritised the *hlādinī śakti* aspect of the divine essence, the power of blissful relation and mutual enjoyment, asserting it to be "absolutely real and eternally displaying the intrinsic nature of Bhagavan."[55] At first glance this may appear to be a mythological bias favouring the content of the related narratives in the *Bhāgavata Purāṇa*, and a Sāṃkhya-influenced bias toward a metaphysical pluralism and dynamism, contradicting the notion seen to be most typical of the Upaniṣadic position that the essence of the divine is pure, undivided being-consciousness-and-bliss. On the Caitanya Vaiṣṇava model, *sat-cit-ānanda* is rather a universal, infinite interrelational plurality of which we are a part. Yet this would also seem to contradict the contemporary eagerness of devotional thinkers to retain certain features of an Advaitic godhead—pure *cit* or consciousness, for instance. But if we see the pure consciousness of Godhead as an infinite field of forms that are *composed* of thought then the contradiction disappears. The claim arises out of a critical process of thought that has dwelt with great rigour on the definition of Being (*sat*) as consciousness (*cit*), and reached the conclusion that phenomenology later reached with revolutionary effects in the West—that by Being we always mean consciousness, that consciousness by definition consists of contents in flux following a diachronic intentional structure, that relationality is a universal and necessary feature of Being. Indeed, it is one of Being's defining features, which, like another such feature, teleology, reveals its true essence. This insight is perhaps the single feature of the ontology of form as realised throughout Caitanya Vaiṣṇava theology, apparently from Caitanya to Jīva Gosvāmi, that is Rūpa's most crucial ontological premise. Accordingly, David Haberman links the *acintyabhedābheda* doctrine directly to Rūpa Gosvāmi's defence of the individual soul's distinction from Krishna as the necessary condition for aesthetic enjoyment, an idea that we will return to later in this chapter, having its correlate in a doctrine of the unified "dual" godhead of Krishna and Rādhā.[56]

MOTION AND DIALECTIC IN SĀṂKHYA

The theistic personality of the divine is, for Rūpa as for other bhaktas in most traditions, the one who creates—yet far from a sudden *ex nihilo* creation of a static substance, this is a *preraṇayā*, an "impelling" or "causing to move" of what has been *pravartita*, "set in motion" or "caused to turn." The dynamic quality of Being is well established in the model of the divine as ultimate reality. Yet in most cases this necessarily shifting, transient, apparently "non-absolute" facet of the divine is relegated to a secondary status relative to the true, changing agent of change. Yet the Caitanya tradition, following the lead of the *Bhāgavata Purāṇa*, does not accept the thoroughgoing character of this separation; rather the form, quality, and movement of the world are the true essence of Krishna, as they are the true way to realising the divine ultimate reality. Rūpa in particular presses this point through rhetorical strategies in his language and through his depiction of the sense-obsessed gopis as spiritual exemplars. This is precisely the kind of emphatically metaphysical point that is repeatedly obscured in translations of Rupa Gosvami's works. Hence lines that are filled with philosophical terminology (in this case Sāṃkhya-Yoga) lose their philosophical context when translated according to different interpretative priorities. In his discussion of *Madhura bhakti rasa* in the *Bhaktirasāmṛtasindhu*, the passionate form of the *rasa* category of refined religious emotion is distinguished by features with a metaphysical significance that Rūpa's later interpreters within the tradition are often reluctant to acknowledge. He describes the divine nature of Krishna as "the container of the perfection of the incomparable height of beauty, play and artful intelligence" (*asamānordhva-saundarya-līlā-vaidagdhya-sampadām*)—his own formulation of *sat*, *ānanda*, and *cit*. Here we discover that Krishna's essential nature also accords with the phenomenal truth of what it is to *be*: in a passage, the implications of which Jīva Gosvāmi resists by glossing *saṃsāra* as *saṃyak sāra*, Rūpa writes that "Rādhā is the vessel (or memory, continued mental impression) of *saṃsāra* (undergoing worldly change) that binds one to the supreme essence of desire" (*saṃsāra vāsanābaddha-śṛṇkhalām*) that Krishna has installed in his heart (*rādhāmādhāya hṛdaye*).

The mutuality and dialectical excitation of *rasa* is expressed again and again in metaphors of flowing and merging waters, and of light and reflection. We see this in the metaphor of *rasa* as "a flood of cool waters," Rādhā as the Ganges and Krishna as the Yamuna river, merging in confluence (BRS, 3.5.14), just as in *rasa*, separate units become a seamless unity (BRS 2.5.83). It can also perhaps be found allusively in texts such as the second verse of the *Vidagdha Madhava*:

> anarpita-carīṃ cirāt karuṇayāvatirṇaḥ kalau samarpayitum unnatojjvala-rasāṃ sva-bhakti-śriyām/ hariḥ puraṭa-sundara-dyuti-kadamba-sandīpitaḥ sadā hṛdaya-kandare sphuratu vaḥ śacī-nandanaḥ.

Here a description of the "compassionate incarnation of the golden-hued [Kṛṣṇa] Caitanya, bringing us the wealth of bhakti in the degenerate Kali age," underlines his identity as incarnation of Krishna in which he chooses to become both himself and Rādhā in a single form, for the purpose of simultaneously enjoying his adoration by Rādhā, and their mutual love, unified in a single experience. Caitanya thus is a physical form of the dialectic of *rasa*. But, as is common in verses referring both to a saint and to a god (e.g., the concluding verse of the Western quadrant), this is juxtaposed with a more theological analysis of the nature of Krishna (Hari) who is to be manifested in the cavern of the mind (*hṛdaya-kandare sphuratu*), and brings *rasa* to his own ever-changing (*anarpita*) treasure (*Śriyā,* also a name of the consort of Vishnu) of self-adoration (*sva-bhakti*), [thus] rejoicing in [his own] grace (*śaci-nandanaḥ*). It can also be read allusively as a metaphor of moonlight, water, and reflection, alluding to *kalā* as moon, *avatirnah* as shining down, *kadamba* as the astronomical ecliptic, and *vaḥ/vār* as pond. Thus, śleṣa-like, it might also read as:

> Of Hari, the moon in its phases, who forever is compassionately descending to dispense sublimely luminous nectar [like moonlight] onto his own-aspect, śriyā; may he, forever illuminated by the lustrous beauty of the gold [sun] at its zenith, shine forth like a reflecting pool in the cave of the heart, rejoicing in his grace.

Later in Rupa's plot (which describes an arc from the *Vidagdha* to the *Lalita Madhava*), Rādhā will indeed be united with Krishna—by drowning in the Yamuna river. In this translation the narrative metaphor is itself a vehicle for expressing the dialectic of Krishna's divinity, which triangulates the light of the sun, moon, and the mirroring pool of the mind (and of Radha), which is able to reflect his shifting (anarpita) light. This is a typical mode of expression for Rūpa, multifaceted and neatly mixing what we might call theological, metaphysical, and poetic discourses. It is in this way that his philosophy has to be teased out of his writings. In the *Ujjvala Nīlamaṇi* Rūpa writes about *nisarga,* one of the types of *svabhāva* or self-sufficient emotion:[57]

> *nisargaḥ sudṛḍhābhyāsa-janyaḥ saṃskara ucyate*
> *tad-udbodhasya hetuḥ syād guṇa-rūpa-śrutir manāk*[58]

The following is an example of a translation by a reader emphasising a devotional axis of interpretation:

> When, by briefly hearing about Krishna's transcendental attributes and handsome form, one's eternal love for him is aroused, this is *nisarga*.

This translation, though imprecise, captures the implication for devotional practice focused around the growing affections of bhakti. However, almost all of the words used also possess concurrent meanings in philosophical and/or other traditions of religious terminology; *ābhyāsa* can mean repetition (or even arithmetic multiplication), arriving at a transcendental truth through such repetition, and in later Vedānta philosophy the continual maintenance of a pure, unmodified mental state in yoga philosophy. For Rūpa then, what is translated as "eternal love" has the cast of a state of tenacious mental focus, which by its allusion to repetition recalls the recitation that is so central to Caitanya Vaiṣṇava practice. Similarly the word *saṃskāra*, barely rendered here in the above translation, can mean a sense impression (i.e., a phenomenon, as at *Yoga-sūtra* 1.18, 1.50, 2.15, 3.9–10, 3.18, 4.9, and 4.27) and also a sacramental ritual—given the divine character of phenomena that we find to be so distinctive for the theology of Rūpa and his tradition, this is a particularly fortuitous conjunction and is often used by Rūpa in his texts. Most explicitly linked to Sāṃkhya philosophy is the phrase *guṇa-rūpa-śrutir*. Literally rendered as "hearing [of] quality [and] form," and translated above as "hearing about [Krishna's] transcendental qualities and handsome form," this simple phrase also suggests that the "hearing" (here using the word *śruti* that most commonly signifies the "hearing" or "perception" of scriptural truths by the ancient sages of the Vedas) that is the cause of enlightenment (*tad-udbodhasya hetuḥ*) is in fact the proper attention to qualities (*guṇa*) and forms (*rūpa*) as designated by those terms in Sāṃkhya metaphysics. Form and quality, the constitution of the world is newly validated as divine in this theology. Thus the line can also be translated:

> That which is aroused by intense proximity or focus, that sense impression, of which the cause of that awakening may merely be the perception of quality and form, that is *nisarga*.

Multiple translations of most of Rūpa Gosvāmi's texts could be done in this way, privileging the narrative, theological, and metaphysical levels of discourse in turn, and it reflects the tradition of *śleṣa* double-meanings in literature, where a verse was designed to be read both with a more literal and a more theological or metaphysical meaning.[59] Here one finds Rūpa weaving meanings concerned not only with practice, but also with the theology of an appropriate attitude to god, and the philosophy underlying that attitude, into a single text. This is rich material requiring careful attention, which aims to substantiate each level (practice, theology, devotional attitude, metaphysics) with an underlying rationale that is not external but rather integral throughout. Here, the implication of this particular passage is again that the changeful phenomena that stand in contradistinction to the ultimate dimension of divinity in most cases are in this case the truth of Krishna to which we must become enlightened.

In Rūpa's doctrine of the divine godhead, this point is pressed further through a Sāṃkhya-influenced feature of the *Bhāgavata Purāṇa*, developed into one of the doctrines that are most uniquely characteristic of Caitanya Vaiṣṇavism: the equal (and, in some lights, superior) importance of Krishna's female consort, Rādhā. Rādhā is said to be not only the second pole, the *viṣaya* or *śakti*, the merely dependent capacity belonging to a relational duality as is common in purāṇic formulations of godhead, but the very principle of relationality and enjoyment itself within the godhead. She is Krishna's *hlādinī śakti*, which in this case links and defines the pole of lover and beloved, enjoyer and enjoyed, that which is same (self) and that which is different (other). Rūpa himself uses the phrase *sādhāraṇyaṃ*, translated by Haberman as "generalisation," also meaning "universalisation" and (according to Monier Williams) a holding of a middle position combining two opposites. He further describes this "generalisation" as an "irreducible reduction of the relation between self and other" (*sva-para-sambandha-niyamānirṇayo*).[60] There is an aesthetic identification with the other, but one that is fundamentally facilitated by separation. The notion is a dialectical one; the transition from unity to duality—neither of which can exist without the other—entails the arising of relationality itself between them. Rūpa recognises the self-perpetuating character of this dynamic—but not, as we will see, as a negative regress, but as a positive intensification. This principle of relationality, the "synthesis" in Hegelian terms, which becomes the second pole of a further movement of the dialectic: a reflective relation with relationality, which is infinitely repeated and deferred. The dialectic can be seen as Krishna loving his own capacity of love, and Haberman clearly recognises it in the *Bhaktirasāmṛtasindhu*:

> Although ultimate reality is recognised as being non-dual, for the purpose of enjoying its own dialectical dynamic of love (*prema*) it splits into the duality of the lover (*āśraya*) and beloved (*viṣaya*). It is very important to remember, however, that according to the theology expressed in Rūpa's text all three of these interrelated aspects—beloved, lover, and love—are divine.[61]

This is an insight that can be shown to pervade the incarnational theology of Krishna throughout many Sanskrit and vernacular, philosophical, and literary manifestations, leading to the conflation of Krishna's incitement of emotion in the characters and through the text, with his cosmogonic role as one who "quickens all things to create bliss in the world."[62] Rādhā's superior capacity to love is often explicitly cited as the reason why Krishna loves her, and indeed worships her. And the observer furthers the dialectic by learning to love Krishna's love for Rādhā's love of him. Rūpa's dramas make it their task to extend this dialectic further in a spirit of speculative, aesthetic participation.[63] We are encouraged not merely to love Krishna (as in Rūpa Gosvāmi's poem *Haṃsadūta*), nor only Rādhā (as in his *Uddhava Saṇdeśa*), nor only the beautiful story of their love (enacted in the plays), but also the observers who love them and who lovingly nurture their love—i.e., the many secondary characters listed in the *Bhaktirasāmṛtasindhu* and the *Ujjvala Nīlamaṇi* as the further "excitants" of ordinary emotion *sthayibhāva* and, in due course, of aesthetic appreciation *rasa*.[64] As Rūpa says: "That emotion that we call 'love' is the play of the great power and participates in the inconceivable nature of God."[65] The terms used in this passage are metaphysical keywords: *rati*, an emotion translated as "love" but also used for enjoyment, fondness, and sexual pleasure, is a type of *līlā*, is therefore also the *mahāśakti* of Krishna, and actually an aspect of the *acintya-svarūpa*—the true form of the divine that is opaque to thought. This statement aims to give a metaphysical status to the bhakti aesthetic theology of *rasa* for which Rūpa Gosvāmi is most celebrated.[66] In his sweeping study of Kṛṣṇa-devotion, F. Hardy is one of the few to note the distinctive character of this "impressive speculative edifice founded on a cosmic conception of bhakti-rasa":

> Here bhakti-rasahas become the fundamental cosmic principle (combining the psychological and the ontological) which underlies Kṛṣṇa's relation to Rādhā, the world, and the souls. The bhakta participates in the emotions of the gopīs (the highest forms of bhakti), because both his and their love is but the outflow of Kṛṣṇa's rasa. There is viraha in so far as Kṛṣṇa and Rādhā, the world and the souls are separate entities (ontology) and separated (psychology); but there is union according to the "unthinkable monism" (acintyādvaita) of the school's philosophical position.[67]

Rūpa's *Bhaktirasāmṛtasindhu* is widely seen as his major theological work, and the fact that it is primarily concerned with the complete, systematic aesthetic analysis of the Krishna narrative in terms of character, settings, and relationships has been taken as an indication that his interests are largely aesthetic rather than metaphysical. Haberman, for instance, notes this prioritising of *hlādinī śakti* and gives a thoroughgoing aesthetic and theological examination of it, but does not seem to even suspect the possibility of an intrinsic and logical reason for prioritising this feature of reality, rather than a practical, historical one.[68] Despite all of the groundbreaking work from David Haberman, Donna Wulff, Neal Delmonico, and others, Rūpa Gosvāmi's literature has not received full attention as an exposition of the metaphysical underpinnings of his views. Hardy recognises this theoretical dimension of Rūpa's work in passing, but as with so many Indian "philosophers," scholarship has been reluctant to see the deep and uncompromising logic behind their religious thought.

Thus it is important to give full recognition to the ontological implications of the dialectic of loving relation between Rādhā, Krishna, and the devotee. Friedhelm Hardy has famously brought to light the importance of the *Viraha Bhakti* or "love-in-separation" genre of narrative in Vaiṣṇava devotional literature, and the importance of this basic structure of deferred love, frustrated fulfilment, and enervated imagination has been further emphasised by many others subsequently.[69] But the metaphysical dimensions of it have yet to be added to this list—it refers not only to the necessary distance from the emotional object that Rūpa, like Paul Ricoeur, sees as essential to aesthetic experience. It is also the essence of ontology—the difference that defines structure, and of dialectic—a way of being not only in relation, but in relation with the principle of relation, thus achieving an understanding of, relation with, and fulfilment of Being itself. With each step back from the fundamental relationality of Rādhā and Krishna, that relationality itself is repeated and expanded and taken deeper into its own essence of relation through relation with itself. Hence the elaborate layers, hierarchies, and mechanisms of "exciting" emotion in his *rasa* theory. Each is a dialectic addition to Being, and fulfilment of it in much the same way that Gadamer encourages us not to transcend Being but to add to it. Just as Gadamer's "vitality" is at the centre of his ontology, and furnishes a eudaimonian ethics realising that vitality in the life of the individual, so the "enjoyment" of relation is shown in the Krishna theology to be both the true nature of Being, and the soteriological destiny of the individual.

In a striking parallel, it is given the same name that Gadamer uses to characterise the true nature of Being: *līlā*, or play. The "play," as Gadamer puts it, "of light, the play of the waves, the play of gears or parts of machinery, the interplay of limbs, the play of forces, the play of gnats, even a play on words" is not merely metaphor but is the meta-principle of Being, universally instantiated and apotheosised in Krishna.[70] Kinsley emphasised the theological importance of this idea, bringing out its implications as an evocation of the divine nature, cosmologically and cosmogonically speaking:

> In its essential form the Godhead is an eternal, playful, delightful dalliance. . . . The Absolute then is an eternal love affair between God and himself (herself) that is played out forever with all its humour and tenderness, frenzy and abandon, pique and reconciliation.[71]

This idea is in evidence in the Krishna literature with rich diversity, and its rhetorical opposition to world-denying philosophies of a still and certain absolute "Other" is unmissable. Kinsley observes this theme:

> The withdrawn, meditating *yogin*, completely closed off from the phenomenal world in trance; the Jain Tirthankara, immobile, statuelike and rigid; and the calm, unrippled countenance of the Buddha all suggest a vision of otherness that is beyond flux and becoming. These models convey the truth that the Absolute, or participation in the Absolute, is silent, still, and unchanging in its

> essence. The topsy-turvy world of Krishna seems to suggest a different vision. Krishna's realm is passionate, frenzied and tumultuous. He is never still in his rambunctious play and intoxicating revelry.[72]

Kinsley rightly highlights the element of theological critique and reformation, so clearly flagged in the many scenes in which the gopīs are used to satirise contemporary theological competitors. The idea of a non-dual absolute is challenged with an affirmation of phenomenological plurality in the play of Krishna. The *līlā* concept had already been applied ontologically in the *Bhāgavata Purāṇa* as a way of tying in the Sāṃkhya theories of plurality with the Vedāntic philosophy of monism.[73] The metaphysical scene for an exploration of change and plurality-in-unity is set by the *Bhāgavata Purāṇa*'s crucial tenth chapter, in which Krishna tells the gopīs: "From myself I create, maintain and destroy myself in myself by means of myself in the form of *guṇas*, senses and elements, through the power of my own *māyā*."[74] This duly provides a discursive framework for relationality that is inherited and deployed by Rūpa Gosvāmi. This Sāṃkhya dimension contributes further means for analysing the fundamental ontological constitution of Being, lending added support to the basic affirmation of necessary relationality as embedded in the cosmogonic theism of the dual divinity. Krishna's energy, his *māyā* in the *Bhāgavata Purāṇa*, is said to be the basis for the existence of the *guṇas*, the three basic constituent qualities of which all phenomenal existence is constituted. These in turn constitute the innate being, or *svabhāva* of all things.

However, A. S. Gupta notes that the *Bhāgavata* takes a turn away from classical Sāṃkhya "where the motive for creation is inherent in primal nature (*prakṛti*) and not in a transcendent reality"; by contrast "[t]he peculiarity of the Bhāgavata lies in the fact that here the supreme self, on its own initiative, has reflected itself in *māyā* and thus fallen under the influence of its own power."[75] Creation is not the willed action of a fully dualistic personal deity. Rather it is a natural product of the self-reflexivity of the divine consciousness; being consciousness it could not do otherwise than reflect in this way and give rise to a dialectical plurality. This divine "personality," critically understood in terms of a reflective consciousness, is an ontologised personalism. The *guṇas* become the dialectical trinity of a threefold ontology and ego of *sattva*, *rajas*, and *tamas*. These are not three separate cosmological elements, like fire, water, earth, and air, but three principles describing the universal and necessary microstructures of Being. In the Sāṃkhya system, operating as symbols of key meta-features of existence they bear much resemblance to the Platonic "transcendentals." The philosophical principle of an "Indeterminate Two" that we find in Indian ontologies as in Plato is once again refigured here. *Rajas* can be seen as the active principle of change and energeia, *tamas* as the inertial principle of unity, and *sattva* as the principle of Being or *sat* that pervades both. One thinks of Aristotle's parable and imagines Being as *sattva,* a moving army, alternately swayed by *rajas* and *tamas* as it shifts from stand to stand in the world of phenomenal forms.

THE APOTHEOSIS OF FINITE BEING

The view that is perhaps most common within the Caitanya tradition is that Caitanya's own theology and his ideological heritage are themselves closest to the radically dualist theology of Madhva. But on a closer examination of the philosophical subtleties that are implicit in Caitanya's ideas and applied to them by his heirs, other parallels suggest themselves. In Jīva's concern to make sense of the relation between ontologically foundational god and ontically plural phenomenal world, one sees a thematic similarity to Rāmānuja's attempt to get to the heart of the nature of the cosmological divide or *chorismos*. Yet the notion that Krishna is in truth Being as a whole, understood in terms of its truly relational essence, has most in common with the thought of Caitanya's contemporary, the Vedāntin scholar Vallabha. It is Vallabha's position that is called *śuddhādvaita,* "Pure Advaita," and with good reason, for it represents an attempt to present a non-dual reality, based on the world that presents itself to our perceptions, "purified" of unwarranted ontological postulates such as a transcendent ground.[76] Vallabha's system has also fallen foul of the Western misconception of Indian philosophy as metaphysically naive, and has been subject to the accusation that his position is "more theological than that of ācāryas like Śaṃkara and Rāmānuja." In addition to this judgement, Pande argues that "the ontological reduction of all things to consciousness as such is not a principle in the thought of Vallabha."[77] But Pande does not grasp the way in which the ontology of "consciousness" can transcend the crude dualism of mind and matter.

From the perspective of post-Heideggerian ontology, Vallabha takes the radical postmodernist position: Supposed Advaitins like Śaṃkara are actually dualists because they maintain the notion that *Brahman* transcends phenomenal reality, and in order to support this they ban the actual pluralistic phenomenality of world from the supposed purity of "Being" in its ultimate truth. From this perspective, Śaṃkara seems like the perfect dualist. Vallabha's departure from Rāmānuja is subtle, but shows that the later Vedāntin is uniquely willing to relinquish the ideal of radical transcendence, as defined by a simple and undivided unity. For Vallabha, the "difference" between Being and beings is neither the relation of a real substrate to an appearance, nor the relation of a substantive to the adjectives that qualify it (as in Rāmānuja's case), but the relation of the unlimited to the limited. There is no wishful desire for simple sovereignty or pure transcendence involved in his position, but only the philosophically honest, religiously serene acknowledgement of an infinity of finitude.

Relative to this position, the Advaitin seems to stubbornly prioritise existence over essence, to the extent of ontologically devaluing essence as mere *māyā*—illusory phenomenal forms. In the same way that Vallabha sees this plurality as the true material of the non-dual reality, so too, based on the theology of the *Bhāgavata Purāṇa*, the Caitanya Vaiṣṇavas embrace the *yogamāyā* of Krishna, his power of manifesting forms, as not only an innate feature but as his true nature both facilitated and personified by Rādhā. Much of what Vallabha does explicitly, the Caitanya Vaiṣṇava perspective does implicitly, and both are in agreement when Vallabha rejects the duality between ultimacy and phenomenality as itself a wilful illusion, instead asserting a true identity between the two. He maintains that Krishna, the ultimate form of the divine and thus the ultimate reality, does indeed have qualities.

Seen in the wider context of the popular rhetoric of the Advaitins, this was a controversial claim, but if one reads even a few pages of any of the centuries of Sanskrit and vernacular poetry devoted to Krishna, it is immediately clear that these qualities are a central and much celebrated feature at ground level in Krishna theology. Further, Krishna's forms are not mere ornaments and aids to worship; they are his own defining features, part of the godhead, much revered as insights into the divine essence. Nowhere are these qualities more central to the theology of Krishna, and elaborated with more care than in Rūpa Gosvāmi's *Bhaktirasāmṛtasindhu*. Like every deity, but perhaps preeminently so, Krishna is not only considered to be a divine personality, but is in addition a thematisation of the philosophy of the divine, and also a meta-discourse on the nature of the bhakti mode of worship itself—psychologically, theologically, sociologically, and, of course, metaphysically.

Vallabha is but one of the philosopher-theologians whose ideas circulated throughout the pan-Indian intellectual discourse of the time; like Caitanya, Madhusūdana Sarasvatī, Nimbārka, and others of that milieu, he was concerned with the idea of a productively, positively pluralistic world and the place of divinity in relation to it. The net may be seen to spread even wider; Sanjukta Gupta (supported by Lance Nelson) argues that Madhusūdana Sarasvatī was another philosopher driven to affirm finitude, in this case through the notion of *savikalpa brahman* ("brahman with parts, a divided brahman")—albeit with greater discomfort about the implications of such an immanentist pluralism.[78] All of these thinkers seem to have followed a contemporary local "zeitgeist" in applying an extremely sophisticated scepticism to the Vedāntic debates, keeping Nyāya and Sāṃkhya to hand as tools for analysis, and Krishna bhakti as the theological framework.

Delmonico is one scholar who places this in the context of a more general humanism toward which Bhakti arguably militates. He writes that "*The*

Sapphire (*Ujjvala Nīlamaṇi*) is a fine example of a humanistic text, provided one understands humanism in a sense that fits the South Asian context," explaining this context in terms of the notion that "the divine has descended from its high, majestic, unapproachable throne into the thoroughly human and humane realm of humble earthly existence, and, by that descent, the value and meaning of human life and passion is exalted."[79] On the one hand, Delmonico draws to the fore a genuine "humanism" of the finite, the earthly, the theologically, metaphysically and aesthetically form-oriented tendencies that developed within much of the bhakti movement per se, and with particular force in Krishna-bhakti as exemplified in Rūpa Gosvāmi's philosophical and literary texts.

On the other hand, one feels that it is not wholly a historical coincidence that in the recent atmosphere of postmodern concerns and historical revisionism, Delmonico should "discover" a gender-, sexuality- and world-affirmative philosophy, reasserting "embodied existence" within the works of a favoured philosopher. His discovery is also a reminder that our own contemporary critical concerns harmonise well with those of sixteenth-century Indian devotionalism. For the realists of Rūpa Gosvāmi's persuasion and the dvaita philosophers before them, it is advaitic monism and Indian asceticism that oversaw an epochal "forgetfulness of Being." The analogy with Gadamer's special brand of "humanism" indicates a genuine similarity in the specific insights of the two men in the face of a similar fabric of larger questions that these writers are addressing.

We have seen that Rūpa's main idea, the ontological and soteriological importance of *rasa*, is a way of enacting the essence of Being. It is a concept that unites ontology with our proper appreciation of it. It is also a eudaimonian conception that sees human flourishing in terms of dialectically appreciating the nature of Being, and instantiating it in a self-reflexively heightened way. The progressive, dialectically structured movements of love, and of an aesthetic love of love, are intended to be a quantitative and qualitative augmentation of Being itself. It is the keynote of his ontology. We have also noted that Rūpa's aesthetic mode of worship is actually both an assimilation to the divine being and a celebration/fulfilment of it through the successive stages of appreciating the essence of Being as relationality through the medium of the Krishna narrative. There is thus a pervasive integrity to the ontological truths of the tradition, their manifestations, and the appreciation that both the scholar, and at a higher level, the devotee can give to these. As a result the "forms" of Krishna worship in art and practice are integrated into the ontological discourse, and this is an explicit feature of his both his fictional and analytical works, imparting a powerful kind of ontological and religious realism to these texts.

While this is here asserted of his thought, as with Gadamer, a certain amount of detective work is necessary to find such assertions in Rūpa

Gosvāmi's own texts. As previously noted, One could read the existing translations of his major texts and remain almost completely ignorant of any metaphysical discourse within them as they tend to be read with aesthetics or devotional practice in mind—like Gadamer, Rūpa Gosvāmi too is a thinker whose practical applications too often obscure his underlying theories. But in texts from the *Bhaktirasāmṛtasindhu* to the *Haṃsadūta*, most of his verses can be read for a primary, secondary or even tertiary metaphysical meaning, so rich had the contemporary devotional literature become, and so complexly coherent is Rūpa's own style.

This is distinctive in his writing but not unique; after all, the Krishna narrative of the *Bhāgavata Purāṇa* is itself myth become metaphysical metaphor, in which Krishna himself provides the justification for this philosophical-theological hermeneutic. He explicitly tells the gopīs that his absence is the necessary catalyst for them to develop their emotions, and also to elaborate their ideas of him.[80] Just as they acquire the hermeneutic talent of learning to see the signs of Krishna in the phenomenal world, so his texts are filled with theological and philosophical "keywords" that alert the different readers of the text to its different discourses. This reflects the importance of reading the text with a sensitivity to contemporary concerns and genre precedents. A multilayered hermeneutic translation would help to clarify the way in which Indian "dogmatic" texts also engage sophisticated critical debates in what we see as quite different types of discourse. Sadly, such a translation is outside the scope of the present study. But as we will see, it is not only different disciplines of inquiry (into practical theology, divine nature, metaphysics, historical, and mythological interpretations, for instance), but also different modes for posing and exploring those questions that are interwoven throughout Rūpa Gosvāmi's texts, from literary metaphors to theoretical treatises to images that are supposed to instantiate what they describe.[81]

While Rupa's formulations of his *rasa* metaphysics are encrypted in this way, properly read they reveal a picture of *rasa* as a model of Being into which individual beings, qualities, aspects, and emotions are taken up. In his extensive discussion of *rasa* in the *Bhaktirasāmṛtasindhu* he writes:

> At first the excitants and the rest (*vibhāvādyāh*) are recognised as separate portions, but upon obtaining the form of rasa they are combined into an undivided unity.[82]

Interestingly, the word rendered as "combined" *(militā)* appears in an augmented form as a word that means both "combined" and "disappeared" (*mīlitā*) in the key scene of the *Bhāgavata Purāṇa*. Here in the *Purāṇa*'s usage we have something close to the German *aufgehoben*; one need only be willing to see hermeneutic complexity where traditionally translators have seen univocal meanings. Later he asserts:

> That emotion called passion (rati) whose true nature is the play of the great śakti and shares in the inconceivable essence [of Krishna]; thus it cannot be invalidated by logic.[83]

We have noted that in Rūpa Gosvāmi's formulations of the metaphysics of divine ultimate reality, the metaphor of pure playfulness gives way to the metaphor of increasingly passionate love-play and the intensifying appreciation of the aesthetic play of forms. The dialectic of love is explicitly described:

> Love makes Krishna and the related factors vessels of sweetness, and then when Krishna and the related factors are experienced as such, they expand the love.[84]

He reiterates this point and also recognises the "fluidity" of this ontological model, as Gadamer does with regard to Hegel's logic (see the quote at the beginning of part I of the present work).[85] Thus *rasa*'s capacity to sublate and unify different features is described as

> just like the ocean which, having filled clouds with its own water, increases itself by means of this very rain water.[86]

This trope of the flow of water is reinforced through other images of nectar, and of rivers uniting and merging. Yet another ontological model that he uses is the familiar metaphor (having some possible provenance in Indian Sufism) of Being as light rather than substance.[87] It is noted of ontologies of light rather than substance that, whereas substance can exist on its own, light requires objects to illuminate in order to meaningfully exist. There is no light in a void—it has a "dialectical" need to exist in relation to an "other." Analogously, Sanskrit aesthetics observes that *rasa* cannot arise without excitants—it too is like the facets of a jewel (hence the title of the book in which he lists those excitants, the *Ujjvala Nīlamaṇi*). The signs, settings, and protagonists of the Krishna narratives also yield powerful emotions of different "hues," refracting the divine light and forming a microcosm of universal cosmogony.[88] This common metaphor is merely another way of expressing the insight into the necessary relationality of Being. The "jewel" itself is defined in terms of the light that illuminates it, relative to the position of the observer that determines its hue; it is an apt illustration of the structure of phenomenal reality.

Literary manifestations of this insight are found in much of the Krishna literature, both before and after Rūpa Gosvāmi. J. S. Hawley shows how the vernacular poem the *Sur Sagar* employs a constantly shifting perspective throughout the stanzas. This ceaseless shifting emphasises the commonality of the aesthetic experience as it bridges the protagonists, writer and reader of the literature.[89] In addition, the *Sur Sagar,* like Rūpa's poetic compositions, employs a basic structural feature of Sanskrit grammar to ontological effect; four-line stanzas may describe four different features of something before letting us finally know in the last word or two what the subject or action of the phrase is. The result is a riddle structure that prioritises the descriptions, facets, and features rather than the subject of the sentence, often putting off our final understanding in order to excite suspense, perpetuate engagement, and defer knowledge of the merely propositional content of the text. This semantic *telos* unifies the verses yet defers fulfilment.

This is a clue to the performative, instantiative nature of the truth discourse in the text, demonstrating ontological truths by virtue of its very semantic structure, in dramatic contrast to the propositional semantics of texts conveying truths on a solely "correspondence" model. Of course, the Indian *dūtakāvya* genre of long poems in the form of speeches given to a messenger to be conveyed to the object of love, explicitly inscribes this same dynamic of teleological and narrative deferral on a larger scale, and both of Rūpa's long poems, the *Haṃsadūta* and the *Uddhava Saṇdeśa,* are in this format. Indeed, both poems describe and excite unfulfilled love. The structures of two of Rūpa's most important aesthetic-theological treatises can appear pedantically concerned with enumerating "in typically scholastic fashion" the attendant details of the Krishna narrative.[90] But on closer examination it becomes clear that these conscientious accounts attempt to map out the variations in the divine essence that are brought into being through these manifestations. They are the particular movements of dialectic within a dialectical ontology for which every ontic particularlity reflects and augments the essence of existence. These are the facets, sparkles, and hues of the "gem" *(nīlamaṇi)* of Being.

"PANTHEISM" AND THE REALITY OF PERCEIVED PRESENCE

There are many devices for manifesting and facilitating this in these ontologically privileged texts with their special brand of semantic integrity. One of the most discussed features of the literature and theology centred on Krishna is its emphasis on *viraha*—"separation" in experiences of romantic and religious love. This separation occurs as a tragic event in a common genre of Indian romantic narrative to which so many of the famous Indian love stories belong. In the ontologised subtext of Krishna and Rādhā's love, it is an expression of the *bheda,* or difference, that is necessary for their love to exist, and for Rādhā, by virtue of their love, to become the true essence of Krishna, thus uniting them across that primeval divide. Thus *viraha bhakti* is not just a stylistic genre, but also a philosophical doctrine in schools that recognise not merely the god-world duality, but also the relational plurality of the cosmos.

Another narrative device with ontological implications and one of the most common, explicitly expresses the monist, identity-oriented theology through the trope of mistaken identity. This longstanding Sanskritic staple of love-in-separation stories (from the *Rāmāyaṇa*, which is referenced by a similar plot device involving Rādhā's kidnapping by a demon in Rūpa Gosvāmi's *Lalita Mādhava*, to Kalidasa's *Vikramorviśiyam*), involves the narrative convention whereby a "beloved," often with some supernatural status, is lost and sought by a delirious lover in the forms of natural beauty that he or she encounters in a pastoral setting. Such an episode has a prominent place in the thirtieth chapter of the tenth book of the *Bhāgavata Purāṇa* in which Krishna disappears from his worshippers' midst leaving them to weep, celebrate, and cavort with diverse objects and aspects of their surroundings, mistaking them for Krishna. In a theologically pivotal moment, Krishna reappears to affirm that their imagined engagement in his midst is actually a legitimate engagement with Krishna himself. This is a scene that adds an explicit theological interpretation to a long tradition of mistaken identity stories (drawing on the concepts of *māyā* and *prakṛti* as manifestations of the divine in nature), and furnishes the template for further illustrations of divine omnipresence in the forms of the perceived world.

Recalling the illusions of the love-maddened gopīs, Rūpa Gosvāmi's *Haṃsadūta* implies the same status for Rādhā's desperate hallucinations of Krishna in the course of her heartbroken response to his absence. She is afflicted with an extreme case of divine madness, classified as *unmāda* in the *Ujjvala Nīlamaṇi*. This madness is by no means a source of pleasure.[91] Its character is not festive or joyful, and it draws into question the character of the bliss *(ānanda)* of which Rūpa Gosvāmi speaks in his opening verse.[92] The scene is nevertheless meant to be paradigmatic for the devotee—by imagining Krishna she makes him present,[93] and he tells her as much when she is pained at his absence: "It is not a dream that you have each night when you are united with me."[94] Thus Rādhā's hallucinations in the grip of *divyonmāda*, "divine madness," are actually the metaphysical insights bestowed by an altered point of view.

Lalita and Krishna, the narrators of the *Haṃsadūta* and *Uddhava Saṇdeśa*, respectively, also demonstrate the possibility of making distant objects present by means of the imagination, in their detailed visual descriptions of distant events that they could not possibly know of.[95] *In the Uddhava Saṇdeśa* Krishna confidently weaves an elaborate portrait of past, present, and future, including much material of which he ought to have no access to such detailed memories.[96] Rūpa also gives the trope a biographical implication; in the *Vidagdha Mādhava* Rādhā finally mistakes the dark waters of the Yamuna river for Krishna's dark limbs and drowns in them, echoing some accounts of the death of Caitanya.[97] The misperception that leads to this love-maddened death is ratified as a case of enlightened perception, according to the underlying theology of Krishna's omnipresence. Others seek union with ultimate reality through long processes of mental training, but according to this ontology Caitanya need only immerse himself in the dark waters—as part of the cosmos they are the reality of Krishna, and also from the perspective of ontology of form, the water's quality of "darkness" also partakes of Krishna's essence in a different way. Rādhā is the envy of the Advaita ascetics, just as the gopīs in the *Bhāgavata Purāṇa* are the envy of passing saṃnyāsins characteristically concerned with enquiry into ultimate reality.

This pattern of mistaken/true perception is explicitly cited as a general characteristic of love-in-separation by Rūpa in the *Ujjvala Nīlamaṇi*, best expressed in the anticipatory excitement of *pūrvarāga*, the early stages of love. The lover achieves the true essence of the beloved through imagination that achieves a special quality of attention to phenomenal form. Rādhā even thinks that she has become Krishna in stanza 55 of the *Haṃsadūta*. Ontologically speaking, she is and becomes the essence of his nature to a greater degree through the intensity of her love, more and more so as it is deferred. Her pantheistic perceptions escalate in the course of the poem: in stanza 54 Rādhā confuses a picture that she herself has produced with Krishna's tangible physical presence; she reaches to embrace it.

This conveys a clear message about the status of art (including the text in which the claim is made) as ontologically equal to its object, having its reality status conferred upon it by the intensity of the aesthetic experience that it provokes. Again the layers of the semantic-ontological integrity of text are present—Rūpa's theology tells us that Rādhā is Krishna, her image in the text is Krishna, the image that she draws is Krishna, the image of that image in the text is Krishna, her "enjoyment" of it is Krishna, our enjoyment of her enjoyment is Krishna. The text tells us about Krishna, is Krishna, and excites Krishna. Like *acintyabhedābheda*, the microcosmic, macrocosmic universal identity portrayed through Rūpa Gosvāmi's narrative devices, just as Gadamer's elusive ontological metaphors are deployed in his, is a universal and pervasive truth.

The semantics of the texts expresses this in ways that are characteristically literal and symbolic, while also instantiating the truths of which it speaks. The initial invocation of the Eastern section of the *Bhaktirasāmṛtasindhu* is an extended metaphor that can be read both as a statement about the moon and its relation to the charms of the night sky, and about Krishna and the charms of the gopīs.[98] Krishna is described as the complete image/manifestation of eternal *rasa* (*akhila rasāmṛtamūrtih*), and these qualities are expressed through the metaphor of the full moon, while the juxtaposition of the two interpretations reflects the truth of Krishna's identity with the world, particularly the natural world, which is a particularly potent symbol of *prakṛti*. Again, the compound *rasāmṛta* can mean many things, both devotional and metaphysical; it can describe *rasa* as a nectar, or it can cite the two things separately—as flavour and nectar (an extended metaphor of taste), or as the fundamental ontological features of enjoyment (*rasa*) and eternality/vitality (*āmṛta*), made "whole" or literally "undivided" (*akhila*) in their single ontological reality. The ambiguity of the semantics of the verse is itself a microcosmic expression of the *acintyabhedābheda* nature of Krishna's various levels of shared identity. The operations of meaning in the text frequently remind us of the presence of Krishna in the text itself, through the literary devices of metaphor, and the semantic deferral that defers, facilitates, prolongs, and nourishes our relation of "enjoyment" of the divine. In addition, we see how it is not only possible but hermeneutically important to bring out the metaphysical implications that pervade Rūpa Gosvāmi's texts.

Interestingly, there is both a deep sense of the constructive virtues in this semantics of instantiation and deferral, and also an acknowledgement of its deconstructive potential. Hence the effects that Krishna can have upon his worshipers are largely characterised by disorder. Famously, the ornaments, clothing, and perceptions of the gopīs are sent into disarray when they hear Krishna's flute. They run off leaving the dinner uncooked and their husbands and mothers-in-law uncared for—a scurrilous subversion of the presiding social order. Strings of pearls are broken and scattered through the forest, clothing falls away, and a divine madness of semantic confusion descends.[99] Yaśodā, Krishna's mother, has a famous experience of this when she accidentally discovers the universe lodged in her baby son's mouth and is briefly overwhelmed—it is not the bliss of *ānanda* that the vision inspires, but a disorder so profound that the intervention of her own infant is required to restore her sanity.

Rādhā's experience of this madness, as portrayed in Rūpa Gosvāmi's *Haṃsadūta*, is one of the darkest instances of the deconstructive disarray that a monist pluralism can produce. Far from being sweetly romantic, Rādhā's intense suffering and her inability to function are central to Rūpa's *kāvya* depictions of her, and in his case they are so harsh that they would seem to act almost as a warning.[100] In other contexts and in the works of other writers, this same potential for disorder hermeneutically reemerges as "freedom and spontaneity." It "expresses the nature of the divine as unconditioned . . . [belonging] to a joyous realm of energetic, aimless, erratic activity that is pointless yet significant."[101] But, as Wulff has implied and we will see, this joyful play is in marked contrast to the position of the individual as portrayed by Rūpa Gosvāmi—bound up in overwhelming and passionate relation, not pointless but rather unwaveringly focused on its goal.

Like Rādhā, others "with sensitive hearts," as Sanskrit aesthetic theory puts it, are also shown noticing Krishna's presence everywhere. Rūpa has Baladeva exclaim:

> "Oh! How is it that I feel such love for this group of cowherds and calves?" the confused Baladeva was astonished and appeared to be frozen in his tracks, like a statue.[102]

There are innumerable examples of Krishna adopting disguises—sometimes by dressing up, sometimes by magically transforming his appearance—such that his various kinds of lover learn to recognise him in diverse forms. But the imagined identity is not a lesser presence—it is still "inconceivably different and non-different" from Krishna himself. Haberman notes that the same principle applies even today in the actual experience of the pilgrim in Vraja—the landscape of the pilgrimage has innate value because "that dirt and mud is considered to be non-different from Krishna."[103]

While the omnipresence of Krishna is enacted through this pervasive literary theme of misperception, a more direct demonstration of Krishna's forms is made through the enumeration of Krishna and Rādhā's literal ornaments—the aspects and ornaments of the beloved become one with him or her.[104] This too is a common device, hence Raghunātha Dāsa Gosvāmi's elaborate and elegant literary confusion of external ornament and internal character in his portrayal of Rādhā.[105] The classical literary technique of pathetic fallacy is theologised in the Krishna bhakti ontology of form. Rūpa gives this monistic identity of Krishna with the things and forms of the world a personal dimension where literary convention demands that he make reference to himself: the invocation at the beginning of the Eastern Section of the *Bhaktirasāmṛtasindhu* elaborately identifies not only Caitanya, but also Rūpa's brother Sanātana (who also acted as his mentor), with Krishna himself.[106] Everywhere, in Caitanya Vaiṣṇava literature as in its practice, the marks of a type of pantheism are evident. God does not dwell in objects as an obscured hermetic essence—purely *puruṣa*, "spirit" seeking to escape the impurities of *prakṛti*, "matter," "form"—but rather is enacted, augmented, and instantiated in the dialectical movement that is the existence of each entity. It is for this reason, as Wulff observes, that Krishna's ornaments, companions, circumstances and lovers do not take on the radically subsidiary role that one might expect.[107] In Rūpa's treatises as in his literature, one does not bypass the accessories of the divine, for they are the divine itself.

RŪPA'S DIALECTICAL ESSENTIALISM: MOTION, TELEOLOGY, AND VALUE

Krishna himself is, as we might expect, both the exemplary enjoyer and the exemplary object of enjoyment. In his drama, the *Lalita Mādhava*, Rūpa has him observe Mount Govardhana and comment with surprise, breathlessly caught up in aesthetic appreciation of his own reflected beauty:

> What is this thing full of sweetness appearing before me? I have never seen anything like it before; it astonishes me with its extreme preciousness. Ah, after seeing it, my heart becomes greedy and I wish eagerly to enjoy it as Rādhā would.

Elsewhere, Krishna rushes toward his own image, mounting the stage to embrace the actor who plays his earlier, sweeter self in the Vṛndāvana-set play within a play that is performed for him in Mathura.[108] Krishna is entranced by his own divinity dialectically coming to light in the world. In the *Uddhava Saṇdeśa* he is portrayed as the exemplary devotee, as full of weakness, excitement, and imaginal yearning as are his consorts and worshipers. Much is made of the theological twist whereby Krishna becomes the devotee to Rādhā's deity. But we must see this too as yet another manifestation of his essential nature—dialectically taken up into the fundamental ontology of *rasa*.

Rasa had always been more than merely a psychological observation about the affective character of art, for the aestheticians were philosophers and thus the main purpose of the Sanskrit critics was to analyse the poetic object rather than primarily to dwell on its psychological effects. Understood in the light of this aim, *rasa* is the objective structure of meaning embodied in the poem, not only the emotion generated by it.[109] At the height of the flourishing of aesthetic thought, the *rasa* theorists and those who held that suggestion (*dhvani*) was the primary feature of aesthetic discourse had argued over whether it was emotional content or semantic reference that should be seen as the essence of poetry.[110] To the objection that some language is merely informative, *rasa* theorists ruled that all propositional information is determined within a context of emotional intention and effect.[111] Abhinavagupta sought to limit this emotive contextuality of meaning to poetry as an otherworldly, *alaukika* discourse; it is primarily in this that Rūpa differed from him. For Rūpa, the problem of deciding between the sovereignty of the formal structure of Being, or its value-imbuing teleological essence, had been raised centuries before in the classical discipline of aesthetics.[112] *In the rasa* theory, metaphysically construed, we see that the traditional Western understanding of monism or pantheism as an identity of divine and worldly *substances* is too crude for this Indian model. It is valid to say that Krishna is the inhabitants, ornaments, and landscapes of Vṛndāvana. But this is not only to say that he manifests in these forms. He is not merely the things, but also the relationships between them, and the experiential enjoyment of those relationships of inherent value and care. This is a "pantheistic" identity understood in a different way.

It could be argued that there is a certain hermeneutic disingenuity in interpreting the divine person of Krishna, subject of religious myth and object of worship, as a cipher for the philosophical constitution of reality.

This surely does not see Krishna's preeminence in the way in which most believers see it (although, remembering the disagreement between Steve Rosen and Shrivatsa Gosvāmi, there are clearly more and less philosophical interpretations even among the relevant communities of believers). There is a danger of reducing the theological aspects of the ultimacy of incarnate divinity to a mere symbol of a philosophical insight. In defence one could argue that this Krishna is a not only a symbol but also an instance of ultimate reality, an incarnation of the ontological truth. But the philosophical foundations of the theology are themselves open to different criteria for examination—logical and hermeneutical ones, which need not compete with the different levels of truth-discourse. Thus, the identity of Krishna as *rūpa* (form) and as *rasa* is less a challenge to the personal identity of the godhead, than a hermeneutic augmentation of the concept which, it turns out, is wholly in keeping with the Upaniṣadic assertion about Brahman: *raso vai sah*—"He is indeed *rasa*"—and further for Rūpa, "the essence of all *rasas*."[113]

It is not difficult to see how the essence of Krishna is form, but it is his essential identification with *rasa* that is most philosophically interesting and most crucial to Rūpa Gosvāmi. Whether Krishna's presiding quality is presence or absence, erotic allure or erotically tantalising cruelty (of which he is frequently accused in Rūpa's poems), all of these qualities are transformed from the perspective of *rasa* into *mādhurya,* sweetness. Shrivatsa Gosvāmi's view is that "the aesthetic experience of rasa is not only the *summum bonum* of life but also the human *raison d'etre.*"[114] In a more dualistic context we would say that *rasa* is *why* the world was created, but here we can say that it is *what* the world is. We can understand *rasa* as the eternal third term of all dialectic, a concept of synthesis and relation personified by Rādhā.[115] As this third term of the dialectic, *love itself* transcends Krishna as lover and object of love, and takes priority, which is why the *hlādinī śakti,* his power of enjoyment, is said to be his true nature. The transition from the Krishna of the *Bhāgavata Purāṇa,* whom Kinsley so vividly describes as spontaneous and free, "unfettered and unconditioned,"[116] to the Krishna of the *Uddhava Saṇdeśa*, unhappily overpowered by his passion, shows the way in which the concept of divinity is "taken up" into what we had supposed to be merely one of its features, which turns out in fact to be pervasive and fundamental.

In Rūpa's *kāvya* Krishna no longer laughs and capriciously disappears from the gopīs in order to reveal his independence and their dependence. Instead, he passively suffers a fervent passion that, theologically, he himself and also the object of his love actually *are*. From this obscure self-transcendence by Krishna of himself through the refining means of his own love, we understand what lies behind Wulff's wonder at the idea that "the absolute for Rūpa is not a metaphysical principle, but an emotion."[117]

Rasa is a metaphysical principle, but it comes from an unexpected kind of metaphysics. *Rasa* explicitly does not refer only to the primary emotion that is inspired by an encounter. Sometimes translated as the "relishing" of an emotion, it is the distinctive further state that we reach upon achieving a certain appreciative awareness of that first emotion—a subtler notion for which there is no such terminology in English. In its literal meaning as the "juice" or inner "nectar" of emotive encounter, the *rasa* concept is a helpful symbolic substantialisation of this ontological quality of dialectical relationship with a particular relation. God is "made" of this "substance," as the devotee is "made" of it.

In her introduction to the *Gītagovinda* B. S. Miller notes that the association of Krishna with *madhu*—meaning "honey" and implying the "sweetness" of romantic-aesthetic enjoyment—is an analogy through which he is often identified with other "sweet" characters or objects assuming a certain malleability of his identity.[118] This same sweet, fluid substantialisation is seen in the use of the word *amṛta*, "nectar," as in the *Bhaktirasāmṛtasindhu* itself. From both an aesthetic and a metaphysical perspective, Caitanya Vaiṣṇava practice sees the goal of the individual as the "distillation" of the essence of being through the filters of dialectical "separation" or *viraha* that yield a pure "juice"—*rasa*—or "nectar"—*amṛta*. In the opening line of the *Vidagdha-Mādhava* Rūpa clarifies the importance of this distillation of emotion, prescribing in the optative that all unwanted desires should be ended, while referring to the concentrated love of Rādhā and the gopīs, which puts the *amṛta* "immortal nectar" of the moon to shame.[119]

Rūpa's concept of *rasa* effects the same change of perspective that Gadamer applauded in Hegel's dialectic, confronting "a problem precisely the opposite of that which the Ancients faced" and making "'fluid' the fixed suppositions of the Understanding, [infusing] them with Spirit."[120] By thinking through the nature of relationship, Rūpa naturally comes to favour a kind of dialectical essentialism. This is reflected in the very methods by which his texts proceed. Rūpa's *Bhaktirasāmṛtasindhu* is considered exemplary in the detail of its elaboration of the modes in which humans approach Krishna, and the modes of the divine in which they are received. His comprehensive detail is celebrated, but there is a danger of missing the hierarchical progression to which these details are subject, elevating the reader to higher levels of appreciation, whether it is through reflection on Krishna's physical ornaments, on the qualities of his wives, or on the provocative qualities of Rādhā herself. The trajectory of his analysis is an increasingly focused one, assimilating the qualities of each stage into the heightened aesthetic response at the next level; the resulting essentialising drive is distinctive in his thought.[121]

Lance Nelson writes that "Bhāva is not phenomenal in nature at all but rather an eternally existent transphenomenal reality."[122] As we have seen, it does indeed describe the relational care or concern that is a basic condition of all phenomena; the "intentional structure" of consciousness, as it were. Thus, we see that when Rūpa Gosvāmi makes a characteristic statement in the *Vidagdha Mādhava* that it is *yogamāyā,* Krishna's personified power of creating phenomenal illusions, that makes Rādhā appear to be married to and separate from Krishna, asserting that in fact she is eternally Krishna's lover, Rūpa's theological opposition of two independent worlds is premised on a philosophical observation about ontic and ontological, phenomenal, and transcendental truths.

Thinkers in Rūpa Gosvāmi's intellectual milieu arrived at conclusions such as these due to: (a) the inclination toward a consciousness-oriented ontology, (b) the inclination toward a monist ontology, and (c) the proximity of those probing philosophers to their main competing models: the nihilism of the Buddhists and materialists, the radical dualism of Madhva, and the absolutism of the Advaitins. Thinkers like Rūpa Gosvāmi were able to affirm change and plurality without the danger of metaphysical (no essences) or semantic (no truths) nihilism. Rūpa affirms radical plurality as the essence of Being, celebrated in each temporary and relative "identity." But where Gadamer focuses on the changefulness of the individual identity and the thread of vital concern that binds it, Rūpa Gosvāmi affirms the individual and his or her purpose primarily as the site in which relation can be self-reflectively realised and heightened. Indeed, he seems almost to make a substance-ontology of pure dialectic with his language of the nectar, juice, *rasa,* or *amṛta* of Being. It is as if the ontological affirmation of the subtle, essentialist structures of Being tips over into a tangible, quantitative conceptual currency of existence again—something more easily handled by the mind. Reintroducing familiar conceptual pitfalls into unfamiliar territory, Rūpa nevertheless gives us a new vocabulary for talking about "realism."

The hermeneutic process of reading Rūpa Gosvāmi's metaphysics is a curious one, for his metaphysical language is found nowhere and everywhere in his writings. Those who expect to find discussions resembling those of Jīva Gosvāmi are disappointed and distracted by the profusion of quite different types of discourse describing theological cosmogonies, analysing the psychology of different states of excited, impassioned, and vitalised reality, using the language of myth, of Sanskritic literary convention, and the folk symbology of flowers and astrology. Yet his style is almost everywhere plurivocal, using metaphysical keywords in consistent extended analogies. He develops precedents in the Krishna literature for discussing the true nature of reality through tropes of love in separation, mistaken identity, and of the nectar of self-reflective relation, and in his plays as in his poems, he is more a narrative realist than a philosophical one; ultimately his concern to give an account of the real serves the purpose of describing what it means to live within it.

Indeed, it is Haberman who most strongly makes the point that the imaginative exercises of the religious practice of *rāgānuga bhakti sādhana* are exercises in realism, even where the metaphysical presuppositions are not fully voiced.[123] Haberman argues strongly for the reality-describing and reality-creating aspects of Rūpa Gosvāmi's thought.[124] His accounts highlight the discourse through which Rūpa analyses and describes the "realism" of religious belief—both in terms of giving detailed accounts of the concerns, setting, atmosphere, characters of a particular "scene" of religious reality, and, by obliquely employing the psychology of truth-discourse, communal world-construction, and role-play as his prescriptive framework for religious practice. This is an immeasurably important insight into the nature of religious experience, differing markedly from the *alaukika*, "otherworldly" position that Rūpa's influential predecessor Abhinavagupta takes on the nature of the aesthetic and religious experience.[125] For Rūpa, religious belief is on a continuum with our everyday truths and processes of reasoning, because it is derived from transcendental metaphysical truths that pervade them.

There remains a major question in the study of religious belief as to whether psychological or linguistic accounts of religious realism do indeed, of their own logic, require a grounding in any underlying metaphysical foundation. The extent to which religious belief engages with existential doubt is questionable in the modern West—how much more so in sixteenth-century India? Rūpa Gosvāmi's work is a perfect example of this debate being implicitly engaged and decided, and this is ignored whenever his work is interpreted as being concerned solely with imaginal practice, literary evocation, or mystical aestheticism. By contrast, Rūpa Gosvāmi's works stand within a discourse of radical questioning, which has centuries of precedent and arguably a greater range and depth of interrogation in India than in the tempest of modern Western debates. For Rūpa Gosvāmi, as for Gadamer, the implicit awareness of epistemological scepticism has contributed to a positive solution that factors in the logical universality of finitude, plurality, and relationality. The imperatives of scepticism were logically bound to drive conscientious philosophers toward an ontology of form that would in turn have to be refined to account for the teleological value, the arché, or dialectic of concern that underlies the directed changefulness of the forms.

In the next chapter we will see that *rasa*, the cornerstone of his metaphysics, is also the cornerstone of his ethics of human flourishing. Rūpa Gosvāmi's realist impulse means that for him as for Gadamer ethics is a eudaimonian affair, involving an attempt to display our ontological nature from the ontic perspective of the view from within Being. Phenomenal or ontic truths must fit with ontological ones, and his prescriptions must be based on accurate descriptions, to somehow help us to do better what we already necessarily do. Yet it is this "somehow" with which we are finally left, facing the problems of what it means to try to be better what we already are, how we should reason toward this conclusion, and what precise ethos it best advocated based on the ontologies that are outlined above.

NOTES

1. These "realisms" stand in contrast to the symbolisms, psychologisms, narrativisms, and other "non-realist" positions of many modern philosophers of religious belief (D. Z. Phillips, Paul Ricoeur, Rudolf Bultmann, Paul Tillich) and plain reductionists (Don Cupitt, Pascal Boyer, etc.).

2. Of his works, the *Bhaktirasāmṛtasindhu* and the *Ujjvala Nīlamaṇi* treat the nature and practice of bhakti religion, the later with particular reference to godhead, the *Nātaka śāstra* discusses aesthetics, the *Bhāgavatāmṛtam* expands on the *Bhāgavata Purāṇa's* narratives, and the *Ganadveśadīpika* expounds the theology of being/becoming Krisna's companions. Of the literary works, the *Vidagdha Mādhava* and the *Lalita Mādhava* are dramas about Krishna and Rādhā while the *Haṃsadūta* and the *Uddhava Sandeśa* are poems on the same theme, and the *Govinda Birudāvali* and *Premendra Sāgara* are verses attributed him. The *Mathura Mahātmya* explores the actual geographical setting in which these divine and literary narratives are set.

3. For details of Jīva Gosvāmi's philosophical and theological position (largely set out in his most famous work, the *Tattvasaṇdarbha*), see Ravi Gupta's *The Caitanya Vaiṣṇava Vedānta of Jīva Gosvāmī* (Oxford: Routledge, 2007).

4. For accounts of Rūpa's life, see David Haberman's introduction to the *Bhaktirasāmṛtasindu of* Rūpa Gosvām*in*, D. Haberman, trans. (New Delhi: Motilal Banarsidass, 2003), and S. K. De's classic *Early History of the Vaiṣṇava Faith and Movement in Bengal* (Calcutta: Firma KLM, 1961) and devotional accounts in the key Caitanya Vaiṣṇava text, the *Caitanya Caritāmṛta* of Krishnadāsa Kaviraja. David Haberman (*Acting as a Way of Salvation: Rāgānuga Bhakti Sādhana*) and Neal Delmonico ("The Blazing Sapphire: A Translation in Progress of Rūpa Gosvāmi's *Ujjvala Nīlamaṇi*") both make a particular effort to bring stress the richness of the contemporary religious and literary culture on which Rūpa Gosvāmi drew.

5. Scholars such as Frank Clooney, and more recently Deepak Sarma, have brought the plurivocity of Indian theological and philosophical writing to the attention of scholars working with such texts. The practical, pedagogical, and hermetic aspects of Indian "theoretical" writings have been brought to light, but little as yet has been said about the methods and reasons by which different disciplinary discourses are merged within a single framework by polymath thinkers like Abhinavagupta and Rūpa Gosvāmi.

6. One example of this is David Haberman's account in *Acting as a Way of Salvation* (New Delhi: Motilal Banarsidass, 1983), 30.

7. Through general cultural transmission from Tamil sources, and biographical encounters between exponents of the two traditions, the Alvars were the main southern influence on the development of the Caitanya tradition, and

already demonstrated the narrativisation, role-play and emotive value of the Vraja legend.

8. The Navya-Nyāya philosophers (also in their second/third generation) revived classical philosophical issues and approaches to other *darśanas,* such as Sāṃ khya, Yoga, Vaiśeṣika, and Vedānta, that had been preserved in purāṇic texts, bhakti poetry, and possibly in broadly yogic practices at the popular level. The influence of Buddhism, Jainism, and even Cārvāka thought would primarily have been mediated through the now-concretised programme of stock philosophical objections to be incorporated into philosophical argument.

9. Orissa in particular remained a centre of Indian Buddhism. See C. Chatterjee, *The Philosophy of Chaitanya and His School* (New Delhi: Associated Publishing Company, 1993), 23. M. T. Kennedy also treats this topic briefly, and not without prejudice as to the possible influence of Sahajiyism (*The Chaitanya Movement: A Study of Vaiṣṇavism in Bengal* (New Delhi: Munshiram Manoharlal, 1925), 11).

10. The mutual exchange of Muslim and Hindu ideas in the Bengali and Gauḍīya Vaiṣṇava contexts is argued for by David Haberman (introduction to the *Bhaktirasāmṛtasindhuh,* trans. Haberman), Richard Eaton ("The Bengal of Sri Caitanya Mahāprabhu" in Steven Rosen's *Vaiṣṇavism: Contemporary Scholars Discuss the Gauḍīya Tradition* (New York: FOLK Books, 1992)), and S. M. Ikram (*Muslim Civilisation in India* (New York: Columbia University Press, 1969), 78).

11. An episode (see Richard Eaton's account in Steven Rosen's *Vaiṣṇavism: Contemporary Scholars Discuss the Gauḍīya Tradition*) recounts how even the Hindu residents of Bengal used to complain to the authorities about the loud noise made by the kirtana-singing of Caitanya's followers.

12. See Richard Eaton's discussion of the Bengal Muslims of this period in the last of his *Essays on Islam and Indian History* (New Delhi: Oxford University Press, 2000).

13. See Deepak Sarma's *Epistemologies and the Limitations of Philosophy: Doctrine in Madhva Vedānta* (Oxford: RoutledgeCurzon, 2005).

14. See F. Matchett, *Krisna: Lord or Avatara? The Relationship between Krishna and Vishnu* (Oxford: Curzon Press, 2001), 107–8.

15. See Daniel Sheridan in *The Advaitic Theism of the Bhāgavata Purāṇa* (New Delhi: Motilal Banarsidass, 1986), 17 ("variegated Vedāntic vocabulary") and 42 ("Sāṃkhya terminology"), respectively.

16. For the historical context of the *Bhāgavata Purāṇa* see the introduction to Edwin Bryant's translation, published by Penguin as *Krishna: The Beautiful Legend of God* (London: Penguin Books, 2003), and also Daniel Sheridan's study, *The Advaitic Theism of the Bhāgavata Purāṇa* (New Delhi: Motilal Banarsidass, 1986).

17. For discussions of the historical development of the Caitanya Vaiṣṇava tradition and its characteristic portrayal of Krishna and Rādhā, see McKenzie Brown, "The Theology of Rādhā in the Purāṇas" in *The Divine Consort: Rādhā and the Goddesses of India* (Boston: Beacon Press, 1982). Also Chhanda Chatterjee, Steve Rosen, and Melville Kennedy. On the background of Bengali or Gauḍīya Vaiṣṇavism, see S. C. Chakravarti, and the essays in Steve Rosen's book. For details of aspects, see Haberman (focus on acting), Hardy (focus on the Alvars) and Donna Marie Wulff (focus on Rūpa's dramas).

18. While Rūpa Gosvāmi was not the first to write on the idea of a type of *rasa* that is specific to bhakti (the *Muktaphala* of *Vopadeva* and the *Kaivalyadīpika* of *Hemādri* both contain seeds of this theory), Rūpa's works were clearly the most extensive development of it in his time, and were to be hugely influential on later theologians and aestheticians.

19. See S. Elkmann's introduction to *Jīva Gosvāmin's Tattva Saṇdarbha: A Study on the Philosophical and Sectarian Development of the Gauḍīya Vaiṣṇava Movement* (New Delhi: Motilal Banarsidass, 1986), xii.

20. Cchanda Chatterjee typically draws almost exclusively on Jīva Gosvāmi's thought to explain *The Philosophy of Chaitanya and His School.* In his essay on "Doctrine and Practice Among the Vaiṣṇavas of Bengal," Edward Dimock makes the same anachronistic generalisation (*Krishna: Myths, Rites, and Attitudes,* M. Singer, ed. (Chicago: University of Chicago Press, 1966)).

21. Gavin Flood, *The Tantric Body: The Secret Tradition of Hindu Religion* (London: I.B. Tauris, 2006), 29.

22. Steve Vertovec, *The Hindu Diaspora: Comparative Patterns* (London: Routledge, 2000), 12.

23. Srilata Raman, *Self-Surrender (prapatti) to God in śrivaiṣṇavism: Tamil Cats and Sanskrit Monkeys* (London: Routledge, 2007), 3–4.

24. Ravi Gupta, *The Caitanya Vaiṣṇava Vedānta of Jīva Gosvāmī* (Oxford: Routledge, 2007), 1.

25. Chatterjee, *The Philosophy of Chaitanya and His School,* 23.

26. Julius Lipner, *The Face of Truth: A Study of Meaning and Metaphysics in the Vedāntic Theology of Rāmānuja* (Hong Kong: State University of New York Press, 1986), 121.

27. Jonardon Ganeri, *The Concealed Art of the Soul: Theories of Self and Practises of Truth in Indian Ethics and Epistemology* (Oxford: Oxford University Press, 2007), 4.

28. M. T. Melville Kennedy, *The Chaitanya Movement: A Study of Vaiṣṇavism in Bengal* (New Delhi: Munshiram Manoharlal Publishers, 1925), 88.

29. F. Hardy, *Viraha Bhakti: The Early History of Kṛṣṇa Devotion in South India* (New Delhi: Oxford University Press, 1983), 557.

30. This is not to suggest that "other realities" are not possible, or a viable theme for speculation. Only that we must be aware that in these cases we are speculating about what is not susceptible to our reasoning, and thus either mistaken in our goals, or using quite particular and indirect means of discourse to refer to semantically empty (if contextually important) concepts.

31. There is also the prior question of whether this philosophy has a realist foundation according to the prevalent Western dualist commonsense meaning of the term "realist." This relates to the question of whether the Vedas are accepted as the ultimate epistemological authority. From the Caitanya Vaiṣṇava perspective, Jīva Gosvāmi in the *Tattvasaṇdarbha* states that only Vedic *śabda* is truly authoritative *pramāṇa* due to the inherent liability of empirical knowledge (*pratyakṣa,* literally "looking toward/ upon," "directional sight") and of inference (*anumāna,* literally after, alongside, assenting, relational, or repetitive thought). Here it is explicitly stated that the basis of the Vedas is itself *vaidusha pratyakṣa* (the empirical perception of the

learned), indicating the idea that the writers of the Vedas had mystical experiences that elude the problems of normal empiricism and are the basis of reliable testimony. The contents of those experiences are then treated as a propositional basis for interpretation and inference. T. K. Stewart argues that the same view is taken of Rūpa Gosvāmi's literary descriptions of Krishna and Rādhā—that they are direct mystical perceptions (see "The Biographies of Sri Caitanya and the Literature of the Gauḍīya Vaiṣṇavas," in S. Rosen's *Vaiṣṇavism*, 122). This is what we would normally think of as a mind-body dualistic empirical analysis based on the "objects" of consciousness, rather than an argument from a phenomenological analysis of consciousness itself. To this extent, an uncritical "realism" of the traditional dualist sort is integrated into this (as into so many) Hindu philosophical tradition.

32. *Bhāgavata Purāṇa*, 2.10.2

33. *Bhāgavata Purāṇa*, 2.10.7

34. *Bhāgavata Purāṇa*,1.2.10

35. It is interesting to note that in the discussion of *acintyabhedābheda* in *Vaiṣṇavism*. Steve Rosen, from the perspective of a practitioner, sees the doctrine as an item of negative theology entailing an inexplicable, "supra-rational" mystery (254). This is a view that Shrivatsa Gosvāmi tries to correct in asserting that there is a carefully thought-out and longstanding course of metaphysical reasoning that has led to this doctrine. Needless to say, the present study agrees with the latter view.

On a separate point, it is difficult to trace this doctrine to pre–Jīva Gosvāmi roots, because while it is attributed to the founder of the school and seen to be an implicit idea in the *Bhāgavata Purāṇa*, Caitanya left no writings by which to test this assertion. A. N. Chatterjee portrays it as an early Vaiṣṇava historical cousin to Rāmānuja's *viśiṣṭādvaita* doctrine, but more generally it is seen to be the product of Caitanya's debates with the Advaitins.

36. See Shrivatsa Gosvāmi in *Vaiṣṇavism: Contemporary Scholars Discuss the Gauḍīya Tradition*.

37. As Caitanya himself left no writings, it is difficult to determine with certainty his own personal ideological affiliations, although B. N. K. Sharma claims that the early Caitanya followers, and Rūpa Gosvāmi in particular, were aware of Madhva and sympathetic to his ideas; Rūpa occasionally cites Madhva in his own works (see Sharma's *History of the Dvaita School of Vedānta and Its Literature* (Bombay: Motilal Banarsidass, 1961)). Yet Sharma does not limit the Caitanya Vaiṣṇavas to this influence alone, as we have seen, and O. B. L. Kapoor explicitly denies that Caitanya or Jīva saw themselves as being in full accord with Madhva (*The Philosophy and Religion of Sri Caitanya* (New Delhi: Munshiram Manoharlal Publishers, 1977), 36–37).

38. See particularly S. C. Chakravarti, *The Philosophical Foundations of Bengal Vaiṣṇavism* (New Delhi: Academic Publishers, 1969), 310. In the light of the centrality of the *Bhāgavata Purāṇa* as an inspiration to both Caitanya and Rūpa, one can certainly identify a "non-dual" element in their thought that correlates with and is corroborated by their purāṇic Sāṃkhya influences. As we will see, the Vaiṣṇava philosophers of the period, for whom the *Bhāgavata Purāṇa* was an axial text, were able to benefit from the realisation that "the non-dualism of the *Bhāgavata* is able to accommodate the pluralism of the world and of the individual selves" (Sheridan, *The*

Advaitic Theism of the Bhāgavata Purāṇa, 42). The theistic, cosmogonic Sāṃkhya of the *Brahmavaivarta Purāṇa* merged with the Vedānta of the *Brahmasūtra* in the many conversations and revelations recounted in the pages of the *Bhāgavata Purāṇa*.

39. See C. Chatterjee's *The Philosophy of Caitanya and His School*, 2, and M. T. Kennedy's *The Chaitanya Movement: A Study of Vaiṣṇavism in Bengal*, 33–34, and, of course, the depiction in Krishnadas Kaviraj's *Caitanya-caritamṛta*.

40. See C. Chatterjee's *The Philosophy of Caitanya and His School*, 4, and M. T. Kennedy's *The Chaitanya Movement: A Study of Vaiṣṇavism in Bengal*, 49.

41. See *Bhaktirasāmṛtasindhu*, 1.2.49–57.

42. *Vadanti tat tattvavidah tattva yaj jñānam advayam/ brahmeti paramātmeti bhāgavan iti ṣabdyate* (*Bhāgavata Purāṇa* 1.2.11, *Tattva-Saṇdarbha* 119: those who know reality say that that truth which is undivided knowledge is called "brahman," "the highest self," and "the Lord").

43. Jīva Gosvāmi's *Tattva Saṇdarbha*, v. 51.

44. Krishna Sharma expresses the common view when he observes that "bhakti in the medieval context is generally understod as an antithesis of Śaṃkara's Advaita Vedānta and his advocacy of jñāna" (*Bhakti and the Bhakti Movement: A New Perspective* (New Delhi: Munshiram Manoharlal, 1987), 130). But this is clearly a simplification of the complex relation of dialogue and assimilation that really existed. Jīva Gosvāmi argues in passing that Śaṃkara was himself a bhakti devotee of a personal divinity, used an oblique way of speaking (*lakṣaṇavṛtti*) to discuss the more monistic and absolutist aspects of the divine, and did so only in order to combat Buddhist philosophy.

45. Shrivatsa Gosvāmi argues for this micro-macrocosmic hermeneutic application of *acintyabhedābheda* in *Vaiṣṇavism: Contemporary Scholars Discuss the Gauḍīya Tradition*, 250–51.

46. *Dialogue and Dialectic*, 92. In "Plato's Unwritten Dialectic" in the same volume he further expounds the centrality of number to Plato's philosophy, as he does in other works in his *Gessamelte Werke*, cited below.

47. See Julius Lipner in *The Face of Truth: A Study of Meaning and Metaphysics in the Vedāntic Theology of Rāmānuja* (Hong Kong: State University of New York Press, 1986), and Gavin Flood in *An Introduction to Hinduism* (Cambridge: Cambridge University Press, 1996), 229–30.

48. O. B. L. Kapoor, "Personalism vs. Impersonalism," in *Vaiṣṇavism: Contemporary Scholars Discuss the Gauḍīya Tradition*, 240.

49. David Haberman, "Kṛṣṇa-Līlā as Perceived in Meditation and Pilgrimage," in *Vaiṣṇavism: Contemporary Scholars Discuss the Gauḍīya Tradition*, 311.

50. See Jīva Gosvāmi's *Bhāgavata-Saṇdarbha*, 4.

51. Sanātana Gosvāmi, *Bṛhad Bhāgavatamṛta*, 2.2.196.

52. See S. C. Chakravarti, *The Philosophical Foundations of Bengal Vaiṣṇavism* (New Delhi: Academic Publishers, 1969), 310.

53. Jīva Gosvāmi himself implies this mere "usefulness" of the distinction in relation to our capacity of discussing its different functions, in his *Sarvasamvādini* (see S. C. Chakravarti, 312).

54. See Plato's lists at *Parmenides*, 1.b.b, and throughout the subsequent sections. As outlined previously, Plato's dyadic concept is not merely of duality, but

of relational differentiation (as of greater and lesser), which relationality allows for simultaneous affirmation and negation of qualities. A classic example is the discussion of unity ("one") and difference ("others") in the final statement of the *Parmenides*: "Let thus much be said; and further let us affirm what seems to be the truth, that, whether one is or is not, one and the others in relation to themselves and one another, all of them, in every way, are and are not, and appear to be and appear not to be."

55. C. Chatterjee's *The Philosophy of Caitanya and His School*, 2, and M. T. Kennedy's *The Chaitanya Movement: A Study of Vaiṣṇavism in Bengal*, 42.

56. See the Introduction to the *Bhaktirasāmṛtasindhu*, lv–lvi.

57. *Svabhāvavāda* is also cited by Monier Williams as the doctrine that the universe was produced and is sustained by the natural and necessary action of substances according to their inherent properties, but it is not clear whether this was a use of the term with which Rūpa Gosvāmi is familiar.

58. See *Ujjvala Nīlamaṇi* chapter 14 (*sthayibhāva prakarana*), v. 32.

59. Ajay Rao writes about the many variations on this strategy used in connection with epic literature, and explores the degree to which they were able to convey strategic sectarian, subversive, or political meanings in his article "Theologising the Inaugural Verse: Śleṣa Reading in Rāmāyaṇa Commentary," in *The Journal of Hindu Studies* 1, no. 1, 2008.

60. *Bhaktirasāmṛtasindhu* (2.5.102).

61. See D. Haberman in *Bhaktirasāmṛtasindhu*, lvi.

62. *Gītagovinda* 1.46, trans. B. S. Miller, in *Love Song of the Dark Lord: Jayadeva's Gītagovinda* (New York: Columbia University Press, 1977), 77. As is so widely noted, Krishna's role in this theology is almost diametrically opposed to his message in the *Bhāgavad Gīta*, in which he features as the paradigmatic advocate of order, duty, and detachment.

63. The Indian view had always been that mere everyday emotions (*sthayi*) such as *rati*, "love," must be heightened and elevated through aesthetic distance, in order for them to become a form of *rasa* such as *śṛngāra*, "passion." But here the elevation of the emotion into *rasa* is achieved by increasing one's *tanmayībhāvana*, "empathetic identification" so that the love featured is amplified by the empathetic response of the observer, and then further intensified by the enjoyer's love for this abundance of love, and further aesthetic appreciation of the whole situation. In focusing on *rasa* as a lens in which other emotions get collected, magnified and reflected, Rūpa draws together the preceding philosophers' insights into the positive feeding-back of meaningfulness and emotional response in the phenomenon of aesthetic experience.

64. *Rasa* is a rich concept with a particularly complex history; it can be translated as taste, flavour, love, affection, pathos, emotion, essence, or understood in terms of a heady combination of all of these connotations (see V. S. Apte's *A Practical Sanskrit Dictionary*, 1331).

65. *Bhaktirasāmṛtasindhu*, 2.5.74, trans. Haberman (with modifications).

66. As S. K. De and D. Haberman note, it is important not to obscure the literal and literary sense of *līlā* with its metaphysical subtext: "The Vṛndāvana *Līlā* is

not a mere symbol or divine allegory, but a literal fact of religious history" (see D. Haberman (1983), 45). Nevertheless, it is the more difficult yet more fruitful duty of the scholar to attempt to account for and integrate *all* of the discourses combined within the intratextual semantics of these works.

67. F. Hardy, *Viraha Bhakti: The Early History of Kṛṣṇa Devotion in South India* (New Delhi: Oxford University Press, 1983), 562.

68. Haberman, *Acting as a Way of Salvation: A Study of Rāgānuga Bhakti Sādhana*, 32.

69. See Hardy, *Viraha Bhakti: The Early History of Kṛṣṇa Devotion in South India*, and also Haberman in conversation with Steve Rosen, 342.

70. *Truth and Method*, 103.

71. D. Kinsley, *The Sword and the Flute: Dark Visions of the Terrible and the Sublime in Hindu Mythology* (Berkeley: University of California Press, 1975), 70–71.

72. Kinsley, *The Sword and the Flute: Dark Visions of the Terrible and the Sublime in Hindu Mythology*, 72.

73. See *Bhāgavata Purāṇa*, 3.7.2. In the introduction to his translation of the tenth chapter, Edwin Bryant gives an excellent summary of the Sāṃkhya and Advaita influences in the *Bhāgavata Purāṇa*. Daniel Sheridan's explores the advaitic aspects of the *Bhāgavata Purāṇa* in detail in his 1986 *The Advaitic Theism of the Bhāgavata Purāṇa* (New Delhi: Motilal Banarsidass), but also investigates its considerable Sāṃkhya elements (42–51).

74. *Bhāgavata Purāṇa*, 10.47.30 (Edwin Bryant, trans., *Krishna: The Beautiful Legend of God* (London: Penguin Books, 2003), 198).

75. A. Sen Gupta, *Classical Sāṃkhya: A Critical Study* (New Delhi: Monoranjan Sen, 1969).

76. Vallabha was a fifteenth-century Telegu Brahmin who wrote commentaries on both the *Bhāgavata Purāṇa* and the *Brahmasūtra*. The subtleties of his position require detailed explanation (which they have too rarely received), but broadly speaking, for Vallabha, "Brahman is the independent reality and is identified with Srī Kṛṣṇa. . . . Souls and matter are his real manifestations. They are his parts. He is the abode of all good qualities and includes even the seemingly contradictory qualities. It is by his will that he manifests himself. . . . The substance and its attributes, the cause and effects are identical" (Chandradhar Sharma, *A Critical Survey of Indian Philosophy* (New Delhi: Motilal Banarsidass, 1987), 378).

77. Susmita Pande, *The Medieval Bhakti Movement* (Jodhpur: Kusumanjali Prakashan, 1989), 66–67.

78. Nelson argues that Madhusūdana Sarasvatī, Vallabha, and Gauḍīya Vaiṣṇavism were all engaged in the affirmation and apotheosis of finitude; see "The Ontology of Bhakti: Devotion as Paramapuruṣārtha in Gauḍīya Vaiṣṇavism and Madhusūdana Sarasvatī," in *The Journal of Indian Philosophy* 32, no. 4 (August 2004). See also Sanjukta Gupta's forthcoming *Advaita Vedānta and Vaiṣṇavism: The Philosophy of Madhusūdana Sarasvatī* (Routledge).

79. Neal Delmonico, "The Blazing Sapphire: A Translation in Progress of Rūpa Gosvāmi's *Ujjvala Nīlamaṇi*," 28–29.

80. E.g., *Bhāgavata Purāṇa*, 32.21–22, and 10.47.23–37.

81. Much recent literature on Indian philosophy, influenced not least by Frank Clooney's work on hermeneutic issues in Indian texts, particularly Indian theological texts, has pursued a heightened hermeneutic sensitivity to excavating neglected modes of discourse. An increasing amount is being done on the practical and hermetic dimensions of what appear to be purely theoretical works (as for instance J. G. Suthren Hirst's *Śaṃkara's Advaita Vedānta: A Way of Teaching* (Oxford: RoutledgeCurzon, 2005), and D. Sarma's *Epistemologies and the Limits of Philosophical Inquiry: Doctrine in Madhva Vedānta* (Oxford: RoutledgeCurzon, 2005)), but justice has not yet been done to the complex discursive modes of philosophical argument that ostensibly *literary* content can take.

82. *Pratīyamānāḥ prathamaṃ vibhāvādyās tu bhāgaśaḥ | gacchanto rasa-rūpatvaṃ militā yānty akhaṇḍatām* (*Bhaktirasāmṛtasindhu*, 2.5.83).

83. *Mahā-śakti-vilāsātmā bhāvo'cintya-svarūpa-bhāk | raty-ākhyā ity ayaṃ yukto na hi tarkeṇa bādhitum* (*Bhaktirasāmṛtasindhu*, 2.5.92).

84. Trans., Haberman, 379 (*Mādhuryādy-āśrayatvena kṛṣṇādīṃs tanute ratiḥ | tathānubhūyamānās te vistīrṇāṃ kurvate ratim—Bhaktirasāmṛtasindhu*, 2.5.98).

85. "The nullity of what is merely there around us, of that which is said to exist in the 'real' world, brings forth the higher truth of 'what is the subject or the concept'" (*Hegel's Dialectic: Five Hermeneutical Studies*, 16).

86. Trans., Haberman, 379 (*Yathā svair eva salilaiḥ paripūrya balāhakān | ratnālayo bhavaty ebhir vṛṣṭais tair eva vāridhiḥ—Bhaktirasāmṛtasindhu*, 2.5.95).

87. The Sufi uses of the imagery of light, jewels, reflection, and refraction to express a philosophy of emanatory oneness between God and world are well-known, as in the works of Ibn al-Arabi (1164–1240 CE), at least five of whose works, the *Mawaqi al-nujum* (*Settings of the Stars*), *Mishkat al-anwar* (*Niche of Lights*), the *Risalat al-anwar* (*Treatise of Lights*), the *Fusus al-hikam* (*Bezels of Wisdom*), and the *Futuhat al-makkiyah* (*Meccan Illuminations*), contain references to the divine light in their title as well as in their content. Tibetan Buddhism had, of course, also adopted this image to express the ultimate realities within the phenomenal self. Sanskritic philosophy had its own tradition of naming treatises after gems, hence Śaṃkara's celebrated *Vivekachudamaṇi* (*Crest Jewel of Discrimination*), and Gangesa's fourtheenth-century Neo-Nyāya text, the *Tattvacintamaṇi* (*Jewel of Reflection on Truth*). Rūpa Gosvāmi continues this trend and makes full use of its assorted implications.

88. This is also true of the personalities of the prophets in Ibn Arabi's medieval Sufi text the *Fusus al-hikam* (*Bezels of Wisdom*), which also uses the metaphor of a jewel refracting the divine nature understood in terms of an emanationist "light" ontology.

89. J. S. Hawley, "A Vernacular Portrait: Rādhā in the Sur Sagar," in *The Divine Consort: Rādhā and the Goddesses of India* (Boston: Beacon Press, 1982).

90. D. Haberman, *Acting as a Way of Salvation*, 33. In the *Ujjvala Nīlamaṇi*, for instance, the divine essence is refracted into the character types, activities, ornaments, social positions, circumstances, and settings of Krishna and the gopīs.

91. *Ujjvala Nīlamaṇi*, ch. 15, 1. Love in Separation, "Unmada."

92. *Ujjvala Nīlamaṇi*, 1.

93. *Haṃsadūta*, v. 107–13.

94. *Uddhava Sandeśa*, 124, trans. Jan Brzezinski, in *Mystic Poetry:* Rūpa Gosvāmi*n's Uddhava Sandeśa and Haṃsadūta* (Hong Kong: Mandala Publishing Group, 1999), 98.

95. *Haṃsadūta*, v. 33–42 and 45–52, *Uddhava Sandeśa*, v. 77–89.

96. E.g., *Uddhava Sandeśa*, 77–90, 98, trans. Jan Brzezinski, in *Mystic Poetry:* Rūpa Gosvāmi*n's Uddhava Sandeśa and Haṃsadūta* (Hong Kong: Mandala Publishing Group, 1999), 98.

97. *Vigdagdha Mādhava*, 5.18

98. See *Bhaktirasāmṛtasindhu*, Eastern Section, 1.1.

99. The trope of the gopīs' confusion and disarray takes on many forms and begins with the *Bhāgavata Purāṇa* itself in which "Krishna, the descendent of Sura, bewilderer of the mind of the mind-bewilderer himself" (10.32.2., trans. Edwin Bryant (2002), 137) again and again causes the gopīs to become dishevelled and disoriented (e.g., 10.29.40, 10.30.40, 10.33.7).

100. Of course, this has crucial implications for Rūpa's prescriptive ethics, which will be explored further in chapter 6.

101. Kinsley, *The Sword and the Flute: Dark Visions of the Terrible and the Divine in Hindu Mythology*, 15.

102. *Bhaktirasāmṛtasindhu*, 2.1.18.

103. David Haberman, "Kṛṣṇa-Līlā as Perceived in Meditation and Pilgrimage," in *Vaiṣṇavism: Contemporary Scholars Discuss the Gauḍīya Tradition* (New York: FOLK Books, 1992), 311.

104. The fourth chapter of the *Ujjavala Nīlamaṇi*, for instance, meticulously (and lovingly) lists Rādhā's ornaments, just as the *Haṃsadūta* lists Krishna's ornaments in a poetic medium in verses 118–26.

105. See quote on 80, *The Divine Consort: Rādhā and the Goddesses of India*.

106. *Bhaktirasāmṛtasindhu*, Eastern Section, 1.2–3.

107. See D. M. Wulff, *The Divine Consort*, 28.

108. *Lalita Mādhava*, 4.32.

109. V. K. Chari, *Sanskrit Criticism* (Honolulu: University of Hawaii Press, 1990), 33.

110. The seventeenth-/eighteenth-century Rajasthani scholar Jagannātha puts this objection in his *Rasangādhara*, 1: 44–46.

111. Seventeenth-century Caitanya Vaiṣṇava scholar Viśvanātha Cakravartin sought to clarify this hermeneutic debate and explicitly championed *rasa* (aesthetic emotion) over *dhvani* (suggestion) as the essence of poetry, on the grounds of a distinctively Caitanya Vaiṣṇava metaphysics.

112. Thanks to Rūpa Gosvāmi's input these linguistic-ontological questions would be continued to be answered in terms of the science of aesthetics centuries later by thinkers such as Visvanātha Cakravartin Thakur (a seventeenth-century Caitanya Vaiṣṇava) and Mahimabhatta (Mahimabhatta's dates are unknown, but the fact that he cites Abhinavagupta and is cited by the eleventh-century theorist Mammaṭa makes him a late contemporary of Abhinavagupta).

113. See *Taittirīyah Upaniṣad*, 2.7., and *Bhaktirasāmṛtasindhu*, 1.1.1.

114. Note to *Bhaktirasāmṛtasindhu*, x.

115. This is why, in the earlier *Gītagovinda* of Jayadeva, there is a scene in which Rādhā immerses herself in yearning for Krishna, even after he has returned to her side.

116. Kinsley, *The Sword and the Flute: Dark Visions of the Terrible and the Sublime in Hindu Mythology*, 73–74.

117. Wulff, *The Divine Consort*, 41.

118. Miller, *Love Song of the Dark Lord: Jayadeva's Gītagovinda*, 19.

119. *Vidagdha Mādhava*, Act 1, v. 1.

120. *Hegel's Dialectic: Five Hermeneutical Studies*, 31.

121. T. R. Sharma notes this dynamic in his study of Rūpa's psychological system in "A Psychological Analysis of Bhakti," in *Love Divine: Studies in Bhakti and Devotional Mysticism*, K. Werner, ed. (Oxford: Curzon Press, 1993), 89.

122. Nelson, "The Ontology of Bhakti: Devotion as Paramapuruṣārtha in Gauḍīya Vaiṣṇavism and Madhusūdana Sarasvatī."

123. Haberman, *Acting as a Way of Salvation: A Study of Rāgānuga Bhakti Sādhana*, 6.

124. It is a weakness of Haberman's account that he vastly simplifies Rūpa Gosvāmi's metaphysical position in terms of a dualistic position aimed at relation with God, in diametric opposition to Abhinavagupta's "monism" aimed at union with God. See the account in *Acting as a Way of Salvation: A Study of Rāgānuga Bhakti Sādhana*, 38.

125. See Haberman, *Acting as a Way of Salvation: A Study of Rāgānuga Bhakti Sādhana*, 37, for a brief account of this disagreement between the two great *bhakti-rasa* theorists.

Chapter 6

Rūpa Gosvāmi's Ethics of Passion

FROM BLISS TO PASSION: THE DEFENCE OF PAIN OVER PLAY

David Kinsley, in placing a coherent and central emphasis on the Vaiṣṇava theology of *līlā*, translated as "play," characterises it as follows:

> *Līlā* is descriptive of the divine activity in Hinduism in at least two ways. First, it underlies the completeness of the gods. The gods need and desire nothing, yet they continue to act. . . . They create the world in play and involve themselves only incidentally or accidentally with the ongoing world order. They do not complete themselves in the creation, maintenance or destruction of the world, they simply amuse and display themselves. Their actions, as such, are not "serious" . . . To play is to be unfettered and unconditioned, to perform actions that are intrinsically satisfying.[1]

This has been the predominant image of *līlā* as a universal feature linking the universe and the gods with all the self-fulfilling, purposeless, blissful connotations that "play" implies. The same qualities have been attributed to "play" by modern Western thinkers such as Huizinga, Gadamer, and Derrida, tapping into a philosophical countercurrent that contradicts the resolute teleologies of critical theory and Semitic eschatologies. But in order to harness these traditionally "playful" virtues, their interpreters typically ignore the competitive, teleological aspects of play, the demand to immerse oneself in the narrative of the game, and the high stakes that it can involve. Consider, in contrast to Kinsley's account, the following portrait of Krishna suffering the consequences of his play in Rūpa Gosvāmi's poem the *Uddhava Saṇdeśa*:

Having anguished alone for a moment,
He returned to his rooftop apartment.
In his desire to find the other shore
of the ocean of troubles
in which he floundered
the killer of Kamsa turned to Uddhava
who stood close beside him,
and began to speak of all that was on his mind,
his voice choked by a wave of love.[2]

Here we have an image of a god who does indeed need and desire; who "flounders" rather than acts; who is involved essentially and purposefully in the world order, caught up by phenomena rather than merely on display in them. His actions are serious. He is fettered and conditioned by his love. Above all, he is helplessly engaged in a loving activity in separation from his beloved that is intrinsically *un*satisfying. And these experiences, as Rūpa Gosvāmi's literature shows, are mirrored in those of humanity.

RŪPA GOSVĀMI'S ETHICAL EXEMPLAR: THE LOVER

Krishna is following Rādhā's lead in this account of distracting, languishing love-addled anguish, following a medieval tradition of poetry in which popular poems such as the *Gītagovinda* seem to mark a turning point between the two portrayals of Krishna and Rādhā's *līlā*.[3] Here the contrast between Krishna's fickle, playful qualities and his passionate, pained, and faithful aspects furnishes the dramatic tension on which the whole narrative is based. The chapters heighten the *rasa* of the situation by veering from his absence to his repentant return, and the psychological consequences are manifested both in Rādhā's inner struggle with her own doubts about whether to pursue this damaging love, and in Krishna's own shame and regret.[4] Images of painful suffering, obsessive attention, of taunting and regret also come to the fore throughout the descriptions of Rādhā and Krishna in Rūpa Gosvāmi's narratives, for which he cites Jayadeva as one of a number of influences.[5]

Rūpa is not unaware of the questions raised by such an ambivalent portrayal of devotional desire and its painful consequences. Indeed, in the wake of longstanding Buddhist discussion on the problem of craving's (*tṛṣṇa*) necessary conjunction with suffering, any theologian advocating an ethos in which passion predominated over peace would almost certainly be aware of the negative implications of desire. In Rūpa's work we find ourselves far from the earlier Advaitic theism of Abhinavagupta who prescribed *śanta-rasa*, the devotional emotion of peace. We are similarly far removed from the Krishna of the *Bhāgavad Gītā* who advocates that his devotee must be free of all passions such as joy and impatience, fear and agitation, expectation, exultation, grief, and desire.[6] Rūpa's notion of bhakti for Krishna evokes all of the above, embracing the pains as well as pleasures.

Moreover, not only does Rūpa refuse to ignore the consequences of such a passionate attachment, but he has his exemplary protagonists, ideal models for the most advanced members of his devotional audience, reflect this knowledge within his texts. His Rādhā is not a blithe and unreflective victim of this feature of bhakti. Other theologians of the Vaiṣṇava tradition often focused on the stories of Krishna as a delightful child, as the close friend of Uddhava, as the guide and protector of the Pāṇḍavas in the *Mahābhārata*, or on altogether less ambivalent manifestations of Viṣṇu, such as Rāma. Still further writers emphasised the pleasurable and the playfully flirtatious aspects of Rādhā and Krishna's temporary separation. But Rūpa's plays portray suffering and resentment without hope of satisfaction, perhaps more than they depict affection or what we conventionally understand as happiness, and as in the *Gītagovinda* rhetorical measures are taken to protest the power relations that it encapsulates. Rādhā is not a suffering saint, and in the literature does not, as Rūpa Gosvāmi suggests in the treatises, patiently and silently suffer the slings and arrows of Krishna's love.[7] Often she appears more as a righteously indignant Job, attracting our sympathy by complaining with "malice and impatience"[8] that she is just a girl, that Krishna's "cruel bumblebee should not blacken [her] flower garland."[9]

Like the divine Rādhā, her mortal friend Lalita is also angry with the god, remonstrating with him and raising the question of his justice. She bemoans the irony of Rādhā's sad change of fate,[10] and a sharp and sarcastic wit is employed again and again: "Krishna promised that he would return [and] he would never lie to us," she tells Rādhā, and goes on to sarcastically assure him, "We do not blame you for forsaking us, for dark persons can rarely relinquish their deceitfulness."[11] Elsewhere, with the same caustic attitude she rebukes him: "Only you continue to torment her for some reason—do you do this because you somehow enjoy yourself in this way?" and "Although you have cruelly cast Rādhā to a mass of suffering, even now she still constantly thinks of you and your acts."[12] She insults Krishna again, calling him a cruel snake[13] and even suggests that Śiva would be a kinder and less harmful god to follow.[14] Her criticism is not merely passively and pitifully pained—it is downright indignant, assuming a position of moral and an empowering ability to subject Krishna himself to her judgement.

Like Job, Rādhā rails against her fate and questions the value of her very life, declaring, "It is a disgrace that this insupportable burden [of my body] is still living," and concluding "my only hope is for my long-determined end [to come]." It becomes clear that Rādhā's true identity as the "blissful" *hlādinī śakti*[15] of Krishna also contains other less pleasant elements than "bliss" as conventionally understood. Play, enjoyment, bliss must all be expanded here to include *bādhā* (pain, suffering, affliction, torment),[16] and *dava* (fire, fever, and pain).[17] In his treatises Rūpa explicitly acknowledges that this phenomenon portrayed in his devotional literature, in which nominally pleasant, or "cool," emotions become painful, "hot," and take on the "appearance of the burden of sorrow" *(duḥkhabharābhāsa)*,[18] lies at the heart of the ethos that he prescribes.

In the many Sanskritic and vernacular literatures focused on these divine lovers, their suffering reiterates a pattern found in the classical *viraha* genre of love story found throughout plays and dūtakāvya, in the epics and many of their Vedic source narratives, and even perhaps the Sufi-influenced Persian trope of the pained lover. The *Haṃsadūta* in particular places Rādhā's suffering as *virahinī*,[19] abandoned and bereft, at the poem's emotional core. This text is a distilled portrait of *vipralambha rasa*, shorn of narrative complications. Rādhā's pain is illustrated in great detail, giving context to the "marks" of love enumerated in the *Bhaktirasāmṛtasindhu* and the *Ujjvala Nīlamaṇi*, and emphasising a particular connection with illness, hallucination and death.[20] The suffering of separation is by no means portrayed as a welcome intensity of feeling for either of these ideal devotees, or by Krishna himself in the *Uddhava Saṇdeśa*. On the contrary, in verses 101–6 Rādhā introduces images of violence and struggle that are echoed throughout the piece and deepened in the omnipresent discourse of Rādhā's imminent death, and Krishna's implied responsibility for it.

Rūpa's texts form a post-sceptical, dialogical discourse in that they allow those who suffer to voice the theological doubts of the reader who sees little to celebrate in a world consisting of attachment to elusive, finite, and situationally circumscribed phenomenal objects: a life of necessary dissatisfaction. But in so doing they intuitively demand a justification or theodicy of the suffering caused by this religious mode that he so eloquently champions. He responds to this by referencing a number of false hopes and genuine answers to the ethical complaint about this realism that he himself is voicing throughout his many writings. These build toward a theodicy that implies a redefinition of suffering, self, and the salvific power of dialectically intensifying desire as a eudaimonian embracing of Being itself.

THE THEODICY OF SUFFERING

Rūpa Gosvāmi begs a theodical question: Why does Rādhā not walk away from this love affair with the dark, beautiful manifestation of ultimate reality, as she threatens to do in certain of the earlier poems in the tradition? Why does she submit to this passion in which she is overwhelmed, pained, and possessed, and why does Rūpa hold her as the ideal? Why, as Donna

Marie Wulff puts it, "should commitment in love be preferred over freedom,"[21] despite its dark and *by definition* dissatisfying side?

The first and perhaps most obvious answer that is referenced in Rūpa Gosvāmi's work is the widespread idea that religious suffering can be beneficially effective in a number of ways: for instance, as an ascetic purification, a yogic means of focus, an accumulation of energy and power, or an atonement aimed at attracting the grace of a deity who is envisioned as a guardian of virtue. Traditions that subscribe to these conceptions of religious suffering are clearly among the many influences on Rūpa's texts and the family of traditions to which he is related. Their traces pervade the logic implied in the strongly tantric and yogic terminology used throughout the genre, which refers to *tāpas, māyā* and the accumulation of powers or *siddhas* through a combination of pain and passion. It is appropriate that Rādhā and Krishna are likened to the ascetic mountain-dwelling divine couple Pārvatī and Śiva, and brought within the theological imaginaire of what Doniger has called the "erotic ascetic" both in texts like the *Gītagovinda* and by Rūpa Gosvāmi.[22] This model implies that the lovers' present suffering will vouchsafe some future reward, and that their currently problematic state is a temporary stage on the way to a future fulfilment.

Yet Rūpā Gosvāmi's portrayal of suffering is more absolute and axiomatic, explicitly contrasting his prescribed attitude of painful intensity with our intuitive commonsensical notion of "what is beneficial or harmful to [us]."[23] It is not in order to obtain merit by which to purchase her entrance to heaven that Rādhā suffers, nor to achieve detachment that will liberate her from the world so that she can enjoy pure union with the divine. Nor is it, as the frequent implicit analogies with the suffering of Pārvatī suggest, in order to win back the favour of her spying lover so that he will approvingly appear and claim her.[24] Rather, Rādhā's suffering will receive no reward within the narrative; it will not be allayed and it is inescapable, and while Rūpa reassures us in his treatises that the pain of devotion is really the highest kind of bliss, his literary portrayals are far more evocative, uncompromising, challenging, and dialogical.

One of the features that makes this pain so philosophically fascinating in Rūpa's work is firstly that it avoids anticipating any structural trajectory toward future union or achievement that will put the *tāpas* of spiritual powers or energies acquired through this painful atonement to use. Despite the frequent fantasised returns to a shared imaginary scene of bliss in the region of Vṛndāvana, there is to be no reunion, no further stage of achievement at which these austerities are aimed. His Rādhā and Krishna predominantly inhabit a landscape of particularly intense suffering in the aftermath of their love affair when there is no longer any hope of earthly satisfaction. According to the popular narratives of Krishna's incarnated earthly life, he eventually leaves the forests of Vṛndāvana and goes on to play his part in the events depicted in the *Bhāgavad Gīta,* never to return to the landscape of his youth as described in the *Bhāgavata Purāṇa.*

But this historical "fact" of the story serves to confirm the metaphysical facts with which Rūpa Gosvāmi is also concerned. By setting most of his literary works in this period after Krishna's departure, Rūpa sustains and centralises the trajectory of *tṛṣṇa,* desire in its dissatisfied, painful form as "thirst" or "craving," by dwelling on a point in the narrative at which physical union has become impossible. Here we see that Gadamer's enlivening swing of the ball from player to player, game to game in a dialectical fusion of horizons, contrasts with this single unending teleological trajectory in which there is no reliance on an external benefit, and no lively movement from goal to goal, but rather an unrelenting and deepening trajectory toward a single goal, entailing the assumption of its intrinsic value.

This provokes questions about what it means to "flourish" and fulfil the goals of human life in the literature associated with this tradition. The *Bhāgavata Purāṇa*'s account of a youthful, mischievous cowherd Krishna was already a significant modification of the tradition of Krishna as the saviour and lawgiver in the *Bhāgavad Gīta.*[25] It is a perfect example of the humanisation and implicit "humanism" that pervades much of the tradition of purāṇic narrative and its development in regional and vernacular, often popular, literatures throughout the medieval period. But with the later texts of Jayadeva, to some extent Sur Das, Vidyāpati, and others, there is a further shift to a more challenging, particularistic, personal portrayal of Krishna's romantic activity. In the widespread movement from the emphasis on the *rasalīlā* dance in which Krishna dances equally with each of his many admirers to the intimate, obsessive relationship between Krishna and Rādhā, Krishna's own vitally playful equally enthusiastic activity with the many gopīs is curtailed in favour of a focused and uncompromising, unequivocal commitment to a love that, in Rūpa's formulation, is without reference to the external rewards enjoyed by the yogis, tantric practitioners, devotees awaiting entrance to heaven's painless "refuge," or the lover who anticipates a long-awaited reunion.

The passion that both Krishna and Rādhā suffer is not like Gadamer's Aristotelian ideal of the life breath of the healthy organism in its growth from form to form; it does not strengthen the individual and encourage its many possible horizons of expansion. Rather, it limits its growth to a single unilateral trajectory. It may weaken the subject, and in Rūpa's literature it may even kill. This violence toward the self could in turn be seen to resonate with the goals of ascetics who aim to weaken and ultimately destroy the personal, particularistic self so that an underlying identity can be revealed. Clearly this could not be true in the simple form to which the radical Advaitic thinker might adhere, for on Rūpa's model the divine is behind *māyā* as well as *brahman,* in *prakṛti* and the *śakti*s as well as in *puruṣa,* and thus the elimination of the embodied dimension of self, world, and perception does not aid realisation of ultimate reality. This cannot be yet another method for minimising the self and reducing ("purifying") its desires, all to the greater magnification of an Other (the universal "I") by which it aims to be displaced.

Yet in reference to Abhinavagupta's tantric theology, which similarly combines Vedāntic and Sāṃkhya influences in a post-Yogic religiosity of shaping interiority, Flood offers a nuanced model of a conciliatory philosophy affirming

> a recognition of human emotion, such as love and tenderness, of anger, of fear and of desire, which can be turned to the service of a spiritual path. Asceticism becomes integrated into subjectivity and becomes not so much an external discipline imposed from without as an internal one, focussing on the transformation of human emotion and the purification of desire.[26]

This is one important modification of the conception of ascesis for a tantric context, suggesting that in passionate and painful emotional bhakti we find intimations of a kind of transformation and purification of self that will also prove pertinent to the bhakti ideal. The replacing of ascetic destruction (or epistemological deconstruction) with a more constructive and creative sense of transformation is very fertile for an improved understanding of this devotional modification of self (yet Rūpa's conception of vitality rejects the notion of religious practice as a self-modification purely aimed at desired future consequences). Clearly physical health and psychological pleasure were not seen as the ultimate virtues of life, but here it is not the emptiness of disillusionment or gnostic purification that he favours, but the fullness of emotional content: "If affection grows even slightly (the image of intensification is central) in the heart, the four goals of man ['desire' (*kāma*), 'liberation' (*mokṣa*), 'wealth' (*artha*), and 'ethical action' (*dharma*)] seem like straw."[27] Any effective theodicy must therefore take into account this portrayal of self-contained suffering as an unending trajectory characterised not by anticipation of closure and reward, but by commitment to an infinite continuation that bears its own intrinsic value.

A second answer suggested by Rūpa is a fundamentally aesthetic one. He implies that Rādhā's very resistance to the situation, far from disrupting the "theme" of love and the successful "play" of Being, furnishes a new kind of play—the play of pain understood as art. This is a classic argument found across cultures, in which the pleasure of tragedy is accounted for through the uniquely transformative lens of aesthetic experience. It is the argument that is particularly close to Gadamer's heart, as developed by Schweiker in his understanding of hermeneutics as "a performative transformation into figuration of both the being of the work and the being of the one understanding."[28] And Rūpa also shows some sympathy with this idea, making recourse to the notion that Rādhā's pain is not the mere emotion (*bhāva*) of suffering (*duḥkha*), but is transformed into the otherworldly (*alaukika*) state of *rasa* in which all pain becomes bliss.[29]

Here Rūpa transcends the pessimism of the *duḥkha* concept by superseding the scale of pleasure and pain with a scale of self-reflective transformation of pain into a dialectically higher form of experience that allows us to appreciate it and its intensity. Haberman is eager to paraphrase this position in simple and pleasing terms, writing: "Ordinary love, dependent on impermanent objects, ultimately resolves into pain, but the unusual (*alaukika*) love for the inexhaustible Krishna brings pure and unending pleasure."[30] The idea can seem to conceal a certain sophistry in redefining pain as "pleasure," but the intention is that the suffering has not merely been defined, but actually transformed. That which ascetics called thirst (*tṛṣṇa*) is assimilated into the higher quality of "relishing" that thirst (*rasa*). This strand of Rūpa's answer is borne out by the many scenes in which the self-referential trope of aesthetic reflection makes its way into the portrayal of Rādhā, such as the scene in the *Haṃsadūta* in which Rādhā creates her own picture of Krishna and worships him in it. Indeed, this answer has a precedent in that famous first sketch of the *viraha bhakti* trope in the *Bhāgavata Purāṇa*, in which the gopīs, lamenting Krishna's absence, act out his presence for each other in a spiritual drama.

Yet at the height of her ecstasy, it is hard to interpret Rādhā as receiving relief from the aesthetic appreciation of her situation that we, the audience, enjoy. She is rather so fully overwhelmed by her suffering that she is said to be near destruction, close to death. Her pain may be aesthetically transformed for us, the spectators, but in Rūpa's portrait there is little evidence of any circumspect reflection that mitigates the raw discomfort. Of course, possibly in order to facilitate this defence, he diverges from the aesthetic theory of Abhinavagupta in his insistence that actors can experience refined aesthetic feeling produced by a performance, along with the audience. It is this that allows his cast of devotional characters to serve in an exemplary way, in addition to their instrumental function as excitants of religious feeling.

Yet there is little we can identify as "relishing," rather than merely suffering, in the experience of the love-maddened Rādhā. She waits for death; in Rūpa's dramas she even seeks it. In tragedy no theodicy is required because the pain is a temporary departure chosen by the audience for its ultimately beneficial effects. But in a text that begs its own theodical questions, this answer seems inadequate for those characters enclosed within the painful situation depicted, particularly when the ultimate goal for the advanced devotee (who has progressed beyond the role of the Lalita-like companion) is to abandon spectatorial distance and follow Rādhā's example by entering into that hopeless, and wholly absorbed, situation.

IS AS OUGHT: REALITY AS THE DIALECTIC OF DESIRE

The third possible solution reflects neither soteriological nor psychological apologetics, but *ontology*. At one level Rādhā's suffering is ill-conceived as an experience of absence, for her separation from Krishna is, in fact, an illusion: she is eternally united with him as his power (*śakti*) and his true form (*sva-rūpa*). They are united by the *abheda* of *acintyabhedābheda*. This answer is stated reassuringly at the end of the chapter on love-in-separation in the *Ujjvala Nīlamaṇi*. Rādhā and Krishna always already possess each other in the unity of their essential being, just as we always already partake in ultimate reality and in the essences of all beings. In this model, as in certain Advaitic formulations of bhakti, pain is caused by the illusion of separation, and so the devotee must simply realise that she is always already in possession of the beloved *at an ontological level* in order to fulfil her craving and end her suffering.

But of course Rūpa has already shown that he is intensely aware of the ambivalent, dual character of this difference and non-difference, and there is little evidence in his narrative that he is recommending Rādhā to use her pain as a spur to new metaphysical realisations that will alleviate her craving. We may make much of her unity with Krishna on a number of metaphysical and symbolic levels, but for the lovesick Rādhā, her ontological one-ness with Krishna is immaterial to her earnest suffering. This theodicy applies well to the forest girls of the *Bhāgavata Purāṇa*, who are taught to be content with his deferred presence in the manifest forms of the natural world (in which they are themselves included), and in their activities, which make him "present" to them. But the Krishna whom Rādhā desires is precisely the impermanent Krishna in his bodily, historically determined, never-to-return human form. For Rādhā the solution cannot be so simple.

For a fourth option one can use the same recognition of unity and difference in another way, giving fundamentally the answer which Donna Marie Wulff gives in marvelling at the intensity of Rādhā's experience in the *Vidagdha Mādhava*. "For the Vaiṣṇava," she writes, "the highest religious ideal is the sweetness of perpetual relatedness in *bhakti*, rather than the release from all bondage that is represented by the goal of *mokṣa*."[31] The previous chapter has argued that this "sweetness of perpetual relatedness" derives at least some of its power as a religious ideal due to its underlying ontological realism: bondage is best because we all are and must be bound. The devotee does not seek refuge from reality; rather, in a love for a divinity that is the ultimate truth, he or she seeks to become a reflection of the underlying metaphysical situation. In Rūpa's literary portrayals of *viraha*, separation is not primarily a theological gap that must be bridged by some soteriological device such as grace. It is an ontological mode of particular being, and a mode of general Being.

On this account, Rādhā's desire is realist not in the sense that it is an epistemological recognition of the unity of *acintyabhedābheda,* but a lived expression of the difference that it entails. Thus, by nature her desire, reflecting the relations of which phenomenal reality consists, cannot be brought to an end. Hence the episode already recounted, in which Krishna's mere presence can no longer fulfil Rādhā's desire for him, is continued and developed here in greater measure by Rūpa Gosvāmi.[32]

It is worth noting that this realism is one that seeks to instantiate the facts, reflecting them at the subjective level, rather than to adjust one's subjective attitude to them in order to preserve pleasure, or at least non-suffering, as a priority for human experience at all costs. Rooting his religious ethos in his reasoned analysis of ultimate reality, Rūpa could choose an option that is realist in the pragmatic sense by redressing Rādhā's inappropriate expectations according to the possibilities for happiness afforded by the situation. This would be a classic realist theodicy in reasoning that her suffering can be put to rest by a better grasp of the truth and a readjustment of one's actions within the context framed by that truth. In this model, one would have expected that as Rūpa's ideal, Rādhā would have been content to love Krishna with a philosophical resignation, and a readiness to enjoy his presence in other forms. Rādhā ought to proceed based on what Haberman, citing Coomaraswamy, asserts as the ethos of the Caitanya tradition: "The best and most God-like way of living is to 'play' the game."[33]

But this reasonable realist resignation is precisely what is not portrayed or advocated by Rūpa. The dissatisfied Rādhā is the one who is celebrated. For Rūpa who is so committed to a reflective analysis of the theology of love-in-separation on many levels, Rādhā's love is a hard-won realist vision of a devotional attitude that is highest precisely because it most fully instantiates the essence of Krishna's ultimate reality. Thus one can argue that it is a full experience of separation is appropriate at the subjective level, because it is a feature of Being itself.

The "passionate" and "painful" expression of this realism highlights a key difference between Rūpa Gosvāmi and Gadamer. Each advocates non-closure on firmly metaphysical grounds, rooted in a realist attempt to realise (in both senses of the word) the intrinsic dualism of a fundamental ontology of phenomena. But where Gadamer is like a positive, exploratory, Odyssean philosopher, multiplying and widening horizons, pursuing our concerns according to a shifting theme, Rūpa Gosvāmi measures our engagement in terms not of infinite directions, but of infinite intensity in a single direction. Despite substantial agreement about basic metaphysical truths and underlying "realist" ways of reasoning about them toward ethical prescription, at this point Rūpa Gosvāmi and Gadamer reach a particularly significant divergence. Given his ethical paradigm of healthy flourishing, Gadamer would doubtless regard Rādhā's situation as a kind of illness—the kind of pathology that results in metaphysically mistaken absolutisms and ethically misconceived fundamentalisms. Rūpa Gosvāmi admits the counterintuitivity of an ideal of flourishing that may culminate in the emptying of the self to the point of death. Yet, in his writing on Rādhā, he defends unilateral unfulfilled passion, not as a mere by-product of theism, but as an attitude that is most appropriate to the ontological truth of the supreme reality of Krishna—hence her status as his truest self.

Interestingly, where the positive rhetoric of *līlā* initially combated the ontological notion of duality and flux as *duḥkha*, "suffering," this new metaphysical vision of *līlā* as a painful type of "play" brought metaphysical debate full circle back to its interpretation of suffering, found notably in and in dialogue with the early discourse of Buddhism, as an inescapable ontological principle of existence. A realist attitude that sought to recognise the true nature of reality had to admit the combination of separation and concurrent relation, desire and inevitable suffering, as a necessary feature of life. But for Rūpa the qualitative particularity of the emotion—whether we subjectively experience it to be pleasurable or painful—is not ontologically significant. For, ultimately, neither suffering nor bliss is at the heart of reality in both its ontological and phenomenological aspects. Both have been taken up into the meta-concept of *rasa*—a brand of engagement that represents relation in its purest form. Suffering then is necessary for reflecting not only the positive sides of ontological relationality, but also the distance, difference, deferral, and what Derrida calls the *différance* that existence entails.

This reflects the locus of truth in the metaphysics informed by *rasa* and *acintyabhedābheda*. It is not that the one who sees correctly is able to spy Krishna as a divine essence *inside* of, or *beyond* the phenomena, like the *puruṣa* hidden within the particulars of the real and the *ātman* hidden in the cave of the heart, but different from them. Rather, Krishna *is* those phenomena and the very principle of their particularity. One is not meant to "look through" the particulars toward something else. Indeed, this is precisely what the extreme attention to sensory details in Rūpa's theory and literature, and the explicit importance placed upon adjuncts (*uddipanas*, of character, narrative, setting, circumstance) and ornamentation (*alaṃkāra*) is aimed at preventing—we are not meant to look beyond or underneath the manifest, we are meant to look at it and understand it in light of its divine status. Part of the argument made here is that this is not advocated merely for aesthetic affect, or devotional practice, but on the *principle* of maintaining an ontological realism.[34]

Thus Rādhā, who has theological connections with *prakṛti* and Krishna's power of creation,[35] suffers her separation from Krishna as a sort of sublimation of creation's continuous birthpangs—a pain in which we all share. She is herself a symbol of realist approaches to the world, for what she *does* (as devotional exemplar) is never separable from what she *is* (as the ultimate truth of existence). This theological justification is omnipresent and pervasive, and often it is given within the very sentence in which he raises the questions and rebukes Krishna, through puns and allegories. When Lalita complains to Krishna with marked exasperation—"I do not know if it is through some magic that you cause us to love you despite your cruelty"[36]—the single word used for magic (*māyā*) within this sentence both asks and answers the question at the same time, invoking the whole theological debate between the dualists and the monists, for *māyā* can mean both illusion, and the formal constitution of the world or procreative power of God to create the world of appearance. It taps into Advaitic rhetoric denigrating phenomenal "reality," and yet reminds us that from a Caitanya Vaiṣṇava perspective (based primarily on the inverted Sāṃkhya ethos of the *Bhāgavata Purāṇa*), *māyā* is a blessing, and the necessary and enabling condition of the world.

Rūpa writes that the devotees should, like sharks, swim in the sea of the nectar of devotional *rasa* (*bhaktirasāmṛtasindhau caratah . . . bhaktamakarān*), surrounded by the nets of time (*paribhūtakālajālabiyah*), and scorn the rivers of liberation (*aśīlitamuktinandīkān*).[37] Again attachment and suffering are not signs of our alienation from truth. Rather, as truth itself they are to be intensified, perpetuated, and heightened. The "view from within" involves instantiating the essence of reality to higher and higher degrees, without end.[38] In the implication that Rādhā should not only manifest the suffering of separation but also cultivate it to ever-greater extremes, we begin to see the extraordinary, extreme implications of this position.

FROM HEALTHY PLAY TO OVERPOWERING ABSORPTION

Following through these implications to their conclusion means tracing the trajectory from an ontological notion of *chorismos* as enabling of pleasurable play in Gadamer's Platonic paradigm, to *bheda* as the inevitable cause of painful passions. Gone is Rilke's "accurate and measured swing" from "the great bridge-building of God." We are far, too, from the recreational and the festive moods to which Gadamer refers, and closer to his examples of the sacred seriousness of the game, and its development into the aesthetics of tragedy.[39]

Haberman notes that even the demons in their hatred for Krishna are said to be bhaktas, because they are overwhelmingly possessed by the intensity of their feeling for him.[40] Hints like these show that Rūpa Gosvāmi's Caitanya Vaiṣṇava soteriology does not involve a scale merely of love, but rather a scale of intensity in which love partakes. This in turn relates to the idea of devotion as unilaterally focussed attention rather than dispersed and plural appreciation. This notion of embracing an obsessive, utterly engaged, perception-distorting, absence-transcending love is already implied in Krishna's theologically crucial speech to the gopīs after the *Kṛṣṇa-līlā* in the *Bhāgavata Purāṇa*, and one can perhaps see its precedent in Krishna's promise of salvation in the *Bhagavad Gītā* to "those people who approach me with unwavering concentration" (*ananyascintayanto māmye janaḥ paryupasate*).[41] But the emphasis is focused and strengthened by Rūpa. Thus the problem of pain appears merely as one way of dealing with the broader philosophy of intensified engagement as the best way to embrace (rather than flee) the ultimate truths of existence.

If the realist religious position advocates that the goal of individuals is to contribute to the transcendental truths of existence through their enactment of those truths—complementing the objective and ontological, with the subjective and ontic—then rather than deferring to either unity or separation as the key feature of existence, it is rather the medial concept that takes both up into a dialectical unity as relation, *rasa*, which is the appropriate way to understand, experience, and contribute to the fundamental ontological truth of which the universe consists. We return again to the logic of dialectic, in which distinctive rules of self-reflective realism apply.

As in Gadamer's model of healthy growth, this dialectical truth should be increased by more and more self-reflective instantiations of relation. But why would the general vitality of Gadamer's play, which also aims to reflect and augment dialectic, or the equivocal enthusiasm of the *rāsalīlā* dance, be considered inferior to the unilateral obsessiveness of Rādhā and Krishna's passionate relationship? If the two conceptions of Krishna's *līlā* as play and passion with which we began this final discussion can be modelled as paralleling the two postmodern ethics of Hans-Gadamer and Rūpa Gosvāmi respectively—one liberal in aspiring to free self-development, the other fundamentalistic in commitment to a particular object, and advocating an intensification of that one trajectory of desire, rather than a multiplication of many such relations—then why does Rūpa make the choice that he does?

Absorption, obsession, passion, and possession all seem to tend toward an unhealthy diminishment of the one who is in their thrall. Why does Rūpa choose to express *bheda* or *chorismos* as an infinite dialectic of single-minded passion qualitatively intensified in a single direction, rather than a play of many loves quantitatively dispersed across many? Is he motivated merely by a cultural "nostalgia for madness,"[42] and a desire to offer a radical and distinctive form of bhakti among many competitors in the place and period in which he wrote? Or is there further philosophical reflection embedded in Rūpa Gosvāmi's ethical ideal?

EMOTION, INTENSIFICATION, AND ONTOLOGY

The question leads us to look deeper into the modelling of dialectic in terms of emotional relation prevalent in his work, conceiving it as something that is not singular or static in its quality, but intrinsically subject to dynamics of invitation and intensification. There is a growing literature in the study of Hindu traditions that affirms their uniquely central and sensitive interest in the analysis and invocation of emotion and its concurrent mechanisms of control—whether in terms of bhakti (as observed by June McDaniel, Madeleine Biardeau, Edward Dimock, David Haberman, and Karen Prentiss), tantra (Gavin Flood), or traditions of possession (Frederick Smith). Rūpa would seem to be a centrally placed commentator on such strands of Indian religious practice, for he is one of the few to make the systematic exposition of religious emotion his primary goal. He gives numerous portrayals of paradigmatic figures acting out the ultimate salvific activity in his poems and plays, and in the verses that are approvingly cited in the *Bhaktirasāmṛtasindhu*, the *Ujjvala Nīlamaṇi*, and the *Padyāvali*, and in them offers ample description in his own words of the type of *rāga*[43] that is "eternal and indestructible, independent and without external ground, eternally increasing and becoming more and more beautiful and bright."[44] Emotion has a cosmic significance both in defining the divine as creator and as transcendent essence, and Rūpa tells us that "passion is the identity of the emanations of the creative energy of the universe, and partakes in the inconceivable emotional true nature [of the divine]."[45] It is this "causeless, independently perfect, ecstatic love," which as we have seen is the *svarūpam*, the own form or essence of Krishna, and which is Rādhā.[46]

But what does this love really consist of? Pertinent to Rūpa's work and a constant challenge to those who study him is the question of how to translate the many words that are used to describe feelings of affection, love, and passion.[47] Of the many terms that he uses, *rati* primarily denotes pleasure and delight, but also love and affection with further connotations of sexual union. *Kāma* is both love itself and its personification in the god of love. Both *rāga* and *rasa* can mean love and affection, but the former is literally a term for the colour red and implies emotional force or passion, while the latter is literally "taste" and suggests the flavour and relishing of love.[48] *Śṛṇgāra* also has the more intense meanings of love, passion, and sexual love rather than of affection, and shares the associations with flavour and with the colour red. *Prema*, on the other hand, has the more tame implications of love, affection, delight, gladness, or tenderness.[49] *Sneha* is more subdued still, translating as affection, love, kindness, or tenderness. Interestingly, *bhāva*, which is usually Being, existence, truth, or reality, can also mean love, affection, and *attachment*, and it is *mahābhāva* with which Rūpa's account of the highest forms of steady love for Krishna culminates in the *Ujjvala Nīlamaṇi*.[50]

Rūpa Gosvāmi's own transformation of bhakti aesthetics shifts from Abhinavagupta's prevailing notion of *śanta rasa*, "holy" or "peaceful" *rasa*, to adopt that most intense of terms available, *śṛṇgāra rasa*, demonstrating his commitment to a radically different, emotionally intense ethos of salvation. He explicitly designates *mādana* love as the highest kind of emotion and the supreme expression of Rādhā as the *hlādinī* essence of the divine—*madana* being that love that is intoxicating and exhilarating, even maddening, with a clear implication that the transformation of the mind is part of passion's goal.[51]

But *detachment* also has an important place in this conception of emotion and intimacy. In Rūpa's theory, as in the general narrative structure of Sanskrit romantic literature, it is separation of the lover from the beloved that most effectively heightens love.[52] Contrary to the view expounded in the *Bhāgavad Gīta*, in which the result of detachment is the gradual eradication of the passions, here the divorcing of desire from its object gradually amplifies passion. He writes that union cannot be attained without prior separation, just as without having been dyed, cloth and other things cannot be made to grow redder.[53]

The usual complex associations of Rūpa's prose are in evidence. *Vivardhate* implies a progressive increase of *rāga*, a word connoting both redness and passion, in the state of union, referring to the whole incremental intensification of emotion in the love-in-separation narratives. The word used for reddening, *kāṣayite*, has connotations of passion, emotion, flavour, and perfume, thus intensifying the romantic metaphor, and also linking with *rasa* as "taste." But, further, it also makes reference to the religio-philosophical implications of the analogy, for in the *Chandogya Upaniṣad* it is used as a word for attachment to worldly objects. In a single pithy verse, Rūpa Gosvāmi incorporates his whole scheme of subverting the transcendence-oriented philosophy of Vedānta in favour of a quality of emotion that can only be achieved by intensifying our attachment to worldly objects.

Thus it hardly seems adequate to speak of Rūpa Gosvāmi's complex mapping of psychological and cosmological dimensions of the emotions associated with intense attachment in terms of a theology of love. As we have seen, his religious philosophy of *rasa*, and the practice that he advocates on its foundation, are both centred around the incremental cultivation of "higher" and "higher" degrees of emotion, that recall the *vilāsa* emanations that lie within the soul of the Mahāśakti. Rūpa follows the picture sketched out by Bharata, the originator of the written theory of *rasa*, in which different emotions have different qualities and stages, may be more or less permanent, and, much like Sanskrit words, meditative states, and the flavour of spiced food to which *rasa* can also refer, can be systematically augmented into stronger and stronger forms. Thus in his works emotion can be intensified (*paropoṣa*: nourished, nurtured, increased as at *Bhaktirasāmṛtasindhu*, 2.1.6–8) through mood and circumstance, and rarefied by the shedding of other concerns leading to the purification of intention. The *Ujjvala Nīlamaṇī*, while asserting that the varieties of transcendent ecstatic love felt by the gopīs is beyond the perception of reason and logic,[54] categorises, divides, and subdivides love into *vṛttis*, or modifications which accumulate, distil, purify, and intensify emotion; the metaphor of juice is apt. This sweetening (*mādhurya*) of the juice (*rasa*) into nectar (*amṛta*) is a crucial part of the religious ethos exemplified in the figure of Rādhā. Thus the engagement that characterises relationality can be mapped according to a continuous scheme of variations and degrees to expand upon Gadamer's less well-developed Platonic-Aristotelian model of vitality (and perhaps harmonising more effectively with Gadamer's Schelerian influences).[55]

As a response to what he perceived as a lamentably emotionless brahminical focus on ritual efficacy (Rūpa reserves some of his greatest disdain for the *mīmāṃsakas*), his soteriological practice of intensification enjoins the devotee to cultivate the highest potency of phenomenal experience, resonating with Nietzsche's urgent invective against the blandness of religious and metaphysical objectivity in the Western tradition cited earlier. Rūpa is concerned that we become galvanised to a new vision of reality, and he is clear that those who feel less than profound passion in their everyday activities are treading a lower path. Indeed, he notes that those who seek "peaceful" forms of emotion through austerities receive only a "segment of that moon of peace."[56] His lists of the external indications of passion, from perspiring and trembling to the rising of the hairs on the skin of the lover, which are borrowed from classical Sanskrit aesthetics, offer visible proof that the devotee has left the null, impassive view of the world far behind.[57]

This vitalised, ecstatic mood, Rūpa tells us, is not arbitrarily designated as the highest path. It is naturally wins out over other approaches to the divine because it is the most potent option, asserting its primacy through its persuasive power and its urgent reminder of phenomenal presence:

> A breeze laden with the sweet scent of Tulasī blossoms mixed with the pollen from the lotus feet of the Lotus-Eyed Lord entered the noses of those ascetics and excited their minds and bodies, even though they were devoted to the formless Absolute (*akṣara*).[58]

The celebrated strong will of the tapasin, who is a specialist at "going-within," is overcome by the mere scent of the blossoms that have "gone in" (*antar-gataḥ*) unbidden, and excited the phenomenal mind and body that the ascetic sought to make still.

A recent growing trend in scholarship has uncovered a highly fruitful model for understanding Rūpa's emphasis on the invasive, compelling power of intense emotion. His comprehensive account of the marks of the passionate state paint a picture of the emotion-possessed devotee dancing, rolling on the ground, singing, shrieking, twisting the body, roaring, gaping, laughing, spinning, salivating trembling, weeping, and even losing consciousness.[59] Such powerful responses, combined with the practice of invoking the identity of a divine person (of Krishna, Rādhā, or one of their servants), suggest that in devotional emotion we can see vestigial elements of divine "possession" emerging with a new emphasis.

Scholars such as Frederick Smith have explicated this neglected ingredient of powerful popular Hindu religious traditions as "a widespread episteme—a historically situated discourse, phenomenon and practice—in Indian thought, culture, religion and medicine," and his project of redefining the notion of possession in terms of its distinctive South Asian framework involves noting that it is to be seen not as a struggle of identities, but as a "passion" in the classical sense, more connected to the overwhelming power of emotions, than to the demonic invasion with which it is often associated in the West. In this context he notes that "emotion itself, [is] the kinder, gentler ancestor of possession,"[60] and this applicability of this possession model of the passionate self to bhakti practice and thought is borne out by June McDaniel's study of "divine madness" in which she locates Vaiṣṇava *mahābhāva* on a scale of Hindu ecstatic traditions that includes *āveśa*—possession.[61]

Understood in the context of a positive religious attitude toward transformative states of emotional intensity, such that theory and practice are devised to invoke and cultivate them, the notion of possession sheds light on this bhakti form of union with the divine, which complements and modifies the Advaitic ideal. An indigenous notion of passion entails developing the indigenous notion of possession, and exploring the willingness of the devotional self to be invaded, kenotically emptied and helplessly filled in ways that may involve "alternating experiences of inner destruction and reintegration" that are fundamentally salvific.[62] It is significant first to note that, while the Śāṃkarite Advaitic model of union rejects the contextual particularity of the devotee's identity and context, the possession model unifies the deity and devotee as personality and situated body, presenting an "immanent presence" of the divine that Kathleen Erndl contrasts with the deity as "just a transcendental ideal."[63] On the bhakti model of emotional possession by the divine there is a sense not of replacing one person with another, but rather of possession as augmenting and fulfilling the potentiality of the mortal person to present a divine form. From ontological principle to instances of its ontic manifestation is a small leap. What is revealed here is a mixture of many forms of unity-in-difference, each of which contributes another layer to this conceptually and experientially rich soteriological experience.

Here too, we see models of nominal suffering in which what appears as the ailing of the self is seen not as ascetic *self-destruction* but as emotional *self-opening* that allows the entry of the heightening and overflowing force of emotion and/or divinity. Indeed, this is one of the central points made in McDaniel's book where Caitanya serves as an exemplar of the idea of apparent suffering as "direct experience" of the divine that may "disrupt and reorganise personality," does not necessarily entail a rejection of the embodied dimension of the self, and entails a "radical alteration of perception, emotion, or personality that brings the person closer to what he regards as the sacred."[64] Rūpa's idea of cultivating intensified emotion lies on a continuum not only with traditions in which the phenomenal self is destroyed in order to reveal an underlying identity (as in much Yogic and Advaitic practice), and those in which the self is invaded by an external force (as in traditions of negative possession by unfavourable spirits, demons, or ghosts), but also with the traditions of incarnation and manifestation that pervade this culture in which the boundary between mortal and divine is rarely firmly drawn. Thus the apparent ailing of a person may merely indicate an advance into a new form, like the flourishing of the sapling into the tree.

Rādhā, Rūpa's exemplar, appears to ail as her attachment intensifies, but she is filled by the purest form of the divine, of which all selfhood is constituted: pure passion. Indeed, in one sense her selfhood is almost erased by her commitment to her divine *telos* in the beloved, as she more and more fully manifests her identity as Krishna's *hlādinī-śakti*. In a classic example of dialectical sublimation, she both kenotically empties her own personality and sacrifices her "self" to the divine, and is raised to a higher level of that which she already is, fulfilling a latent potential. This is not an Advaitic realisation of identity in which I realise that "I" consist in consciousness, but rather a new and more complex form of identity in which I realise (i.e., bring into being) that "I" consist in teleology, motion, motivation, and desire.

It is important to note the distinction between the kenotic unity of the self-denying ascetic who abandons his particularity for an undifferentiated (*akṣara*) universalised reality with no place for situated identity and desire, and this kenotic unity through complete instantiation of the situated desire in which ultimate reality consists. Rūpa prioritises the love described as *samartha* in which the lover and the beloved become one—the most intense type of love for Krishna. As *manjistha rāga* it is eternally increasing. In Krishna's voice, Rūpa writes that

> as sages in samādhi merging in self-realisation like rivers into the ocean forget the names and forms of the world, so the gopīs were so preoccupied with me that they could not think of their own bodies, the world, nor their future lives.[65]

The continuation of craving as an open trajectory is essential to this process of intensification, and here we see how Rūpa does not merely depict the suffering of *viraha bhakti* as an apologetic portrayal, but uses it as a mechanism for achieving this effect in the devotee. In both of Rūpa Gosvāmi's poems the anticipation of Krishna's return is invoked again and again in expressions that are full of hope and full of irony, and the framing narrative of Lalita's initial message to the swan messenger culminates in the direct request to know when he will return.[66] Again and again one or other voice asks "O when . . . ?" invoking the dramatic irony that characterises the whole piece. In verses 93–96 of the *Haṃsadūta* this hope is cited as the reason that she stays alive in her pain—life itself consists of this open-ended, dynamic form of engagement.

This is a theological notion with a history that reaches well beyond India and beyond those forms of religion that we would typically see as robustly devotional. Numerous modern Western writers develop images of open teleologies and non-closure in relation to religious yearning.[67] Caputo, seeking to paraphrase Derrida, aptly expresses this postmodern trend by writing:

> I am the one who finds his life a question, whose life is always being put in question, which is what gives life its salt. We seek but do not find, not quite, not if we are honest, which does not discourage the religious heart but drives it on and heightens the passion, for this is one more encounter with the impossible.[68]

Replace "salt" with "sweetness" and we have something resembling the Caitanya adage that one should seek to *taste* sugar, not to *become* sugar (although on this phenomenological interpretation tasting sugar *is* becoming sugar—i.e., from a phenomenal perspective both involve bringing the experience of sweetness into being). Caputo's quote conveys the vitalist ethos of reviving religious feeling against the sway of scepticism and instrumental, utilitarian approaches to religion: we are excited, enthused, and enlivened by the "encounter with the impossible." It encourages the religious heart, driving it on. Caputo's language discloses his characteristically postmodern anxiety that the dispassionate cloud of nullity be lifted and religion restored to a lively and driving concern. Despite his criticism of Gadamer's metaphysical essentialism, he too seeks to be reinvigorated by an idea from the realm of the real: the impossibility of complete closure.

But, as we have stated, Rūpa's position is subtly different from this, adding ontology to rhetoric. The goal is not merely to wake us up with insoluble aporias and heighten our attentiveness to reality. Rather, in this way, as well as reflecting the real we invoke in a heightened degree a kind of realist "presence" according to which obliqueness, deferral, and indirectness all deliver the beloved in a finer form. Rūpa's literature is full of celebrations of the circuitous forms, curves, and dialectic of the media through which divinity is hidden and yet all the time present. In part, this is a stylistic mark of the tradition, extending "the process of increasing elaboration and specificity that one sees in the development from the *Harivaṃṣa* through the *Viṣṇu* and the *Bhāgavata Purāṇas* to the *Gītagovinda*."[69] But it also reflects and instantiates the deeper truths of form and deferral. The curves seen in Krishna's pose, his curls and ornaments, reflect those of Rādhā's lovely physical form, and of the beauty of the natural forms in the forest, of her oblique glances, of the circuitous and complicating games that they play to heighten their passion, and of the curving, oblique dialectic of the grammatical structure of the Sanskrit stanzas of Rūpa Gosvāmi's verses. The use of poetic suggestion (*dhvani*), the anticipatory deferral of open-ended semantics, and the thematisaton of elusiveness is elevated from a mere stylistic convention to a way in which the divine is made present in the evocation of beauty and of open-ended engagement itself. It serves a purpose that is at once psychological and invocatory, ontic and ontological.

This theme of elusiveness and deferral as enjoyment-enabling separation, and indeed as a symbol of ultimate reality and a form of divine presence, is made concrete in many forms throughout the texts. Thus, recalling Krishna's purānic encouragement to Yaśodā to perceive him in his incarnate, particularistic embodied form, and his injunction to the gopīs to perceive him in the phenomenal forms around them ("I cannot repay you gopīs, so please be satisfied with your activities"),[70] Rūpa places particular emphasis on the various vessels of Krishna's manifestation through ornaments, incarnations, companions, and situations.[71] The obstructions to the divine lovers (characters such as Jāṭila, the mother-in-law, and rivals such as Candramukhi) are actually positive forces insofar as they are the accessories and enabling features of *rasa*.

The devotee aims at the *mādhurya* of intimately, subjectively enjoying Krishna rather than the *aiśvarya* or majesty of his direct "objective" apprehension. Duly, it is not the purely virtuous heroine whom Rūpa lauds in the *Ujjvala Nīlamanī*, but rather the "saucy and soft" heroine whose paradoxical nature hooks our interest and perpetuates it, far from assuaging it with easy answers. Many of the verses take the form of riddles, and the obliqueness of sarcasm, irony, metaphor, and of the gopīs' teasing glances is celebrated in the rich language of the text. We are told that

> Rādhārani dispatches many darting glances from the corners of her playfully oblique, glimmering eyes . . . every word fragment she speaks is an inscrutable, powerful mantra to invoke the presence of the God of love.[72]

It is these qualities that contribute to her being an expert "enjoyer" of reality.[73]

All of this contributes to the cultivation of intensity as a realisation of the divine, in both senses. We can see this argument as underlying Rūpa's defence of the primacy of Rādhā. In his chapter on her in the *Ujjvala Nīlamanī*, he prefaces his detailed exposition of her qualities with a short defence of her preeminence above all other lovers of Krishna. Krishna's two chief gopīs, Candrāvalī and Rādhā, are said to be almost equal in status. This in itself is interesting, not least because historically Candrāvalī has failed to attain anything like the devotional or theological preeminence enjoyed by Rādhā. She is noted for her *ghṛta-sneha*—a category of affection (*sneha*) that is metaphorically linked to ghee and the ritual religion of reverence for the gods. Rādhā, by contrast, is the advocate of *mādhurya-sneha*, affection characterised by honeyed intimacy, sweetness, and a certain irreverence. Rūpa makes this clear in his list of the relevant qualities enumerated in chapters of the *Ujjvala Nīlamanī*—including Radha's ability to keep Krishna under control, and her skill at concealing her true feelings beneath a wrathful or taunting exterior. It is tempting to characterise these contrasting relationships in terms of an axial duality of religious moods—between personal and impersonal relationships with the divine, between the objective and the subjective mood, the abstract and the particular focus. The intuition of a structural duality is rooted firmly in the text, offering devotees two valid modes of religiosity *within* the tradition.

Rādhā's intimate, honeyed love is "in every way superior" because its qualities make it the "true essence of the great emotion."[74] From the philosophical perspective it is satisfying to note that this same phrase, *mahābhāva svarūpa iyam*, can also mean the "true essence of the great Being" or "great becoming." It is the true nature of devotional emotion, and implicitly the true nature of all emotion and all being. To this extent, we may say that the self-conscious, distant, and awed love of Candrāvalī exemplifies the qualities (good and bad relative to their context of application) of objectified concern, but she suffers the self-alienation of postmodern thinkers who have learned to consider their own "care" as something separate from themselves, about which they have a choice.

In defence of Rādhā, Rūpa cites her longstanding high rank in an impressive list of authoritative texts, including the Ṛg Veda, the Upaniṣads, and Purāṇas.[75] In so doing he roots the theology of Rādhā in the ancient literatures that underpin many, if not most, schools of *astika* (orthodox) Hindu thought. He assimilates Rādhā to Lakṣmī, the consort of Viṣṇu,[76] calling on the support of a wider field of Vaiṣṇava adherence, and also linking the particularity of the Krishna incarnation and its narrative to the cosmic order represented by Viṣṇu. Having dealt with the Caitanya bhakti, Vedic, and Vaiṣṇava reasons for Rādhā's importance, he shifts into the discourse of purāṇic Sāṃkhya by pointing out that as the *hlādinī-śakti*, she is the best and the truest form of all the great *śaktis* of Krishna.[77] Here he is restating explicitly what has been said previously in the text and elsewhere in his works: all powers or energies are really the power of *hlād*—enjoyment, gladness, exhilaration, and delight.

Ganeri offers a striking parallel in one early Vedāntic answer to the question of how one can experience one's true nature, bringing the higher truth of universal consciousness to presence in our own subjective consciousness. Even here, according to Ganeri, where emotion is seen as part of the phenomenal reality that needs to be removed from the equation in order to reveal a value-neutral truth, there is the acknowledgement that any soteriology that aims at eudaimonia through realisation of the truth must achieve it by means of some sort of dialectical, qualitative self-enjoyment:

> [W]hen a sensation is being sensed, you catch the sensing self only by getting hold of the sensing; when a cognition is being cognised, you catch the thinker only by getting hold of the thinking. Here is a way to reach the self—not by grasping it as an object, but catching it in its activity of sensing and thinking . . . the self is caught in the phenomenological quality of thinking, in the flavour of the experience of what it is like to think.[78]

Thus, from a philosophical perspective one can see a logical progression from the consciousness-based "onto-theology" of Advaita to the "enjoyment" of the "flavours" of consciousness advocated in many of its later bhakti manifestations. "How exactly *does* it feel to experience the self?" asks Ganeri, and draws his answer from the Upaniṣads:

> It is like this [says Yajnavalkya, this time to Janaka]. As a man embraced by a woman he loves is oblivious to everything within or without, so this person embraced by the self consisting of knowledge is oblivious to everything within or without. Clearly this is the aspect of his where all desires are fulfilled, where the self is the only desire.[79]

Even here, where the language of "self consisting of knowledge" seems to preclude the emotionalism of bhakti, one can see how qualitative experiences redolent of love and desire arise as our best way of expressing the dialectic of experience experiencing itself. Whether we speak of the mind knowing, the heart feeling, or the senses enjoying, all self-reflectivity must entail a qualitative experiencing, an "enjoyment" of self, for it is only experience's qualitative content that can be grasped by experience. The point illuminates the reasoning behind the inclusion of "bliss" in the "being-consciousness-bliss" formulation of *Brahman* in Vedānta, and points toward the harmonious union of the blissful Gopala myth with the Vedānta philosophy. Thus it is important to note the theological point embedded in the devotional exaltation of enjoyment—it is not that enjoyment is the best way to worship Krishna, nor that it is his most characteristic quality, nor even that it is his best. It is that he himself *is the quality of enjoyment*. Only in enjoyment, in experiencing or "tasting" him, can we both *be* and *see* him.

If Being is enjoyment then we can enjoy as much as we like, wherever and whenever we like, indiscriminately without prejudice as to the object of our desire. But if it is also attachment, directedness, *telos*, then this too must be exemplified in an appropriate attitude to our object(s) of desire. For Gadamer, passion is like a mathematical quantity that can be quantitatively added and increased, as if "passion for *x*" plus "passion for *y*" equals passion times two. But for Rūpa, enjoyment, desire, passion, and thirst all have degrees of intensity, represented by his metaphors of distillation and purification, as of a substance. He is committed to a position in which dialectic can indeed deepen as well as widen its scope, thereby improving its reflection of Being's essence. We are to proceed with an attitude "not subsumed to knowledge and action" (*jñānakarmādyanāvṛtam*)[80] of "bhakti [which is] service, with the senses, to the lord of the senses" (*hṛṣīkeṇa hṛṣīkeśasevanaṃ bhaktiḥ*).[81]

Rūpa Gosvāmi's prioritisation of value and teleology as a central and celebrated feature of ontology highlights the absence that Gadamer laments in Plato as opposed to Aristotle, and in Husserl as opposed to Scheler. It is an oversight that underlies Plato's hostility to the poets, and Aristotle's defense of the *phronetic* model of truth and the dynamic, diachronic model of beings. It reflects an insight that has its roots in the "the concept of 'life', which is fundamental to Greek thinking about reality," understanding "that which moves itself or that which has the origin of motion in itself, as primary."[82]

But Rūpa Gosvāmi's worldview is less preoccupied by the unrestrained, irreducible, opaque freedom of Being's vital dynamism than are the post-Heideggerian philosophers—perhaps "selfhood" and "freedom" were not held as highly *qua* cultural ideal in his own tradition, and perhaps because his own historical arena of discourse was already more multifaceted and filled with contradictions. This is also perhaps the case because his cultural emphasis is less on the problem of meaning than on the meaningfulness of meanings—which is partly to say that he is a more explicitly ethical and religious thinker. Perhaps another way of putting this subtle but axial difference between Gadamer and Rūpa Gosvāmi, is that while both acknowledge flux, transformation, and mutual constitution, for Gadamer the "theme" to which we must devote ourselves is the Self—a free and vital interiority that the "other" illuminates. For Rūpa Gosvāmi, however, it is the renunciant sages taking pleasure in the self who, on the one hand, are clearly mistaken in choosing this will-oriented, overtly interior path of *jñāna* that Rūpa so meticulously rejects, yet on the other hand are still appropriated in his path to Krishna as ultimate reality through their "motiveless attachment to the idea of the self."[83]

Gadamer too speaks approvingly of the dialectical identity of self in the object of desire. *Rasa* appears more apt to express dialectical truths than Gadamer's governing trope of "play," yet in his studies on Hegel with whom he expressed such an affinity, Gadamer too writes of the intrinsic deferral of desire and its elevation into a medial category of "life" in which the self is happily both preserved and destroyed. He writes: "It is all too clear that the self-consciousness of desire or of satisfaction of desire, respectively, provides no lasting certainty, for 'in pleasure I thirst for desire.'" His words apply to Rādhā's state, continuing:

> Desire is as little interested in the differences which various "objects" might have as the species is in the life of the individual, or the organism in the particular foodstuffs which it assimilates. He who is hungry wants "something to eat"—it does not matter what.[84]

This is the sort of statement that would seem to accord very well with his idea that we can move from arc to arc of *telos*, from game to game, and object to object of desire or belief without prejudice as to continuity or commitment. But he also writes that

> [c]onsequently, the object of desire is itself "life"—precisely because the object for the consciousness of desire is "everything else" besides that consciousness . . . [Hegel] is asserting that the object of desire as such, i.e., as it is, not only for us, but for desire itself, has the structure of life.[85]

His words are a reminder of the way in which we should interpret Rūpa Gosvāmi's portrayal of Rādhā's passion. Krishna is not any mere object or *telos*, engaged with a vitality that enlivens her. This would be what Gadamer speaks of as the mere "condition of animal desire" in which the individual is "absorbed in the single dimension of its instinctual desires."[86] As it turns out, both thinkers believe in the absorption of the identity of the individual into a medial identity of the whole which encompasses the other, and both believe that this involves elevating mundane desire into a relationship with Being or "life" as a whole. And while Gadamer seems again and again to be motivated by a concern for the good of the individual in this relationship (i.e., to be seeking "the certainty of self reached in its satisfaction"),[87] elsewhere this emphasis is modified by a recognition that this self is in fact not a witness to the *telos*, or a bearer of it, but the integral consistency of the *telos* or *desire* itself:

> In order that desire might attain true self-consciousness, the object of desire must, in all of its "nothingness of the other," still not cease to exist. It must be living self-consciousness in the "particularity of its distinctness." To be sure, as desire, the desire seeking real self-consciousness also knows only itself and

> seeks nothing but itself in the other. But such desire is only able to find itself in the other if . . . it does not exist in its own right, but rather, in disregard of itself, it "is for another." Only consciousness is able to be the other of itself in this way and to cancel itself in such a fashion that it does not cease to exist.[88]

Note that the terms designating the individual have here become replaced by "desire," and that this is also revealed to coincide ontologically with consciousness—the only medium in which self and other can be unified.

The difference in emphasis between Gadamer's notion of self and Rūpa Gosvāmi's notion of other comes into focus in one way: the confusion arises by a last stubborn reassertion of dualism. The desire is not the desire "of" the individual. The desire is the individual itself. The fulfilment of desire is not satisfaction of arbitrary states of the self. It is the satisfaction of the self and it is the satisfaction of Being *qua* its particularity. It is in this light that we desire, and find our "Self" in the passion of that desire.

This makes one further point to be noted. As stated in chapter 2, a rigorous phenomenologist must eventually admit values to be intrinsic to Being, and as Heidegger says, the attempt at a purely "objective" assessment and grounding of value misunderstands the nature of its object, which in fact stands as part of the ontological ground beyond the objectifying frameworks of realism and idealism. He writes:

> Thinking is judged by a standard that does not measure up to it. Such judgement may be compared to the procedure of trying to evaluate the essence and powers of a fish by seeing how long it can live on dry land. For a long time now, all too long, thinking has been stranded on dry land. Can then the effort to return thinking to its element be called "irrationalism?"[89]

He continues:

> Where else does "care" tend but in the direction of bringing man back to his essence? What else does that in turn betoken but that man (homo) become human (humanus)? Thus humanitas really does remain the concern of such thinking. For this is humanism: meditating and caring, that man be human and not inhumane.

This then was the definition of humanism that Gadamer inherited from Heidegger—a humanism with ethical and ontological implications, understood "as a concern that man become free for his humanity *and find his worth in it*."[90] If ontology is rightly understood, value needs no "grounding" for we realise that there is no such thing as a primordially value-neutral field of truth, or human life above which questions of worth float untethered. Rather, learning to dwell in Being means learning to dwell in value: to live as Rādhā rather than as Candrāvalī. Value is ingrained into the world.

This is a slippery but important truth, clarifying many modern and ancient difficulties in conjoining accounts of ethics to accounts of reality. Other Western philosophers concerned with the need to return to questions of value and the mechanisms by which value operates in the world have not been ignorant of the ways in which those questions have been knit through the philosophies of other cultures. Martha Nussbaum, a contemporary thinker who shares with Gadamer the agenda of seeking to restore our passions and prejudices to their natural and necessary place in life, wrote in an essay dedicated to Bimal Matilal (whom she described as "a paradigm of cross-cultural historical and philosophical inquiry")[91] that

> [t]he story of an emotion . . . is the story of judgements about important things, judgements in which we acknowledge our neediness and incompleteness before those elements that we do not fully control.[92]

In the essay that follows this assertion she argues that emotions are a form of judgement on those things before which we are helpless and disempowered. She speaks of the "urgency and heat" of these judgements, and perhaps most importantly of the way in which they seem unlike our usual forms of "reflection" and "judgement" because of our passivity before them, and their power to overwhelm and "dismember" the very self that is normally in control. Rādhā too is overwhelmed in the state that Rūpa considers ideal; lost, confused, her ego disrupted by what Gadamer would normally consider an overattachment. She cries: "I trembled with longing to be touched by the lotus-hand of that boy who is dark as a lotus' blue petal: where was I? Who was I? What was I doing? Friend, I did not know."[93]

Nussbaum seeks to restore value to our accounts of truth—the problem of "the passion of the real," which Badiou coined in such pithy and prophetic tones. In many respects, while this study aims to draw limited but instructive parallels between Rūpa Gosvāmi's and Gadamer's positions, it often seems that Rūpa Gosvāmi's insights are the more critically modern of the two; his optimism resonates with that of many of Gadamer's contemporaries and successors. He displays an eagerness to affirm the validity and importance—indeed, the ontological importance—of emotion as our epistemological guide to the centrality of value in ontology. There is a willingness to explore that which infringes upon and overwhelms the self. All of this also helps to explain why Gadamer has his exemplary poet engaged in the self-reflexive appreciation of many goals or objects, while Rūpa Gosvāmi has Rādhā absorbed in an unwavering self-reflexive passion for a single object of desire.

Finally, we can see a further parallel in Rūpa Gosvāmi's notion of the ideal ethical activity as an intensification of Being. Gadamer, as we have said, affirms the Hegelian formulation of Being's intrinsic relationality as "dialectic." But he rejects the culmination of dialectic in a totality of absolute spirit. Badiou agrees with this—infinite deferral as opposed to totality is a key tenet of the postmodern position. Thus, he also speaks for the Heideggerian and Gadamerian traditions when he writes that "we share with Hegel a conviction about the identity of being and thought. But for us this identity is a local occurrence and not a totalised result."[94] Gadamer's goal then is to extend this local occurrence, which is also the occurrence of truth, in many directions, extending the horizons of Being, just as Heidegger advised us to become Being's shepherd or midwife. Again, we see the mathematical paradigm of this tradition of thought for which Being can be increased, but as a single type cannot be intensified—a conclusion that Badiou problematises in his set-theoretical model.

Badiou explores the parameters and presuppositions of such a perspective, and provides a critical model for comparing Gadamer's and Rūpa Gosvāmi's models of dialectic. On his ontological conception of mathematics, multiples are not merely many accumulations or aggregates of equal units. Rather, in the set-theoretical model of mathematics that Badiou champions, each unit is itself a quantity that is able to become greater or lesser. He further sheds light on Rūpa Gosvāmi's ideal of self-reflexive enjoyment of enjoyment by addressing the broadly Hegelian faith in the reflexivity of Being, through his own model of ontological plurality:

> We will agree to call reflexive a multiple (a being) which has the property of presenting itself in its own multiple composition. Engaging in an altogether classical consideration, we have just said that if the Being of the Whole is presupposed, it must be presupposed as reflexive. Or that the concept of universe entails, with regard to its being, the predicate of reflexivity.[95]

The multiplicity of which we all consist is reflected in the multiplicity of Being, and yet in its totality Being must itself contain awareness of itself—Badiou formulates this in terms of a multiplicity which must finally encompass the fact of itself in its wholeness.[96] This self-reflexivity of the whole, it becomes clear, is the essence of Rūpa's religious insight, and the precise tenet that Gadamer does not accept. This position, philosophically equivalent to Gadamer's assertion that the fusing of horizons is an infinite process without completion, is what Badiou calls the project of "detotalisation." In these terms, Rūpa Gosvāmi's theology of Krishna's identity with, reflection upon, and fulfilment of relation with the universe addresses this problem of totality and detotalisation that preoccupies other heirs of Hegel, Gadamer's philosophical "cousins," including Deleuze. On this view, what is distinctive about Hegel is his commitment to the idea that the individual can, as part of Being, reflect upon and fulfil Being itself. Speaking of human attempts at a method of thinking the Whole, Hegel himself gives an account in *The Science of Logic*, cited by Badiou, that effectively explains one of the functions of Rūpa Gosvāmi's ethics of *rasa*:

> The method is the pure concept that relates itself only to itself; it is therefore the *simple self-relation* that is *being*. But now it is also *fulfilled being*, the *concept that comprehends* itself, being as the *concrete* and also absolutely *intensive* totality.[97]

The intensifying of enjoyment in *rasa*, through its repeated dialectic of relation to relation, is indeed conceived as a fulfilment of Krishna. The neo-Vedāntic mutuality and self-divided identity of Krishna and world, the plurality and dynamism of Sāṃkhya *śaktis*, the introduction of the aesthetic concept of *rasa* as vehicle of ultimate enjoyment is all aimed at the goal not of making humans happy, but of serving reality itself in its true essence. This is the meaning of soteriology in what we have called a realist theology—an inversion and transformation of what is meant by "human flourishing." Devotees do not seek heaven in order to find a pleasant refuge. Even in what the West sees as a soteriological fulfilment in Krishna's "heaven," each devotee continues to consecrate the self to a fulfilment of the divine *līlā*. There is no rest from Being, only its continued and perfected activity. In Rūpa Gosvāmi's ontologically grounded ethics, parallel but contrary to Gadamer, we see a model in which, in Badiou's words:

> through successive subsumptions, thinking appropriates the movement of the whole as constituting its own being, its own identity. . . . Here one can see that the axiom of the whole leads to a figure of thought as the saturation of conceptual determinations—from the exterior toward the interior, from exposition toward reflection, from form toward content—as one comes to possess, in Hegel's vocabulary, "fulfilled being" (*das erfullte Sein*) and the "concept comprehending itself."[98]

Without imputing a simple correspondence between the two, we can note how Badiou draws out the ideals that Hegel shared with Rūpa Gosvāmi (ironically, his near contemporary), and from which Gadamer ultimately turned away. In this final respect, then, despite their common ontological subscription to brands of dialectic, their difference lies in the post-Heideggerian resistance to totality and the Indian tendency as described at the beginning of part II, to seek an intimate connection between the particular and the axiomatic truths of the Whole.

RŪPA GOSVĀMI'S REALISM AND RELIGIOUS BELIEF

One of the features of Rūpa's works that is most fascinating for the theologian and the philosopher is that they are filled with thought-provoking, theologically illuminating illustrations of the implications of these ideas for religious belief. Elaborating on the theme of the gopīs' *līlā,* he cites Rādhā's imitation of Krishna, a guise assumed in order to console herself at his absence.

> Limbs anointed with black musk, garlanded and dressed in yellow silk garments, having placed a peacock feather in her braided hair, and playing a bamboo flute tilted to touch her shoulder; thus made into the sweet lord, may Rādhā protect us.[99]

In this plaintive verse, Rādhā alleviates her cravings by pretending to be Krishna, offering up a concrete illustration of her recognition of their dialectical identity. Can we imagine Rilke's lover or Blanchot's believer pretending to *be* the object of their desire in order to console themselves? It is difficult even to imagine the thought arising as a natural step in the logic of their craving. Symbolically, this is a reminder that the aporia of separation, in the Indian context as in Gadamer's, is founded upon a monistic rather than a dualistic metaphysics (granted the specific refinements in those ill-defined taxonomies that we have discussed).[100] Yet it is also a powerfully paradoxical image of the psychology of Rādhā as devotee, lost in forever-unsatisfied, forever-possessing assimilation to the beloved. Her own identity has been eternally and essentially transformed by her consuming love, and her efforts to imitate him are both charming and pitiful. We see that she eternally possesses the means for a bittersweet partial satisfaction of her love, and that in this peaceless union, at once charming, provocative, and foolish, she is made worthy of worship—and emulation. In Rūpa's vision Rādhā offers a newly rich philosophical and psychological, ontological, and ontic elaboration of the *Bhāgavata Purāṇa*'s model of bhakti:

> Not Brahma's supremacy, nor great Indra's region, nor the world's conqueror's sway, nor rule over the underworld, neither yogic accomplishments nor release from rebirth does he desire whose mind is fixed upon me. He desires nothing other than me.[101]

Again and again, this study has used the term "realism" in the sense of a perspective that locates the highest value, and the foundation for all other knowledge and action, in the correct apprehension of ultimate reality. Here we see a religious expression of the same impulse, framed in a mode of expression that is too easily identified as "devotional" without acknowledging the concurrent "philosophical" dimension of such religiosity. Krishna speaks simultaneously as deity and ultimate reality. Both philosophers and religionists are all too often wont to miss the connection between the two, which one might otherwise think to be a natural conjunction in any mildly reflective person in any minimally questioning period of thought.

Badiou writes of philosophy's commitment to truth that "it is like a love without object."[102] Paraphrasing Badiou's notion of the faith-event (whether political, religious, ethical, or otherwise personal), O. Feltham and J. Clemens highlight the preeminent, ever-returning trope of the lover. They write:

> When two people fall in love, their "meeting"—whether that meeting be their first hours together, or the length of their entire courtship—forms an event for them in relation to which they change their lives. This certainty does not mean that their lives are simply going to be the better for it; on the contrary, love may involve debt, alienated friends and rupture with one's family. The point is that love changes their relation to their world irrevocably.[103]

Yet the tendency in postmodern writers, including Caputo, Levinas, and Badiou,[104] is to prefer a model of the faith-event as a commitment to an irrational transcendence, a narrative of mysterious logic that controverts and contends with the "real" context. This is not the case for Rūpa Gosvāmi, who grounds his ethos of transformative passion in the very fabric of reality, both as it is rationally analysed and as it is emotionally experienced. As in the case of Gadamer, his religion does not contend with, but arises from the nature of Being and therefore his own nature also. For both writers, the discovery of the self, which is the essence of realist "soteriology," does indeed lie in attempting to align the intuitive *phenomenal* self with its true *ontological* nature. In both cases the goal of the self, in reawakening to the passion of the real, is to discover its own nature as freedom (plurality, difference, motion), harnessed to a theme (unity, non-difference, form, *telos*).

On this account, poetry is an exemplary truth discourse because it best expresses the world in which we live as a world of meaning, rather than a purportedly neutral field of contingent signs. Poetry is for Gadamer the matrix in which the inner essence is enshrined, and called forth to revitalise experience by expressing the freedom, ambiguity, and ever-potential vitality that most aptly returns to us what we most desire *pace* Badiou—the passion of the real.[105] For many, religious belief must be "poetic" in this way. But in Rūpa Gosvāmi's model we see that rigorous truth-inquiry can also integrally coincide with religious forms that are more committed to particularity in their character. Rādhā is an exemplary model of Tillich's classic definition: "Religion is the state of being grasped by an ultimate concern, a concern which qualifies all other concerns as preliminary and which itself contains the answer to the question of the meaning of our life."[106] Rūpa describes the experience of being impassioned and possessed by a religious "reality," reminding us of a neglected cornerstone of realist religious experience. This is a vision that offers to balance out our often overly clinical notions of belief, caricatured in terms of social control or dogmatic rule following. It gives an alternative account of such religious forms, reinvested with passion, and shows how they can arise from the same critically sophisticated, philosophically "sceptical" foundations as other visions of human good.

CONCLUDING REMARKS

This chapter has sought to show some of the philosophical, humanistic, and religious reasoning that inform Rūpa Gosvāmi's metaphysical and ethical positions, taking as its foundation the assumption that his richly multivocal and syncretic works do indeed reflect a process of profound reflection, undertaken in many forms that are both theoretical and enacted, tending toward a systematic rationale. While, seen in this light, his work stands as an example of the complexity and depth that remains to be uncovered in the works of many Indian thinkers, the ultimate goal of the chapter has been a philosophical one—to show how his approach addresses an aporia that is common throughout Western and Indian thought, and arrives at an alternative result from that of Gadamer.

Gadamer and Rūpa Gosvāmi offer models for a healthy human life that not only acknowledges, but also celebrates and contributes to the truths of phenomenal form, flux, and teleology. Both vitality and passion offer potentially fruitful modes for living within such an ontological framework, but it is the unfolding understanding of dialectic that illuminates Rūpa Gosvāmi's belief that our goal should be "the highest bhakti of feeling for Krishna [i.e., for ultimate reality] alone . . . devoid of other desires."[107] For Rādhā, the object that "confirms" her individual particularity is itself Being, and that same object also is her—in *becoming* engagement with the fact of her engagement in the world, Rādhā gains a simultaneous confirmation of self and whole as a multifaceted single process.

"Reason," says Gadamer, "is reconciliation with ruination."[108] Rūpa agrees, but embraces that ruination in a more personal way, discovering that, far from sacrificing her salvation in the kenotic absorption of the self to Being, Rādhā is saved by the "passion of the real" precisely as the self is breached, overwhelmed, saturated, and heightened by it. This is at once an ascetic "voluntaristically self-oppressive"[109] subjugation of the self, and a dynamically self-nurturing increase of it; at once an emptying and a filling to overflow by a reality that is both self and other. Its binary function is fundamentally facilitated by the eudaimonian character of this soteriology, binding the identity of the particular to the nature of the whole, making us ever more what we must be. For this, we must be in love with reality—a reading of much bhakti devotion that counterbalances and complements its personalisation of the divine.

Radha's reason then is a "passionate reason" leading her to choose, on rational as well as purely involuntary, instinctive, and psychological grounds, to be guided by her passions. Her courageous choice to abandon freedom, a blank plain on which no values can be found, for an unending pilgrimage through the rich topography of the passions, is the "choice" that Being has already made, and it is a path that, for Rūpa, it is our most fitting destiny to follow.

NOTES

1. D. Kinsley, *The Sword and the Flute: Dark Visions of the Terrible and the Sublime in Hindu Mythology* (Berkeley: University of California Press, 1975), 73–74. Kinsley's thematic approach, in which theological themes are explored through almost literary critical means, provides a useful reference point for exposing the implicit ethos of Rūpa Gosvāmi's narratives. It will be augmented by the kind of literary approaches that are commonly taken to other Vaiṣṇava bhakti literature, but applied here with novel application to metaphysical discussions.

2. Jan Brzezinski's translation in *Mystic Poetry: Rūpa Gosvāmin*'s *Uddhava Sandeśa and Haṃsadūta* (Hong Kong: Mandala Publishing Group, 1999), 48. All other quotes from Rūpa Gosvāmi are original translations from editions as cited.

3. Friedhelm Hardy has shown how far the northern Sanskritic depictions of the love of Krishna and the gopīs, including the *Gītagovinda*, draws on the literature of the Alvars, in much of which suffering is a particularly prominent theme (see F. Hardy, *Viraha Bhakti: The Early History of Kṛṣṇa Devotion in South India* (New Delhi: Oxford University Press, 1983)). It is not unlikely Rūpa Gosvāmi had direct or indirect knowledge of those works, but it is the northern tradition that he references in his own works, and it is arguably in the *Gītagovinda* that the theme of suffering first reaches a watershed in being attached primarily to Rādhā.

4. Jayadeva has Rādhā say in imagined conversation: "Cheat, the image I have of you now/flaunting our love's break/causes me more shame than sorrow" (*Gītagovinda*, 9.1), while his Krishna yearning for her is duly likened to Shiva with "a necklace of snakes," smeared with ash on his lovelorn body (3.10), and laments: "I was too ashamed, too afraid to stop her. Damn me! My wanton ways made her leave in anger" (3.3), in Barbara Stoler Miller's translation *Love Song of the Dark Lord: Jayadeva's Gitagovinda* (New Delhi: Columbia University Press, 1977).

5. See *Haṃsadūta* verses 2–6 and the section that the narrator Lalita herself calls a "drama in the rasa of separation" (*tasyā rasād ākhyātavyam parikalaya tan nātakam idam*), verses 74–126. Also *Uddahava Saṇdeśa* verses 1–3 and 103–6 in reference to Krishna.

6. See *Bhagavad Gītā*, 12.14–19.

7. He describes her in the *Ujjvala Nīlamaṇi* as the *uttama*, or highest heroine, partly on account of this virtue.

8. *Vidagdha Mādhava*, 2.3.

9. As paraphrased by Mukhara in *Vidagdha Mādhava*, 2.1.

10. *Vidagdha Mādhava*, 2.74.

11. *Vidagdha Mādhava*, 2.72.

12. *Vidagdha Mādhava*, 2.86.

13. *Vidagdha Mādhava*, 2.80.

14. *Vidagdha Mādhava*, 2.90.

15. *Hlādinī* is a feminine adjective from the verbal root *hlād*, to rejoice, delight, be glad or joyful (see V. S. Apte's *The Practical Sanskrit Dictionary* (New Delhi: Motitlal Banarsidass, 1998), 1768).

16. *Haṃsadūta*, 2, V. S. Apte (1998), 1161.

17. *Haṃsadūta*, 3, V. S. Apte (1998), 804.

18. See *Bhaktirasāmṛtasindhu*, 2.5.78.

19. The *virahinī*, is the separated one (feminine) (see *Haṃsadūta*, verse 2).

20. The main depiction of Rādhā's suffering is in verses 74–106, although it is in verses 112–13 that it culminates in the divine madness of hallucination.

21. Donna Marie Wulff, "A Sanskrit Portrait: Radha in the plays of Rupa Gosvami," in *The Divine Consort: Radha and the Goddesses of India*, J. S. Hawley and D. M. Wulff, eds. (Boston: Beacon Press, 1982), 33.

22. As at *Gītagovinda*, 3.11 and 4.4, and at *Haṃsadūta*, 82–84. Rūpa Gosvāmi explicitly takes his "saucy and soft," innocent and mature heroine from the *Gītagovinda*, as attested under the list of "different varieties of heroines" in chapter 5 of the *Ujjvala Nīlamaṇi*. See O'Flaherty's *Śiva: The Erotic Ascetic* (New York: Oxford University Press, 1981) for discussion of Śiva's paradoxical qualities.

23. *Haṃsadūta*, verse 77.

24. Frequent references to Śiva implicitly place her in the role of Pārvatī, who chose to undergo purifying austerities, to the admiration of others, in order to please her *sādhu* beloved (see verses 11, 68, 83, 90 of the *Haṃsadūta*).

25. D. Haberman and J. O'Connell both interpret the shift to the Krishna of Vṛndavan as an anti-political escapism resulting from the loss of Hindu political power to the Muslim rulers in the period immediately preceding Rūpa Gosvāmi. Kinsley also attributes it to the general dissatisfaction with the Brahminical religious mode that is seen in the growth of numerous Bhakti traditions.

26. Gavin Flood, *The Ascetic Self: Subjectivity, Memory and Tradition* (Cambridge: Cambridge University Press, 2004), 104.

27. *Bhaktirasāmṛtasindhu*, 1.1.33, *manāgevaprarudhāyām hṛdaye bhagavādratau/ puruṣarthāstu catvārāstṛṇāynate samantataḥ.*

28. William Schweiker, *Mimetic Reflections: A Study in Hermeneutics, Theology and Ethics* (New York: Fordham University Press, 1990), 2.

29. See *Bhaktirasāmṛtasindhu*, 1.3.6, 1.4.1, 2.5.73, and 2.5.132 for various accounts by Rūpa of the transformation of mere emotion into *rasa*.

30. D. Haberman, *Acting as a Way of Salvation: A Study of Rāgānuga Bhakti Sādhana* (New Delhi: Motilal Banarsidass, 1983), 39.

31. *The Divine Consort: Rādhā and the Goddesses of India*, 41. Unfortunately, Wulff's engagement with this conundrum of Caitanya Vaiṣṇava theology, the psychology of love, and the philosophy of religious belief stops here.

32. Rūpa Gosvāmi recounts this episode as an instance of *prema-vaicittyam* in *Ujjvala Nīlamaṇi*, chapter 15.

33. Haberman, *Acting as a Way of Salvation: A Study of Rāgānuga Bhakti Sādhana*, 37.

34. See the *Haṃsadūta* and *Bhaktirasāmṛtasindhu*. Of course, such details also lend a certain fantastical realism to these works.

35. While the *Bhāgavata Purāṇa* outlines a clear allegory of *puruṣa* and *prakṛti* intended by the story of Krishna and the gopīs, it does not identify Rādhā explicitly with any one of these characters, never mind laud her cosmogonic status as the preeminent goddess who is *prakṛti* itself. This is done in the *Brahmavaivarta Purāṇa*, where Sāṃkhya ideas are given a theistic, cosmogonic, and metaphysical application. Here Rādhā is *prakṛti*, but in this text as in the *Bhāgavata Purāṇa* this does not automatically relegate her to a lower, inferior status to that of Krishna. Rather, although he is *puruṣa* and substance, and she is *prakṛti* and attribute, both are said at different times to be the *ādhāra*, the foundation and support for the other. This sets an important precedent for the cosmological and ontological elevation of Rādhā.

36. *Haṃsadūta*, v. 91.

37. *Bhaktirasāmṛtasindhu*, 1.1.4.

38. There remains unclarity in the way and degree in which Lalita, Rādhā, and indeed Krishna are to be taken as models for the devotee on one hand, and the everyday, uncommitted reader on the other. The question of the degree to which Rādhā is a paradigmatic figure, and the degree to which she is an unapproachable goddess, is much debated in existing scholarship on Caitanya Vaiṣṇava literature. Chapter 3, section two of the *Ujjvala Nīlamaṇi* emphasises that Krishna should be served, not imitated. But one suspects this to apply to his capricious behaviour with regard to the gopīs, rather than to his penitent sadness at the suffering he has caused, or that which he himself experiences.

39. Gadamer constrasts the recreational and "sacred, serious" aspects of play in *Truth and Method*, 102, and similarly contrasts the festive and tragic manifestations at 121 and 125 respectively.

40. D. Haberman, *Acting as a Way of Salvation: A Study of Rāgānuga Bhakti Sādhana*, 52.

41. *Bhagavad Gītā*, 9.22.

42. June McDaniel, *The Madness of the Saints: Ecstatic Religion in Bengal* (Chicago: University of Chcago Press, 1989), 1.

43. *Rāga*: "love, passion, affection," in V. S. Apte, 1333.

44. This is the description of *manjistha rāga* of which the love of Rādhā and Krishna is the highest paradigm, given in the *Ujjvala Nīlamaṇi*, chapter 14.

45. *"Mahāśaktivilāsātmā bhāvocintyasvarūpabhāk/rati," Bhaktirasāmṛtasindhu*, 2.5.92.

46. See *Ujjvala Nīlamaṇi*, chapter 14.

47. Additional to this problem are the complications of the many theological connotations that key words such as *rasa* and *bhāva* have.

48. All of the terms listed below are used by Rūpa in his study of love for Krishna in the *Ujjvala Nīlamaṇi*, and the translations given are based on V. S. Apte's *The Practical Sanskrit Dictionary*.

49. See the discussion of *prema-vaicittyam* in chapter 15 of the *Ujjvala Nīlamaṇi*.

50. See *Ujjvala Nīlamaṇi*, chapter 14.

51. *Ujjvala Nīlamaṇi*, v. 207, "*sarvasya bhāvodnamollāsī madano 'yam parātparah.*"

52. In the varieties of the passionate love (*sṛṇgāra*) of the gopīs recounted by Rūpa, he lists love in separation (*vipralambha*) as the penultimate category, preparing the way for the ultimate *sambhoga*, union.

53. *Ujjavala Nīlamaṇi*, "*Sṛṇgārabheda*," v. 3, 560.

54. See *Ujjvala Nīlamani*, the summary of the *Sthayibhāvaprakaraṇa* chapter.

55. In a non-Sanskritic context June McDaniel gives an excellent account of the hugely diverse ways in which emotion and its vocabulary have been expanded in contemporary Bengali culture (see *The Madness of the Saints: Ecstatic Religion in Bengal* (Chicago: University of Chicago Press, 1989), 21–27).

56. *Bhaktirasāmṛtasindhu*, 3.1.7, "*śāntākhyabhāvacandrasya hṛdākāśe kalāṃ.*"

57. See the *Ujjvala Nīlamaṇi*, chapters 12 and 13.

58. *Bhaktirasāmṛtasindhu*, 3.1.23.

59. *Bhaktirasāmṛtasindhu*, 2.2.1–60.

60. Frederick Smith, *The Self Possessed: Deity and Spirit Possession in South Asian Literature and Civilisation* (New York: Columbia University Press, 2006), 3–4.

61. McDaniel, *The Madness of the Saints: Ecstatic Religion in Bengal*, 280.

62. McDaniel, *The Madness of the Saints: Ecstatic Religion in Bengal*, 280.

63. Kathleen Erndl, "The Mother Who Possesses" in *Devi: Goddesses of India*, John Hawley and Donna Wulff, eds. (Berkeley: University of California Press, 1996), 176.

64. McDaniel, *The Madness of the Saints: Ecstatic Religion in Bengal*, 2–3.

65. *Ujjvala Nīlamaṇi*, *Sthayibhāvaprakaraṇa*, v. 157.

66. *Haṃsadūta*, v. 116.

67. Levinas illustrates a type of anti-absolutist ethics that balances between quietism and vitalism in the advocation of an unrelenting passive devotion to the "Other" that keeps us ethically "on our toes." Rather like Krishna who can be seen in so many forms, this other is (among other things) a cipher with the function of maintaining us in a state of mind. Blanchot, as we have seen, sees Messianism as an ethical method rather than a salvific fulfilment. Pattison likens similar strategies in Heidegger to the expectation-deconstructing methods of Zen Buddhism.

68. John Caputo, *On Religion* (Oxford: Routledge, 2001), 18.

69. *The Divine Consort: Radha and the Goddesses of India*, 27.

70. *Bhāgavata Purāṇa*, book 10, chapter 32.

71. The *Ujjvala Nīlamaṇi*, for instance, has a single particularly detailed chapter enumerating Krishna's ecstatic love stimulating qualities, which include his youthfulness, beauty, and sweetness, his many delightful names, his charming pastimes such as dancing, playing the flute, and milking the cows, his garments and ornaments, his flute, horn, singing, fragrance, peacock feathers, the remains of love tokens given to him, his footprints and the dust raised by the cattle, the birds, bees, and flowers, and even the moonlight, the springtime, and its fragrant breezes. All of these are listed as vessels that help to stimulate the main emotion that he provokes, and that are, in a cosmic sense, considered to be part of him.

72. *Ujjvala Nīlamaṇi*, chapter 4, verse 41.

73. Rādhā's talent at enjoying is cited as one of the qualities justifying her supremacy (in the *Rādhāprakaraṇa* chapter in the *Ujjvala Nīlamaṇi*), under the name of *suvilasa*.

74. "*tayor apy ubhayor madhye radhikā sarvathādhikā/ mahābhāva svarūpa iyaṃ guṇaiḥ ati varīyasī,*" *Rādhāprakaraṇa*, v. 3. Rūpa Gosvāmi had, of course, developed "Mahābhāva" as a technical term for the highest stage of devotional emotion.

75. These texts are the *Gopālatapani Upaniṣad, Uttara Khaṇḍa*, the *Ṛg Veda Pariśiṣṭa*, and the *Padma Purāṇa* (see *Rādhāprakaraṇa*, v. 4).

76. She is *vishnoranyanta vallabhā*, "Vishnu's perfect or unceasing companion" (*Rādhāprakaraṇa*, v. 5).

77. "*hlādinīyī mahāśaktiḥ sarvaśaktivarīyasī/tat sārvabhāva rupeyaṃ sarvadā vārṣ abhānavī*" (see *Rādhāprakaraṇa*, v. 6).

78. Jonardon Ganeri, *The Concealed Art of the Soul: Theories of Self and Practises of Truth in Indian Ethics and Epistemology* (Oxford: Oxford University Press, 2007), 34–35.

79. Ganeri, *The Concealed Art of the Soul: Theories of Self and Practises of Truth in Indian Ethics and Epistemology*, 34–35.

80. *Bhaktirasāmṛtasindhu*, 1.1.11.

81. *Bhaktirasāmṛtasindhu*, 1.1.12.

82. *Hegel's Dialectic: Five Hermeneutical Studies*, 29.

83. "*atmarāmāśca munayo nirgranthā apyurukrame/ kurvantyahaitukiṃ bhaktimittham,*" *Bhaktirasāmṛtasindhu*, Eastern Section, 2.54.

84. *Hegel's Dialectic: Five Hermeneutical Studies*, 60–61.

85. *Hegel's Dialectic: Five Hermeneutical Studies*, 60.

86. *Hegel's Dialectic: Five Hermeneutical Studies*, 61.

87. *Hegel's Dialectic: Five Hermeneutical Studies*, 61.

88. *Hegel's Dialectic: Five Hermeneutical Studies*, 61.

89. Martin Heidegger, "Letter on Humanism," in *Basic Writings* (Oxford: Routledge, 1978), 223–24.

90. Heidegger, "Letter on Humanism," in *Basic Writings*, 225.

91. Martha Nussbaum, "Emotions as Judgements of Value and Importance," in *Relativism, Suffering and Beyond: Essays in Memory of Bimal Matilal*, P. Bilimoria and J. N. Mohanty, eds. (New Delhi: Oxford University Press, 1997), 248.

92. Martha Nussbaum, "Emotions as Judgements of Value and Importance," in *Relativism, Suffering and Beyond: Essays in Memory of Bimal Matilal*, 232.

93. *Vidagdha Mādhava*, 2.6, "*daronmīlannīlotpaladalarucastasya nibiḍādvirūḍ hāṃ sadyaḥ karasarasijaspaśakutukāt/vahantī kṣobhānāṃ nivahamiha najnasiṣamidaṃ kvavāhaṃ cakara kimahāṃ vāsakhi tadā.*"

94. Alain Badiou, from "The Transcendental," in *Theoretical Writings*, Ray Brassier and Alberto Toscano, trans. and ed. (London: Continuum, 2004), 223 (original essay in *Logiques des Mondes*).

95. Alain Badiou, from "The Transcendental," in *Theoretical Writings*, 190.

96. Badiou also introduces the notion of "the chimera," an unthinkable mathematical boundary between the plurality of non-reflexive beings, and the single reflexive totality of Being itself. This concept plays a very similar philosophical role to the idea of *acintyabhedābheda*.

97. Alain Badiou, from "The Transcendental," in *Theoretical Writings*, 222.

98. Alain Badiou, from "The Transcendental," in *Theoretical Writings*, 223.

99. *Ujjvala Nīlamaṇi, Anubhāva, līlā*, v. 30.

100. Of course, the scene is also a reference to the real life *līlā* plays practised by devotees as a form of worship and remembrance, and to the interchangeability of Krishna and Rādhā in their conjoined dual divinity as *rādhā-kṛṣṇa*. But both references intimate Krishna's omnipresence.

101. *Bhāgavata Purāṇa*, 11.14.14.

102. Alain Badiou, *Infinite Thought: Truth and the Return of Philosophy*, O. Feltham and J. Clemens, trans. and ed. (London: Continuum Press, 2003), 166.

103. Introduction to *Infinite Thought: Truth and the Return of Philosophy*, 7.

104. O. Feltham and J. Clemens write of Badiou's notion of religious decisions and actions as those that "isolate an actor from their context . . . who act[s] in *fidelity* to a chance encounter with an *event* which disrupts the *situation* they find themselves in" (see the introduction to *Infinite Thought: Truth and the Return of Philosophy*, 7).

105. Badiou inadvertantly summarises Gadamer's esteem for the poets, writing that "since Nietzsche, all philosophers claim to be poets, they all envy poets, they are all wishful poets or approximate poets." But it is not mere orientalism that leads him to continue: "[E]ven Jambet or Lardneau salute the ineluctable poetic slant of the Orient's metaphysical elevations" (*Manifesto for Philosophy*, Norman Madarasz, trans. and ed. (Albany: State University of New York Press, 1999), 70).

106. Paul Tillich, *Theology of Culture*, Robert C. Kimball, ed. (New York: Oxford University Press, 1959).

107. "*Anyābhilāṣita śūnyaṃ . . . kṛṣṇānuśīlanam bhaktiruttamā*" *Bhaktirasāmṛta-sindhu*, 1.1.11.

108. *Hegel's Dialectic: Five Hermeneutical Studies*, 105.

109. Flood, *The Ascetic Self: Subjectivity, Memory and Tradition*, 249.

Conclusion

> To think is to confine yourself to a single thought that one day stands still like a star in the world's sky.[1]

Gadamer shows us a finite, self-grounding, intrinsically value-filled world viewed from the perspective of our own necessity of making ethical choices within it. Rūpa Gosvāmi shows us a similarly constituted metaphysics and ethics in which subtle differences result in a profound change of tone. In both cases the intrinsic, *necessary* combination of finitude and value that characterises our situation (by which we mean to say "reality itself") is a positive factor in informing how we live. It shows us that truth is not elsewhere, eluding capture by our falsifiable beliefs and metaphors. Rather, it dwells in our existence and must be captured according to our own particular, problematic, phenomenal way of knowing and acting.

The hermeneutic readings found in the two parts of this study have sought to show that "realism," defined as a model of reality derived from "transcendental" truths and used as the ground of ethical conclusions, can be figured according to a range of ontological models. Against the fears to which the radical critiques of traditional metaphysics have given rise, one can offer alternative non-dual ontologies that yield transcendental truths and ethical grounds. Indeed, *within* the Western tradition there exist a range of alternatives to the tradition of onto-theological substantialism rejected by Heidegger, including classical Greek philosophies that have provided a fruitful resource for modern attempts to rethink the dominant principles of Western metaphysics. The ontology of forms, qualities, or structures described in chapter 2, reflected by Gadamer in his synthesis of Plato, Aristotle, and others, is one of these.

As we learn to recognise alternative ontologies in the works of Western thinkers like Heraclitus, Democritus, Plato, Aristotle, Spinoza, Hegel, and Heidegger, so we must acknowledge that Indian philosophy has, from its earliest periods and throughout its history, incorporated sophisticated arguments for varieties of scepticism, nihilism, and relativism. Recognition of this rights a longstanding prejudice regarding the supposed credulity and lack of complexity in Indian thought. It also opens the way for more advanced philosophical dialogue with other "post-Enlightenment" traditions. As we have seen, on the whole the Indian philosophical tradition (to include much theological, poetic, and aesthetic discourse) has leaned away from the realist-idealist, monist-dualist axes as they are figured in Western analysis, due—I would argue—to a predominantly phenomenological approach to epistemology, and a resulting "formal" approach to metaphysics. Philosophical issues raised by this metaphysics were explored in the gradual synthesis and reinterpretation of Indian philosophical positions through debate and exegesis, and engaged with particularly fruitful vigour throughout the theological self-definitions of the bhakti thinkers and later Vedāntins. Rūpa Gosvāmi was part of a fruitful contemporary dialogue exploring particularly sophisticated, self-reflective versions of these debates, and his theology is founded on a particularly rigorous understanding of the wholesale finitude, relativity, ontological unity, mutual constitution, relationality, and innately teleological, prejudicial, or passionate character of Being.

In Rūpa's various routes of reasoning through the problem of finding and framing the ideal response to the real, not merely in theoretical but also in lived terms, it is fascinating to see exposed in his verses, as if captured in ice, a process of theological synthesis and rationalisation that every thinker enacts. In order to justify the tradition and give it a rational shape that will persuade opponents and strengthen its future heirs, he has to juggle the implications of incarnate and cosmic deities, of the awed and intimate forms of bhakti devotion, of Vedic, purāṇic, and tantric texts, and also of the *rasa* theory that he has inherited from Bhārata, Mammata, Abhinavagupta, and nandavardhana and seeks to yoke to his own tradition. Each thinker weaves a complex tapestry from the threads provided by his tradition, and must often find or create new methods and ideas in merging those raw materials into a successful synthesis. But we cannot make sense of the pattern he creates, unless we admit the presence of the thinker in the text as the locus of a careful, syncretic process of logic that we trace in our reading. And we cannot decipher those ideas unless we are willing to doggedly pursue that other path of reasoning, regardless of the distances that divide us.

Such interpretations of Gadamer and Gosvāmi have been founded on a not-uncontroversial definition of realism: that a "realist" ethics may be derived from a "realist" logic that reasons "This *x* is what is the case, thus this *x* is what ought to be the case." This raises the aporia of whether a being can *more* or *less* instantiate ontological facts about Being. How can Rilke and Jayadeva extol the virtue of any hero who merely does more what we all do to some extent? Why should axiomatic truths about our essential nature guide us toward any particular position of affirmation or rejection with regard to that nature? One can only reply that while Gadamer and Gosvāmi do not believe the insight into the One and the Many to be optional, the choice to adopt a realist attitude toward them must be—an option that not all philosophers in India or the West have taken. Levinas, for instance, might be interpreted as a thinker who holds out for something that might be "other" than Being, as might Kierkegaard and certain other post-Enlightenment theists.

Yet in their stubborn refusal to flee what they believe to be the facts, the standpoints of both Gadamer and Gosvāmi are useful paradigms through which to shed light on the division of "postmodern" religiosity into at least two major positions. On the one hand there is the freedom of non-committally engaging with whatever religious perspective enthuses us *while* it enthuses us. This is a liberal approach that places emphasis on the freedom and decisionmaking capacity of the individual. On the other hand there is the commitment to a particular, reality-determining unconditional truth in such a way that it is not really a decision but a passionate process of being overwhelmed and determined. Writing about the Indian paradigm of the sacrifice of the self in passionate commitment to a chosen value, Jonardon Ganeri makes comparison with Bakunin and Nechaev's description of the revolutionary who roots his life's value in his passion:

> The revolutionary is a lost man; he has no interests of his own, no cause of his own, no feelings, no habits, no belongings; he does not even have a name. Everything in him is absorbed by a single exclusive interest, a single thought, a single passion.[2]

One can see Rādhā's exemplary model as a paradigm for a wider range of commitments than merely those of the lover and the devotee. One may also see in her a fuller exposition of the "lost man" of political or religious commitment, who finds himself in his passion.

By way of contextualising the scope of this enquiry, it is important to emphasise that these are only two possible worldviews, and it is possible that in other Western thinkers we might have found models more similar to certain aspects of Rūpa Gosvāmi's work from which Gadamer departs—perhaps in the self-abnegation of the I in Husserl, in Levinas and in Weil's ascetic observation that "the power to say 'I'" is "what we have to give to God—in other words, to destroy,"[3] in the fulfilment of the self through aesthetic reflexivity in Ricoeur, or in Derrida's equation of the relinquishing of ego-awareness with the gaining of a kind of God-and-reality-immersed immortality. But the particular route from Gadamer's reasoning to that of Gosvāmi shows how logical paths that share a family resemblance may arrive at different destinations.

All of the above arguments have been sustained by certain underlying premises of comparative work: that it is valid and possible to identify common philosophical questions, themes, and conclusions across different historical traditions and cultural terminologies, on the model as it were of a common mathematics. Thus, for instance, our investigation begins and ends with reference to the critically useful insights of Alain Badiou, who is one of the modern philosophers most committed to revigorating philosophy as an exploration of universal analytic structures of knowledge and existence. There will always be larger or smaller degrees of difference between such contrasts and comparisons, but this is not a problem unique to cross-cultural dialogue, and should not thus be seen as a *special* intrinsic problem of cross-cultural comparative philosophy. One goal of this book has been to demonstrate a way of comparing worldviews that achieves a degree of hermeneutic sensitivity through a groundwork of *philosophical* questions. These questions have guided the comparative structure of this study, hoping to avoid superficial bilateral comparisons. This is in keeping with the aim stated in the introduction, to avoid the traditional comparitivist difficulties of direct one-to-one analogy, by triangulating larger fields of complex discourse within each culture.

We can ask whether Hans-Georg Gadamer and Rūpa Gosvāmi would agree with the conclusions that have been excavated from their dense works. It is true that Gadamer does not give a single, coherent, explicit analysis of Being in this way in his works, yet the bulk of his writings in studies such as *Dialogue and Dialectic*, and *Hegel's Dialectic*, are devoted to explicitly metaphysical concerns, and, despite their hermeneutic style, address explicitly metaphysical truths. His position can clearly be derived from his scattering of direct statements on the subject, his ontological metaphors, and his exegeses of many voices in the Western philosophical tradition. Badiou, who seeks a similar depth-analysis of the ontological problematic that persists from Plato to Heidegger, has been harshly criticised for his "monstrous" (mis)representation of Deleuze's thought as addressed toward ontological concerns. His defence is that it is valid and significant to see what results when ideas that do not necessarily intend a "fundamental" ontology are pressed to reveal their fundamental ontological implications.[4] In Gadamer's case the same kind of hermeneutic attention is ratified by an explicit concern in the works of the author in question—and indeed the methodological example of Gadamer himself. An interesting and valid criticism of such approaches can be made, such that the complexity of discourse and philosophical intention is said to make it impossible and unjust to reduce the *oeuvre* in question to a single systematic doctrine.[5] Yet this book contends that while multiple discourses cohabit within each set of writings, the systematic attempt to describe consistent, well-founded truths is an important feature of the works of both Gadamer and Rūpa Gosvāmi, and to ignore this is to monstrously misrepresent their own lives' work.

Doubtless Rūpa Gosvāmi might feel that the psychological pursuit of "religious realism" involved in generating a compelling personal relationship with Krishna takes priority over the "metaphysical realism" of analysing the ontological basis of that relationship. Many devotees, ancient and modern, may find the latter perspective marginal to the importance and all-determining reality of the relationship with Krishna and his actions in the world. But this study assumes that these dimensions of Rūpa Gosvāmi's work stand in a relation of complementarity, rather than one of conflict. One need not refuse to hear the philosopher, just because he is also a fine poet, or ignore his thought where he also offers feeling.

A philosophical "realism" is described here that differs from classic Western realism only insofar as the touchstone of the real and our referential grammar in relation to it have been altered—but not capriciously. However, we can also ask whether this ontologically foundational realism, grounded in the fundamental necessity of truth-inquiry, really has anything to do with the quality of "literal realism" that applies to much religious belief. The problem of religious realism remains crucial in the field of religious studies and in public life—and, of course, has concrete implications for dealing with decisionmaking and conflicts in more social and political contexts.[6] But one of the premises of this study has been that what we think of as "literal" or "naïve" realism almost always has one eye trained on the question of foundations.

D. Z. Phillips writes of a Ho dirge that cries to the dear departed, "We have ever loved and cherished you; and have lived long together under the same roof; Desert it not now! . . . Come to your home!" that "If someone asked, 'And did the departed spirit actually come home?' would not this be an example of a supremely foolish question?"[7] Contrary to Phillips, one should not assume that it is a foolish question, as believers of so many traditions wait to discover whether their prayers are answered, and wonder whether they will indeed be confirmed by promised experiences after death. Rūpa Gosvāmi explores the attitude of the believer tempted to doubt by the perceived absence of the objects of belief, but we must not think that Krishna ever becomes only a symbol for Rādhā, or her love a mere gesture toward infinity. Like Gadamer's poet, Rilke's lover, or so many religious believers, Rādhā's imagination strains toward the tangible touch of the beloved, the audible sound of his return, and the intimate, immediate realisation of the real, for only in this way can she truly make him infinitely and eternally present.

NOTES

1. Quotation translated by Albert Hofstadter in "From the Experience of Thinking" (1947), and cited as the preface to "Letter on Humanism," in Heidegger's *Basic Writings* (Oxford: Routledge, 1978), 213.

2. Jonardon Ganeri, *The Concealed Art of the Soul: Theories of Self and Practises of Truth in Indian Ethics and Epistemology* (Oxford: Oxford University Press, 2007), 204.

3. Simone Weil, "The Self," in *An Anthology* (London: Penguin Classics, 2005), 99.

4. See Louise Burchill's introduction to Badiou's *Deleuze: The Clamor of Being*, trans. Burchill (Minneapolis: University of Minnesota Press, 2000), xv–xvi.

5. Thomas A. Wartenberg makes this point with regard to precisely the Hegelian metaphysics that Gadamer reproduces in his own work. Wartenberg suggests that Hegel's thought here is not "metaphysical" insofar as it eschews propositional statements about reality, but concerned instead with useful categorical tools for thinking about reality. His concerns here reflect a wider movement of critique, and are eminently applicable to both Gadamer and Rūpa Gosvāmi. However, the reluctance to designate statements of what can universally and necessarily be said of all that is as "propositional" or "metaphysical" statements seems to be a reluctance to acknowledge the goals and standards that are normally engaged in metaphysics (see Wartenberg's essay "Hegel's Idealism: The Logic of Conceptuality," in *The Cambridge Companion to Hegel*, Frederick C. Beiser, ed. (New York: Cambridge University Press, 1993)).

6. See J. B. Elshtain's "Just War, Realism and Humanitarian Intervention" and R. S. Appleby's "Serving Two Masters? Affirming Religious Belief and Human Rights in a Pluralistic World," in *The Sacred and the Sovereign: Religion and International Politics*, J. D. Carlson and E. C. Owens, ed. (Washington, D.C.: Georgetown University Press, 2003).

7. D. Z. Phillips *Death and Immortality* (London: Macmillan and Co. Ltd., 1970), 70–71.

Bibliography

Unless otherwise cited, translations of texts in languages other than English are by the author.

Acharjee, Ranjit Kumar. *A Discourse on Bengal Vaiṣṇavism*. Kolkata: Punthi Pustak, 2002.

Apel, Karl-Otto. *Transformation der Philosophie, Band I: Sprachanalytik, Semiotic, Hermeneutik*. Frankfurt am Main: Suhrkamp, 1973.

Arendt, Hannah. "Martin Heidegger at Eighty." *The New York Review of Books*, October 21, 1971.

Arya, Devkanya. "*Acintyabhedābheda* or inconceivable difference-non-difference." *Philosophical Quarterly* (Amalner) 38 (1965), 191–98.

Badiou, Alain. *Manifesto for Philosophy*, translated and edited by N. Madarasz. Albany: State University of New York Press, 1989.

———. *L'Etre et l'Evenement*. Paris: Editions de Seuil, 1998.

———. *Deleuze: The Clamor of Being*, translated by Louise Burchill. Minneapolis: University of Minnesota Press, 2000.

———. *Infinite Thought: Truth and the Return of Philosophy*, translated and edited by O. Feltham and J. Clemens. London: Continuum, 2003.

———. "One Divides into Two," translated by Alberto Toscana. Malden, Mass.: Polity Press, 2007.

Bartel, T. W., ed. *Comparative Theology: Essays for Keith Ward*. London: SPCK, 2003.

Benesch, Walter. *An Introduction to Comparative Philosophy: A Travel-Guide to Philosophical Space*. London: Macmillan, 1997.

Berger, Douglas. *Veil of Maya: Schopenhauer's System and Early Indian Thought*. Binghamton, N.Y.: Global Academic Publishing, 2003.

Bernstein, Richard. *Beyond Objectivism and Relativism: Science, Hermeneutics and Praxis*. Oxford: Basil Blackwell Publishers Limited, 1983.

Bhattacharya, H. "*Acintya-bheda-abheda-vada*." *Indian Philosophy and Culture* 9, no. 4 (1964), 42–45.

Bhattacarya, Kalidas. *On the Concepts of Relations and Negation in Indian Philosophy*. Calcutta: Sanskrit College, 1977.

Biardeau, Madeleine. *Hinduism: The Anthropology of a Civilisation*, translated by Richard Nice. New Delhi: Oxford University Press, 1989.

Biderman, S., and B. Scharfstein, eds. *Rationality in Question: On Eastern and Western Views of Rationality*. Leiden: Brill, 1989.

Bilimoria, Purusottama, and Peter Fenner, eds. *Religions and Comparative Thought: Essays in Honour of the Late Dr Ian Kesarcodi-Watson*. New Delhi: Sri Satguru Publications, 1988.

Blackburn, Simon. *Knowledge, Truth and Reliability*. Oxford: Oxford University Press, 1985.

———. *Essays in Quasi-Realism*. New York: Oxford University Press, 1993.

———. *Ruling Passions: A Theory of Practical Reasoning*. Oxford: Clarendon Press, 2000.

———. *Liberalism, Religion, and the Sources of Value*. Lawrence: University Press of Kansas, 2005.

Blackburn, Simon, and Keith Simmons, eds. *Truth*. Oxford: Oxford University Press, 1995.

Blackwood, R. T., and A. L. Herman, eds. *Problems in Philosophy, West and East*. Upper Saddle River, N.J.: Prentice-Hall, 1975.

Brockington, J. L. *The Sacred Thread: Hinduism in Its Continuity and Diversity*. Edinburgh: Edinburgh University Press, 1981.

Brodbeck, Simon. "Observations on the idea of non-attached action (asakta karman) in the Mahābhārata." Spalding Symposium, 2005.

Bronkworst, J. *Karma and Teleology: A Problem and Its Solutions in Indian Philosophy*. Tokyo: International Institute for Buddhist Studies, 2000.

Bryant, Edwin, ed. *Krishna: A Sourcebook*. New York: Oxford University Press, 2007.

Bultmann, Rudolf. *New Testament and Mythology*. Norwich: SCM Press, 1985.

Cadava, Eduardo, Peter Connor, and Lean-Luc Nancy, eds. *Who Comes After the Subject?* New York: Routledge, 1991.

Caputo, John. *Radical Hermeneutics: Repetition, Deconstruction and the Hermeneutic Project*. Bloomington: Indiana University Press, 1987.

———. *The Prayers and Tears of Jacques Derrida*. Bloomington: Indiana University Press, 1997.

———. *More Radical Hermeneutics: On Not Knowing Who We Are*. Bloomington: Indiana University Press, 2000.

Chakrabarti, K. K. *Definition and Induction: A Historical and Comparative Study*. Honolulu: University of Hawaii Press, 1995.

Chakravarti, Ramakanta. "Gauḍīya Vaiṣṇavism in Bengal." *Journal of Indian Philosophy* 5 (1977), 107–50.

Chaturvedi, Hermaba. "Role of *bhakti* in Chaitanyism." *Bharati: Bulletin of the College of Indology* (Banaras Hindu University) 22–23 (1995–1997), 49–57.

Clarke, J. J. *Oriental Enlightenment: The Encounter between Asian and Western Thought*. London: Routledge, 1997.

Clarke, Timothy. *The Poetics of Singularity: The Counter-Culturalist Turn in Heidegger, Derrida, Blanchot and the Later Gadamer*. Edinburgh: Edinburgh University Press, 2005.

Coburn, Thomas. *Devī Mahātmya: The Crystallisation of the Goddess Tradition*. New Delhi: Motilal Banarsidass, 1984.

Coltman, Rod. *The Language of Hermeneutics: Gadamer and Heidegger in Dialogue*. Albany: State University of New York Press, 1998.

Copleston, F. C. *Philosophies and Cultures*. Oxford: Oxford University Press, 1980.

———. *Religion and the One: Philosophies East and West*. London: Search Press, 1982.

Corbin, H. *The Concept of Comparative Philosophy*, translated by Peter Russell. Ipswich: Golganooza Press, 1981.

Coward, Harold. *Derrida and Indian Philosophy*. Albany: State University of New York Press, 1990.

Cunningham, Conor. *Genealogy of Nihilism*. Oxford: Routledge, 2002.

Dallmayr, Fred. *Beyond Orientalism: Essays on Cross-Cultural Encounter*. Albany: State University of New York Press, 1996.

———. "The Enigma of Health: Hans-Georg Gadamer at 100." *The Review of Politics* 62 (2000), 327–51.

Dalmia, Vasudha, Angelika Malinar, and Martin Christof, eds. *Charisma and Canon: Essays on the Religious History of the Indian Subcontinent*. New Delhi: Oxford University Press, 2001.

Davey, Nicholas. "Hermeneutic Passions: Gadamer versus Nietzsche on the Subjectivity of Interpretation." *International Journal of Philosophical Studies* 2 (1994), 45–60.

Davidson, Donald, *Truth and Predication*. Cambridge, Mass.: The Belknap Press, 2005.

Das, Rahul Peter, ed. *Essays on Vaiṣṇavism in Bengal*. Calcutta: Firma KLM, 1997.

De, Sushil Kumar. *Early History of the Vaishnava Faith and Movement in Bengal*. Calcutta: Firma KLM, 1961.

Derrida, Jacques. *Dissemination*, translated by B. Johnson. London: Athlone Press, 1981.

———. *The Problem of Genesis in Husserl's Philosophy*, translated by Marion Hobson. Chicago: University of Chicago Press, 1990.

Derrida, J., and G. Vattimo, eds. *Religion*. Cambridge: Polity Press, 1998.

Dicenso, James. *Hermeneutics and the Disclosure of Truth: A Study in the Work of Heidegger, Gadamer and Ricoeur*. Charlottesville: University of Virginia Press, 1990.

Dilworth, David. *Philosophy in World Perspective: A Comparative Hermeneutic of the Major Theories*. London: Yale University Press, 1989.

Dimock, Edward C. "Doctrine and Practice among the Vaiṣṇavas of Bengal." *History of Religions* (Chicago) 3 (1963), 83–105.

Dostal, Robert J., ed. *The Cambridge Companion to Gadamer*. New York: Cambridge University Press, 2002.

Dragonetti, Carmen, and Fernando Tola, eds. *On the Myth of Opposition between Indian Thought and Western Philosophy*. Hildesheim: Georg Olms, 2004.

Dravid, Raja Ram. *The Problem of Universals in Indian Philosophy*. Varanasi: Motilal Banarsidass, 1972.

Droit, Roger-Pol. *L'Oublie de l'Inde: Une Amnīsie Philosophique*. Paris: Presses Universitaire de France, 1989.

———. *The Cult of Nothingness: The Philosophers and the Buddha*. Chapel Hill: University of North Carolina Press, 2003.

Dube, Manju. *Conceptions of God in Vaishnava Philosophical Systems*. Varanasi: Sanjay Book Centre, 1984.

Dubey, S. P. *Idealism, East and West*. New Delhi: Bharatiya Vidya Prakashan, 1983.

Eaton, Richard. *Essays on Islam and Indian History*. New Delhi: Oxford University Press, 2000.

Faulconer, James, ed. *Transcendence in Philosophy and Religion*. Bloomington: Indiana University Press, 2003.

Flood, Gavin. *An Introduction to Hinduism*. Cambridge: Cambridge University Press, 1996.

———. *The Ascetic Self: Subjectivity, Memory and Tradition*. Cambridge: Cambridge University Press, 2004.

———. *The Tantric Body: The Secret Tradition of Hindu Religion*. London: I.B. Tauris & Co., 2006.

Foster, Matthew. *Gadamer and Practical Philosophy: The Hermeneutics of Moral Confidence*. New York: Oxford University Press Inc., 1991.

Gadamer, Hans-Georg. *Kleine Schriften*. Tübingen: Mohr, 1967–1979.

———. *Hegels Dialektik*. Tübingen: Mohr, 1971.

———. *Truth and Method*, translated by G. Barden and J. Cumming. London: Sheed and Ward Ltd., 1975. (All references to *Truth and Method* are from the 1975 edition unless otherwise stated.)

———. *Hegel's Dialectic: Five Hermeneutical Studies*, translated by P. Christopher Smith. New Haven, Conn.: Yale University Press, 1976.

———. *Letter to Leo Strauss* (1961), published in *The Independent Journal of Philosophy* 2 (1978).

———. *Dialogue and Dialectic*, translated by P. Christopher Smith. New Haven, Conn.: Yale University Press, 1980.

———. *Reason in the Age of Science*, translated by F. Lawrence. Cambridge, Mass.: MIT Press, 1981.

———. *The Beginning of Philosophy*, translated by P. Christopher Smith. New Haven, Conn.: Yale University Press, 1983.

———. *Philosophical Apprenticeships*, translated by R. Sullivan. Cambridge, Mass.: MIT Press, 1985.

———. *Philosophical Hermeneutics*, translated by D. Linge. Cambridge, Mass.: MIT Press, 1985.

———. *The Relevance of the Beautiful and Other Essays*, translated by N. Walker, and edited by R. Bernasconi. Cambridge: Cambridge University Press, 1986.

———. *Hermeneutics Versus Science*, edited by Gadamer, Stegmuller, and Specht. Notre Dame, Ind.: University of Notre Dame Press, 1988.

———. *The Idea of the Good in Platonic-Aristotelian Philosophy*, translated by P. Chris-

topher Smith. New Haven, Conn.: Yale University Press, 1988.
———. *Gesammelte Werke*. Tübingen: J.C.B. Mohr, 1991.
———. *Plato's Dialectical Ethics: Phenomenological Interpretations Relating to the "Philebus"*, translated by R. M. Wallace. New Haven, Conn.: Yale University Press, 1991.
———. *Hans-Georg Gadamer on Education, Poetry and History: Applied Hermeneutics*, edited by D. Misgeld and G. Nicholson, and translated by L. Schmidt and M. Ruess. Albany: State University of New York Press, 1992.
———. *Hermeneutik, Ästhetik, Praktische Philosophie: Hans-Georg Gadamer im Gespräch*, edited by Carsten Dutt. Heidelberg: Universitätsverlag, 1993.
———. *Über die Verborgenheit der Gesundheit: Aufsätze und Vorträge*. Frankfurt: Suhrkamp Verlag, 1993.
———. *Heidegger's Ways*, translated by John W. Staley. Albany: State University of New York Press, 1994.
———. *Literature and Philosophy in Dialogue: Essays in German Literary Theory*, translated by R. H. Paslick, and edited by D. J. Schmidt. Albany: State University of New York Press, 1994.
———. *The Enigma of Health: The Art of Healing in a Scientific Age*, translated by John Gaiger and Nicholas Walker. Oxford: Polity Press, 1996.
———. *Der Anfang der Philosophie*. Stuttgart: Reclam, 1997.
———. *Gadamer on Celan: "Who am I and Who Are You?" and Other Essays*, edited and translated by R. Heinemann and B. Krajewski. Albany: State University of New York, 1997.
———. "Dialogues in Capri," in *Religion*, edited by J. Derrida and G. Vattimo. Cambridge: Polity Press, 1998.
———. *Praise of Theory: Speeches and Essays*, translated by Chris Dawson. New Haven, Conn.: Yale University Press, 1998.
———. *Hermeneutics, Religion and Ethics*, translated by Joel Weinsheimer. New Haven, Conn.: Yale University Press, 1999.
———. *Hermeneutische Entwürfe*. Tübingen: Mohr Siebeck, 2000.
———. *Gadamer in Conversation; Reflections and Commentaries*, translated and edited by R. Palmer. New Haven, Conn.: Yale University Press, 2001.
———. *"Sein, das Verstanden Werden kann, ist Sprache": Hommage an Hans-Georg Gadamer*, edited by Rüdiger Bubner. Frankfurt am Main: Suhrkamp, 2001.
———. *The Beginning of Knowledge*, translated by R. Coltman. New York: Continuum, 2002.
———. *A Century of Philosophy: A Conversation with Ricardo Dottori*, translated by R. Coltman and S. Koepke. New York: Continuum, 2003.
———. *Truth and Method*, translated by J. Weinsheimer and D. G. Marshall. London: Continuum, 2004.
Ganeri, Jonardon. *Semantic Powers: Meaning and Means of Knowing in Classical Indian Philosophy*. Oxford: Oxford University Press, 1999.
———. *Indian Logic: A Reader*. Richmond: Curzon, 2001.
———. *Philosophy in Classical India: The Proper Work of Reason*. London: Routledge, 2001.

———. *The Concealed Art of the Soul: Theories of Self and Practises of Truth in Indian Ethics and Epistemology*. Oxford: Oxford University Press, 2007.

Ganguly, H. K. *Philosophy of Logical Construction: An Examination of Logical Atomism and Logical Positivism in Light of the Philosophies of Bhartṛhari, Dharmakīrti, and Prajñāparagupta*. Calcutta: Sanskrit Pustak Bhandar, 1963.

Ghosh, Raghunath. "Some Reflections on the Concept of *Mukti* in Vaiṣṇava Philosophy." *Journal of Religious Studies* (Patiala) 25 (1995), 148–52.

———. "The *Āvirbhāva* and *Tirobhāva* Theory in Vallabha Vedānta: Some Philosophical Problems." *Indian Philosophical Quarterly* 30 (2003), 553–62.

Gier, N. *Spiritual Titanism: Indian, Chinese and Western Perspectives*. Albany: State University of New York Press, 2000.

Gorner, Paul. "Heidegger's Phenomenology as Transcendental Philosophy." *International Journal of Philosophical Studies* 10, no. 1, February 2002.

Gosvāmi, Jiva. *Tattvasaṇdarbha*, edited by Stuart Elkmann. New Delhi: Motilal Banarsidass, 1986.

Gosvāmi, Rūpa. *Ujjvalanīlamaṇi*, edited by P. Kedaranatha and W. L. S. Panashikar. Bombay: Tukaram Javaji, 1932.

———. *Vidagdha Mādhava*, edited by Bhavadatta Shastri. Bombay: Nirnaya Sagar Press, 1937.

———. *Nāṭakacandrika*, edited by B. S. Sastri. Varanasi: Chowkambha Sanskrit Series Office, 1964.

———. *Lalitamādhavanāṭakam*. Varanasi: Caukhamba Samskrta Sirija Aphisa, 1969.

———. *Dāna Keli Kaumudi*. Indore: Gaurahari Press, 1976.

———. *Padyāvali*. Navadehalirajadhanitah: Navaranga, 1990.

———. *Śrī Upadeśāmṛta*. Mathura: Gauḍīya Vedānta Publications, 1997.

———. *Haṃsadūta*, edited by V. S. Apte. 1998.

———. *Mystic Poetry:* Rūpa Gosvāmin*'s Uddhava Saṇdeśa and Haṃsadūta*, translated by Jan Brzezinski. Hong Kong: Mandala Publishing Group, 1999.

———. *Haṃsadūta*, edited and translated by A. K. Bhattacaryya. Calcutta: Orion Publications, 2000.

———. *Bhaktirasāmrtasindu of Rūpa Gosvāmin*, translated by D. Haberman. New Delhi: Motilal Banarsidass, 2003.

Greisch, J. "Bulletin de Philosophie Hermeneutique: Heidegger, Schleiermacher, Ricoeur, Gadamer." *Revue des Sciences Philosophiques et Thīologiques* 80 (1996), 639–56.

Grondin, Jean. *Introduction to Philosophical Hermeneutics*, translated by Joel Weinsheimer. New Haven, Conn.: Yale University Press, 1994.

———. *The Philosophy of Gadamer*, translated by Kathryn Plant. Montreal: McGill-Queens University Press, 2003.

Gupta, A. Sen. *Classical Sāṃkhya: A Critical Study*. New Delhi: Monoranjan Sen, 1969.

Gupta, Bina. *The Disinterested Witness: A Fragment of Advaita Vedānta Phenomenology*. Evanston, Ill.: Northwestern University Press, 1998.

Gupta, Bina, and J. N. Mohanty, eds. *Philosophical Questions East and West*. Lanham, Md.: Rowman and Littlefield Publishers, 2000.

Gupta, Ravi. *The Caitanya Vaiṣṇava Vedānta of Jīva Gosvāmī*. Oxford: Routledge, 2007.

Gupta, Santosh. The *Conception of Bhakti in the Gauḍīya Vaiṣṇava Philosophy*. Vrindavan: Sri Rādhā Madhva Prakashan, 1998.

Haberman, David L. "Entering the Cosmic Drama: *Lila-smaraṇa* Meditation and the Perfected Body." *South Asia Research* 5 (1985), 49–58.

Habermas, Jurgen. *The Philosophical Discourse of Modernity*, translated by Frederick Lawrence. London: MIT Press, 1980.

Halbfass, Wilhelm. *Tradition and Reflection: Explorations in Indian Thought*. Albany: State University of New York Press, 1991.

———. *On Being and What There Is: Classical Vaiśeṣika and the History of Indian Ontology*. Albany: State University of New York Press, 1992.

———. *India and Europe: An Essay in Understanding*. Albany: State University of New York Press, 1988.

Hall, D. L. *The Uncertain Phoenix: Adventures Towards a Post-Cultural Sensibility*. New York: Fordham University Press, 1982.

Hall, E. W. *Philosophical Systems: A Categorical Analysis*. New York: University of Chicago Press, 1960.

Haney, David P. "Aesthetics and Ethics in Gadamer, Levinas and Romanticism: Problems of Phronesis and Techne." *Publications of the Modern Language Association of America* 114 (1999), 32–46.

Haq, M. Emmanuel. "Impact of Islam on the Gauḍīyan Form of Vaishnavism." *Journal of the Asiatic Society of Pakistan* 13 (1968–1969), 125–36.

Hardy, Friedhelm. *Viraha Bhakti: The Early History of Krishna Devotion in South India*. Oxford: Oxford University Press, 1983.

———. *The Religious Culture of India: Power, Love and Wisdom*. Cambridge: Cambridge University Press, 1994.

Hawley, John Stratton. *Krishna, the Butter Thief*. Princeton, N.J.: Princeton University Press, 1983.

Hawley, John Stratton, and Donna Marie Wulff, eds. *The Divine Consort: Rādhā and the Goddesses of India*. Boston: Beacon Press, 1982.

———, eds. *Devī: Goddesses of India*. Berkeley: University of California Press, 1996.

Heidegger, Martin. *What is Called Thinking?* edited by Fred D. Wieck and J. Glenn Gray. New York: Harper and Row, 1968.

———. *Basic Writings*. Oxford: Routledge, 1978.

———. *Being and Time*, translated by J. Macquarrie and E. Robinson. Oxford: Blackwell Publishers, 1978.

———. *Pathmarks*, translated and edited by William McNeill. Cambridge: Cambridge University Press, 1998.

Hein, Norvin. *The Miracle Plays of Mathura*. London: Yale University Press, 1972.

Hemming, Lawrence. *Heidegger's Atheism; the Refusal of a Theological Voice*. Notre Dame, Ind.: University of Notre Dame, 2002.

Hempel, H-P. *Heidegger und Zen*. Frankfurt am Main: Athenaum, 1987.

Hintikka, J. "Gadamer: Squaring the Hermeneutical Circle." *Revue Internationale de Philosophie* 54 (2000), 487–98.

Hollinger, Robert, ed. *Hermeneutics and Praxis*. Notre Dame, Ind.: University of Notre Dame Press, 1986.

Horton, R., and R. Finnegan, eds. *Modes of Thought: Essays on Thinking in Western and Non-Western Societies*. London: Faber, 1973.

Hosaku, Matsuo. *The Logic of Unity: The Discovery of Zero and Emptiness in Prajñāpāramita Thought*, translated by Kenneth Inada. Albany: State University of New York Press, 1987.

How, Alan. *The Habermas-Gadamer Debate and the Nature of the Social: Back to Bedrock*. Aldershot, UK: Avebury, 1995.

Jankovic, Zoran. *Au-dela du Signe: Gadamer et Derrida; Le Depassement Hermeneutique et Deconstructiviste du Dasein*. Paris: Harmattan, 2003.

Jha, V. N., ed. *Relations in Indian Philosophy*. New Delhi: South Asia Books, 1993.

Johnson, Patricia. *On Gadamer*. London: Wadsworth, 1999.

Joshi, M. V. "The Concept of Brahman in Vallabha Vedānta." *Journal of the Oriental Institute* 22 (1973), 474–83.

Kahrs, Eivind. *Indian Semantic Analysis: The Nirvacana Tradition*. Cambridge: Cambridge University Press, 1998.

Kaplan, Stephen. *Hermeneutics, Holography and Indian Idealism: A Study of Projection and Gauḍapāda's Māṇḍūkya Kārikā*. New Delhi: Motilal Banarsidass Publishers, 1987.

Kapoor, O. B. L. "The Absolute in Bengal Vaishnavism." *Agra University Journal of Research* 7 (1959), 13–22.

Katz, N., ed. *Buddhist and Western Philosophy*. New Delhi: Sterling Publishers, 1981.

Kennedy, Melville T. *The Chaitanya Movement: A Study of Vaishnavism in Bengal*. Calcutta: Association Press, 1925.

King, Richard. *Early Advaita Vedānta and Buddhism: The Mahāyana Context of the Gauḍapadīyakārikā*. Albany: State University of New York Press, 1995.

———. *Orientalism and Religion: Postcolonial Theory, India and "The Mystic East."* Oxford: Routledge, 1999.

Kojeve, Alexandre. *Introduction to the Reading of Hegel: Lectures on the Phenomenology of Spirit*, translated by James Nichols. Ithaca, N.Y.: Cornell University Press, 1980.

Koţgler, Hans Herbert. *Power of Dialogue: Critical Hermeneutics after Gadamer and Foucault*, translated by Paul Hendrickson. Cambridge, Mass.: MIT Press, 1999.

Krajewski, Bruce, ed. *Gadamer's Repercussions: Reconsidering Philosophical Hermeneutics*. Berkeley: University of California Press, 2003.

Kuk-Won, Shin. *A Hermeneutic Utopia: H.-G. Gadamer's Philosophy of Culture*. Toronto: Tea for Two Press, 1994.

Kunihiko, N. *Das Ich im Deutschen Idealismus und das Selbst im Zen-Buddhismus*. Freiburg: Alber, 1987.

Kupperman, Joel. *Learning from Asian Philosophy*. Oxford: Oxford University Press, 1999.

Kusch, Martin. *Language as Calculus vs. Language as Universal Medium: A Study in Husserl, Heidegger and Gadamer.* Dordrecht: Kluwer Academic Publishers, 1989.

Lacoue-Labarthe, Philippe. *Poetry as Experience*, translated by Andrea Tarnowski. Stanford, Calif.: Stanford University Press, 1999.

Lampert, Jay. "Gadamer and Cross-cultural Hermeneutics." *The Philosophical Forum* 28 (1997), 351–69.

Larson, G., and R. S. Bhattacharya, eds. "Sankhya: A Dualist Tradition in Indian Philosophy." *Encyclopedia of Indian Philosophies*, Volume 4. Princeton, N.J.: Princeton University Press, 1987.

Lawn, Christopher. *Gadamer: A Guide for the Perplexed*. London: Continuum, 2006.

Lee, Mi-Sook. *Sein und Verstehen in der Gegenwart : Die Frage nach dem Sein in der Philosophischen Hermeneutik von Hans-Georg Gadamer*. Dissertation, Bochum, 1994.

Levinas, Emmanuel. *God, Death, and Time*, translated by Bettina Bergo. Stanford, Calif.: Stanford University Press, 2000.

Lipner, Julius. *The Face of Truth: A Study of Meaning and Metaphysics in the Vedantic Theology of Ramanuja*. Hong Kong: State University of New York Press, 1986.

Loy, David. *Non-Duality: A Study in Comparative Philosophy*. London: Yale University Press, 1988.

Lynch, Owen, ed. *Divine Passions: The Social Construction of Emotion in India*. Berkeley: University of California Press, 1990.

Lyotard, Jean-Francois. *Moralitis Postmodernes*. Paris: Gallilee, 1993.

Mahoney, William K. *The Artful Universe: An Introduction to the Vedic Religious Imagination*. Albany: State University of New York Press, 1998.

Malpas, Jeff, Ulrich Arnswald, and Jens Kertscher, eds. *Gadamer's Century: Essays in Honour of Hans Georg Gadamer*. Cambridge, Mass.: MIT Press, 2002.

Marks, J., and Ames, R. T., eds. *Emotions in Asian Thought: A Dialogue in Comparative Philosophy*. Albany: State University of New York Press, 1995.

Matchett, Freda. *Kṛṣṇa: Lord or Avatāra? The Relationship between Kṛṣṇa and Viṣṇu*. Oxford: Curzon Press: 2001.

Matilal, Bimal Krishna. *Perception: An Essay on Classical Indian Theories of Knowledge*. Oxford: Oxford University Press, 1986.

———. *The Character of Logic in India*, edited by Jonardon Ganeri and Heeraman Tiwari. Albany: State University of New York Press, 1998.

———. *Ethics and Epics: The Collected Essays of Bimal Krishna Matilal*, edited by Jonardon Ganeri. Oxford: Oxford University Press, 2002.

———. *Mind, Langage and World: The Collected Essays of Bimal Krishna Matilal*, edited by Jonardon Ganeri. Oxford: Oxford University Press, 2002.

———. *Epistemology, Logic and Grammar in Indian Philosophical Analysis*, edited by Jonardon Ganeri. Oxford: Oxford University Press, 2005.

Matilal, B. M., and A. Chakrabarti, eds., *Knowing from Words: Western and Indian Philosophical Analysis of Understanding and Testimony*. London: Kluwer, 1994.

May, Reinhardt. *Heidegger's Hidden Sources: East Asian Influences on His Work*, translated by Graham Parkes. Oxford: Routledge, 1996.

McDaniel, June. *The Madness of the Saints: Ecstatic Religion in Bengal*. Chicago: University of Chicago Press, 1989.

———. "Divine Love in Gauḍīya Vaiṣṇava and Catholic Mysticism." *Journal of Vaishnava Studies* 5, no. 1 (1996–1997), 83–102.

McDermott, C., ed. *Comparative Philosophy: Selected Essays*. Lanham, Md.: University Press of America, 1983.

McDowell, John. *Mind and World*. Cambridge, Mass.: Harvard University Press, 1996.
———. *Mind, Value and Reality*. Cambridge, Mass.: Harvard University Press, 2001.
McEvilley, Thomas. *The Shape of Ancient Thought: Comparative Studies in Greek and Indian Philosophies*. New York: Allworth Press, 2002.
Michelfelder, Richard, and Diane Palmer, eds. *Dialogue and Deconstruction: The Gadamer-Derrida Encounter*. Albany: State University of New York Press, 1989.
Miller, Barbara Stoler, ed. *Love Song of the Dark Lord: Jayadeva's Gītagovinda*. New York: Columbia University Press, 1977.
Mohanty, J. N. *Essays on Indian Philosophy: Traditional and Modern*. Oxford: Oxford University Press, 2002.
———. *Reason and Tradition in Indian Thought: An Essay on the Nature of Indian Philosophical Thinking*. Oxford: Oxford University Press, 2002.
Morrison, Robert. *Nietzsche and Buddhism: A Study in Nihilism and Ironic Affinities*. Oxford: Oxford University Press, 1999.
Muses, Charles. *East-West Fire: Schopenhauer's Optimism and the Lankāvatāra Sūtra; An Excursion toward the Common Ground between Oriental and Western Religion*. London: J. M. Watkins, 1955.
Nakamura, Hajime. *A Comparative History of Ideas*. Oxford: Routledge and K. Paul, 1986.
Narayanan, Vasudha. *The Way and the Goal: Expressions of Devotion in the Early Sri Vaiṣṇava Tradition*. Washington, D.C.: Institute of Vaiṣṇava Studies and Center for the Study of World Religions, 1987.
Neville, R. C. *Normative Cultures*. Albany: State University of New York Press, 1995.
———. *Religion in Late Modernity*. Albany: State University of New York Press, 2002.
Norris, Christopher. *Against Relativism: Philosophy of Science, Deconstruction and Critical Theory*. Oxford: Blackwell Publishers, 1997.
Odin, Steve. *Process Metaphysics and Hua-Yen Buddhism: A Critical Study of Cumulative Penetration versus Interpenetration*. Albany: State University of New York Press, 1982.
O'Flaherty, Wendy Doniger. *Śiva: The Erotic Ascetic*. New York: Oxford University Press, 1981.
Olsen, Carl. *The Indian Renouncer and Postmodern Poison: A Cross-Cultural Encounter*. New York: Peter Lang, 1997.
Ormiston, Gayle, and Alan Schrift, eds. *The Hermeneutic Tradition*. Albany: State University of New York Press, 1990.
Palmer, Richard E. *Hermeneutics: Interpretation Theory in Schleiermacher, Dilthey, Heidegger, and Gadamer*. Evanston, Ill.: Northwestern University Press, 1969.
Parkes, Graham, ed. *Heidegger and Asian Thought*. Honolulu: University of Hawaii Press, 1990.
Patton, Kimberley, and Benjamin Ray, eds. *A Magic Still Dwells: Comparative Religion in the Postmodern Age*. Berkeley: University of California Press, 2000.
Phillips, S. H. *Classical Indian Metaphysics: Refutations of Realism and the Emergence of "New Logic."* Chicago: Open Court, 1995.

Prasad, Rama. *Rāmānuja and Hegel: A Comparative Study*. New York: Prometheus Books, 1984.

Prentiss, Karen Pechilis. *The Embodiment of Bhakti*. New York: Oxford University Press, 1999.

Raman, Srilata. *Self-Surrender (prapatti) to God in Śrivaiṣṇavism: Tamil Cats and Sanskrit Monkeys*. London: Routledge, 2007.

Ram-prasad, Chakravarti. *Advaita Epistemology and Metaphysics: An Outline of Indian Non-Realism*. Oxford: RoutledgeCurzon, 2002.

Rauch, Angelika. *The Hieroglyph of Tradition: Freud, Benjamin, Gadamer, Novalis, Kant*. London: Associated University Presses, 2000.

Reynolds, F. E., and D. Tracy, eds. *Religion and Practical Reason: New Essays in the Comparative Philosophy of Religions*. Albany: State University of New York Press, 1994.

Rilke, Rainer Maria. *Selected Poems*, translated by J. B. Leishman. London: Penguin, 1964.

Ringma, Charles Richard. *Gadamer's Dialogical Hermeneutic: The Hermeneutics of Bultmann, of the New Testament Sociologists and of the Social Theologians in Dialogue with Gadamer's Hermeneutic*. Heidelberg: Universitatsverlag C. Winter, 1999.

Risser, James. "Poetic dwelling in Gadamer's hermeneutics." *Philosophy Today* 38 (1994), 369–79.

———. *Hermeneutics and the Voice of the Other: Re-reading Gadamer's Philosophical Hermeneutics*. Albany: State University of New York Press, 1997.

Roberts, David, ed. *Reconstructing Theory: Gadamer, Habermas, Luhmann*. Melbourne: Melbourne University Press, 1995.

Rorty, Richard. *Philosophy and the Mirror of Nature*. Princeton, N.J.: Princeton University Press, 1981.

Sarkar, A. K. *Dynamic Facets of Indian Thought*. New Delhi: Manohar, 1980.

———. *Buddhism and Whitehead's Process Philosophy*. New Delhi: South Asian Publishers, 1991.

Sastrik, Asoke Chatterjee. "Śrimadbhāgavata and Caitanya-Sampradāya." *Journal of the Asiatic Society of Bengal* 37, no. 4 (1995), 1–14.

Sax, William, ed. *The Gods at Play: Līlā in South Asia*. Oxford: Oxford University Press, 1995.

Schaffer, Jonathan. "Is There a Fundamental Level." *Nous* 37 (September 2003).

Scharfstein, Ben-Ami. *Philosophy East/ Philosophy West: A Critical Comparison of Indian, Chinese, Islamic and European Philosophy*. Oxford: Basil Blackwell, 1978.

———. *A Comparative History of World Philosophy: From the Upanishads to Kant*. Albany: State University of New York, 1998.

Scheibler, Ingrid. *Gadamer: Between Heidegger and Habermas*. Lanham, Md.: Rowman & Littlefield Publishers, 2000.

Schmidt, Lawrence. *The Epistemology of Hans-Georg Gadamer: An Analysis of the Legitimization of Vorurteile*. Frankfurt am Main: P. Lang, 1987.

Schrift, Alan, ed. *Nietzsche and the Question of Interpretation: Between Hermeneutics and Deconstruction*. Oxford: Routledge, 1990.

———. *The Logic of the Gift: Toward an Ethic of Generosity*. New York: Routledge, 1997.

Schwarz, Regina, ed. *Transcendence: Philosophy, Literature and Theology Approach the Beyond*. Oxford: Routledge, 2004.

Scott, Charles E. "Mnemosyne's Loss: Lethe, Gadamer, Heidegger and Derrida." *Internationale Zeitschrift für Philosophie* 2 (1996), 274–85.

Sharma, Arvind. *Modern Hindu Thought: The Essential Texts.* Oxford: Oxford University Press, 2002.

———. *Hinduism and Its Sense of History.* New Delhi: Oxford University Press, 2003.

Sharma, B. N. K. *History of the Dvaita School of Vedānta and Its Literature*. Bombay: Motilal Banarsidass, 1961.

Sharma, Chandradhar. *A Critical Survey of Indian Philosophy*. New Delhi: Motilal Banarsidass, 1987.

Sharma, Krishna. *Bhakti and the Bhakti Movement: A New Perspective—A Study in the History of Ideas*. New Delhi: Munshiram Manoharlal, 1987.

Sharpe, Eric. *Comparative Religion*. London: Duckworth, 1975.

Silverman, Hugh J., ed. *Gadamer and Hermeneutics*. New York: Routledge, 1991.

Sinha, Debabrata. *Understanding in Human Context: Themes and Variations in Indian Philosophy*. New York: P. Lang, 1996.

Sinha, Jadunath. *A History of Indian Philosophy*. Calcutta: Sinha Publishing House, 1952–1971.

Sinha, R. S. S. *Contemporary Indian Philosophy*. New Delhi: Munshiram Manoharlal Publishers, 1983.

———. *Comparative Religion*. Delhi: Munshiram Manoharlal Publishers, 1996.

Smith, David. "The Premodern and the Postmodern: Some Parallels with Special Reference to Hinduism." *Religion* 23 (1993), 157–65.

Smith, Wilfred Cantwell. *The Meaning and End of Religion*. San Francisco: Harper and Row, 1978.

Srinivasan, Gummaraju. *The Phenomenological Approach to Philosophy, Indian and Western*. New Delhi: Caravan Publishing Co., 1980.

Staal, J. F. *Advaita and Neo-Platonism: A Critical Study in Comparative Philosophy*. Madras: Madras University Press, 1961.

Staals, Frits. *Universals: Studies in Indian Logic and Linguistics*. Chicago: University of Chicago Press, 1988.

Stewart, Tony K. "*Bhāva* and Divinity in the Caitanya Bhāgavata." *South Asia Research* 6 (1986), 61–76.

Sullivan, Robert. *Political Hermeneutics: The Early Thinking of Hans-Georg Gadamer*. Philadelphia: Pennsylvania State University Press, 1990.

Sundararajan, K. R., and Bithika Mukerji, eds. *Hindu Spirituality, Postclassical and Modern*. London: Herder and Herder, 1997.

Taylor, Charles. *Sources of the Self: The Making of the Modern Identity*. Cambridge: Cambridge University Press, 1989.

Taylor, Mark C., ed. *Critical Terms for Religious Studies*. Cambridge: University of Chicago Press, 1998.

Thiselton, Anthony C. *Two Horizons: New Testament Hermeneutics and Philosophical Description*. Grand Rapids, Mich.: Eerdmans, 1996.

Tymieniecka, A-T. *The Logic of the Living Present: Experience, Ordering, Onto-Poiesis of Culture*. London: Kluwer Academic, 1995.

Vattimo, Gianni. "Histoire d'une Virgule: Gadamer et le Sens de l'Etre." *Revue Internationale de Philosophie* 54 (2000), 499–514.

Vaudeville, Charlotte. *Myths, Saints and Legends in Medieval India*. New Delhi: Oxford University Press, 1999.

Vertovec, Steve. *The Hindu Diaspora: Comparative Patterns*. London: Routledge, 2000.

Vico, Giambattista. *The New Science*, translated by David Marsh. London: Penguin, 1999.

Vitsakis, V. G. *Plato and the Upanishads*. New Delhi: Arnold-Heinemann, 1977.

Wachterhauser, Brice. *Beyond Being: Gadamer's Post-Platonic Hermeneutic Ontology*. Evanston, Ill.: Northwestern University Press, 1999.

———. *Hermeneutics and Truth*. Evanston, Ill.: Northwestern University Press, 1994.

Wallulis, Jerald. *Hermeneutics of Life History: Personal Achievement and History in Gadamer, Habermas, and Erikson*. Evanston, Ill.: Northwestern University Press, 1991.

Warnke, Georgia. *Gadamer: Hermeneutics, Tradition and Reason*. Cambridge: Polity Press, 1987.

Weber, Edmund, and Tilak Raj Copra, eds. *Shri Krishna Caitanya and the Bhakti Religion*. Frankfurt am Main: Peter Lang, 1988.

Webermann, David. "A New Defense of Gadamer's Hermeneutics." *Philosophy and Phenomenological Research* 60 (2000), 45–67.

Weinsheimer, Joel. *Gadamer's Hermeneutics: A Reading of Truth and Method*. New Haven, Conn.: Yale University Press, 1985.

———. *Philosophical Hermeneutics and Literary Theory*. London: Yale University Press, 1991.

———. "Charity Militant: Gadamer, Davidson and Post-critical Hermeneutics." *Revue Internationale de Philosophie* 54 (2000), 405–22.

Werner, K., ed. *Love Divine: Studies in Bhakti and Devotional Mysticism*. Oxford: Curzon Press, 1993.

Williams, Bernard. *Truth and Truthfulness: An Essay in Genealogy*. Princeton, N.J.: Princeton, 2004.

Wolin, Richard. *Labyrinths: Explorations in the Critical History of Ideas*. Amherst: University of Massachusetts Press, 1995.

Wright, Kathleen, ed. *Festivals of Interpretation: Essays on Hans-Georg Gadamer's Work*. Albany: State University of New York Press, 1990.

Zizek, Slavoj. *The Ticklish Subject: The Absent Centre of Political Ontology*. London: Verso, 2000.

———. "Welcome to the Desert of the Real; Reflections on WTC," in *Welcome to the Desert of the Real: Five Essays on September 11th and Related Dates*. London: Verso, 2002.

Zuckert, Catherine. *Postmodern Platos: Nietzsche, Heidegger, Gadamer, Strauss, Derrida*. Chicago: University of Chicago Press: 1996.

Index